SAGE was founded in 1965 by Sara Miller McCune to support
the dissemination of usable knowledge by publishing innovative
and high-quality research and teaching content. Today, we
publish over 900 journals, including those of more than 400
learned societies, more than 800 new books per year, and a
growing range of library products including archives, data, case
studies, reports, and video. SAGE remains majority-owned by
our founder, and after Sara's lifetime will become owned by
a charitable trust that secures our continued independence.

Los Angeles | London | New Delhi | Singapore | Washington DC | Melbourne

Learn English

(Second Edition)

Learn English

A Fun Book of Functional Language, Grammar, and Vocabulary

(*Second Edition*)

Santanu Sinha Chaudhuri

English Language Teacher and Author

Los Angeles | London | New Delhi
Singapore | Washington DC | Melbourne

First published in 2018 by

SAGE Publications India Pvt Ltd
B1/I-1 Mohan Cooperative Industrial Area
Mathura Road, New Delhi 110 044, India
www.sagepub.in

SAGE Publications Inc
2455 Teller Road
Thousand Oaks, California 91320, USA

SAGE Publications Ltd
1 Oliver's Yard, 55 City Road
London EC1Y 1SP, United Kingdom

SAGE Publications Asia-Pacific Pte Ltd
18 Cross Street #10-10/11/12
China Square Central
Singapore 048423

Published by Vivek Mehra for SAGE Publications India Pvt Ltd, typeset in 10/12 pts Garamond by Zaza Eunice, Hosur, Tamil Nadu, India.

Library of Congress Cataloging-in-Publication Data Available

ISBN: 978-93-528-0801-4 (PB)

SAGE Team: Amit Kumar, Indrani Dutta, Vandana Gupta and Kanika Mathur

To Nishaant and Aneesh

Thank you for choosing a SAGE product!
If you have any comment, observation or feedback,
I would like to personally hear from you.

Please write to me at **contactceo@sagepub.in**

Vivek Mehra, Managing Director and CEO, SAGE India.

CONTENTS

PART 2:   Let's Talk About the Present

PART 8:   Language 'Clear as Sunlight, Crisp as Sand'

PART 9: From Simple to Complex Language

PREFACE

Is This Book for You?

I believe you will find this book useful if

- you use English at your workplace, but aren't confident about it,
- as a student at a college/university, you find it difficult to follow lessons and textbooks in English,
- you are looking for a job or planning to go abroad,
- you are going to take the IELTS or similar exams and wish to improve your English language skills,
- you are a parent and teach your child English, or
- you are just one of those millions who missed the opportunity to learn English at school.

This book will also help proficient users of English, who may need to check some points. For example, an English teacher or a literature student will find the answers to a large number of tricky questions on grammar and vocabulary in these pages. And of course, teachers will find it useful in classroom. However, let me quickly add that this book is not for beginners. You will find it useful only if you can write—not necessarily accurately—simple sentences in English, and if you can talk about things familiar to you, even if with some effort.

Also, I have written this book with the South Asian learner in mind. I believe they will identify with the contexts given in the book easily. Besides, while learning English, most South Asians face similar problems partly because of the vernacular influence of their languages, which are similar in many ways. While speaking English, we often follow rules that are valid in our regional languages but not in English. This book points out a large number of such problem areas and helps the reader overcome them.

What Can You Get Out of This Book?

As of now, one-fourth of the world population speaks English. 'English has established itself as the lingua franca throughout the world, so that Chinese airlines pilots overflying Eastern Siberia communicate with (Russian) ground controllers in English ....'[1]

Indeed, English is the language in which Indians do business with Brazilians, Bangladeshis with Europe, and Chinese with everyone else in the world. Even *within* non-English speaking countries, English plays a

---

[1] J. A. Simpson and E. S. C. Weiner, *Oxford English* (Oxford: Oxford University Press, 1989).

major role in higher education, commerce, and public administration. However, many, if not most, of our schools do not equip students with the English language skills they require. And this is a huge problem.

The aim of this book is to address this problem. This book contains:

- ✓ detailed analysis of *all* the grammatical forms a person like you requires,
- ✓ a large amount of the vocabulary used in everyday situations,
- ✓ lots of practice exercises and tests, and
- ✓ functional language.

Let me explain the fourth component. Every language contains certain expressions that are used frequently in lots of situations. For example: *It's so nice of you*, or *You had better not go out without an umbrella*. Expressions like these are known as functional language and you should be able to use them *without thinking*.

I have tried to write in an informal, reader-friendly style, and I would suggest that you don't approach the business of learning English too seriously, with taut[2] muscles and a frown on your face! Relax, smile, and work through this book at your own pace. Most importantly, enjoy! Your language will certainly improve even *without the guidance of a teacher*.

Please tell me what you think about the book and how it can be made better. You are welcome to write to me at santanusc@yahoo.com.

How to Use This Book?

The first chapter of the book, '*Secret Mantras for Assured Success*' discusses how people learn a second language and offers some practical tips. I would suggest that you first read this chapter, draw a plan of action, and then begin working through this book.

Beginning with the basics, this book discusses *all* the complex structures you will need in academics, business, and in most other professions. To help you test your own learning, I have provided activities within each chapter and a set of practice exercises at the end of most of the chapters. There are also 10 tests covering different aspects of English.

The book has been organized in 10 parts. Part 1 ('*The Rules of the Game*' Chapters 1–6) sets the tone and introduces definitions of terms that are used throughout. Chapters 16 and 17 too introduce some key concepts that are used in the subsequent chapters. Please check these definitions first.

The remaining chapters are such that each part is independent in itself; you can go through *any part* (not any chapter) depending on your needs. For example, if you have questions about articles and prepositions, you can straightaway go to Part 6 ('*Nuts and Bolts of the English Language*' Chapters 35–38). Or you can *work through* the chapters from the beginning. By 'working through', I mean that you learn the concepts and do the activities, exercises, and tests. You will find a key to the activities in each unit and a key to all the exercises and tests at the back of the book.

Throughout the book, I have added text boxes highlighting meanings of confusing words and their usage, and other common problem areas. The detailed table of contents at the beginning and the index at the back will help you identify the topics to study depending on your specific personal needs.

---

[2] **taut:** pulled tight, not relaxed.

To conclude, I would like to add that besides going through this book, you must read authentic English texts, watch films and television programmes that have fine speakers, and listen to videos on the Internet. Non-native speakers improve their English by consciously noting new language and using it whenever they get an opportunity.

The key is *using new language*. You don't learn English by memorizing the 'rules' of grammar and applying them to write or speak. While reading this book, note and remember how English is used, and store the information in the back of your head. But most importantly, read, listen to, and practise speaking and writing. *Use the language in real life.*

Learning a language is not a hundred-metre dash; it is a long-distance race that never ends. Enjoy the exciting journey!

ACKNOWLEDGEMENTS FOR THE FIRST EDITION

The first words of thanks must go to my students, who have not only helped me look at language teaching from the learner's point of view but have also augmented my confidence by acquiring fair amount of command on English themselves. I am indebted to them.

My wife Arundhati read the first drafts of all the chapters—usually at odd hours—and helped me polish the rough edges. My friends K.T. Rajagopalan, Damodar Menon, and Uma Sankar were with me throughout the process of writing and revising this book. They corrected the manuscript and offered wonderful suggestions. But more importantly, they encouraged and supported me throughout. Without them, this book would not have been possible.

My senior colleague Krishna Koyal suggested some changes. The alterations proposed by her, I believe, have improved the book significantly. My colleagues at the British Council Teaching Centre in Kolkata, Chitra Velayudh, Poushali Dutta Purakaystha, and Smita Saha also gave their input in some of the chapters. Finally, my senior friend, K.S. Narasimhan, scrutinized every word of the final draft and identified some errors and inaccuracies that I had missed. I cannot thank them enough. My daughter Sohini's specialist input on current business vocabulary has been a great help.

My late friend Chandrachur Sarkar was the main protagonist in the incident described at the beginning of Chapter 49. I found the Oraon folk tale used in the same unit in Sandeep Bandyopadhyay's Bengali book *Katha Brittanta*. I thank all of them. I also thank Gautam Basu for the illustrations and Srikumar Chatterjee for helping me acquire the map used in Chapter 15.

I owe a huge debt of gratitude to Professor K.A. Jayaseelan of English and Foreign Languages University, Hyderabad, for checking the manuscript. His corrections and suggestions for improvement have saved me from many inky embarrassments.

Finally, Ray Mackay, a well-known Scotland-based ELT expert who was in Kolkata on a state government project in 2010, read through the book and pointed out its merits and shortcomings. Ray's critique opened a few unknown windows before my eyes and helped me revise the book. Thank you very much, Ray.

Acknowledgements for the Second Edition

Writing a perfect, error-free book on second language acquisition is like attaining Nirvana. I am far from there, but I am trying.

Over the last year or so, I have been revising this book, making minor corrections and major changes, adding six chapters, and sprinkling new lessons on vocabulary throughout the book. During this time, I made myself perfectly unbearable to some of my former colleagues at the British Council, a few students, and a few other friends by badgering them to review my manuscript. Apologies to all of you, but this book wouldn't have been possible but for your gentle patience and unstinting support.

With deep gratitude I acknowledge the thorough and consistent support of my close friends K.T. Rajagopalan and Damodar Menon. Since I started working on this book, that is, over almost 12 years, they have spent innumerable hours for the cause. And recently, I rediscovered another old friend, Philip Abraham, who too gladly extended a helping hand. All of them speak and write excellent English, and I have had much to learn from them. 'Thank you' will be too inadequate a word for them.

My senior colleague Krishna Koyal has been an inspiration from the day I joined her as a colleague in the British Council. She guided me when I first wrote the book and has helped me ever since. Thank you, Krishna di, you are such a darling!

Among my colleagues, Ruchi Jain has made a stupendous contribution towards this edition. She has checked all the new/revised chapters and I do not know how she managed to find the time despite her hectic work schedule. More significantly, every time Ruchi disagreed with me, or when she had a different take, she added some value to the book.

A number of colleagues and friends have gone through one or more of the chapters and have contributed in different ways. I owe a huge debt of gratitude to them all: George Thomas, Chitra Velayudh, Poushali Dutta Purakayastha, Brian Beaton, James Bradbury, and Animesh Mitra. My friend Mohan Sivanand reminded me of the beautiful poem by Nissim Ezekiel which I have used in the last chapter of the book. Thanks, Mohan.

Moving on to my students, Dipayan Chatterjee, Manami Saha, Arpita Pal, and Milan Kamilya too have helped significantly. I reached out to them particularly because I wanted to get the reader's perspective. All of them have contributed, and in particular, Milan has convinced me to modify my text at several places. Thank you all.

All the new illustrations for this edition have been drawn by my friend Amit Kumar Saha. Thank you, Amit.

Every boat needs a port, and every author, a publisher. Thank you Amit Kumar and Indrani Dutta for being where you are and for the confidence you have in me.

Finally, my wife Arundhati Sinha has not only checked every word written in this edition and helped me refine them, she has also lived—at a conservative estimate—a year with a self-absorbed and unsupportive husband, not always with a smile! I have been fortunate to have shared my life with a person who has such forbearance.

ABOUT THE AUTHOR

Santanu Sinha Chaudhuri, a teacher who worked for the British Council Teaching Centre (Kolkata), teaches General English, Business English, and Spoken English to adult learners. He has conducted numerous workshops at renowned institutions on diverse topics such as presentations, International English, and dealing with difficult people. Presently, he is a freelance English teacher and corporate trainer specializing in business communication and training IELTS examinees.

Santanu also translates Bengali literary fiction into English, and writes essays and creative non-fiction, some of which are available on his blog.[1] His translated books such as *Of Man and Earth, The Mountain of the Moon,* and *Faces and Other Stories* have been brought out by some of the leading publishers of India. He has also contributed articles and translations to a number of newspapers, magazines, and literary journals.

---

[1] http://www.santanusc.blogspot.in/

PART
1

THE RULES OF THE GAME

Secret Mantras for Assured Success

1.1 A COMMON QUESTION

At some time or other, every adult learner of English asks themselves: 'How can I improve my English?' As you are reading this book, I presume you too have thought about it. In the following pages, I will try to answer the question.

Let me begin by telling you that you can certainly become an effective speaker and writer in English. To help you reach the goal, I am going to give you some simple tips which you can follow, besides working through this book.

Let me also tell you that language is a skill, it can't be taught. *It has to be learned.* The statement is also true for other skills, such as cooking, singing, and driving. For example, in India, you get a driving licence typically after 30 hours and 300 kilometres of training. But do you become a driver the day you get the licence?

No, you don't, unless you are a genius at the wheel. You become a driver only after you have driven a car alone at Flora Fountain in Mumbai, Burrabazaar in Kolkata, or Mirpur Road in Dhaka. The journey between getting a licence and driving in a busy marketplace is a long and difficult one, and you must travel this distance alone.

The process of learning a foreign language is similar. You have got to do it alone. And it isn't easy. You must work hard, consistently, over a period of time. From my experience of teaching English, I would say that you need at least two years of systematic practice to become fluent and reasonably accurate in English.

1.2 THE PROBLEM

Let's now move on to what you should do to achieve your goal. First, check these sentences:

1. Smoking is injurious to health.
2. She got off the bus.

I am certain that you won't have a problem with the first sentence. If there is an occasion to tell someone why he/she shouldn't smoke, you'll use the first sentence easily, without hunting for words. However, when it comes to the second sentence, most South Asians would say:

She got down from the bus. ✗

It may look like a fine sentence, but it isn't. A native speaker of English will perhaps never use it. They would say: *She got off the bus.*

Why don't we have a problem with the first sentence, although 'injurious' is not a common word, but we're unsure about the second? Please think and write down the answer before you move on to the next section.

1.3 THE FIRST RULE

You have possibly got it: We don't have a problem with the first expression because we've heard and read it thousands of times. That brings us to our first mantra.

> We learn English by reading and listening to good, accurate English repeatedly.

When you read, it helps you to improve your written language. When you listen to good speakers, it helps you speak better. Therefore,

- ✓ Read books, particularly the ones that have been around for 20 years or more.
- ✓ Read newspapers that use accurate English (e.g., *The Hindu*). Read the Internet editions of leading newspapers such as *The Guardian* or *The New York Times*. If you can't find a top-drawer newspaper, in any of them, focus on the centre-page, which carries editorials and articles. You find the finest language in a newspaper in its editorials.
- ✓ Read magazines such as *The Frontline, Outlook, The Scientific American,* and *The New Yorker.* All good magazines are available online. For most online magazines, you have to pay a subscription. But you can read a few articles for free.
- ✓ Watch news programmes and debates on TV. But be selective and do not watch channels where the anchor and the participants fight all the time. I would recommend NDTV 24×7, BBC, Al Jazeera, and CNN IBN.
- ✓ Follow speeches and debates on the YouTube, which has a vast collection. Another wonderful resource of our time is the TED talks.[1]
- ✓ Watch English films as often as you can.

The best way to learn a foreign language is to follow good speakers/writers. The operative word here is 'follow'. If you read or listen passively, or if you do not make notes of the new language, you won't improve. You must focus on new words and expressions, remember them, and use them when you get an opportunity.

---

[1] Visit www.ted.com/ if you haven't been there already.

1.4 WHAT SHOULD YOU FOCUS ON?

Before answering the question, here is a word of caution: Some people believe—may God forgive them—that good English means long sentences with impossible-to-pronounce words like subdermatoglyphic. It is not true. Language is a tool to communicate, and for practical purposes, simpler the words you use, the better it is. However, you may have to write long sentences with uncommon words if you are an academic,* diplomat,[2] or lawyer.

So, instead of difficult words, look for words and expressions you are likely to use more often in your life. Like *She got off the bus.* Let me give you

> ### * Academic/Academician
>
> An *academic* is a teacher or scholar at an institute of higher education like a university.
>
> In British English, an *academician* may or may not be a teacher, but he/she is a member of an academy like *The National Academy of Sciences* (India) or *The Royal Academy of Music, England.*
>
> Very often, people use the word *academician* to refer to a college or university teacher, which is not Standard English.

another example. You know what 'look' means. But the meaning alone doesn't help. You must learn how to use the word. For example: *Look at me.*

Here are a few more sentences with *look:*

- ✓ Sir, can you please <u>look into</u> the problem of shortage of space? (=examine)
- ✓ Our company is <u>looking for</u> graduates with strong communication skills. (=searching)
- ✓ Radhika has a nanny[3] to <u>look after</u> her children during the day. (=take care of)

You don't have to learn all of them at a go. But whenever you read or hear a word, note what other words go with it. And remember the combination.

But how can you remember the combination?

1.5 ROLE OF A GUIDE

Every language follows certain *patterns.* The rules for forming these patterns are collectively called grammar. Let's recall that you speak your mother tongue perfectly even if you didn't know the rules of **grammar**. However, can people who don't live in an English-language environment speak or write English accurately without some knowledge of English grammar and vocabulary?

If you are not a native speaker[4] of English and if you don't know the rules of grammar, you will find it extremely difficult to identify the correct sentences given in Activity 1 on the next page. The English language is so counter-intuitive[5] at times! Do the following activity and check the answers given at the end of this chapter. (If you've got all the answers correct, please do not waste your time on this book. You should have better things to do!)

---

[2] **diplomat:** an official working for the foreign ministry of a country, for example: an *ambassador* or a *high commissioner.*

[3] **nanny:** someone, especially a woman, who is paid to look after a child at his/her home, *ayah* in India.

[4] A *native speaker* of English is a person whose mother tongue is English.

[5] **counter-intuitive:** something that goes against common sense or intuition.

ACTIVITY 1

In the pairs of sentences below, either A is correct, or B. Please tick (✓) the correct sentence before you move on:

Sentence A	Sentence B
I trust you.	I am trusting you.
I did a project on robotics[6] at college.	I had done a project on robotics at college.
If I were you, I would look for another job.	If I were you, I will look for another job.
I've been living in Colombo for 10 years.	I am living in Colombo for 10 years.
She studies in Bishop Cotton High School.	She studies at Bishop Cotton High School.
I prefer coffee than tea.	I prefer coffee to tea.

A language teacher often fills in this gap, analyses another language, and helps you understand the rules of grammar and vocabulary so that you can speak/write accurately.

The principal aim of this book is just that. This book, I believe, answers most, if not all, of the questions that an average learner of the English language has in his/her mind.

But let me add a word of caution here. You cannot memorize the rules of grammar and apply them to frame sentences. It should be the other way around: read and write, listen and speak, and also learn the patterns of the language.

1.6 REMEMBERING AND USING A NEW LANGUAGE

Language experts tell us that unless you go back to a new word or expression four to five times, you might not remember it. And that brings us to our second mantra.

I will record new expressions in a personal wordbook and review them from time to time.

Here is what you can do:

1. Write down new words, their meanings, and one or two sentences with them in a personal wordbook. If necessary, refer to a dictionary that gives illustrative sentences.[7] Listen to how the word is pronounced. Write down the pronunciation in your own language.
2. Simultaneously, work through this book and understand the patterns of English.
3. Go back to every new word/expression after a day, a week, a fortnight, a month, and whenever you can.

---

[6] **robotics:** the subject of designing, constructing, and using robots.
[7] For example: https://en.oxforddictionaries.com/

Most importantly, practise writing and speaking, and try using the word. First, you should use the new language in your mind. Think about them, think of a situation when you can use the expressions you've just learned, and use them whenever you get an opportunity. So our next mantra is:

> I will imagine situations where I can use the new language I've just learned, and frame sentences in my head. I'll wait for an opportunity and use the new expression the moment I find one.

To sum up:

1. Read and listen to good, accurate English regularly.
2. Record the new language you come across and review them.
3. Work through this book to learn the patterns of English.
4. Practise using the new language in your head.
5. Use the new language whenever you find an opportunity.

Mastering a second language is not a hundred-metre dash, it is a fascinating journey that never ends. But for you, the most important point is: *You can teach yourself to become a fine speaker and writer.*

PRACTICE

1. Jot down your personal strategy to improve your English.

KEY TO ACTIVITY

Activity 1: For each of the first four pairs, Sentence A is correct. For the remaining two, Sentence B is correct.

Communication and Language

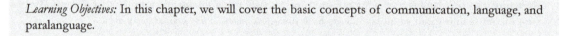

Learning Objectives: In this chapter, we will cover the basic concepts of communication, language, and paralanguage.

A politician communicating with people

She too has something to communicate

2.1 WHAT IS COMMUNICATION?

If I asked you, why you have chosen to read this book, you would perhaps say, *To communicate better in English*, or *To improve my communication skills*. To understand your needs better, let's check what **communication** means. According to the *Oxford Advanced Learner's Dictionary*:

Communication is the activity or process of expressing ideas and feelings or of giving people information.

When people express ideas and feelings, or give information to someone else, they communicate. And such expression or giving of information is done mainly, but not only, through language.

2.2 LANGUAGE

The question that follows is: *What is **language?*** We may say:

> Language is:
>
> - a system of spoken sounds to which meanings have been added, and which is used by humans to communicate with others; and
> - the written representation of such a system.

Language, therefore, is a medium of spoken and written communication. But communication does not happen only through language. We may even communicate without using language. As we grow up, we learn how to emphasize or change the meaning of what we say with the help of facial expressions, gestures,[1] and subtle changes in our way of speaking. We learn these techniques mainly by observing others. No one teaches us these tools at school, and most of us don't even know that we communicate in many different ways without using language. **Non-verbal communication**, that is, communication without words, plays a major role when we speak.

These other forms of communication, like gestures, are collectively known as **paralanguage.** When we talk face to face with someone, paralanguage is often more important than the words we use. It may sound strange, but it is true!

2.3 PARALANGUAGE

The most important form of paralanguage is the **body language.** This is the language of facial expressions, gestures, and postures.[2]

Some expressions like a smile convey the same thing to all human beings. But often, peoples from different cultures have different body languages. For example, Europeans or Americans do not stick out their tongue to express a feeling of guilt or shame, unlike Indians or Bangladeshis.

This is what some of our facial expressions and gestures convey:

Body Language	What It Conveys
Nodding of head	Agreement
Shaking of head	Disagreement
Wrinkling the forehead	Surprise, anxiety

---

[1] **gesture:** a movement of hand or head to show a particular meaning.

[2] **posture:** how you sit or stand while talking.

Body Language	What It Conveys
Raising eyebrows	Enquiry, surprise, or doubt
Staring with an open mouth	Surprise
Twisting one's lips	Dislike or hatred
Stooping shoulders	Lack of confidence or spirit
Shrugging of shoulders	Indifference
Clenching fists	Anger, aggression
Tapping fingers	Impatience
Index and middle finger raised	Victory
Thumbs up	Wish you good luck!

We use body language all the time without being aware of it. Often, our body language gives us away. You may not shout, but a tightened fist or blazing eyes might tell people that you are angry. We have to be careful about body language. We cannot click our fingers or shrug in front of our college principal. And often it might be necessary to see that our body language doesn't tell people that we are angry, irritated, or unhappy.

ACTIVITY 1

What Are They 'Saying'?

These people are saying something without using words. Write down what they are saying:

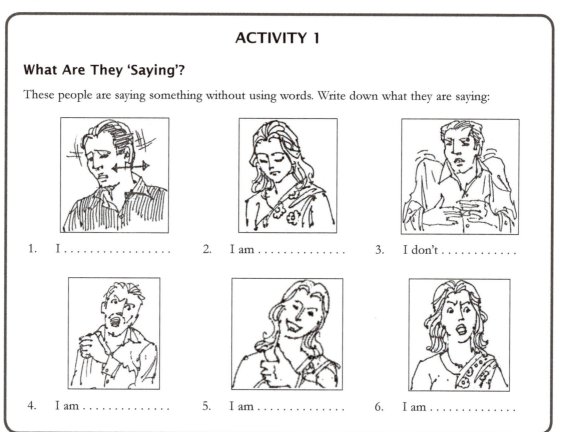

1.   I . . . .

2.   I am . . . .

3.   I don't . . . .

4.   I am . . . .

5.   I am . . . .

6.   I am . . . .

2.4 TONE AND NATURE OF VOICE

The **tone** or nature of your voice significantly changes the meaning of what you wish to say. For example, consider the sentence: *It's all right.*

If you say this slowly and in an even voice, it would mean you are happy (about something). But if you say the same thing quickly, in a rising voice and end the sentence abruptly, it would mean you are unhappy or angry, but you do not wish to discuss the matter. Our voice has many characteristics: it can be quick, slow, rising, or falling. And it can be loud or a whisper. All these characteristics convey some special meaning.

2.5 COMMUNICATING THROUGH CLOTHES

The clothes you wear also says something about you. That is, your clothes too communicate silently. You must dress appropriately for different occasions. For example, if you face a job interview in faded jeans, you are unlikely to be selected, however brilliant you may be. Also, if you are a young man, you shouldn't go to meet your girlfriend's parents wearing, say, shorts and bathroom slippers; it is likely to create an unfavourable impression. The colour and design of your clothes are important. If you went to a funeral wearing garish[3] clothes, you would seem to be disrespectful.

2.6 DISTANCE BETWEEN THE SPEAKER AND THE LISTENER

When you talk with another person or group, the distance between you and your listener(s) is important. Every one of us has a sense of comfortable distance from the person we are speaking with. If that person gets closer, we feel uneasy, or even threatened. I am sure you have met at least a few people who tend to come too close for comfort? And for the same reason, when people are tightly packed with others, for example, in a Delhi metro coach, or in an office lift, they avoid making eye contact, let alone talking. On the other hand, if someone talks to you from far away, you feel he/she is not interested in you.

The average comfortable distance in the Indian subcontinent is roughly as follows:

Distance Between Two Faces	Speech	Kind of Message
Very close (3 to 6 inches)	Soft whisper	Secret or intimate, like the boy and the girl in the picture on the first page of this chapter
Close (12 to 24 inches)	Audible whisper	Confidential
Neutral (2 to 3 feet)	Low volume	Personal discussion
Neutral (3 to 5 feet)	Full voice	Non-personal exchange
Distant (5 to 20 feet)	Loud voice	Talking to a group

---

[3] **garish:** brightly coloured and unpleasant to look at.

If you address someone from too far away, he or she will not pay attention. And if you get too close, the listener will feel uncomfortable. So the distance between you and the listener has a role to play in the success or failure of communication.

2.7 SUMMARY

The graphic below gives a summary of the different aspects of communication:

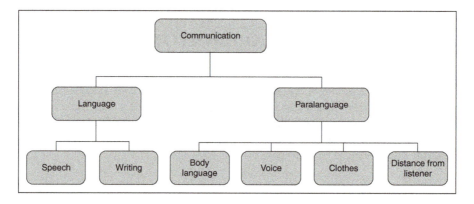

PRACTICE

1. Match the words with their meanings:

1	**garish**	A	to move your head up and down
2	**gesture**	B	without words
3	**nod**	C	how you stand or sit while talking
4	**non-verbal**	D	brightly coloured in an unpleasant way
5	**posture**	E	movement of hands or head to show something

KEY TO ACTIVITY

Activity 1: 1. No, I don't agree. 2. I am ashamed. 3. I don't care. 4. I am angry. 5. I am happy. 6. I am surprised.

Words and Sentences 3

Learning Objectives: Once you have worked through this chapter, you will know what the terms 'word', 'vocabulary', and 'sentence' mean. You will see that English has a huge collection of words; and you will also realize why you must improve your stock of words.

3.1 A TREE CALLED LANGUAGE

A language is like a tree. A tree has three main parts—roots, stem, and branches (comprising leaves, flowers, and fruits). As an analogy, we can say that for any language:

- ✓ the roots are the grammar, that is, the rules of combining words to form sentences,
- ✓ the stem consists of speech and writing, and
- ✓ branches (flowers, fruits, and leaves) consist of beautiful phrases, idioms, and proverbs that add beauty to the language.

To speak and write English fluently, we must learn new words and expressions.

3.2 WORDS, SENTENCES, AND VOCABULARY

- A **word** is a single distinct meaningful element of speech or writing, used with others (or sometimes alone) to form a sentence.
- A **sentence** is a set of words that is complete in itself, conveying a statement, question, or an instruction.

Words are like stand-alone railway coaches. They have meanings, but don't convey any message. But a sentence is like a train that conveys a message (people) to a reader/listener (destination).

> **Vocabulary** means all the words that a person knows or uses.

Therefore, everyone has his/her own vocabulary. Your vocabulary is different from mine. Also, we have two kinds of vocabulary—*active* and *passive*. Your **active vocabulary** is all the words that you know and use. Your **passive vocabulary** is all the words that you know, but cannot use.

> ### * *Its* and *It's*
>
> *My dog's name is Chakradhar.* **It's** *extremely sensitive about its tail.*
>
>   We can rewrite the second sentence as: **It is** *extremely sensitive about its tail.*
>
> - *it's* (with an apostrophe) is a short form of: *it is* (or *it has*) and
> - *its* (without an apostrophe) stands for *Chakradhar's,* to show possession or some other connection.

If a word is in your passive vocabulary, you will understand its* meaning when you read or hear it, but you won't be able to use it while speaking or writing. How do you move words from passive to active vocabulary?

The answer to the question has been given in Chapter 1. Please go through the chapter if you haven't already.

3.3 ENGLISH IS A TREASURE HOUSE OF WORDS

Let's take the word *hand.* Its Hindi equivalent, *haath,* means everything from *shoulder to the finger tips.* But in English, *hand* means *the part of your body that is attached to your forearm,* that is, *your wrist to fingers.* English has three words—*arm, forearm,* and *hand*—for *haath,* which is one word in most Indian languages.

Synonym means a word that has the same or nearly the same meaning as another. English has more synonyms for a word compared to any other language in the world. Let's check the synonyms of the word **break.**

Synonym	What It Means	Example
Break	To separate into two or more parts by force	Be careful, don't break the flower vase.
Burst	Break because of pressure from inside	The dam burst after heavy rains.
Crack	Break without the parts separating	The mirror cracked when I was trying to fix it on the wall.
Fracture	Break or crack a hard substance	I fractured my forearm last night.
Shatter	Suddenly break into small pieces	The bowl shattered into tiny bits when she dropped it.
Smash	Break or to be broken into many parts with a noise	The angry mob smashed the window panes of the bus.
Snap	To break suddenly with a noise	A big branch of the tree snapped in the storm.
Stave	Break something by part of it falling inwards	The roof of our cottage staved in when the branch fell on it.
Split	Divide a collection of something	The teacher split the class into two groups.

And this is not the complete list! There are more. Also, note that usually these words are not interchangeable: You cannot use *snap* instead of *fracture* and so on.

I am explaining this to highlight that English has lots of words, and it is necessary that we keep adding words to our active vocabulary.

ACTIVITY 1

Different ways of seeing: These words mean similar actions, but they are not the same: *look, see, watch, observe,* and *notice.*

Read the following paragraph and guess what these words mean:

When Detective Bhola Singh **looked** inside the restaurant, he **saw** the dangerous criminal Bullet Singh sipping lassi. Bullet **was watching** a yoga guru on TV, and **didn't see** Bhola. Bhola also **noticed** the wedding ring on Bullet's index finger. Detective Bhola **had been** secretly **observing** the movements of Bullet's gang for over a year now. But he had never come across Bullet himself. A smile crossed Bhola's face, he **looked** happy!

Now match the words with the meanings:

1. look	A. to become aware of someone or something by looking at it
2. (to) look	B. to fix your eyes at something
3. see	C. to watch something carefully in order to learn about it
4. observe	D. to look at someone/something for some time, paying attention to details
5. notice	E. to see something and become aware of it
6. watch	F. (to) appear/seem

ACTIVITY 2

Fill in the blanks with:

didn't see	**looked**	**noticed**	**observe**	**saw**	**was looking at**	**watched**

After many years, Ayesha[1]................. her former boyfriend Aneesh at Pune railway station. Aneesh[2].................................. a display board and[3]........................ her. Ayesha[4]................. Aneesh carefully. With a tinge of sadness, she[5]................. the wedding ring on his right index finger. She walked up to Aneesh and[6]................. at him. A surprised Aneesh said, 'Wow! Ayesha! It's great to meet you again. What brings you here?'

'I work in the Girawali Observatory nearby.'

'Observatory?'

'I am an astronomer. I [7]................. stars.'

KEY TO ACTIVITIES

Activity 1: 1. B, 2. F; 3. A, 4. C, 5. E, 6. D

Activity 2: 1. saw; 2. was looking at; 3. didn't see; 4. watched; 5. noticed; 6. looked; 7. observe

Language and Style 4

Learning Objectives: In this chapter, we are discussing how you can make your language more attractive. In particular, we are going into phrases, clauses, idioms, and proverbs.

Shakespeare was not a genius. He was, without the distant shadow of a doubt, the most wonderful writer who ever breathed. But not a genius. No angels handed him his lines, no fairies proofread for him. Instead, he learnt techniques, he learnt tricks, and he learnt them well.

Mark Forsyth, in the preface to *The Elements of Style*

4.1 HOW TO SPEAK SO THAT PEOPLE LISTEN

As we have seen in Chapter 2, we express ourselves mainly—but not only—through language. Some people speak so well that we are forced to listen to them. On the other hand, some people are so boring that the moment they open their mouth, we say, 'Not again!' And this is true about the written language too.

Have you ever thought what makes you listen to some speakers/read some writers with rapt attention, while you find others boring? Effective communication has two main aspects:

1. How you organize[1] what you are going to say
2. The beauty of your language

The first aspect is beyond the scope of this book. In this chapter, we are going to discuss a few ideas to make your speech and writing more beautiful so that people fall in love with your language!

---

[1] **organize:** to arrange thoughts (or things) in a systematic way.

4.2 PHRASES

Many years ago, I went trekking[2] in the jungles of Palamou along with two friends. Palamou, which is in Jharkhand, is a monsoon forest. The lines below are from an account of the trip I wrote later:

> We were camping **in a forest** near Daltongunj. It was **early in the morning** and the sun was rising **in the east**. We **broke camp**[3] at sunrise, had **a cup of tea,** and started off.

Each group of words highlighted here represents a single thing or idea. We call them phrases.

A **phrase** is a sequence of two or more words carrying a single thought.

ACTIVITY 1

I have not highlighted all the phrases in the short passage on camping. Underline the other phrases in the passage and check your answers with the key given at the end of this chapter.

4.3 CLAUSES

Consider the following sentences:

1. We broke camp *at sunrise.*
2. We broke camp *when the sun rose in the east.*

---

[2] **trek:** to travel on foot.

[3] **(to) break camp:** to take down tents.

At sunrise and *when the sun rose in the east* describe the same situation. We call *at sunrise* a time phrase. And if you remove *when* from the second highlighted expression, you get a complete sentence:

The sun rose in the east.

Therefore, we can say that the sentence *We broke camp when the sun rose in the east* is a combination of two sentences: *We broke camp + the sun rose in the east,* joined together by *when.*

If such simple sentences are parts of a longer sentence, we call them clauses.

A group of words that is part of a sentence, but is like a sentence in itself, is called as a **clause**.

4.4 IDIOMS

An **idiom** is a combination of words that convey a meaning different from what is usually understood from the individual words.

Let me give you some examples. ***To keep one's fingers crossed*** means to hope that your plan will work. *I am keeping my fingers crossed that you'll love this book and read it till the end.*

If I told you: ***You should cross the bridge when you get to it,*** I would not be talking about crossing any bridge physically. What I would mean is: *You shouldn't worry about imaginary problems; rather, you should take care of difficulties when you actually face them.*

The Hindi idiom *kebab me haddi (a bone in the kebab)* has an equivalent in English. It's a ***fly in the ointment.*** The same problem is referred to by the French as *a hair in the soup.* In my mother tongue Bangla, to describe a person who is cunning[4] but pretends to be innocent, we use the expression *it seems he can't turn a fried fish around.* We have similar idioms in other South Asian languages too. The same person is described in Malayalam as someone *who chews water before drinking it.* In English, he is known as someone who ***looks like butter doesn't melt in his mouth.*** The concept of idioms is universal, but every language has its own set of idioms. So do not translate idioms literally, that is, word for word. It may not make sense in the target language.

4.5 PROVERBS

Over the ages, people have put some significant and useful truths in simple, catchy sentences and passed them down through generations. They are called ***proverbs*** or ***sayings.*** They too are idiomatic expressions because they convey a meaning which is different from the usual meaning expressed by the words. For example: *All that glitters is not gold,* which means we should not judge things (or people) by their appearance.

---

[4] **cunning:** (adjective) a person who gets what he/she wants by cheating or tricking, FOXY.

A **proverb** (or saying) is an idiom that tells us an age-old truth.

Here are a few other frequently used English sayings:

- ✓ Empty vessels make the most noise. = Ignorant people tend to be talkative or noisy.
- ✓ The darkest hour is just before dawn. = Bad times are never permanent.

There are also a lot of English proverbs that are self-explanatory:

- ✓ It is never too late to learn.
- ✓ Don't cry before you are hurt.
- ✓ A drowning man will clutch at straws.
- ✓ A deaf husband and a blind wife are a happy couple.

A proverb conveys some truth that crosses borders of cultures and times. But many proverbs are culture-specific. In other words, they make sense only to the native speakers of that language. Interestingly, there are often exactly parallel proverbs in English and Indian languages that are expressed differently but still convey the same idea.

TABLE 4.1   Proverbs and Their Literal Translation

Original Proverb	Literal Translation	English Equivalent
Vinash kaale vipreet buddhi (Sanskrit)	Calamities[5] often result in bad judgement.	Whom the gods would destroy, they first make mad.
Aag lagi tyare kuvo khodiyo (Gujarati)	You're digging a well when a fire is raging.	A stitch in time saves nine.
Payye thinnaal panayum thinnaam (Malayalam)	If you eat slowly, you can eat even a palm tree.	Slow and steady wins the race.
Gaachhe kaanthal gonfey tel (Bangla)	The jackfruit is on the tree and you think you've eaten it.	Don't count your chickens before they hatch.

Beautiful phrases, idioms, and proverbs are like ornaments to a language. Try to learn, remember, and use them when you speak and when you write informally. Proper use of idioms, including sayings, add beauty and sharpness to your speech and writing. They also make your language sound *natural*.

However, do not use idioms or proverbs in official letters or formal essays.

Another word of caution: Idioms, including proverbs, are language-specific. They are often understood only by the native speakers of the language. And as Table 4.1 shows, literal translation of a proverb from your mother tongue may not make sense in English. Therefore, let's learn English idioms.

---

[5] **calamity:** (noun) an event that causes huge damage: *The commonest natural calamity in India is flooding of rivers during monsoons.*

PRACTICE

1. Write down what you understand by the following idioms:

   a. Somebody's bark is worse than their bite

   ....

   b. Between the devil and the deep blue sea

   ....

   c. Be out of one's depth

   ....

   d. To make hay while the sun shines

   ....

   e. To make heavy weather of something

   ....

   f. Running with the hare and hunting with the hound

   ....

   g. Sleep like a log

   ....

   h. Stepping into someone else's shoes

   ....

2. Some common English proverbs have been jumbled below. Arrange them in order. Also, write down what you understand by these sayings and check your answers with the key given at the back of the book.

	The Proverb	*It Means*
→ port /in/storm/a/any	Any port in a storm.	We cannot be choosy during an emergency.
a. in hand/bird/is/ two/worth/a/in the bush		
b. cloth/ cut/according to/your/your/coat		
c. vessels/the most/sound/empty/make		
d. rush in/angels/fools/where/fear to tread		
e. an/brain/idle/workshop/brain/devil's/the/is		
f. is/it/too/never/late/to learn		
g. a/time/in/stitch/nine/saves		
h. spilt milk /crying over/there is no use		
i. cooks/too many/the broth/spoil		
j. a will/where/there's/a way/there's		

3. Read the complete proverbs and think if you have a similar proverb in your mother tongue. Write them down.

KEY TO ACTIVITY

Activity 1: 1. were camping; 2. near Daltongunj; 3. the sun; 4. was rising; 5. at sunrise; 6. started off.

Different Classes of Words

Learning Objectives: Words are grouped into eight categories on the basis of their functions in sentences. In this chapter, we are going to study these categories, which are called word classes.

5.1 CLASSES OF WORDS

Shankar had a very strange dream …. He is in a dense jungle of tall bamboo grass. He and another man are climbing up a huge mountain. The views around them are stunningly beautiful. Around them are bamboo stalks and tall trees with creepers[1] …. And far away, there is a snow-clad mountain peak

---

[1] **creeper:** (noun) a plant that climbs trees or walls.

washed by moonlight. A clear sky with countless stars scattered around. He hears trumpeting of wild elephants. The whole jungle shakes with the sound. (*Source: The Mountain of the Moon*, a children's novel by Bibhuti Bhushan Bandyopadhyay)

English words are classified into eight groups called ***word classes*** or ***parts of speech:***

1. Nouns	5. Adverbs
2. Pronouns	6. Prepositions
3. Verbs	7. Linking words
4. Adjective	8. Determiners

5.2 DEFINITIONS OF DIFFERENT CLASSES OF WORDS

1. **Verb:** A word or a group of words that expresses an action (such as *climb up*), an event (such as *happen*) or a state, condition, or location. (*Shankar is in a dense jungle.*)
2. **Noun:** A word that refers to a person, place, thing, quality, or an activity. (*Shankar, dream, bamboo grass* [a noun phrase], *views*)
3. **Pronoun:** A word that is used instead of a noun or a noun phrase. (*I, we, she, they, her, them,* and so on)
4. **Adjective:** A word that describes a person or a thing. (The underlined words in: *strange dream, dense jungle, huge mountain*)
5. **Adverb:** A word or a phrase that adds more information about the place, time, manner, cause, or the degree to a verb, adjective, or another adverb. (The underlined words in: *Shankar thinks of adventures all the time. They moved slowly through the jungle. A very strange idea.*)
6. **Preposition:** A word that connects a noun/pronoun and someone or something else. (*There was a lake between the jungle and the mountain. Shankar made friends with Diego Alvarez.*)
7. **Linking words:** Words such as *and, so,* and *but* that join two words or two parts of a sentence.
8. **Determiner:** Most English words belong to one or more of the seven categories described above. The words that do not fit any of these categories are called *determiners*. A determiner comes before noun phrases, but it is not an adjective. There are five groups of them:

   a. A unique group called **articles;** the group has only three words: *a, an,* and *the*.
   b. Words that indicate possession or some other connection: *my book, your boyfriend, her, his, their, its, whose,* and so on.
   c. Words that point at things: *this, these, that, those*.
   d. A group called **quantifiers** that indicate how much or how many we are talking about: *one, ten, some, any, each, every, much, many,* and so on.
   e. Some other words: *which, whichever, what,* etc.

Let's identify the word classes for the first three sentences from the passage at the beginning of this chapter:

Shankar	had	a	very	strange	dream
noun	verb	determiner	adverb	adjective	noun

He	is	in	a	dense	jungle	of	tall	bamboo grass
pronoun	verb	preposition	determiner	adjective	noun	preposition	adjective	noun phrase

He	and	another	man	are climbing up	a	huge	mountain
pronoun	linking word	determiner	noun	verb phrase	determiner	adjective	noun

5.3 SAME WORD, DIFFERENT WORD CLASSES

Each one of us belongs to several groups. For example, I belong to my family, a country called India, and also to the teaching fraternity.[2] Similarly, most words belong to several word classes. A word which is a noun in one sentence can be an adjective in another. In fact, we usually assign a word to a word class only with reference to a context. For example:

- ✓ I <u>dream</u> of going to the moon.   ⇨ *dream* is a verb here
- ✓ I have a <u>dream.</u>   ⇨ *dream* is a noun
- ✓ Sunil Gavaskar made a <u>dream</u> debut[3] in 1970. ⇨ *dream* as adjective

Another example:

- ✓ The teacher said <u>that</u> Ravi had done well.   ⇨ *that* is a linking word
- ✓ I knew <u>that</u> all along.   ⇨ *that* is a pronoun
- ✓ Please give me <u>that</u> book.   ⇨ *that* is a determiner

---

ACTIVITY 1

1. Underline the nouns or noun phrases in the following sentences:

    The jungle is dense. Around them are bamboo stalks and tall trees with creepers. And far away, there is a snow-clad mountain.

2. Underline the verbs in the following sentences:

    They are walking through a jungle of bamboo stalks and tall trees with creepers. Far away, there is a snow-clad mountain. Shankar suddenly hears trumpeting of wild elephants.

3. Underline the adjectives in the following sentences:

    Above, a clear sky with millions of twinkling stars. He hears trumpeting of wild elephants. The dark jungle shakes with the sound.

---

[2] **fraternity:** (noun) a group of people who are in the same profession.
[3] **debut:** (noun) the first public appearance of a performer or sportsperson, pronounced DE**BIU.**

4. Underline the adverbs in the following sentences:

   The jungle shakes violently with the sound. Suddenly, he hears trumpeting of wild elephants. Shankar and Diego Alvarez climb the hill silently.

5. Underline the prepositions in the following sentences:

   Shankar was in bed. Early sunlight was streaming in through the window. He had just dreamed of a snow-clad mountain.

6. Underline the determiners in the following sentences:

   That morning, Shankar took an early bath and went to the village library. He borrowed three adventure stories based in Africa.

PRACTICE

1 Identify the class to which the following words belong:

a	Mother	gave	me	a	book	yesterday	

b	The	book	is	*The Old Man and the Sea*			

c	It	is	a	novella	by	Ernest Hemingway	

d	It	is	about	Santiago	an	old	fisherman

e	I	am reading	the	book	now		

2 Complete the grid in the following page with names of word classes (or parts of speech).

A1: A word such as *a, this,* and *my* that comes before a noun/ noun phrase, but is not an adjective

A2: A word or group of words that expresses an action, an event, or the state of something

A3: A word used instead of a noun or noun phrase

D1: A word that describes a person or a thing, such as *beautiful, tall, angry, huge, black,* or *white*

D2: A word that establishes the relationship between a noun/pronoun and someone or something else

D3: A word or phrase that adds more information about the place, time, manner, cause, or the degree to a verb, adjective, or another adverb

D4: A word that refers to a person, place, thing, quality, or an activity

3. Name the missing word class in the above grid ……………………….

KEY TO ACTIVITY

Activity 1:

1. <u>Nouns</u> or <u>noun phrases</u>: jungle, bamboo stalks, trees, creepers, mountain
2. <u>Verbs</u>: are, is, hears
3. <u>Adjectives</u>: <u>clear</u> sky, <u>twinkling</u> stars, <u>wild</u> elephants, <u>dark</u> jungle
4. <u>Adverbs</u>: The jungle shakes <u>violently</u> …. <u>Suddenly</u>, he hears …. Shankar and Diego Alvarez climb the hill <u>silently</u>.
5. <u>Prepositions</u>: Shankar was <u>in</u> bed. Early sunlight was streaming in <u>through</u> the window. He had just dreamed <u>of</u> a snow-clad mountain.
6. <u>Determiners</u>: <u>That</u> morning, Shankar took <u>an</u> early bath and went to <u>the</u> village library. He borrowed <u>three</u> adventure novels based in Africa.

6

Sentence Patterns

Learning Objectives: Every language has its own patterns. In this chapter, we are going to discuss the basic patterns of the English language, and how words are combined to frame sentences. Among the different classes of words, the most complex are the verbs. When you have studied this chapter, you will identify the factors that determine the forms of verbs and also how words are combined in English.

6.1 SYNTAX: THE BASIC PATTERN OF ENGLISH

When we frame a sentence, we either make a *positive statement* or a *negative one*, or ask a *question*.

- Raju is a good boy.   ⇒ Positive
- Raju is not/isn't a good boy.   ⇒Negative
- Is Raju a good boy?   ⇒ Question

We don't say: ~~Raju a good boy is~~. Or: ~~Raju is a good boy not~~. Or: ~~Is a good boy Raju?~~

We don't say these because to frame sentences, we arrange words following *some fixed patterns*. Collectively, these patterns are known as **syntax.** (Perhaps you know that the software on your phone or laptop too is written in computer languages that follow fixed 'syntax'?)

The way in which words and phrases are combined to frame sentences in a language is called the **syntax.**

Every language has its own **syntax.** And the rules for framing sentences are called **grammar.** Learning a language is basically learning words and learning how to combine them.

Let me say here that there are many similarities between the syntax (the plural too is **syntax**) of modern North Indian languages such as Hindi, Assamese, Bengali, Gujarati, Marathi, Punjabi, and Urdu. This is because all these languages (except Urdu) evolved from Sanskrit. Urdu is a hybrid language, a combination of Persian and Hindi. Dravidian languages such as Tamil, Telugu, Kannada, and Malayalam have a history independent of Sanskrit, but at present, there are many similarities between them and the North Indian languages that originated from Sanskrit. Together, they are known as the *Indic languages.*

Certain European languages such as French, Spanish, Portuguese, and Italian belong to a particular group. They all originated from Latin and are collectively known as the *Romance languages.* On the other hand, English, German, Dutch, Swedish, etc., form another language group known as the *Germanic languages.*

6.2 'OUR' SYNTAX, 'THEIR' SYNTAX

If you are from India, Pakistan, Bangladesh, Nepal, or Sri Lanka, please keep in mind that the English syntax is completely different from the syntax of the South Asian languages. To appreciate the point, translate the following into your mother tongue: *I went to my brother's home yesterday.*

I don't know what language you speak, but I know that your translation reads:

('I' in your language) + (a word for 'yesterday') + (a word for 'my') + (a word for 'brother's') + (a word for 'home') + (a word/words for 'went')

This illustrates an amazing fact: *Most South Asian languages follow similar syntax, which is completely different from English.*

English →	I	went	to	my	brother's	home	yesterday
Our languages →	I	yesterday	–	my	brother's	home	went

Therefore, it will be difficult for you to learn English if you try to frame sentences in your head in a South Asian language and translate them into English. *You must **think** in English.*

6.3 COLLOCATION

From Section 6.2, it follows that if we wish to speak or write effectively in a language other than our mother tongue, it will be good to have a clear idea of the syntax of the second language. The next factor that you should also keep in mind is: *collocation.*

To explain collocation, let me first ask a question. Are the following phrases (that is, combinations of words) all right?

- global heating, central warming
- travel operator, tour agent
- powerful coffee, strong engine

Heating and warming mean the same thing, just as *operator–agent* and *strong–powerful*. Yet, no one ever uses these combinations. You say: *global warming, central heating, travel agent, tour operator, strong coffee,* and *powerful engine*.

To a native speaker of English (that is, someone who speaks English as mother tongue), *powerful coffee* or *global heating* would sound strange and incorrect. This means we cannot combine words randomly. We must learn which words *go together,* which combinations sound *natural*.

Collocation refers to the usual combinations of a particular word with another word or other words.

Continuing with collocation, let's recall that a verb is often a word that describes an action. [More about verbs in a moment.] Let's check a few collocations with verbs.

1. **answer:** You *answer* (or *respond to*) a question; you also *answer the door* or *answer the phone* (but you don't ~~respond~~ *to the door* or *a phone!*).
2. **going home/going abroad:** You *go to school* or *to office* or *to the cinema,* but you *go home, go abroad,* and *go there.*
3. **whisk:** To make an omelette, you have *to whisk an egg*. You cannot replace *whisk* with any other verb. For example: *you do not ~~stir~~ an egg* ✘.

Keep the idea of collocation in the back of your head. If you come across a *combination of two (or more) words* which is seen 'at a frequency greater than chance', try to remember the combination or collocation.

Going Abroad

The word ***abroad*** means **in** or **to a country other than your own:**

✓ *Ravi lived abroad for a year as student (=lived in a foreign country).*
✓ *I have never gone abroad (=never gone outside my country).*

Learners often have problem with *abroad*. I've heard people say:

✘ *I want to go ~~to~~ abroad.*
✘ *Her brother ~~lives in an abroad country~~.*

The last two sentences are not fine. You **go abroad** and **live abroad.**

ACTIVITY 1

Combine a word or phrase each from the two boxes below to form 12 phrases:

(to) answer, balanced, central, fully, (to) go, lunch, open-air, powerful, strong, tour, travel, (to) whisk	abroad, agency, an egg, aware, box, tea, diet, engine, heating, operator, theatre, the door

1. .... 2. .... 3. .... 4. ....
5. .... 6. .... 7. .... 8. ....
9. .... 10. .... 11. .... 12. ....

6.4 IS THERE A GENERAL PATTERN OF ENGLISH SENTENCES?

When we frame a sentence, we talk about a person or a thing. The person or the thing is called the *subject* of the sentence. We also need a *verb* to say something about the subject. A sentence usually (not always) begins with the subject. The simplest English sentence would look like:

Subject	Verb
The fish	swims
Men	talk

Obviously, we cannot go very far with just a subject and a verb. We need more parts, and these are broadly classified as *object, complement,* and *adverbial.* We will discuss them in a moment, but before that, let's look at *verbs* more closely.

6.5 ACTION VERBS/STATE VERBS

Note the verbs in the following sentences. (They are in italics.[1])

Mom *gave* me a book on my birthday. It *is* a novel. It's fantastic! I *am reading* it now.

The verbs in the first and the fourth sentences above are about *actions:* giving and reading. In this book, we will call verbs like these, which describe an action (or an event), *action verbs.*

The verbs in the second and third sentences do not talk about any action. In the second sentence, the verb *is* identifies the book. In the third, the verb tells you what kind of a book it is (*It's fantastic!*). Let's say the verbs in these sentences describe the *identity, quality* or *state* of the book. Looking at it from a different angle, in these two sentences, the verb *is* links the subject with other words.

Verbs that play these roles are called either *link verbs* or *state verbs.* We will refer to them as *state verbs* throughout this book. Here are some frequently used state verbs: *be, become, believe, know, seem, understand,* and so on. We will discuss state verbs in more detail in Chapter 8 [*I Am Fine,* pp. 49–51].

The commonest state verb is *be. Am* (or *'m*), *is* (or *'s*), and *are* (also, *'re*) are the three forms of the verb in the present tense. For example:

✓ I am happy. Also: I'm happy.
✓ Why are you angry?
✓ He is not well, but he's full of spirit.

Some verbs may be used both as action verbs or state verbs:

Action verb	*State verb*
✓ She looked into the mirror.	✓ She looked happy.
✓ She has appeared in a few films.	✓ She appears sad.
✓ The nurse is feeling her pulse.	✓ I feel happy.

---

[1] **italics:** sloping letters that are used in printed books to highlight points.

6.6 ESSENTIAL ELEMENTS OF AN ENGLISH SENTENCE

Continuing from where we left in Section 6.4, here are a few examples of the essential elements of an English sentence.

S.No.	Subject	Verb	Object(s)	Complement	Adverbial
1	Mother	gave	me a book		on my birthday
2	It	is		*The Old Man and the Sea*	
3	*The Old Man and the Sea*	is		a novel by Ernest Hemingway	
4	It	is		about Santiago, an elderly fisherman	
5	I	am reading	the book		now

Let me now define the terms *object, complement,* and *adverbial:*

An *object* is a word or phrase that refers to either <u>a person or a thing affected by the action of the verb</u> (called the *direct object*) or <u>a person/thing which is the recipient of that action</u> (called the *indirect object*).

In the first sentence in the above table, the verb <u>gave</u> has two objects: (a) the *direct object,* <u>a book,</u> because the action of *giving* happens on it and (b) an *indirect object,* <u>me,</u> because <u>me</u> is the recipient of the action. In the fifth sentence, the verb is <u>am reading</u> and the only (*direct*) object is <u>the book</u>.

* Compliment/Complement

These words are pronounced in the same way, but they mean completely different things.

- If you say you love this book (I hope you do!), you will be paying me a *compliment*.
- In grammar, a *complement* is a word or a phrase that comes after a state verb and completes the sentence.

A *complement** is a <u>noun</u>, <u>noun phrase</u>, or a <u>pronoun</u> which comes after a state verb (such as *be, become,* and *seem*) and <u>completes the sense conveyed by the verb</u>.

Without the complements, the second, third, and fourth sentences in Section 6.1 read:

- It is
- *The Old Man and the Sea* is
- It is

They mean nothing. They become meaningful only when we add a complement after the verb.

- An *adverbial* is a word or a phrase that gives us more information about <u>the state/condition of something</u> or about <u>an action</u>, such as the <u>place</u>, <u>time</u>, or <u>manner</u> of the action.

Therefore, we can say that the simplest sentences may have one of the following patterns:

- ✓ Subject + action verb + object
- ✓ Subject + action verb + object + adverbial
- ✓ Subject + state verb + complement

Note this structure in your head. However, this is not a rule; it just gives you a general idea. Sentences are actually framed in many different ways as we will see throughout this book.

ACTIVITY 2

Read the sentence below and answer the questions that follow:

The boy spread a blanket over Santiago when it was dark.

Question	Answer
1. Which word describes the person doing the work?	The boy
2. Which word describes the action?	
3. Which words describe the thing on which the action is done?	
4. Which word describes the person who receives the blanket?	
5. Which words give information about the time of the action?	
6. Which word connects *a blanket* with *Santiago?*	

ACTIVITY 3

1. Match the words in the two columns below:

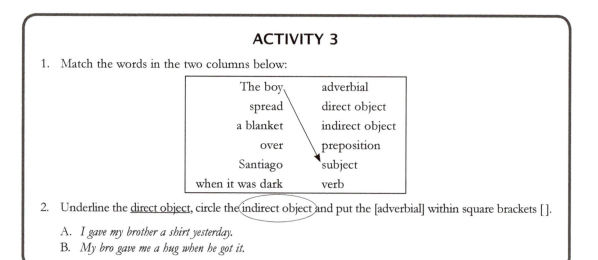

2. Underline the <u>direct object</u>, circle the indirect object and put the [adverbial] within square brackets [ ].

   A. *I gave my brother a shirt yesterday.*
   B. *My bro gave me a hug when he got it.*

6.7 PERSON, NUMBER, AND TENSE OF A VERB

The form of the verb depends on the nature of the subject. By nature, we mean two things: ***person*** and ***number*** of the subject. The table below explains the concept.

Person	Singular Number	Plural Number
First person	I	we
Second person	you	you
Third person	he, she, it, my city, Deepika, Sri Lanka …	They, Sharukh and Aamir, five cars, our cities …

The form of the verb also depends on its ***tense.*** The tense of a verb tells us whether it describes the present, past, or the future.

The following table shows some sentences where the verbs have been highlighted. Can you tell us the person, number, and the tense of these verbs?

	Person	Number	Tense
Gabbar Singh **sings** bhajans.	third	singular	present
I **studied** with Gabbar at college.			
Are you students of this college?			
We **study** English.			
Students **will not/won't accept** this.			

Key: 1. first person, singular number, past tense; 2. second person, plural, present tense; 3. first person, plural, present tense; 4. third person, plural, future tense.

You will see it is easy to identify the tense, but you might find it a little confusing to determine the person and number of the subject. Let's check a few sentences to get a clearer idea on this.

The Subject in Bold	The Person and the Number Are
Tausif and I were students at Cotton College.	*Tausif and I* mean 'we'; so the subject is *first person, plural*
One of my friends is a TV newscaster.	*Third person, singular*, because we are talking about only one person here
The number of students in this school is 800.	*Third person, singular number*; the subject here is *The number*, which is a singular noun
All the photos in his album were faded.	The subject is *All the photos*, not the *album*; so *third person, plural*
The books in this shelf belong to my dad.	Third person, plural
Two weeks is sufficient time to do this.	Here, *two weeks* is considered as a period of time; hence, *third person, singular number*

The Subject in Bold	The Person and the Number Are
Either he or you are responsible.	The complete sentence is: *Either he is responsible or you are responsible*. The sentence on the left is a shortened version without the words 'is responsible'. So *second person, singular number*.
A majority of Indians live/lives in villages.	Third person. We can treat *A majority of Indians* as either *plural* or *singular*.

You can read more about this aspect in Section 12.8 (Page 86).

PRACTICE

1. Strike off the incorrect words.

   To make an omelette, you have to first break an egg, as the saying goes. And after that, you **¹stir/whisk** the egg. Nandini is doing precisely that at the moment. Next, she will **²toast/roast** two slices of bread and make herself a **³strong/powerful** cup of tea.

   The weather is **⁴sunny/golden**, but Nandini is tense. From her **⁵native/hometown** near Kolkata, she has come to the **⁶olden/historic** city of Hyderabad to join a badminton academy. It's not just any other academy, it is the same institution that has produced **⁷champions/victors** such as Saina Nehwal, P.V. Sindhu, and Srikanth Kidambi.

   Nandini has been staying at her uncle's home at Banjara Hills. Her uncle and aunt are in office at the moment. She is all alone. **⁸Last/Yesterday** night, she **⁹gave/took** the first round of her selection test. She thinks the coach who had played against her was **¹⁰fully/completely** impressed. In a short **¹¹period/while** from now, she is going to meet the **¹²chief/head** of the academy, Pullela Gopichand, who himself was a champion badminton player in the past. He is among the top coaches in the world today.

2. Complete the definitions by filling in the blanks with one of these:

adverbial   complement   direct object   indirect object   state   subject   syntax

   a. The way in which words and phrases are combined to frame a sentence is called the ....
   b. A sentence usually tells us about a person or a thing. That person or thing is called the .... of the sentence.
   c. A/An .... is a thing or person that is affected by the action.
   d. A/An .... is a noun, noun phrase, or pronoun that tells us about the person to whom the action is done.
   e. A/An .... is the word that comes after verbs such as be, become, seem, and appear, and completes the sense conveyed by the verb.
   f. A/An .... is a word or a phrase that adds place, time, manner, cause, or the degree to a verb, adjective, phrase, or another adverb.
   g. A verb that talks about the state or identity of a thing has been referred to as .... verb in this book.

3. Strike off the incorrect verb:

   a. Only one of the answers **is/are** correct.
   b. Mother and I **am/are** shifting to a new house.
   c. Either he or you **is/are** wrong.
   d. She told her husband, 'You want to go abroad for two years? Two years **is/are** a long time.'
   e. The number of cars in our cities **is/are** increasing every day.
   f. The consequences of our action **was/were** grave.
   g. Two little boys and a woman **is/are** waiting at the door.
   h. Time and tide **wait/waits** for no man.

4. Fill in the blanks with *is, are, has,* or *have*:

   a. The chairman of the board and all the members _____ present.
   b. Most of the songs by Geeta Dutt _____ superb.
   c. One of my friends _____ a Harley Davidson bike.
   d. In India, everyone over 18 _____ eligible to vote.
   e. It is a tough paper. Three hours _____ not enough to complete it.

5. Underline the <u>direct object</u>, circle the (indirect object,) and put a bracket () around the adverbial in the sentences below:

   a. Ravi repaired his motorbike last Sunday.
   b. Inspector Bhola put a handcuff on Bullet Singh.
   c. Mother gave Kuttan a music system on his birthday.

KEY TO ACTIVITIES

Activity 1: 1. (to) answer the door; 2. balanced diet; 3. central heating; 4. fully aware; 5. (to) go abroad; 6. lunch box; 7. open-air theatre; 8. powerful engine; 9. strong tea; 10. tour operator; 11. travel agency, 12. (to) whisk an egg

Activity 2: 2. spread; 3. a blanket; 4. Santiago; 5. when it was dark; 6. over

Activity 3: 1. The boy → subject; spread → verb; a blanket → direct object; over → preposition; Santiago → indirect object; when it was dark → adverbial; 2. A. I gave my (brother) a <u>shirt</u> [yesterday]. B. My bro gave (me) a <u>hug</u> [when he got it].

Test 1:
Reviewing the Basics

1. Given below are some pieces of advice for improving your English. If you think the idea is good, put a ✔ next to the sentence. If you think it is not, put a ✘.

   A. Read English books, magazines, and newspapers, and also, watch films, YouTube videos, and TV programmes in English. ☐
   B. Read and follow English from wherever you find the language, including signboards. ☐
   C. Pick up words randomly from a dictionary and memorize their meanings. ☐
   D. When you read or listen, focus on *how words are used*. ☐
   E. Record new words and expressions in a personal wordbook and go through them regularly. ☐
   F. Write down at least 10 sentences with every new word you come across. ☐
   G. Think about how you can use the new words you have learned. Frame sentences with them in your head. ☐
   H. Practise speaking and writing as much as you can. ☐
   I. Take a grammar book, memorize the rules, and apply them when you speak or write English. ☐
   J. Write and speak naturally, without worrying too much about grammar, but follow a dependable grammar book to understand the patterns of the language. ☐

2 Fill in the blanks to complete the sentences:

   Communication happens mainly through ¹l _ _ _ _ _ _ _ and also, through paralanguage. ²L _ _ _ _ _ _ _ means both ³s _ _ _ _ _ _ _ and writing. Paralanguage means ⁴_ _ _ _ _ _ _ l_ _ _ _ _ _, the nature of your ⁵v _ _ _ _, what kind of clothes you are wearing, and also, how close you are to your listener or listeners.

3. Read the sentences and put the highlighted words or phrases in the correct box below. (If necessary, go back to Chapter 5 and check the definitions of the word classes.)

   After many years, Ayesha saw her former boyfriend Aneesh at the crowded railway station in Pune. Aneesh was looking at a display board and didn't notice her. Ayesha watched Aneesh carefully. With a tinge of sadness, she noticed the shining wedding ring on his finger. She walked up to him and looked at him.

Nouns or noun phrases	
Pronouns	
Verbs or verb phrases	
Adjectives	
Adverbs	
Prepositions	
Linking words	
Determiners	*many;*

4. In the sentences below, I have underlined the verbs. What kind of verbs are these? Write either *Action Verb* or *State Verb* in the blank spaces next to the sentences.

   A. After many years, Ayesha <u>saw</u> Aneesh at a railway station. ....

   B. She <u>noticed</u> the wedding ring on his ring finger ....

   C. She <u>felt</u> a little sad. ....

   D. She <u>walked up</u> to Aneesh and said 'Hullo!' ....

   E. Aneesh <u>was</u> surprised to see his former girlfriend unexpectedly. ....

5. Fill in the blanks with *am, is, are, has,* or *have*.

   A. Tausif and I .... teachers at this language school.

   B. Either Tausif or I .... going to receive our guests at the airport.

   C. One of my friends .... a famous TV actor.

   D. The number of cars in Bengaluru .... increasing every day.

   E. All the shopping malls in this city .... large parking lots.

   F. All the saris in this store .... expensive.

   G. Either you or he .... responsible for this mess.[1]

   H. A significant[2] number of Indians .... vegetarians.

6. In the sentences below, underline the <u>direct objects</u>, circle the (indirect objects,) and put the adverbial within square brackets [].

   A. Radhika bought a camera at the duty-free shop.

   B. She gave it to Ravi on his birthday.

   C. Ravi held the camera with evident delight.

---

[1] **mess:** (noun) untidiness or confusion.

[2] **significant:** (adjective) large, sizeable.

PART

2

LET'S TALK ABOUT THE PRESENT

7
Everyday Activities and Universal Truths

Learning Objectives: In this chapter, we are going to discuss the language used to talk about (a) what people do regularly and also, (b) statements that are always true.

7.1 INTRODUCTION

Let us begin with everyday activities. We use the **simple present tense** for these. This is how verbs are used in this tense:

- ✓ love ⇒ I <u>love</u> mangoes.
- ✓ like ⇒ We <u>like</u> mangoes.
- ✓ enjoy ⇒ You <u>enjoy</u> mangoes.
- ✓ sell ⇒ They <u>sell</u> mango juice.

But the rule is different when a sentence talks about a single person (or a thing) other than *you* and *I*.

- ✓ love ⇒ Ravi <u>loves</u> mangoes.
- ✓ hate ⇒ Radhika <u>hates</u> mangoes.

The rules for using verbs are also known as **conjugation** of verbs. The conjugation of verbs in the simple present tense is shown in Table 7.1.

TABLE 7.1 Conjugation of Verbs in the Simple Present Tense

I	**like**	mangoes
We		reading storybooks
You		classical music
All of you		to visit different places
They		listening to music
He/She	**likes**	dancing in rain

The rules for using a verb in the simple present tense are:

1. When the subject is in the first person (I or we) or second person (you), we don't change the verb.
2. When we talk about the third person singular number (he, she, my grandma,[1] the train), we add either *s* or *es* after the base verb; if the verb ends with *y*, we replace the *y* with *ies* (cry → cries).
3. But if the subject is 'in the third person, but more than one' (they), we leave the verb unchanged.

This is one of the first rules of English grammar. It isn't too complex, is it? And the other rules of English grammar are simple too. You can learn them easily.

7.2 SAYING NEGATIVE THINGS

The negative forms of verbs are given in Table 7.2.

TABLE 7.2 Negative Forms of Verbs

	Positive Sentences	Negative Sentences
1.	I **eat** fried ice cream every day.	I **don't/do not eat** fried ice cream.
2.	We **study** English.	We **don't/do not study** English.
3.	You **drive** very well.	You **don't/do not drive** very well.
4.	Grandpa **plays** kabaddi.	Grandpa **doesn't/does not play** kabaddi.
5.	Radhika **rides**[2] a scooter to office.	Radhika **doesn't/does not ride** a scooter to office.
6.	Express trains **stop** at this station.	Express trains **don't/do not stop** at this station.

Note the use of *do not* (don't) and *does not* (doesn't). The negative sentences are framed this way:
Framing Negative Sentences

I	**don't like** or **do not like**	mangoes
We		classical music
You		reading
All of you		visiting different places
They		Mondays
He/She	**doesn't like** or **does not like**	Bollywood films

---

[1] **grandma:** (noun) a shortened form of *grandmother*. Similarly, *grandpa* stands for *grandfather*.

[2] You **drive** a car, but **ride** a bike/scooter. You don't drive a bike. You **sail** a boat, **fly** an aircraft.

Let's practise conjugations. Please go back to Table 7.2. Cover the second column and write down the negative sentences in a notebook. If you have got them right, move to the next section. If you haven't, check your answers and repeat the activity.

In Sections 7.1 and 7.2, we have discussed the negative forms of ordinary verbs such as *run*, *stop*, and *like*. The rules are different for some special verbs such as **be** (*am*, *is*, and *are* in the simple present tense), **can**, and **may**. We will discuss these verbs later.

Doesn't/Does Not

When we speak, we normally don't say *Grandpa **does not play** kabaddi*. We say:

*Grandpa **doesn't play** kabaddi.*

Even when we write informally (that is, when we write to our parents or a friend), we use **doesn't** and **don't** instead of *does not* and *do not*. I have often used the informal style in this book.

7.3 WHEN DO WE USE THE SIMPLE PRESENT TENSE?

✓ Raghu <u>works</u> in a government office. He joined the office sometime last year. He <u>goes</u> to office by bus. Sometimes he <u>takes</u> a taxi. After reaching office, he <u>drinks</u> a glass of water and <u>sleeps</u> for some time.

These sentences (except the second) talk about the present. The underlined verbs tell us about an *everyday activity*, that is, an activity that is *part of someone's routine*. We use the **simple present tense** to describe these.

The following sentences too are in the simple present tense, but they don't talk about a regular activity. Instead, they express some *universal truths*, that is, statements which are always true.

✓ Learning another language <u>is</u> fun.
✓ Knowledge of grammar <u>helps</u> us learn a second language.
✓ However, almost everyone <u>hates</u> grammar.

The simple present is also used to describe something that is happening at the moment, such as in a running commentary:

- ✓ Rabada **bowls** another bouncer.
- ✓ Here **comes** the team bus.
- ✓ There he **goes**!

Finally, this tense is used to describe the state of something that is currently true:

- ✓ You **look** sad and troubled. I **understand** your difficulties.

To summarize, we use the simple present tense to:

1. Describe things that happen regularly, or things we do regularly
2. Express universal truths
3. Describe something that is happening right now
4. Describe the state of something that is currently true

▌ 7.4 WHEN WE SPEAK…

The spoken language is often different from the written language. If someone asks you a question, usually you give only a partial answer. For example, if I ask you, *'Do you study at Cotton College?',* you say:

- ✓ Yes, I do.

    Or,

- ✓ No, I don't.

You don't say: *Yes, I study at Cotton College.* Or, *No, I don't study at….*

Some time, Sometime, and *Sometimes*

- We use **some time** for 'a period of time' if we don't state the period precisely. For example:

After reaching office, Raghu sleeps for <u>some time</u>.

- We use **sometime** to talk about a time that we don't know exactly, or a future time that has not been decided yet:

Raghu joined this office <u>sometime</u> last year. Or, I'll telephone you <u>sometime</u> next week.

- **Sometimes** means occasionally:

He goes to office by bus. <u>Sometimes</u>, he takes a taxi.

Please and *Thanks*

Please and **Thanks** are two power words that are used in English often. In many South Asian languages, we don't use the equivalent of these except in very formal situations. But in English, if you say, 'Give me a glass of water', it would be considered rude.

Give me a glass of water. ✗
⇨ **Please give** me a glass of water. ✓

Sign here. ✗
⇨ **Please sign** here. ✓

How are you?—**I am fine**. ✗
⇨ **I'm fine, thanks. How are you?** ✓

Shall I give you a cup of tea?—**No!** ✗
⇨ **No, thanks.** Or, **No, thank you.** ✓

Thank you is more formal than plain **thanks**. When your boss sanctions your leave, you normally say: *Thank you.* Not just *thanks.*

ACTIVITY 1

Aju, an upholsterer, makes cushions, sofa covers, curtains, and seat covers for cars. Given below are a few questions that a customer asks him. Write down the expected answers from Aju. Follow the model given:

→ Do you stitch sofa covers?

Answer: Yes, I do.

1. And do you stitch curtains?
   Answer:..
2. And cushions?
   Answer:..
3. Do you make furniture?
   Answer: No, ...

ACTIVITY 2

Answer the questions in the table below following the model answers:

Question	Answer
→ Do you drive a car?	No, I don't. I ride a motorbike.
→ Are there penguins in the Sundarbans?	No, there aren't. There are tigers in the Sundarbans.
1. Do you study Chinese in school?	No, we don't. We study ....
2. Do people play football in museums?	
3. Do Indians live in caves?	
4. Do they show films in libraries?	
5. Do we buy fish at the bus station?	
6. Does your computer have a soft disc?	No, it doesn't. It has a ....
7. Does your maths teacher teach history?	
8. Does the postman deliver railway tickets?	

PRACTICE

1. Given below are some jumbled sentences. Rearrange the words to form proper sentences:

   i. in a/I/boarding school/live ....
   ii. up/all of us/before 5.15 AM/wake/ ....
   iii. prayer room/go to/we/by 5.30 AM/the ....
   iv. the prayers/we hate/in winter/particularly ....
   v. breakfast/after/the prayers/have/we ....
   vi. at 4/our school/in the afternoon/ends ....

    vii. we/football/play/school/after ....

   viii. the boys/supper[3]/have/9 PM/at ....

     ix. we/by 10/to/bed/go ....

     x. switches off/the warden/the lights/at/time/that ....

2. I have written down a description of a typical morning in my life. Use appropriate verbs to fill in the blanks. You may use the verbs given below:

be	blow in	come	drink	gather	make/prepare	rise	run
see	start	stop	swing	talk	wait		wake up

I _____ ____ early, at 5.00 in the morning. At that time, the sky ____ still dark. Soon, the darkness fades away and the sun _____ in the east. A pleasant breeze _____ ____ from the north. Birds wake up too and _____ chirping. Mohan _____ a teashop near my house. He lights his stove and _____ tea. Rickshaw-pullers _____ hot, steaming tea and rush to the station to pick up the passengers who arrive by the first train. Soon, the milkman arrives, riding his old bicycle, with two noisy milk cans hanging on either side. After some time, little girls _____ at the junction and _____ for their school bus. Their plaits[4] and ponytails _____ as they _____ excitedly. From my balcony, I _____ all this. Oh! Here _____ the yellow school bus. And I must _____ writing, my cup of tea is ready.

3. Complete the sentences following the pattern given below. For the first three, the verb has been given.
⇨ *The carpenter makes furniture.* ⇨ *The cobbler repairs shoes.* ⇨ *The milkman brings us milk.*

     i. The newspaper vendor .... (deliver)

    ii. The doctor .... (treat)

   iii. The architect .... (design)

   iv. The English teacher ....

    v. The vet[5] ....

   vi. The pilot ....

4. Given below are some common proverbs or sayings. Complete them with suitable verbs:

     i. Time and tide _____ for no man.

    ii. A _____ in time _____ nine.

   iii. A bad workman _____ his _____.

   iv. Don't _____ your chickens before they are _____.

5. Make a list of things you do from morning to evening. Use the sentences that you have learned in this chapter. Read out the list to a friend. Ask him/her to tell you what he/she does every day. Correct his/her mistakes.

I wake up at ....
....
....
....

---

[3] **supper:** (noun) the last meal of the day, usually smaller and less formal than dinner.

[4] **plait:** (noun) long hair divided into three parts and woven together; anything else woven similarly. Pronounced as PLAT, like cat.

[5] **vet:** (noun) the short, informal form of *veterinary doctor,* that is, a doctor who treats animals.

....
....
....
....
....
....
....
....
....
....
....

KEY TO ACTIVITIES

Activity 1: Yes, I do. 2. Yes, I do. 3. No, I don't.

Activity 2: 1. No, we don't. We study English and Hindi at school. 2. No, they don't. They play football on playgrounds. 3. No, they don't. They live in cottages and buildings. 4. No, they don't. They show films in cinemas. 5. No, we don't. We buy fish at the fish market. 6. No, it doesn't. It has a hard disc. 7. No, she doesn't. She teaches us maths. 8. No, he doesn't. He delivers letters and telegrams.

I Am Fine, How Are You?

Learning Objectives: In English, the most frequently used verb is 'be'. It follows a different pattern of conjugation compared to all the other verbs. In this chapter, we will learn how to use the 'be' verb in the present tense.

8.1 A SPECIAL VERB: *BE*

After teaching adult learners for nearly two decades, I have realized that South Asian learners face some common stumbling blocks while learning English. Often, there is no one to tell them how to tackle those blocks, and consequently, they get stuck. The **be** verb is one such block, and in order to get a grip on English, you must learn how to use it.

Check how the **be** verb is used, and also understand how the following forms are different from the forms of ordinary verbs such as *sit, study,* and *sing,* which we discussed in the last chapter.

In the simple present tense, this verb has three forms: *am, is,* and *are.* We frame sentences with the *be* verb as shown below:

I +	am +	
We/You/They +	are +	complement
He/She/It +	is +	

You can use the *be* verb to express ideas conveyed by action verbs:

Statements with Action Verbs	Same Facts Using the 'Be' Verb
I teach English.	I am an English teacher.
You study English.	You are students of English.
You write computer software.	You are a programmer.
Virat Kohli plays cricket.	Virat Kohli is a cricketer.

Saudamini Desmukh flies aircraft.	Saudamini Desmukh is a pilot.
Brinda designs buildings and bridges.	Brinda is an architect.
Aju makes sofa covers.	Aju is an upholsterer.
Raju repairs cars.	Raju is a car mechanic.
Ismail lives a saintly life.	Ismail is a saint.
They grow crops and vegetables.	They are farmers.

We use the *be* verb often. Also, we use it not only to say who is a saint or a sinner,[1] but also used to describe *feelings, states, where someone is, conditions,* and *opinions:*

I am fine.	The sky is dark.	The girls are at the bus stop.
You are late.	Sir, here is your coffee.	The birds are in the sky.

8.2 MAKING NEGATIVE STATEMENTS

This is how we frame negative sentences with the *be* verb:

I am a car mechanic.	I am/I'm not a car mechanic.
You are right.	You aren't/are not right.
Ramu is involved in politics.	Ramu is not/isn't involved in politics.
Ramu is involved with Rita.	Ramu is not/isn't involved with Rita.
Ramu is crazy about Rita.	Ramu isn't/is not crazy about Rita.
They are farmers.	They aren't/are not farmers.

Compare these with the negative sentences with action verbs in Sections 7.2. Do you see the difference?

Involved In/Involved With

Ramu is <u>involved in</u> politics = Ramu takes part in politics.
Ramu is <u>involved with</u> Rita = Ramu is emotionally attached to Rita.
Ramu is <u>crazy about</u> Rita = Ramu is madly in love with her.

The word ***involved*** is always followed by ***with*** or ***in***. And only ***about*** goes after the word ***crazy***. We do not say *Ramu is ~~crazy of~~ Rita.* ✖

In Sections 6.2 and 6.3, we have seen that in English, words are not combined randomly; certain words often go only with certain other words and this is known as ***collocation***. When you read or listen to good English, keep noting collocations. Any good dictionary gives illustrative sentences after many words. Read them. You can also use a collocation dictionary.[2]

---

[1] **sinner:** someone who lives an immoral life; the opposite of *saint*.
[2] http://www.freecollocation.com/

8.3 OF 'THIS' AND 'THAT'

We often point at a thing and then describe it. To do so, we use these words:

	Singular	Plural
When something is close to you	*this*	*these*
When something is away from you	*that*	*those*

For example:

- ✓ This is a ballpoint pen. And these are some refills.
- ✓ That is our headmaster's car. Those cycles belong to students.

This and *that* are also used to refer to ideas and abstract things:

- ✓ This is not true. ◊ These are lame excuses. ◊ That's great!

PRACTICE

1. Rewrite the following sentences using *am, is,* or *are:*

   a. I fix and repair bathroom fittings.   I am a ....
   → We study history.   We are students of history ....
   b. You cook well.   ....
   c. Raju makes wooden furniture.   ....
   d. Sachin builds buildings and bridges.   ....
   e. Wasim manages a bank.   ....
   f. They grow crops and vegetables.   ....

2. Invert the meanings of these sentences by adding *not* or *n't* at appropriate places:

   a. I am a plumber.[3]   ⇨   ....
   b. You are a great storyteller. ⇨   ....
   c. The players are tired.   ⇨   ....
   d. The light is dim.   ⇨   ....
   e. That is my view on the topic. ⇨ ....
   f. That's an important point.   ⇨   ....

3. Here is a passage written by a budding[4] cricketer about himself. You can see that he is not very modest. Can you transform the positive sentences into negative and the negative into positive?

---

[3] *Plumber* is pronounced as **PLUHM**-ER, with stress on the first part; the letter *b* is silent.

[4] **budding:** (adjective) a budding cricketer is someone who is in the process of becoming a successful cricketer.

Although I don't play cricket regularly, I am a great cricketer. I'm an excellent all-rounder. I don't have to try too hard. I don't think Virat Kohli is a great batsman. He has many weaknesses in his batting. Therefore, he is not my idol. I am sure I will be a great success in cricket. But unfortunately, my coach doesn't think so. He doesn't even pick me for the school team!

4. What is common among them?

   → Salman Rushdie, Amitabh Ghosh   ⇨ They are writers ....
   a. Shakira, Sonu Nigam, Shreya Ghoshal   ⇨ They are ....
   b. Naseeruddin Shah, Kajol, Tom Hanks   ⇨ ....
   c. Pablo Picasso, Jatin Das, Anjolie Ela Menon   ⇨ ....
   d. Barack Obama, L.K. Advani, Angela Merkel   ⇨ ....

Special Test:
Vocabulary around Occupations[1]

A. To solve this crossword puzzle, use names of professionals or words relating to different professions. Check the clues given on the next page.

	1		2R					3U	4S	H	E	R		5
6			E											
			7P								8R			
9			R								10E			
			O		11	12					A			
13			G								L			14
			R				15				T			
			A	16							O			
	17		P								R			
			H											
	18		E			S			19	20				
	21M		R											
22	O				23		24							
	L													
25	E									26				

[1] **occupation:** (noun) your job or profession. For example: *What is her occupation? —She is an English teacher.*

Across	**Down**
1. He cuts men's hair (6) 3. He shows your seat in a cinema (5) 7. She flies aircraft 9. A film _____, or one in the sky (4) 10. The ophthalmologist works on this organ (3) 11. You have to do this well to succeed as a salesperson (5) 13. He tries and punishes criminals (5) 15. He treats patients (6) 17. He makes sofa covers (11) 18. He removes painful teeth (7) 19. He represents a company in another place (5) 22. A professor in Oxford/Cambridge or a mafia boss! (3) 23. He repairs your car and scooter (8) 25. His work is to make laws, but we often see him fighting with his colleagues (10) 26. A vet treats him, among others (3)	2. He microfilms and preserves documents in a library 4. He takes care of guests in a restaurant and takes down orders (7) 5. A computer programmer often writes this (4) 6. He plays records at a restaurant or club to make a living (4, 6) 8. An agent for sale and purchase of buildings and land (7) 12. They offer puja in temples (7) 14. S/he designs buildings and other structures (9) 16. He makes clay pots (6) 20. He protects buildings and factories (5) 21. Another name for a spy (4) 24. A driver often drives this (3)

B. Guess the professions:

→	Bhawani doesn't go to office every day. She goes to different places and observes interesting things, people, and events. She writes about them in different newspapers/periodicals.	Bhawani is a f r e e l a n c e [2] j o u r n a l i s t.
1.	Rani is attached to a hospital. She advises patients about what they should eat. Generally, she advises people about the right kind of food.	Rani is a d _ _ _ _ _ _ _ _.
2.	Anjali works irregular hours and often works on Sundays. As a part of her work, she travels thousands of miles every day. While on duty, she smiles all the time.	Anjali is an a _ _ h _ _ _ _ _ _ .
3.	Sehnaz's clients are women. She works from 10 AM to 8 PM. She has weekly off on Thursdays. Saturdays and Sundays are the busiest days of her week. She often works with brides on their wedding day.	Sehnaz is a b _ _ _ _ _ _ _ _ .
4.	Bipasha is tall, slim, and beautiful. She is seen on TV, asking you to buy things such as shampoos and gel pens. She also exhibits new clothes.	Bipasha is a _ _ _ _ _ .
5.	Mani works in a bank. She sits at the front desk, accepts and pays cash, and updates records in the bank's computer.	Mani is a t _ _ _ _ r.

---

[2] A *freelance* professional is someone who doesn't work for a salary, but instead, sells his/her services to different organizations.

6.	Deepak stands behind a counter and serves drinks to his customers. He is busy in the evenings, particularly at weekends.	Deepak is a b _ _ _ _ _ _ _ r. He's also called a b _ _ m _ _.
7.	Sanjeev cooks in a hotel. In fact, he is a master cook.	Sanjeev is a _ _ _ _.
8.	You will find Raghubir at a railway station. He wears a black coat even in summer. He stands at the station gate and checks if passengers have proper tickets.	Raghubir is a _ _ _ _ _ _ _ x _ _ _ _ _ _.
9.	Ram too wears a black coat. He works at a court of law and represents people who fight legal battles.	Ram is a l _ _ _ _ _.
10.	Sucharita writes texts for advertisements.	Sucharita is a c _ p y w _ _ _ _ _.

C. Fill in the blanks to match the pictures:

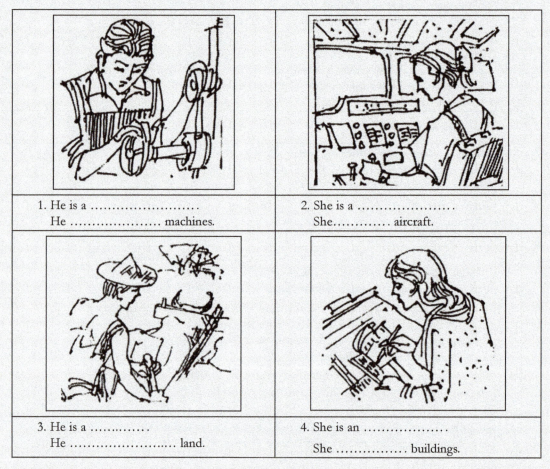

1. He is a ....
   He .... machines.

2. She is a ....
   She............. aircraft.

3. He is a ....
   He .... land.

4. She is an ....
   She .... buildings.

D. Given below are names of some people and their occupations. Write a few sentences on each of them:

→	Savitri is a bus conductor. She works in shifts, helps the bus driver, and issues tickets. Her work is not easy. She is on her feet for hours at a stretch and often has to tackle angry passengers. Initially, people were surprised to see her. But now, they are comfortable with the idea of having a female bus conductor.
1.	Angelica is a nurse. She works at a hospital. She ....
2.	Gayatri is a fashion designer. She ....
3.	Shatarupa is an architect. She ....
4.	Sudeep is a freelance photographer. He ....
5.	Barkha is a TV anchor. She ....
6.	Jagdeesh is a doctor. He works at a hospital. He ....

Talking About Yourself

Learning Objectives: You have to introduce yourself whenever you meet someone in a formal situation. This chapter deals with the functional language you will use to talk about yourself.

9.1 INTRODUCING YOURSELF

You often have to talk about yourself, for example, when you face an interview to join an institute, or for a job. Generally, the first question you face is: *Present yourself* or *Introduce yourself*. In informal situations too, when you meet a new person or group of people, you tell them who you are. When we talk about ourselves, we often use the following expressions:

- ✓ My name is ….
- ✓ I am … (years)
- ✓ I am married/unmarried
- ✓ I have a daughter and a son ….
- ✓ My father works for ….
- ✓ My mother is a ….
- ✓ I come from …./I'm from ….

- ✓ I live in ….
- ✓ I am a student/carpenter ….
- ✓ I study ….
- ✓ I work for ….
- ✓ I work as a ….
- ✓ I love ….
- ✓ My hobbies are ….

9.2 RITA INTRODUCES HERSELF

Rita Menon is a software engineer. This is how she introduces herself during a job interview:

Good morning! My name is Rita Menon. I am 23 and I'm from New Delhi. My father is a lawyer and my mother is a homemaker. I am a BTech in CST from JU, Kolkata. At university, I specialized in RDBMS. I currently work as a network engineer for a company called Network Solutions Limited.

My present job doesn't match my specialization and my core strengths. So I am looking for a change. I strongly wish to work as a software developer.

However, Rita introduces herself differently to the members of a trekkers' club she has just joined.

Hi! It's nice to be with you all. I am Rita Menon from Chanakyapuri. My dad is a lawyer and my mom, a homemaker. I've a bro. He's in class XI. I am an engineer from JU, Kolkata, with a specialization in computer science and tech. I work for a company called Network Solutions. I enjoy working with computers. But I like reading and travelling even more. In particular, I love trekking. I trekked for seven days in the Nilgiris last year, from Udhagamandalam to Bandipur. My dream is to visit the Manas Sarovar someday. I am delighted to join the Trekkers' Club of South Delhi.

What are the differences between the two introductions?

✓ In the first, Rita talks only about things relevant[1] to her job.
✓ Her tone is formal.
✓ She uses the short forms CST (and not computer science and technology) and RDBMS (relational database management system) as the interviewers are familiar with these terms.

But when she speaks to the members of her new club, she talks less about her profession and more about her interests and hobbies. She also explains why she has joined the trekkers' club. Her language is informal. She uses *dad/mom* instead of *father/mother*, and *bro* instead of brother.

When you make a presentation about yourself:

1. Mention facts that are relevant to the situation
2. Depending on the situation, speak either formally or informally

---

My father is ….

I often hear young people saying: '*My father is a serviceman.*'
The word *serviceman* means *a member of the armed forces.* You should say:
My father works for ….
For example, if your father is in a bank, you say:

• My father works for a bank.
  Or,
• My father is a bank employee.

---

[1] **relevant:** (adjective) closely connected to the situation you are discussing.

ACTIVITY 1

Write a short paragraph to introduce yourself (a) formally and (b) informally. Keep the following points in mind as you prepare your presentation:

- Frame sentences in English in your mind. Do not think in your mother tongue and then translate into English.
- After writing, read the sentences aloud. Do they sound good? Rewrite them. Even the best of writers revise their language several times.
- Use the expressions given in Section 9.1.

ACTIVITY 2

I am your friend and I can say the following things about myself:

1. I am Dinesh Thakur from Pune.
2. I am 20 years old.
3. I study economics at Fergusson College, Pune.
4. I come from a family of musicians.
5. My mother, Smt. Roshni Thakur, is a playback singer for Hindi movies.
6. I am a budding[2] singer. I sing both classical and modern songs.
7. I was the winner of a talent contest organized by the ABC TV last year.
8. Besides singing, I also play the sitar.
9. I learn playing the sitar from the maestro[3] Rahamatullah Khan.
10. I am the lead singer of the musical band Cactus Flowers in Pune.
11. The band is very popular among the youth of our city.

Using these pieces of information, introduce me to the audience in a musical concert, where I am going to sing a few songs. Also, as you can see, I am quite modest. I haven't said a good word (such as brilliant and talented) about myself! But you are expected to add a few fine adjectives about me in your introduction! Present me in a way that the audience can't wait for me to pick up the mike.

ACTIVITY 3

Imagine that you are a budding cricketer. In the first column of the following table, I have given a set of objectives to become a great cricketer. In the second column, I have noted down some of the actions required to achieve these objectives. Match the objectives with the required actions:

---

[2] **budding:** (adjective) someone who shows promise and is expected to become successful.

[3] **maestro:** (noun) a master of any art, especially a great composer or a teacher of music.

My Objectives	Actions Required
✓ To remain physically fit	practising regularly at the nets
✓ To improve concentration	learning the finer points of cricket from our coach
✓ To improve my cricketing skills	doing yoga every morning
✓ To understand the game better	watching cricket matches on TV
✓ To follow the masters of the game	jogging and exercising every day

Now complete the paragraph combining the objectives and required actions:

I am a young cricketer. I want to be a great player and I work hard to achieve my goal. I jog and exercise regularly to remain physically fit. To improve my concentration, I ....
....
....
....
....
....
....

KEY TO ACTIVITIES

Activity 2: If I was given the task of introducing Dinesh, I would say something like this, but your introduction would naturally be different from mine.

Good evening, ladies and gentlemen! I am delighted to introduce a talented young musician who is with us tonight. His name is Sri Dinesh Thakur. Although he is only 20 years old, he has already made a name for himself. He is studying economics at Fergusson College, Pune. A very important fact about him is that he comes from a family of illustrious musicians. His mother is none other than Smt. Roshni Thakur, the famous playback singer for Hindi films. Dinesh, a budding singer with tremendous potential, sings both classical and popular songs. He was the winner of a talent contest organized by ABC TV channel this year. Besides singing, he also plays the sitar. He learns the sitar from the maestro Rahamatullah Khan. He is also the lead singer of the musical band Cactus Flowers in Pune. As you all know, this band is immensely popular among the youth of our city.

I am sure you will enjoy Dinesh's performance. I will now leave the floor to our guest this evening—Sri Dinesh Thakur. Please give him a big hand!

Activity 3: I am a young cricketer. I want to be a great player and I work hard to achieve my goal. I jog and exercise regularly to remain physically fit. To improve my concentration, I practise yoga every morning. I practise regularly at the nets to improve my cricketing skills. I learn the finer points of the game from our coach. I also watch cricket matches on TV to follow the masters of the game.

Talking About Others

Learning Objectives: *This chapter focuses on vocabulary. Here, we are discussing the language used to describe people, their appearance, qualities, and the state of their mind at a particular time. We will also learn compound adjectives here.*

10.1 HOW DO WE DESCRIBE OTHERS?

In Chapter 9, we discussed how to talk about ourselves. Now, we are going to talk over how to describe others. To describe someone, we give details of their *physical features* (*tall, short, thin, overweight,* and so on) and qualities (*hardworking, lazy, generous, mean,* and so on). Also, we recount their physical or mental states (*happy, sad, tired, angry,* etc.).

10.2 PHYSICAL DESCRIPTION

To describe people, we often use expressions like what you read below:

Radhika is tall and slim. Her husband Ravi is stout[1] and a little short. Both of them are around 30. Ravi has a dark complexion; Radhika is fair. Ravi is in a kurta and a pyjama; Radhika is wearing a salwar suit.

Radhika has short curly hair. Her daughter Rani's hair is long and straight. She has a sharp nose and full lips. Her dress has a floral design.

---

[1] **stout:** (adjective) strongly built.

Rani is a somewhat chubby[2] girl; her brother Rohan is thin. He has a wide forehead, high cheekbones, a rather flat nose, and thin lips. Rohan is in a striped shirt.

Rani has large eyes. Her friend Alverin has slanting eyes. Rani is wearing a bindi on her forehead; Alverin isn't.

Ravi is strongly built, but his friend George is rather thin and frail. George has broken cheeks and a beak nose. He has a shock of salt-and-pepper hair. He wears spectacles. He is in a checked shirt.

Ravi's father, Dr Ram, has a bald pate with a few strands of hair. His wife, Rukmini Devi, has completely grey hair. She wears a nose ring and earrings.

Avoid negative language while describing others. Don't say: *She is ugly* or *he is mean*. Similarly, it doesn't sound nice if you say *someone is obese*.[3] Also, we often use words such as *rather*, *somewhat*, or *slightly* to soften negative expressions:

- ✓ Rani is a beautiful girl, but she's **a little** chubby.
- ✓ George is **rather** thin.

In another context:

- ✓ Your essay is fine, but **slightly** long.

---

[2] **chubby:** (adjective) round and full in shape; another word for chubby is PLUMP.
[3] **obese:** (adjective) very fat.

ACTIVITY 1

It's a cold winter afternoon, the roads are empty. As you approach a bank, you notice a man and a woman walk out hurriedly, get into a car, and drive away. A few minutes later, an elderly woman rushes out of the bank screaming, followed by several people. They tell you that a man and a woman have just cheated the old lady of a large sum of money. The cheats pretended to be bank employees, took the money from her, and went behind the counter, as if to deposit it. Then they were seen no more.

  This is the mental picture you have of the cheats. Can you describe them?

Yes, I have seen a man and a woman rushing out of the bank. I think they are both in their mid-twenties. The man is ....

....

....

....

....

....

....

10.3 VOCABULARY: DESCRIBING SOMEONE'S QUALITIES

Often, we use short words such as *able, kind, lazy,* and *rude* to describe qualities. Given below are some longer adjectives. The second column tells you whether the word is positive or negative. (The synonyms are in the UPPER CASE like elsewhere.)

Word	(+)/(−)	Meaning/Synonym/Illustrative Sentence
1. Accessible	(+)	Someone who is easy to talk to/*Our new boss is a little short-tempered, but he is always* **accessible.**
2. Ambitious	(+)	Someone keen to go up in life/*When I met Sharukh, he was a young and* **ambitious** *TV actor.*
3. Arrogant	(−)	Full of pride, but with little substance/HAUGHTY/*We should be polite, no one likes* **arrogant** *people.*
4. Brilliant	(+)	Exceptionally clever or talented, EXCELLENT/*Kishore Kumar, a* **brilliant** *Indian singer, is revered[4] by all.*

---

[4] **(to) revere:** (verb) to have deep respect for someone.

5. Cheerful	(+)	Someone who is happy and shows he/she is happy/*She looks **cheerful**. No wonder, she's just been promoted out of turn.*
6. Confident	(+)	Someone who is sure of his/her ability/opposite of NERVOUS/*Be **confident** about the exam, you have prepared really well.*
7. Enthusiastic	(+)	A person who shows a lot of energy and excitement/opposite of LETHARGIC/*Ramu is an **enthusiastic** reader, he reads all the time.*
8. Focused	(+)	With your mind firmly set on what you are doing/SINGLE-MINDED/*At office, Ranjana thinks of nothing but work, she is indeed **focused**.*
9. Generous	(+)	KIND, HELPFUL, opposite MEAN/*A **generous** man, he goes out of his way to help his colleagues.*
10. Hardworking	(+)	Someone who works hard/opposite of LAZY.
11. Hypocrite	(–)	Someone who makes false, exaggerated claims about him or herself/PRETENDER, TWO-FACED/*People trusted him earlier. Now everyone knows him as a **hypocrite**.*
12. Jealous	(–)	Someone who feels unhappy if fortune smiles on anyone else/*We had excellent teamwork in our small office, no one was **jealous** of anyone else.*
13. Lively	(+)	Full of life and energy/ENERGETIC, ACTIVE/*Rani is so **lively**, she can lift the spirit of any party.*
14. Resourceful	(+)	Good at finding solutions and getting things done/*Ravi is so **resourceful**, everyone in office falls back upon him in tricky situations.*
15. Sincere	(+)	Someone who says what he genuinely believes/GENUINE, HONEST.
16. Unfriendly	(–)	Opposite of FRIENDLY.

ACTIVITY 2

In the grid below, there are four short and seven long adjectives from Section 10.3 above. We have marked one of them. Search diagonally, across, and down to find the remaining words:

L	A	Z	Y	B	F	C	D	F	A	H	J
C	K	L	M	N	K	O	P	Q	C	R	C
S	H	T	V	X	I	Z	C	B	C	D	O
F	S	E	G	G	N	H	J	U	E	K	N
F	R	I	E	N	D	L	Y	T	S	V	F
L	M	N	N	R	P	Q	R	S	S	E	I
W	X	Y	E	C	F	Z	A	B	I	C	D
D	F	G	R	H	E	U	B	J	B	K	E
L	M	N	O	P	Q	R	L	S	L	T	N
V	W	R	U	D	E	X	E	Y	E	Z	T
B	R	E	S	O	U	R	C	E	F	U	L

ACTIVITY 3

Fill in the blanks with the words you have found in the grid above:

A. Raghu is an _____ tennis player, he has been the district tennis champion for the last two years. He is agile[5] on the court, but at office he is known to be _____. He does little work, and often sleeps at his desk. But when he is awake, he is c_____, he smiles all the time. And as an individual, he is _____. He gives 5% of his salary to charities every month.

B. Raju gets on with people easily. He is _____ with everyone. Also, if you have a problem and ask him for help, he will find a way, like the legendary Jeeves in P.G.Wodehouse novels. His friends say, he can get you a bottle of chilled water in the middle of a desert. He is the most r_____ person I have ever seen. However, on the flip side, he is quick-tempered, and at times, he can be _____ with people.

ACTIVITY 4

I manage a small office with four colleagues who are interesting in different ways. In the note below, I have given short sketches on them, but have erased some of the adjectives fully or partly. Fill in the blanks with these words:

aggressive	ambitious	brilliant	cheerful
focused	~~generous~~	hardworking	jealous
resourceful	sincere	unfriendly	

A. Amrindar, my assistant, is a[____], [generous], and a little [____] about others' success. Amri— as we all call him—is keen to go up in life. He works hard to develop himself. He also has a big heart and helps colleagues. But on the downside, he seems unhappy if the company rewards anyone else. In fact, he looks sad when someone else gets a big pay hike.

B. Krishnan manages our marketing desk. He is [____], [____], and always [____] on work. He has a great sense of humour and smiles and jokes all the time. But when he works on his computer, he forgets everything else. Many a time, I stood before his desk while he was working, but he did not even notice. Finally, he is the opposite of people who are called two-faced. He means what he says.

C. Give our computer specialist Rehna any problem related to her work, she will find a way to solve it. She is genuinely [____]. She was a [____] student; she always came at the top of her class at college. But sadly, she gets angry easily, and if someone made even a minor mistake, she would tell him off[6] rather rudely. I would reluctantly say that she is a little a[____].

D. Our driver Murty never smiles and doesn't talk with anyone. He is aloof and rather [____]. But he can drive long hours and never grumbles even if he has to go to the airport in the middle of the night. I haven't seen many [____] people like him.

---

[5] **agile:** (adjective) able to move quickly and easily.

[6] **tell off:** (verb) if you tell someone off, you speak to them angrily.

ACTIVITY 5

Follow the text above and the adjectives you have come across in this chapter. Using these words, write five sentences each about any four of your colleagues, classmates, friends, or neighbours.

10.4 IS SHE HAPPY/IS SHE SAD?

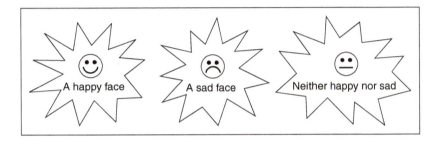

A happy face | A sad face | Neither happy nor sad

In Section 10.2, we discussed physical description, and in Section 10.3, we talked about qualities. Let's now move on to **states of the mind and the body**. You perhaps use these emoticons in text messages. An emoticon is an icon[7] that expresses a particular emotion. It's a relatively new word, a combination of *emotion* and *icon*.

My Webster Dictionary gives more than 100 synonyms of the word *happy*. The words *sad, angry,* and *tired* too have lots of synonyms. And these synonyms are often not interchangeable; different synonyms convey different shades of meanings. The list below gives you some frequently used synonyms of these adjectives and their meanings:

Happy	GLAD (not before nouns), PLEASED—happy about a particular thing: *I'm glad to meet you.* Or *Pleased to meet you.*
	DELIGHTED—very pleased
	SATISFIED—pleased because you have achieved something, or something that you wanted to happen has happened
Sad	SORRY—sad and sympathetic about something: *I am sorry to hear your dad has had an accident.*
	DEJECTED, DESPONDENT—unhappy and disappointed DISPIRITED—having no hope or spirit
	UPSET—(not before nouns) unhappy because something unpleasant has happened: *Don't be upset because you haven't done well in a class test. Relax!*
Angry	ANNOYED (usually not before nouns), IRRITATED—slightly angry
	ENRAGED, INFURIATED, LIVID, FUMING, FURIOUS—very angry: *Our flight was delayed by 10 hours. The passengers were furious but could do nothing.*

---

[7] **icon:** (noun) a picture that stands for something. *You see icons on your laptop screen.*

	OFFENDED—upset because someone has behaved badly with you
	IRATE—very angry: *As a bus conductor, Savitri has to deal with irate passengers every day.*
	Opposite of *angry:* calm, cool, composed
Tired	EXHAUSTED—very tired
	WORN-OUT—very tired because of overwork
	BURNT-OUT—tired of doing the same thing for a long time: *I am burnt-out after working continuously for years, I must go on a vacation.*
	Opposite of *tired:* active, lively, energetic, full of life

ACTIVITY 6

Given below are a few sketches. Rani, Fatima, Rohan, and their friend Boogie have different words to talk about the moods of the people in the sketches. Write down what they might say:

	Rani:	I think this young man is happy.
	Fatima:	Well, he seems to be delighted.
	Rohan:	I think he is ....
	Boogie:	He is ....

	Rani:	I think she is sad.
	Fatima:	....
	Rohan:	....
	Boogie:	....

	Rani:	....
	Fatima:	....
	Rohan:	....
	Boogie:	....

ACTIVITY 7

Psychologists tell us that every language all over the world has the words: ***happy, sad, angry, afraid, disgusted,*** and ***surprised.*** They relate to our basic emotions. In Section 10.3, we have discussed the English synonyms of three of these. Check the synonyms of the remaining three words and note them down.

10.5 TWO WORDS, ONE ADJECTIVE

So far in this chapter, we have come across words that are used to describe people: *cheerful, kind, generous,* and so on. Let's now check **compound adjectives**, that is, adjectives made up of two or more words which are joined with hyphens. For example, a *down-to-earth* person is a practical person. An insincere man is also called a *two-faced* man.

ACTIVITY 8

A. Take a word from the left and another from the right, and join them with a hyphen to form a compound adjective:

1. easy	2. dim	3. level
4. high	5. open	6. quick
7. self	8. stuck	9. two

assured	faced	going
headed	minded	spirited
tempered	up	witted

1. *easy-going* ....   2. ....   3. ....

4. ....   5. ....   6. ....

7. ....   8. ....   9. ....

B. Among the nine compound adjectives above, four are critical or negative. Can you write them down here?

1. .... 2. .... 3. .... 4. ....

ACTIVITY 9

Match the compound adjectives from Activity 8 with their definitions below:

a. A confident person ....
b. A calm person, someone who behaves sensibly ....
c. Someone who behaves in a lively and cheerful way ....
d. Someone who is willing to consider and accept new ideas ....
e. A person who gets angry easily ....
f. Someone who finds it difficult to grasp ideas, unintelligent ....
g. A person who keeps away from others and thinks he is superior ....
h. Someone who is insincere and who lies and cheats ....
i. A relaxed and tolerant person ....

PRACTICE

1. Most of the words in the crossword puzzle on the next page are words that describe people:

Clues

Across	Down
1 Not likely to change (4)	2 Good at understanding and thinking logically (11)
5 New to a job, INEXPERIENCED (3)	3 'Could you pass _____ the salt?' (2)
9 Full of enthusiasm (9)	4 Someone who handles difficult tasks effectively (11)
10 Giving or willing to give freely (8)	5 A negative word for a communist (3)
12 A synonym of IRRITABLE (5)	6 Same as 18 Across (2)
15 Easy to approach or to talk to (10)	7 He/she makes sensible decisions and gives good advice (4)
16 A short form for gentleman (4)	8 If you don't know something clearly, you are said to have a _____ idea. (4)
17 A synonym of TIRESOME (6)	11 about to fall asleep, DROWSY (6)
18 A preposition of place (2)	13 a _____ person, one who hates to spend (7)
19 Slow in understanding, STUPID (4)	14 very happy: He was _____ to win the gold medal. (9)
21 IRRITATED or ANNOYED (5)	18 (informal) expert or first rate (3)
22 Full of life and vigour (6)	20 the opposite of hardworking (4)
23 Very angry (5)	

2. Match the *opposites*:

1.	quick-tempered	dim-witted
2.	brilliant	sad
3.	self-assured	calm
4.	delighted	nervous
5.	down-to-earth	mean
6.	friendly	absent-minded
7.	generous	stuck-up
8.	alert	impractical

3. Find the word that is nearest to the meaning of the word given in the first column of the following table:

		A	B	C	D	Answer
→	**annoying**	angry	irritating	negative	forceful	B
1	**dejected**	very sad	exhausted	laid-back	rejected	
2	**delighted**	lit up	warm-hearted	very happy	relaxed	
3	**exhausted**	asleep	bankrupt	poor	very tired	
4	**focused**	photographer	intense	tense	steadfast	
5	**upset**	marginal	overbearing	upside down	sad	
6	**joyful**	happy	bottle shaped	furious	beloved	
7	**irate**	very angry	highly rated	jealous	obese	
8	**obese**	oblong	overweight	basic	circular	
9	**sensitive**	sympathetic	toothpaste	skin	weak	
10	**energetic**	active	overfed	overweight	irritated	

4. In the sentences below, replace the underlined words with the following: *bad-tempered, happy-go-lucky, laid-back, open-minded, self-centred, stuck-up,* and *two-faced*.

A. People who are <u>relaxed</u> and <u>unconcerned about what is going to happen tomorrow</u> live longer.
B. People who are not <u>open to new ideas</u> often slow down progress.
C. When we choose friends, we avoid <u>arrogant</u> and <u>insincere</u> people.
D. No one likes <u>irritable</u> people.

5. Here is a brief write-up about my friend Gautam. Read it, and then write a paragraph to describe your best friend.

My Friend Gautam

Gautam is one of my best friends. He is about 25. He is not very tall, but is slim and quite handsome. He has curly hair, deep, enquiring eyes, and a sharp nose. He wears a full-sleeve shirt even in summer just like late Dev Anand, the Bollywood superstar of the past. His principal hobby is trekking. Fortunately for him, it is his profession too.

Gautam works for an adventure tourism company and accompanies tourists going on treks to the Himalayas. He is focused on his work and is exceedingly knowledgeable about the Himalayas. When he is not travelling, he studies the history and geography of the Himalayan region. Every evening after coming home, he reads about the Himalayan people, plants, and animals on the Internet.

As a person, he is self-assured and warm-hearted. An easy-going person, he makes friends easily and never criticizes people. I am fortunate to have a friend like him.

My friend ....

.... is one of my best friends. He/She is ....

....

....

....

....

....

....

....

....

....

....

....

....

....

KEY TO ACTIVITIES

Activity 1: (Suggested answer, your answer will be different.) Yes, I have seen a man and a woman rushing out of the bank. They got into a parked car and drove away. The man, thin and tall, was in his mid-twenties. He was wearing sneakers, a white shirt, and a sleeveless jacket. The woman was wearing salwar kameez. Her kameez had polka dots. She had large eyes, sharp nose, thin lips, and straight hair up to her shoulders.

Activity 2:

L	A	Z	Y	B	F	C	D	F	A	H	J
C	K	L	M	N	K	O	P	Q	C	R	C
S	H	T	V	X	I	Z	C	B	C	D	O
F	S	E	G	G	N	H	J	U	E	K	N
F	R	I	E	N	D	L	Y	T	S	V	F
L	M	N	N	R	P	Q	R	S	S	E	I
W	X	Y	E	C	F	Z	A	B	I	C	D
D	F	G	R	H	E	U	B	J	B	K	E
L	M	N	O	P	Q	R	L	S	L	T	N
V	W	R	U	D	E	X	E	Y	E	Z	T
B	R	E	S	O	U	R	C	E	F	U	L

Activity 3: A. able, lazy, cheerful, generous; B. friendly, resourceful, rude

Activity 4: A. ambitious; jealous; B. cheerful, focused, sincere; C. resourceful, brilliant, aggressive; D. unfriendly; hardworking

Activity 8: A. 2. dim-witted; 3. level-headed; 4. high-spirited; 5. open-minded; 6. quick-tempered; 7. self-assured; 8. stuck-up; 9. two-faced. B. 1. dim-witted; 2. quick tempered; 3. stuck-up; 4. two-faced

Activity 9: a. 7 (self-assured); b. 3 (level-headed); c. 4. (high-spirited); d. 5. (open-minded); e. 6. (quick-tempered); f. 2. (dim-witted); g. 8. (stuck-up); h. 9. (two-faced); i. 1. (easy-going)

Asking Questions

Learning Objectives: In this chapter, we are going to discuss the grammatical forms used to ask simple questions.

11.1 EVERY STATEMENT ANSWERS A QUESTION

Every statement can serve as an answer to one or more questions. For example, the statement *I play football* answers the question *Do you play football?*

In fact, we can write down a question for almost every statement. In the first column of the Table 11.1, I have jotted down some statements. And in the second, I have framed the relevant questions.

TABLE 11.1 Framing Questions from a Statement

Answer	Question
I **love** mangoes.	**Do** you **love** mangoes?
We **study** English.	**Do** you **study** English?
No, we **don't study** Chinese.	**Do** you **study** Chinese?
You **sing** well.	**Do** I **sing** well?
Yes, you **look** good.	**Do** I **look** good?
She **doesn't eat** fried cockroaches.	**Does** she **eat** fried cockroaches?
Raghu **sleeps** in office.	**Does** Raghu **sleep** in office?
Express trains **stop** at this station.	**Do** express trains **stop** at this station?

As you can see, the rules for framing questions are slightly different for *Raghu* or *she*. The forms are:

Do	I/we/you/they	verb	object/complement?
Does	he/she/it		

ACTIVITY 1

Use the above forms to frame questions for the answers given in the second column:

1. .... I wake up early in the morning.
2. .... I study physics at Cotton College.
→ Do you play computer games in the afternoon? I play computer games in the afternoon.
3. .... We go to bed at 10 in the night.
4. .... My father runs a milk depot.
5. .... My mother manages an old people's home.[1]
6. .... Grandma reads the Quran every day.
7. .... I have two sisters.
8. .... They study medicine.

11.2 PARTIAL QUESTIONS

The activity above would not be useful in real life. Normally, you don't ask questions like: *Do you study physics at Cotton College?*

You would ask this only if you knew what I did, and in that case, it would be a pretty pointless question to ask. More likely, you would ask questions to find out *what* I do or *where* I study:

✓ What do you do?
✓ Are you a student?
✓ What subjects do you study?
✓ Where do you study?
✓ At which college do you study?
✓ What city do you live in?

Reading, Learning, and Studying

Read: 1. To look at and understand the meaning of written words. ➤ *Rohan is only four, but he can read.*
　　　 2. To go through written or printed words either silently or aloud. ➤ *Grandma reads the Bible every day.*
Learn: To gain knowledge or skill by reading, or from experience or a teacher. ➤ *Nandini is learning music.*
Study: To learn something by reading, going to school, and so on. ➤ *She studies physics at Bethune College.*

---

[1] **old people's home:** an establishment where old people live and where they are taken care of.

11.3 WE ASK THESE QUESTIONS EVERY DAY

The following table provides a list of some questions against question-words such as *where*, *which*, *when*, and *why*. We call them **wh-questions.** You will use questions like these often. Memorize the sentences if necessary.

Where		When	
Where does the bus stop?		When does the train start?	
Where is the toilet?		When do we meet?	
Where is your car?		When do you start for office?	
		When do you go to bed?	

What*		Which*	
What's your name?		Which is your favourite colour?	
What station is this?		Which book do you want?	
What is the time now?		Which key opens this door?	
What can I do for you?		Which road goes to heaven?	

How		Why	
How do you start this machine?		Why are you sad?	
How do you know (this)?		Why is he late?	
How can I help you?		Why is the office closed today?	
		Why is she crying?	

* Use **which** if there is a choice between two or more options. Otherwise, use **what.**

ACTIVITY 2

Let's frame more meaningful wh-questions with **when, what,** and **how.** The table below gives parts of some questions. Complete them:

1.	When do you	I wake up early in the morning.
2.	What ...., and at which college?	I study physics at Cotton College.
→	What do you do in the afternoon?	I play computer games in the afternoon.
3.	When	We go to bed at 10 in the night.
4.	What .... do?	My father runs a milk depot.
5.	....	My mother manages an old people's home.
6.	....	Grandma reads the Quran every day.
7.	How many	I have two sisters.
8.	....	They study medicine.

11.4 HOW ARE YOU?

We ask people *what* they do or *how/when* they do something, as shown in the table below. We also ask *how* people are or *who* they are. And the forms are:

Who	am	I?
Who/How/ How old	are	you?/they?
Who	is	he?/that girl in red?
What	is	this?/that? your phone number?

The above table shows the questions that are asked often. But of course, unless we are insane (or philosophers), we don't ask ourselves: *Who am I?* In real life, we ask questions like those in Activity 3.

What's Your Name Please?

This is how many Indians speak:
Q: What is your good name?
A: Myself, Mr Lucky Singh.

'Good name' is not good English and never begin a sentence with 'myself'.
Also do not put Mr (or Mrs/Miss) before your own name.

The correct forms are:
Q: What is your name?
A: My name is Lucky Singh.

ACTIVITY 3

Given below are some questions and answers. Write down the missing questions:

→	How are you?	I'm fine, thank you.
1.	………………………………………………	I am 25.
2.	………………………………………………	My mother is better now, thanks.
→	Who is the girl in red?	She's Diya Mirza, a budding actress.
3.	And who……………………………………	He's Diya's boyfriend.
4.	What………………………………………	This is an e-reader, a Kindle.
5.	………………………………………………	You read books on this.
6.	………………………………………………	These kids? They are terribly naughty.

11.5 HAVE YOU?/HAVE YOU GOT?/DO YOU HAVE?

A surveyor has come to Ravi's house to do a market survey. She asks these questions:

Surveyor: Sir, do you have a car?
Ravi: No, I don't.
Surveyor: Do you have any other vehicle?
Ravi: Yes, I have a bike.
Surveyor: Bike?
Ravi: I mean, a motorcycle.

Instead of saying 'Do you have a car?', the girl could have said:

✓ Have you got a car?

Have and *have got* are both used in British English to show possession or ownership, but *have got* is more informal.

- ✓ I have got a small flat. = I have a small flat.
- ✓ You've got the right attitude. = You have the right attitude.

The negatives and questions are shown in the following table:

Negative	I haven't got a house.
	You haven't got the right attitude.
	The minister hasn't got the time to meet you.
Questions	Have you got a passport? —Yes, I have. Or—No, I haven't.
	Has your sister got a house? —Yes, she has. Or—No, she hasn't.

Notes: 1. Don't use *have got* in short answers. Say *we have* or *we haven't*.

2. Indian languages don't have a precise equivalent of the verb **have**. Translate *I have a book* into our mother tongue and you will appreciate this statement. The syntax is different, isn't it? Because of this difference, we are often confused about how to use the verb *have*.

ACTIVITY 4

Ravi has just left his house. He is riding his motorcycle with George on the pillion. Complete the following conversation using: **'ve got, have … got, haven't, haven't got,** and **has got.**

Ravi: George, I have almost run out of petrol and I .... any cash
                 .... you .... five hundred rupees on you?
George: Sorry, I ....
Ravi: It's all right. I'll will go home and get some money from Radhika. I am sure she
                 .... some cash at home.
George: You don't have to. I .... my debit card with me. We can pay with my
                 card.
Ravi: Thanks. I will pay you back tomorrow.

ACTIVITY 5

Mrs Sikha Ray has applied for a passport. An officer has come to her house to verify the information she has furnished in her application. Complete the conversation below:

Officer   **Mrs Ray**
What is your name, madam?   Sikha Ray.

(A) And your husband's...............?   Sri Aniruddha Ray.
(B) ....?   I am a homemaker.
How many children (C) ....?   We've a son.
(D) ....?   He's a software engineer.
He works for?   He works for Tata Consultancy Services.
Where is he posted?   At the moment, he is in Houston, USA.
Why (E)...................................? I'd like to visit my son in America.
(F) .... a bank passbook? Yes, I have.
And your birth certificate?   Sorry, I (G) .... a birth certificate.

PRACTICE

1. Complete the questions with *what, where, how many, how, when:*

    a. .... is your name?
    b. .... do you live?
    c. .... children do you have?
    d. At .... school do you work?
    e. .... children study in your school?
    f. .... are the backgrounds of the students of your school?
    g. .... do you spend your day?
    h. .... do you go to school?
    i. .... are your hobbies?
    j. .... kind of books do you like?

2. You and I are friends, but we live in different countries. We have never met, we only chat on the Internet. One day, we discussed my obsession with computer games. I have erased some of the questions either partially or fully. Can you complete the following dialogue?

    You: (a) What do _____ _____ _____ _____ afternoon?
    I: Well, ... most of the days, I play games on the Internet.
    You: (b) _____ you _____ a computer at home?
    I: Yes, I do.
    You: (c) _____ _____ _____ _____ _____?
    I: I play Scrabble, Sudoku, and of course, card games.
    You: (d) For how many hours _____ _____ _____?
    I: For about four to five hours.
    You: (e) In that case, when _____ _____ study?
    I: I don't have to study. I did my masters 60 years ago.
    You: (f) Oh, really! How _____ _____ _____?
    I: I am 80.
    You: I am sorry. I always thought you were my age.
    I: That's all right. We can only try to know people. We never know anyone completely.

3. A lifestyle magazine is interviewing Mr Vagle for a story titled 'An Unknown Indian'. Given below are the answers given by Mr Vagle. Frame the questions from the statements on the right:

i.	My name is Manjunath Vagle.
ii.	I speak Marathi, Hindi, and English.
iii.	I am a teller in a bank.
iv.	Kolhapur Samavaya Bank Limited.
v.	My office is at Deccan Gymkhana, Pune.
vi.	Yes, I've got a car.
vii.	It's a Maruti Alto.
viii.	Normally by bus, but sometimes by car.
ix.	Yes, I am married.
x.	My wife is a dietician.
xi.	I have a daughter.
xii.	My daughter is a freelance photographer.
xiii.	Well, I travel a lot and I also love reading.
xiv.	I mostly read fiction.
xv.	My favourite author is Amitav Ghosh.

4. Mrs Gayetri Mahadevan has just been honoured as 'The best primary school teacher' by the President of India. You are a journalist who has interviewed Mrs Mahadevan on behalf of your paper. The short interview focuses on Gayetri's school and the kind of person she is. Imagine and write down the conversation that occurred between you and Mrs Mahadevan. Also, remember that there is always a shortage of space in a magazine, and as such, your interview should be precise and not exceed 200 words.

The interview covers the following points:

✓ How does she feel?
✓ Gayetri's school, its location, background of the children who attend her school, the number of classes in her school, and the number of children studying
✓ Her family, daily routine, interests, her likes, and dislikes

KEY TO ACTIVITIES

Activity 1: 1. Do you wake up early in the morning? 2. Do you study physics at Cotton College? 3. Do you go to bed at 10 in the night? 4. Does your father run a milk depot? 5. Does your mother manage an old people's home? 6. Does grandma read the Quran every day? 7. Do you have two sisters? 8. Do they study medicine?

Activity 2: 1. When do you wake up? 2. What do you study and at which college? 3. When do you go to bed? 4. What does your father do? 5. What does your mother do? 6. What books does your grandma read? 7. How many brothers and sisters do you have? 8. What do they do?

Activity 3: 1. How old are you? 2. How is your mother now? 3. And who is the boy sitting beside her? 4. What is this? 5. Kindle? What do you do with it? 6. How are these children?

Activity 4: Ravi:… and I haven't got any cash. Have you got five hundred rupees on you?/George: Sorry, I haven't./Ravi:… I am sure she has got some cash at home./George:… I've got my debit card with me.

Activity 5: (A) name is? (B) What do you do? (C) do you have/have you got? (D) What does he do? (E) Why do you require a passport? (F) Do you have/Have you got…? (G) don't have/haven't got….

Counting Things

People think they don't understand math, but it's all about how you explain it to them. If you ask a drunkard what number is larger, 2/3 or 3/5, he won't be able to tell you. But if you rephrase the question: what is better, 2 bottles of vodka for 3 people or 3 bottles of vodka for 5 people, he will tell you right away: 2 bottles for 3 people, of course.

Israel Gelfand, Mathematician

12.1 COUNTING, NOT COUNTING

A **noun** is a word used as the name of a person, place, thing, or an idea. When we have to say how many or how much of something, we say:

- ✓ Give me <u>a pen</u>.
- ✓ Give me <u>some sugar</u>.

We can count pens, men, and machines, but not sugar, milk, or happiness. Nouns are classified as **countable nouns** and **uncountable nouns** (also sometimes called **mass nouns**). Most *countable nouns* are words for things that can be counted. *Uncountable nouns* are names of things that we think of as *quantity* or *mass*: <u>milk</u> or <u>sand</u>, and *abstract concepts* such as <u>anger</u> or <u>time</u>.

In a dictionary, a countable noun is marked by the symbol [C] and an uncountable noun either [U] or [M]. If you see [U] or [M] next to a noun, you would know it doesn't have a plural form. You'll also find some words are marked [U] in one sense, but [C] in another sense. More about such nouns shortly.

12.2 COUNTABLE NOUNS

Countable nouns can be singular or plural. This is how you form plurals:

Plural Countable Nouns

Rules for Forming Plurals	Examples
1. Generally, add *s* to get the plural	*book → books, class → classes, taxi → taxis*
2. For nouns ending with *s, sh, ch,* and *x,* add *es* to the word	*bus → buses, bush → bushes, box → boxes, one inch → two inches*
3. If a noun ends with a ***consonant + y,*** replace the last *y* with *ies*	*army → armies, baby → babies*
4. But for a noun ending with a ***vowel + y,*** you add just an *s*	*boy → boys, key → keys, monkey → monkeys*
5. For most nouns ending with *o,* you have to add *s*	*disco → discos, kilo → kilos, radio → radios, piano → pianos, zero → zeros*
6. But for some nouns ending with *o,* you have to add *es*	*hero → heroes, mango → mangoes, tomato → tomatoes*
7. These examples show that for words ending with *f,* plurals may have different endings	*cliff → cliffs, belief → beliefs*
	thief → thieves, leaf → leaves
	Also, life → lives, knife → knives
8. For some nouns, the plural is the same as the singular	*one aircraft → two aircraft, spacecraft → spacecraft, bison → bison, deer → deer, sheep → sheep, offspring[1] → offspring, species[2] → species*
9. But often, there is no rule	*man → men, woman → women, child → children*

12.3 UNCOUNTABLE NOUNS

When we talk about a non-specific quantity of something that cannot be counted, we use words or phrases such as *some, any, a little, a lot of, lots of, much,* and *a large quantity of.* Note how *some* and *any* are used:

Nandini: Shall I make <u>some</u> tea for you?
Catherine: Thanks, but please don't put <u>any</u> sugar.

Some is used in positive statements and *any* in negative statements. Also, while we use *a lot of* (a rather formal expression), or *lots of* (informal) in positive sentences, we use *much* in questions and negative sentences.

Radhika: How <u>much</u> time do we have before the movie?
Ravi: Not <u>much</u> really. But after the film, we'll have *lots of* time.

---

[1] **offspring:** (noun) a son or a daughter.
[2] **species:** a closely related group of animals or plants. *Which species of dog is it? —It's a Labrador.*

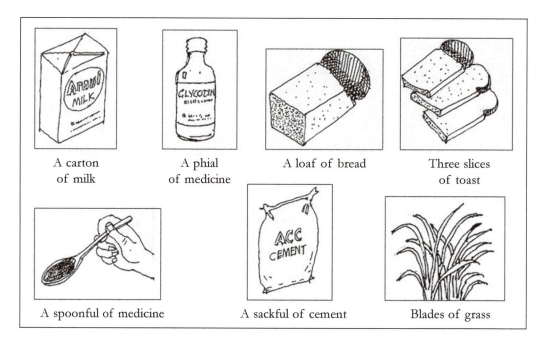

| A carton of milk | A phial of medicine | A loaf of bread | Three slices of toast |
| A spoonful of medicine | A sackful of cement | Blades of grass |

When we talk about a specific quantity of uncountable things, we say:

- ✔ a drop of milk, a bottle of milk, two cartons of milk
- ✔ a grain of rice, a handful of rice, a morsel of rice
- ✔ a loaf or slice of bread, a slice of cake, a slice of toast
- ✔ a sackful of or 10 tonnes of cement, 50 wagons of iron ore
- ✔ a strand of hair
- ✔ a blade of grass
- ✔ a phial (pronounced **PHAI**-UHL) of medicine
- ✔ *A spoonful of sugar as my medicine*

That is how we express specific quantities of rice or cough syrup. But what are the units of *truth, jealousy,* or *illness?*

I was suffering from a <u>bout of influenza</u>. My friend George telephoned and told me he had just seen my girlfriend with another guy. Normally, I would have felt a <u>pang of jealousy</u>, but it was a <u>stroke of good luck</u> that my girlfriend was with me at that time. I asked George, 'Is there an <u>iota of truth</u> in what you say?'

George laughed, 'Oh! I was just having <u>a little</u> fun!'

If the subject is an uncountable noun, the verb is singular.

✓ This <u>luggage belongs</u> to Georgy. It's quite heavy. A lot of money <u>is required</u> to ship it to London, where he lives now.

✓ <u>Grass is</u> always greener on the other side of the fence.[3]

ACTIVITY 1

Fill in the blanks with appropriate words. You will find all of them in Section 12.3.

1. Shall I make............... coffee for you?
2. Yes, thanks. I'd like to have a............... of sugar in my coffee.
3. Mother, can you give me............... cash?
4. Sorry, I don't have............... right now.
5. I can see a few............... of grey hair on your head.
6. It is spring............... of grass have sprouted everywhere.
7. There is not an............... of truth in this press statement.
8. When Calvin won a lottery, Hobbs suffered a............... of envy.
9. I had a............... of fever last month.
10. When the waiter brought the bill, I realized I had lost my wallet. It was a............... of fortune that a friend walked into the restaurant just then.

12.4 THE GANG OF FIVE

Some English nouns look like countable but they are not. *Furniture, equipment, information, news,* and *advice* are five commonly misused uncountable nouns. We do not say ~~two furnitures~~ or *this is ~~a good~~ news*.

Common Problems with Uncountable Nouns

Incorrect	Correct
You'll get all the ~~informations~~ at our head office.	You'll get all the information at our head office.
This is ~~a good news~~.	This is good news. Or... a piece of good news.
Our gym is small, but we have state-of-the-art[4] ~~equipments~~.	Our gym is small, but we have state-of-the-art equipment.
You have given me ~~a good advice~~.	You have given me good advice. Or... a piece of good advice.

---

[3] This proverb means we often think that other people are happier or are in a better position compared to us. Another variation of this saying is: *Blue are the hills that are far away.*

[4] **state-of-the-art:** (noun) the latest in the field of a product, machine, and so on.

Besides these, some frequently used uncountable nouns in British English are ***bread, clothing*** (= things that you wear), ***luggage, rubbish, traffic, toast, transport*** (= a system of carrying people and goods), and ***work*** (in the sense of employment, activity, or duty).

12.5 NOUNS ALWAYS PLURAL OR SINGULAR

Plural nouns: Some nouns refer to a group of people, animals, or things. For example:

- ✓ **crew** (= the people who operate a ship or an aircraft) and
- ✓ **staff** (= all the people working in an organization)

They are always plural and take plural verbs. Dictionaries often use the symbol [Pl] for them. Here are some examples:

- ✓ **cattle:** cows or bulls kept in a farm. *The cattle are fed on barley.*
- ✓ **clothes:** things you wear. *Your clothes say a lot about you.*
- ✓ **folk:** people in general. *The village folk in India may not read or write, but they are not politically illiterate.*
- ✓ **goods:** things that are produced to be sold. *My brother deals in consumer goods.*
- ✓ **police:** *Police are trying to identify the burglars from the CCTV footage.* Do not say: *Police is...* ✗ If you wish to talk about men or women in the police force, say a **policeman,** two **policewomen,** or 20 **police officers.**

Also, ***people*** is a plural noun when you mean more than one person: *Two hundred people are attending the meeting.* But when you talk about the entire population of a country, it is a countable noun: *Peoples of India and Pakistan want to live in peace.*

Singular nouns: Some nouns are always singular and have no plural form.

- ✓ **fillip** (= boost): *The new policies will give a fillip to agriculture.*
- ✓ **whiff** (= a smell, particularly what you smell just for moments): *Aneesh caught a whiff of perfume when he crossed Ayesha.*
- ✓ **jot** (= a small amount to speak of negatives): *The report doesn't contain a jot of truth.*

12.6 PAIR NOUNS

Objects that have two parts joined at one end are called ***pair nouns:*** *a pair of jeans, a pair of shorts, a pair of spectacles,* and so on.

The words *jeans, trousers, shorts, spectacles, sunglasses, scissors, binoculars,* and such others are plural in English. You do not use singular verbs with them:

- ✓ His jeans are dirty. (His jean is dirty ✗. His jeans is dirty ✗.)
- ✓ You look good in these spectacles. (Not in this spectacle)

ACTIVITY 2

Correct the following sentences:

1. I have only two luggages.
2. The furnitures in his house are beautiful.
3. I always give you good advices.
4. Don't throw rubbishes here.
5. Ramu is a police; his wife Shanta too is a police.
6. The rush hour traffics are terrible in Bengaluru.
7. I have to give you two news.
8. I bought a trouser yesterday.
9. Two hundred aircrafts land at this airport every day.
10. The police is searching for a dangerous criminal.

12.7 NOUNS: BOTH COUNTABLE AND UNCOUNTABLE

There are many words in English which are uncountable in one sense, but countable in another sense. For example:

✓ When you talk about *a number of **fish**,* they are still fish. You do not say: *I caught two fishes.* ✗ You say: *I caught two fish.* However, when you talk about *different kinds,* you use *fishes: Sardine and tuna are the two common fishes we find in Goa.*

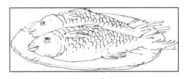

Two fish

✓ ***Food*** is uncountable if you are referring to things people eat: *Indians eat a wide variety of food.* It is countable if you are talking about a particular kind: *Frozen foods, baby foods,* and so on.

Three pieces of fish

✓ ***Iron*** is uncountable when you think of it as metal, but when you talk about the tool to press clothes, it is countable. Similarly, ***paper, glass, space, time,*** and ***light*** can be either countable or uncountable depending on the context.

Several fishes

If you do not know if a word is a countable or not, check in a dictionary. There is no shortcut!

12.8 SOME COMMON PROBLEMS

If the subject is singular, it takes a singular verb and when it is plural, it takes a plural verb. But at times, we make mistakes when the subject is one of many things:

- One of my friends ~~work~~ in a call centre. ✗
- Correct: One of my friends **works** …. ✓

Another source of error:

- Most of the books in this library ~~is~~ old. ✗
- Most of the books in this library **are** old. ✓

These errors are rather common.

Don't Say	Say
One of the **policeman** was rude. ✗	One of the **policemen** was rude. ✓
I told you many a **times**. ✗	I told you **many a time**. ✓
	'I'm sad to say/I'm on my way,/Won't be back in **many a day**.' (A Caribbean song)

ACTIVITY 3

Fill in the blanks with one of the options given within the brackets:

1. Only one of the students………(is/are) wearing proper uniform.
2. The cartons found in the truck……… (contains/contain) old books.
3. The flowers in the vase……… (is/are) stale.
4. The soil in all the flowerpots……… (is/are) dry.
5. News from all corners of the country……… (is/are) bad.
6. The consequences of my action……… (was/were) bad.

ACTIVITY 4

Put the words in the appropriate sections:

advice	anger	bread	clothes	clothing
crew	expertise	equipment	fish	food
language	luggage	manners	milk	news
paper	people	police	information	scissors
shorts	staff	toast	traffic	whiff

Uncountable Nouns		Countable Nouns	
		Nouns that can be both singular and plural:	
Pair nouns:	*Always plural*	*Always singular*	

PRACTICE

1. Complete the rules using either *singular* or *plural*:

   a. Countable nouns take .... verbs if the subject is singular and .... verbs if it is plural.
   b. Uncountable nouns take .... verbs.
   c. Pair nouns take .... verbs.
   d. Plural nouns take .... verbs.

2. Fill in the blanks with one of the following: *blade*, *grain*, *iota*, *pair*, *piece*, and *strand*.

   a. a _____ of grass   b. a _____ of salt
   c. a _____ of furniture   d. a _____ of hair
   e. not an _____ of truth   f. a _____ of trousers

3. Fill in the blanks with either is or are:

   i. Happiness .... not the same as satisfaction.
   ii. The clothes .... in the washing machine.
   iii. These goods .... of poor quality.
   iv. In a democracy, people .... the supreme authority.
   v. Money .... not everything in life.

4. There are eight mistakes in the following paragraph. Underline them:

   When we reached Darjeeling, all the hotels of the town was full. We had to walk from place to place, carrying our luggages. The tourist office was closed and we could not get the necessary informations. There were lots of policemen on the roads. There had been a murder in the town the day before. The police was looking for the criminal. To make matters worse, I broke my spectacle and couldn't see anything. We went into a restaurant. The food was good; they served two fishes to everyone. My wife complained, 'I told you many a times not to go to a new place without booking hotel accommodation in advance!' I said, 'One of my friend works for the All India Radio here, let's go and look for him.'

5. a. Jot down the pair nouns that you can remember

    ....

    b. Write down the plural nouns that you can recall.

    ....

KEY TO ACTIVITIES

Activity 1: 1. some; 2. spoonful; 3. some; 4. any; 5. strands; 6. Blades; 7. iota; 8. pang; 9. bout; 10. stroke

Activity 2: 1. I have only two pieces of luggage. 2. The furniture in his house is beautiful. 3. I always give you good advice. 4. Don't throw rubbish here. 5. Ramu is a policeman; his wife Shanta too is a policewoman. 6. The rush hour traffic is terrible in Bengaluru. 7. I have to give you two pieces of news. 8. I bought a pair of trousers yesterday. 9. Two hundred aircraft land at this airport every day. 10. The police are searching for a dangerous criminal.

Activity 3: 1. is; 2. contain; 3. are; 4. is; 5. is; 6. were

Activity 4: *Uncountable nouns:* advice, anger, bread, clothing, expertise, equipment, luggage, milk, news, information, toast, traffic; *Countable nouns:* language; *Nouns that can be both singular and plural:* fish, food, paper, people; *Pair nouns:* scissors, shorts; *Always plural:* clothes, crew, police, staff; *Always singular:* whiff

13

A School of Fish or Group Nouns

Learning Objectives: In English, you come across words that describe specific groups of animals and things. In this chapter, we are going to study these widely used words.

13.1 A VISIT TO THE ZOO

Last Sunday, a strange thing happened during our visit to a zoo. We saw a few elephants and in a vast open space behind a fence, we found a **herd of deer** and a **herd of bison.** We also saw a **pack of hyenas.** A **troop of monkeys** entertained us. A **flock of geese** had come to spend their winter holidays at a lake in the zoo. Then we went to see hippopotamuses. The hippos were kept in a marshy enclosure surrounded by a high wall. The viewing platform is 10 feet above the ground. We climbed a **flight of stairs** to reach there. In the end, we went to see tigers. The tigers' area is separated by a low wall and a wide moat.[1] There was a **shoal of fish** in the water. A few tigers were lazing around in the winter sun. A **litter of tiger cubs** were playing among themselves. Suddenly, two young men jumped over the wall, swam across the moat and rushed towards the nearest tiger. They were carrying a **bouquet of flowers** and a garland. They were shouting, 'Jai Sherawali Mata!' As the **crowd of people** watched in horror, the young men tried to put the garland around a tiger's neck. But the big cat, unlike humans, wasn't fond of garlands. It growled and slapped the man with its paw. Then it turned round and walked away calmly. But its casual blow was enough to break the man's neck. His friend jumped back into the moat and swam to safety. Later, he said that he and his friend belonged to **a group of devotees** of the Sherawali Mata, a goddess who rides a tiger. These young men wanted to offer flowers to the mount of the goddess.

We often refer to a collection of things, animals, or people as one whole. In this true story, the highlighted phrases (*flock* of geese, *flight* of stairs, and so on) talk about collections of animals or things.

A noun, such as *committee, herd,* or *pack,* which refers to a group of people, animals, or things is known as a **group noun** or **collective noun.**

---

[1] **moat:** (noun) a broad ditch dug around an area (particularly a castle) and filled with water.

The English language is unusual in many ways and the *group noun* is something unique in English; most languages don't have it. There are hundreds of them and all of them mean 'a group (of something)'. But each one of them is specific to one or a few particular things or animals: a *pride* of lions, a *crowd* of people, a *pack* of cards, and so on. A *pride* of lions means a group of lions. *Pride* cannot be used for any other animal; you cannot say a ~~*pride*~~ *of monkeys* ✘. But the group noun *herd* can be used for the following animals and many more:

✓ A herd of buffalo ✓ A herd of bison   ✓ A herd of cattle ✓ A herd of cows
✓ A herd of deer   ✓ A herd of elephants ✓ A herd of zebras ✓ A herd of whales

There is great diversity of group nouns associated with animals, from a *murder* of crows to a *zeal* of zebras! People do not use most of them in their lifetime. In this chapter, we are going to check a handful of them, the ones you are likely to come across.

13.2 SOME COMMON GROUP NOUNS

The table below lists some common group nouns:

Group Nouns—Animals	
An army of	ants
A colony of	
A swarm of	
A swarm of	bees
A flock of	birds
A flight of*	
A rainbow of	butterflies
A brood of	chicken
A shoal of	fish
A school of	
A pack of	dogs
A flock of	geese
A litter of	kittens[2]
A litter of	puppies
A horde of	mice
A flock of	sheep
A pack of	wolves

Group Nouns—Others	
A pile of	bricks
A shower of	bullets
A pack of	cards
A wad of	currency notes
A block of	flats
A bouquet of	flowers
A bunch of	
A bunch of	grapes
A cluster of	huts
A ring of	keys
A collection of	paintings
A team of	players
A fleet of	ships
A flotilla of	
A troop of	soldiers
A flight of	stairs
A chain of	stores
A convoy of	trucks

* We use a *flight of birds* only to describe flying birds.

---

[2] **kitten:** (noun) a young cat.

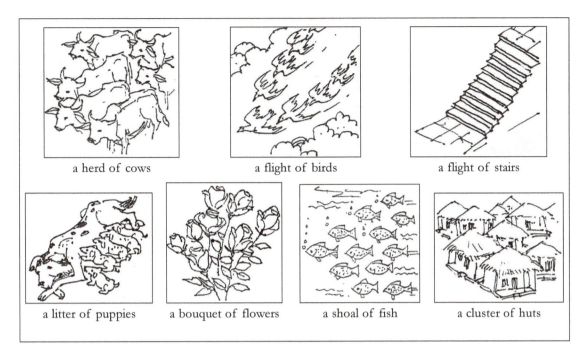

a herd of cows   a flight of birds   a flight of stairs

a litter of puppies   a bouquet of flowers   a shoal of fish   a cluster of huts

13.3 SINGULAR VERBS OR PLURAL VERBS?

Do group nouns take singular verbs or plural verbs? Fill in the blank below:

•   A fleet of ships............ (pass/passes) through this channel every day.

While framing sentences, group nouns are usually treated as singular, although they are actually a collection of many. For example:

1.   A fleet of ships **passes** through this channel every day.
2.   A committee of students **is empowered** to decide this.
3.   The pride of lions in this jungle **has** limited supply of food.

In India, we generally follow the rules of British English where many collective nouns such as <u>company</u>, <u>committee</u>, <u>parliament</u>, and so on can be treated as both singular and plural verbs. For example, both these sentences are correct:

1.   The committee **has decided** to change the rules.
2.   The committee **have been arguing** on this issue.

In the first example, we use the singular verb as we think of the committee as a unit. But in the second, we are talking about the individual members of the committee who have been arguing on *this issue*. So we use a plural verb here. Another example:

1.   The Indian football team **is** on the field.
2.   Have you noticed? The team **are wearing** socks of different colours!

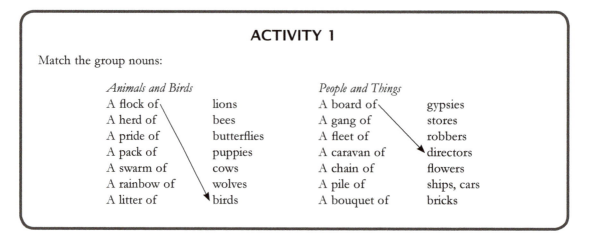

A School of Fish

What do you understand by a **school of fish?** Clearly, it is not a place where young fish go every day. The expression means a large *number* of fish *swimming together*. Another collective noun for fish is a **shoal** (*of fish*).

Some More ...

Here are a few interesting group nouns. If you wish to know more, please search for the following on the Internet: *group nouns* or *collective nouns*.

- A clutter of cats
- A murder of crows
- A leap of leopards
- A parliament of owls
- An ambush of tigers or
- A swift of tigers

13.4 NAMES OF INSTITUTIONS

The names of institutions, companies, and clubs are also collective nouns: the United Nations, the All India Radio, East Bengal (football club), the Union Bank, and so on. You can use singular or plural verbs with them depending on the situation:

- ✓ East Bengal is in good form this year. Or: East Bengal are playing badly today.
- ✓ The Union Bank is planning to open an office in China.

Note: Use *the* before names of organizations. However, don't use *the* if the name begins with the name of a person or place: *Jawaharlal Nehru University.*

ACTIVITY 2

There are two blanks in each of the following sentences. Fill in one of the blanks with the appropriate group noun (there may be more than one correct answer), and the other with the correct verb:

1. A .... of soldiers .... (march/marches) along this highway every morning.
2. The .... of directors of the company .... (decide/decides) about payment of bonus.
3. A .... of people .... (wait/waits) at this bus stop every morning.
4. A .... of puppies .... (is/are) suckling at their mother's breast.
5. Walmart .... (has/have) a .... of retail stores all over the world.
6. This .... of footballers often .... (fight/fights) among themselves.

PRACTICE

1. Fill in the blanks using words that you have come across in this chapter:

   One of the special features of the English language is ¹g............. or ²c............. nouns. These nouns represent a collection of something. For example, a ³........ of keys, a ⁴f........ of stairs, or a ⁵c............. of cottages.

   There are some interesting words to describe groups of animals. A ⁶............. of lions refers to a group of lions that live together as a social unit. If you see in the sky a formation of birds flying together, you call them a ⁷f............. of birds. But when the same birds come down, you them a ⁸f........... Also, you call a large number of fish swimming together either a ⁹s............. or a ¹⁰sc............. of fish. However, for a number of ships sailing together, you use the term ¹¹............. of ships.

   English has some strange group nouns like a ¹²m............... of crows or ¹³p................. of owls, but you may not use most of them ever. Another interesting point to note is that they are used for ¹⁴s............... things or animals. For example, no one ever says a pride of elephants or a herd of lions.

2. Fill in the blanks with group nouns and delete the inappropriate verbs:

   i. There is/are a .... of ants under this building.
   ii. A .... of migratory birds come/comes to this lake every year.
   iii. Sometimes, a .... of elephants enter/enters our village in search of food.
   iv. Be careful! A .... of wolves live/lives in this jungle.
   v. Mr Rao's .... of paintings is/are worth millions of rupees.
   vi. There is/are a .... of huts between the highway and the forest.
   vii. Our football .... win/wins most of the matches.
   viii. A .... of army trucks pass/passes through this road every day.
   ix. It was a beautiful palace once. But now, only a .... of bricks stand/stands at the place.
   x. 'How do I go to the post office?'—'Go straight. The post office is after that .... of flats.'

KEY TO ACTIVITIES

Activity 1: ANIMALS AND BIRDS: A flock of birds, a herd of cows, a pride of lions, a pack of wolves, a swarm of bees, a rainbow of butterflies, a litter of puppies. PEOPLE AND THINGS: a board of directors, a gang of robbers, a fleet of ships and a fleet of cars, a caravan of gypsies, a chain of stores, a pile of bricks, a bouquet of flowers.

Activity 2: 1. A <u>troop</u> of soldiers <u>marches</u> along the highway every morning. (A battalion, a brigade, a platoon, an army are some other group nouns that go with soldiers.) 2. The <u>board</u> of directors of the company <u>decides</u> about payment of bonus. (It is a collective decision of the board.) 3. A <u>crowd</u> of people <u>waits/wait</u> at this bus stop every morning. 4. A <u>litter</u> of puppies <u>are</u> <u>suckling</u> at their mother's breast. 5. Walmart <u>has</u> a <u>chain</u> of retail stores all over the world. 6. This <u>team</u> of footballers often <u>fight</u> among themselves.

14

Where Are You Going, My Pretty Maid?

Learning Objectives: In this chapter, we are going to study the grammatical forms used to describe incomplete actions in the present.

14.1 A MAN MEETS A PRETTY YOUNG GIRL

'Where are you going, my pretty maid?'
'I'm going a-milking, sir', she said.
　　　'May I go with you, my pretty maid?'
　　　'You're kindly welcome, sir', she said.
'What is your father, my pretty maid?'
'My father's a farmer, sir', she said.
　　　'What is your fortune,[1] my pretty maid?'
　　　'My face is my fortune, sir', she said.
'Then I can't marry you, my pretty maid.'
'Nobody asked you, sir', she said.

Have you heard this nursery rhyme? It tells us about a man who approaches a pretty girl but turns away when he comes to know that the prospective[2] father-in-law is not exactly rolling in wealth. Let's wish the man better luck next time and concentrate on the first two sentences:

'Where <u>are you going</u>, my pretty maid?'
'<u>I'm going</u> a-milking, sir', she said.

We use sentences like 'I'm going' when we talk about an incomplete action in the present time. We call this the ***present continuous form***:

———————————
[1] **fortune:** (noun) a lot of money. *She inherited a fortune when her aunt passed away.*
[2] **prospective:** (adjective) a person who is likely to become someone for you: *a prospective employer.*

I	am/'m	<u>climbing</u> down a tree
We/you/ they	are/'re	<u>eating</u> boiled biscuits
		<u>fixing</u> a burglar alarm
		<u>playing</u> Scrabble
		<u>singing</u> a Scandinavian bhajan
He/she	is/'s	<u>watching</u> a film

You will find more of the present continuous form in the following dialogue:

Tania:	What <u>are you cooking</u> for lunch, ma?
Mother:	Biriyani.
Tania:	Great! I <u>love</u> biriyani.
Mother:	I <u>know</u>; <u>I'm trying</u> to do a good job.
Tania:	Ma, your biriyani is heavenly, always! <u>I'm going out</u> now. Shall we have lunch after an hour?
Mother:	Sure. Where <u>are</u> you <u>going</u>?
Tania:	My mobile has broken down. I've to get it fixed. I'll be back soon.
Mother:	What<u>'s</u> your papa <u>doing</u>?
Tania:	I guess he<u>'s taking</u> a nap. He <u>dozes off</u> every Sunday before lunch.

Tania and her ma use *the present continuous* for actions that are taking place at the moment: *I am cooking*, *I'm trying*, and so on. But they use the simple present to talk about what is usual. (*I love biriyani*. *He dozes off every Sunday*….)

ACTIVITY 1

Given below are four pictures. Look at them and complete the sentences to describe them. (Use the verbs given within brackets.)

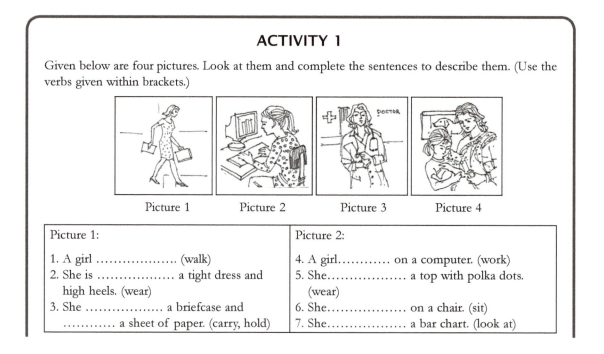

Picture 1	Picture 2	Picture 3	Picture 4

Picture 1:	Picture 2:
1. A girl .... (walk)	4. A girl............ on a computer. (work)
2. She is .... a tight dress and high heels. (wear)	5. She.................. a top with polka dots. (wear)
3. She .... a briefcase and .... a sheet of paper. (carry, hold)	6. She.................. on a chair. (sit)
	7. She.................. a bar chart. (look at)

Picture 3:	Picture 4:
8. A doctor .... (stand) 9. She ...... not .... (smile) 10. She .... a white coat. (wear) 11. She .... a folder.[3] (hold)	12. A small girl .... a cat in her arms. (hold) 13. A vet .... the cat some medicine. (give) 14. A dog .... behind them. (stand)

14.2 ANOTHER USE OF THE PRESENT CONTINUOUS

We also use the *present continuous form* when we are involved in an activity but are not actually doing it at the time of speaking:

Radhika <u>is doing</u> her PhD. Her husband, Ravi, is an engineer. He <u>is planning</u> to go to Argentina. In Argentina, people speak Spanish. So Ravi and Radhika <u>are taking</u> Spanish lessons.

14.3 A COMMON ERROR

The *present continuous tense* is used to describe (a) an incomplete action in the present (*Mom is cooking biriyani*), and (b) an activity we are presently involved in (*Ravi and Radhika are taking Spanish lessons*).

Some people incorrectly use the continuous tense for habitual things:

It would be incorrect to say: ✖ *Narasimhan is living in Coimbatore.* ✖ *He is going to office by bus every day.* Say: *Narasimhan lives in Coimbatore. He goes to office by bus.*

Also, the sentence *Virat Kohli is playing for India* will be fine when a match is in progress and Kohli is in the team. Otherwise, you say: *Kohli plays for India.*

14.4 THE NEGATIVE FORM

To get the negative form of the present continuous, just add **n't/not** after **am/is/are**.

Transform the sentences in the table below by following the examples given:

	Positive	Negative
→	I am reading a book.	I am not reading a book.
→	We are cleaning the house.	We aren't/are not cleaning the house.
1.	You are telling the truth.	

---

[3] **folder:** (noun) a plastic or cardboard cover for holding loose papers.

2.	Kuttan is riding his dad's bike.	
3.	They are talking nonsense.	

Key: 1. You aren't/are not telling the truth. 2. Kuttan isn't/is not riding his dad's bike. 3. They are not/aren't talking nonsense.

▌14.5 QUESTIONS

To frame questions in the present continuous, we begin with a question word (*what*, *how*, and so on) and bring the helping verb before the subject. In the table below, some answers (statements) are given. Write down the relevant questions:

	Question	**Answer**
→	What are you doing?	I am writing a letter.
1.	Whom .... you .... to?	To my mom.
2.	What .... eating?	I am munching peanuts.
3.	Whose bike ....?	Kuttan is riding his father's bike.
4.	What ...... your grandpa ....?	Grandpa is playing kabaddi.
5.	....	Yes, sir, I am telling the truth.

Key: 1. Whom are you writing to? 2. What are you eating? 3. Whose bike is Kuttan riding? 4. What is your grandpa doing? 5. Are you telling the truth?

ACTIVITY 2

Simple Present or Present Continuous?

A.   Strike off the incorrect words:

1.   We live/are living in India.
2.   I can't answer the door. I talk/am talking on the phone.
3.   I wake up/am waking up early.
4.   I love/am loving mangoes.
5.   You don't do/aren't doing the right thing.
6.   My sister studies/is studying the last lesson before her exam.
7.   My father works/is working for a bank.
8.   Grandpa eats/is eating chapattis every day.

B.   Fill in the blanks with appropriate forms of the verbs given within brackets:

1.   Look, they .... (close) the shop. Please go and get this medicine.

2. The shop .... (close) at 8 PM.
3. He normally .... (speak) English. But now he .... (talk) in Hindi.
4. 'Can you come for a moment?'—'Sorry, I' .... (watch) TV.'
5. Rekha came here last night. She .... (stay) in a hotel for three days.
6. They .... (play) football on Sundays.
7. Usually they .... (play) football, but today, they .... (play) hockey.
8. 'What .... you .... (do)?'—'I .... (work) for a travel agency.'

14.6 I BELIEVE GOD EXISTS

In Section 6.5, we defined *action verbs* and *state verbs*:

- Verbs that describe an action (or event) are called **action verbs.**
- Verbs that tell us about the state, location, nature, or identity of a thing are called **state verbs.**

The most common state verb is *be.* Here is a list of some frequently used *state verbs:*

States of your mind	adore, admire, believe, feel (= think), imagine, know, like, dislike, love, hate, recognize, recall, remember, realize, trust, understand, want, wish
Senses	the five sensory verbs: feel, hear, see, taste, touch, and also sound
Conveying/receiving ideas	agree, disagree, appear, disappear, deny, look (= appear), mean, please promise, satisfy, seem, surprise
Others	be, belong, contain, depend, deserve, include, need, owe, own, possess

Here is an important point to note.

Normally, state verbs are not used in continuous tenses.

Don't Say	Say
I am believing in God. ✘	I believe in God. ✔
I am not believing that God is existing. ✘	I don't believe that God exists. ✔
I am liking you. ✘	I like you. ✔
Are you understanding me? ✘	Do you understand me? ✔

Some verbs function both as action verbs and state verbs.

In the sentences below, check how *feel, touch,* and *see* are used first as an action verb, and then as a state verb:

Action Verb	State Verb
The nurse <u>is feeling</u> the patient's pulse.	I <u>feel</u> sad to hear that you are unwell. (Don't say: *I am feeling sad.* ✗)
Please do not talk, I <u>am thinking</u>.	I <u>think</u> (= I feel) you are right. (Not: *I am thinking you are right.* ✗)
After the accident, I <u>wasn't seeing</u> at all.	I <u>see</u> your point. (Not *I am seeing your point.* ✗)

ACTIVITY 3

Fill in the blanks with appropriate forms of the verb given within brackets:

A.   These trousers .... me now. (not fit)
B.   I'll call you back. Right now, I .... a CCTV camera in my factory. (fit)
C.   That umbrella .... to me. (belong)
D.   It was pitch dark, I .... my way to the bed when someone sighed. (feel)
E.   I was with my old friends after decades. It .... great. (feel)
F.   I .... the gorgeous sunset when my phone .... (admire, ring)

▌ PRACTICE

1.   Fill in the blanks to complete the descriptions of the pictures. Fill in the first blank with what 'he/she is' and the second blank with what 'he/she is doing'. Follow the model given:

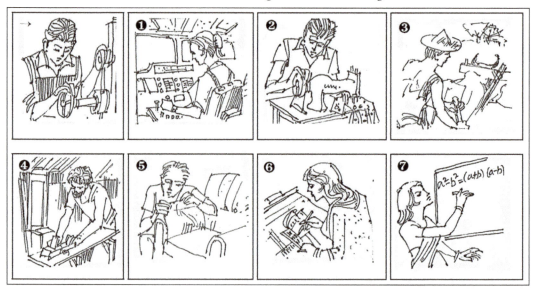

→ Mangal is a me<u>chanic</u>. He's <u>repairing</u> a machine. (repair)

1. Saudamini is a .... She' .... an aircraft. (fly)
2. Raju is a .... He' .... a frock. (stitch)
3. Balu is a .... He' .... (farm)
4. Ismail is a .... He' .... a table. (make)
5. Aju is an .... He' .... a sofa. (repair)
6. Brinda is an .... She' .... a building plan. (draw)
7. Nandini is a .... She' .... maths. (teach)

2. Correct the following sentences:

   a. I do not sleep, I am listen to music.
   b. My brother is not play the match today.
   c. The Indian Republic is consisting of 28 states and 7 union territories.
   d. The power supply is erratic here; we are depending on diesel generators.
   e. My uncle is owning two houses.
   f. I am not remembering his phone number.

3. Frame questions for the following answers:

a. Yes, I am reading the Gita.	.... you....... the Gita?
b. I am reading the Gita.	What......... you............?
c. No, Virat isn't playing today.	
d. No, I am not reading the newspaper.	
e. I am going to the market.	
f. No, I don't believe in God.	

4. Fill in the blanks using the verbs given within brackets:

   Ravi: Why .... you .... (repeat) the same point?
   Radhika: Because you .... (not pay) attention.
   Ravi: Oh no! I .... (listen to) you.
   Radhika: Are you? I think you .... (think) of someone else.

5. Look out of your window and see what is happening. Write down the scene using both the simple present and the present continuous. [For example: *There are lots of people on the road. A man is walking his dog. Some children are waiting for their school bus. The sky is clear. Some birds are flying. ...*]

   ....
   ....
   ....
   ....
   ....
   ....
   ....
   ....
   ....

....
....
....
....
....
....
....
....
....
....
....
....
....
....
....

KEY TO ACTIVITIES

Activity 1:
A. 1. A girl is walking. 2. She is wearing a tight dress and high heels. 3. She is carrying a briefcase and holding a sheet of paper. 4. A girl is working on a computer. 5. She is wearing a top with polka dots. 6. She is sitting on a chair. 7. She is looking at a bar chart. 8. A doctor is standing. 9. She is not smiling. 10. She is wearing a white coat. 11. She is holding a folder. 12. A girl is holding a cat in her arms. 13. The vet is giving the cat some medicine. 14. A dog is standing behind them.

Activity 2:
A. 1. We live in India. 2. I am talking over the phone. 3. I wake up early. 4. I love mangoes. 5. You aren't doing the right thing. 6. My sister is studying the last lesson.... 7. My father works for a bank. 8. Grandpa eats chapattis....

B. 1. ... they are closing the shop. 2. The shop closes at 8 PM. 3. He normally speaks English. But now he is talking in Hindi. 4. 'Sorry, I'm watching TV.' 5. She is staying in a hotel for three days. 6. They play football on Sundays. 7. Usually they play football, but today, they are playing hockey. 8. 'What do you do?'—'I work for a travel agency.'

Activity 3: A. don't fit; B. am fitting; C. belongs; D. was feeling; E. felt; F. was admiring, rang

15

We Eat ...

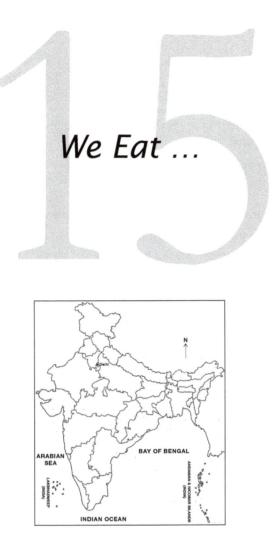

Disclaimer: This figure has been redrawn by the author and is not to scale. It does not represent any authentic national or international boundaries and is used for illustrative purposes only.

Write a heading for the essay below:

....

Indians speak different languages, follow different religions, and eat different foods. The diversity[1] in their food habits is quite remarkable. If you wish to understand India, a good way to begin might be to check what kind of food Indians eat.

The food habits change as you travel from the coasts to the interior parts of the vast country. In the coastal states, from Gujarat to Kerala on the west coast and from Tamil Nadu to Bengal on the east, and also in the North East, rice is the staple food. However, in the interiors of North India, chapatti and dal are the most common dishes. In Bihar, people eat both rice and chapattis. Chapattis are made from wheat and millets, that is, raagi, baajra, or jowar.

---

[1] **diversity:** (noun) a variety of different things or ideas.

Coastal regions and the plains on either side of the River Ganga receive a lot of rainfall. The climate and the soil in these areas are ideal for growing paddy, which gives us rice. But Rajasthan, Madhya Pradesh (MP), Chhattisgarh, and the interiors of Gujarat, Maharashtra, and Karnataka get very little rain. The only crops that grow in these areas are millets. Cultivation of wheat requires a lot of water. As Punjab, Haryana, and western Uttar Pradesh (UP) have excellent irrigation systems, they produce large quantities of wheat, from which flour is made.

So we can say that the geography of an area determines the food habits of its people. Here are a few more examples to illustrate[2] the point: Kerala has lots of coconut trees, and hence the people there often use coconut (and coconut oil) for cooking. There are many rivers in Assam, West Bengal, Odisha, and Kerala, and the people in these states eat a lot of fish.

Cereals such as rice and wheat are rich in carbohydrates and give us energy. Besides these, we need proteins and vitamins for a healthy body. We get protein from dal, but it is not enough, particularly for growing children. So many of us eat fish, meat, and poultry, all of which are rich in proteins. But as many Indians are vegetarians, they drink milk and eat curd, which too are also excellent sources of proteins. Also, as vegetables are the best and the least expensive source of vitamins, most people eat vegetables. A diet that has the right proportion of carbohydrates, proteins, and vitamins is called a balanced diet.

Just as the food varies from place to place, so does the cooking medium. People of Punjab, Haryana, UP, Bihar, and West Bengal use mustard oil as mustard seeds are widely grown in these regions. Similarly, Gujarat, Maharashtra, Andhra Pradesh (AP), Telangana and Tamil Nadu use groundnut oil, whereas sesame oil is used in Rajasthan, MP, and Tamil Nadu. Recently though, there has been an increase in the consumption of sunflower oil. Commercial farming of sunflower for extraction of oil from its seeds is relatively new in India.

Other major agricultural products of India are tea, coffee, and sugarcane. UP, Punjab, Haryana, Maharashtra, and AP are the major producers of sugarcane. Coffee is produced mainly in the Nilgiri hills of Karnataka, Tamil Nadu, and Kerala. The hills of the Nilgiris, Assam, and West Bengal have a large number of tea gardens too.

Salt is an essential part of our diet, and a proper amount of salt is crucial for our body. It is interesting that this vital ingredient of our diet is the only thing that does not grow on plants. Do you know how salt is produced?

ACTIVITY 1

Read the essay again. Eight words/phrases have been highlighted in the text. If you don't know what they mean, try to guess their meanings from the context. Match the words with their meanings in the table below:

1. staple food	A. use of land for growing crops and vegetables
2. climate	B. the basic or most important part of your diet
3. cultivation	C. the pattern of weather condition of an area

---

[2] **illustrate:** (verb) to show with the help of examples, graphs, or picture.

4. irrigation	D. completely necessary
5. balanced diet	E. a diet with a good mix of proteins, vitamins, and carbohydrates
6. extraction	F. one of the things that go into making something
7. essential	G. a system of providing water to fields to help crops grow
8. ingredient	H. the process of getting useful things from something

ACTIVITY 2

Write *T* if the statement matches what has been given in the essay, write *F* if it does not match, and *NG* if the information has not been given in the essay:

A.   People of Haryana generally eat chapattis, dal, and vegetables. ......
B.   In West Bengal, people mainly use groundnut oil for cooking. ......
C.   In Bihar, people eat both chapattis and rice. ......
D.   In the North East, people are generally non-vegetarian. ......
E.   People of Odisha eat fish and rice. ......
F.   Sugarcane is not cultivated in UP. ......
G.   In Tamil Nadu and Kerala, people don't drink tea. ......
H.   We add salt to our food only for taste. ......

ACTIVITY 3

Fill in the blanks with one word from the text given above:

a.   Punjab, Haryana, and western UP have good .... systems.
b.   Carbohydrates give us ....
c.   Milk is an important source of protein for ....
d.   Our food habits depend on the .... of our region.

PRACTICE

1.   What is your idea of a balanced diet? Write five sentences on the topic.
2.   Write a short paragraph (approximately 10 sentences) on the diet of your family.

KEY TO ACTIVITIES

Activity 1: 1-B, 2-C, 3-A, 4-G, 5-E, 6-H, 7-D, 8-F

Activity 2: A-T, B-F, C-T, D-NG, E-T, F-F, G-NG, H-F

Activity 3: a. irrigation, b. energy, c. vegetarians, d. geography

Test 2:
Present Tenses

1. Strike off the incorrect options and fill in the blanks with appropriate verbs:

    I **wake up/am waking up** early, at five in the morning. At that time, the sky ...... still dark. As I **w**......, darkness fades away and the sun .... in the east. A pleasant breeze **blows in/is blowing in** from the north every day. Birds wake up too and s......... chirping. Mohan **runs/ run** a teashop near my house. He lights the stove and m......... tea. Rickshaw pullers **d**........... hot, steaming tea and **rush/rushes** to the station to pick up the passengers who arrive by the first train. Soon, the milkman **a**......, riding his old bicycle, with two noisy milk cans hanging on either side. After some time, little girls **gathers/gather** at the junction and **w**........... for their school bus. Their plaits and pony tails **s**...........**g** as they **t**...... excitedly. From my balcony, I **s**......... all this. Ah! Here **c**......... the yellow School bus. And I must .... writing. My cup of tea is ready.

2. Rearrange the words to form sentences:

    i. in/I/a boarding school/live

       ⇨ ....

    ii. All of/5.15/wake up/us/before

       ⇨ ....

    iii. go/the/hall/prayer/to/We/by 5.30

       ⇨ ....

    iv. the prayer/We/in winter/hate/particularly

       ⇨ ....

3. Fill in the blanks using the *be* verb in the present tense:

    i. Tausif and I .... students of Cotton College, Guwahati.
    ii. Only one of the answers ...... correct.
    iii. One of my friends ...... a TV newscaster.
    iv. The number of students in this school ...... 800.

4. Frame questions for the following answers:

    i. My name is Dibakar Das.

       ⇨ ....

ii. I work in a school.
⇨ ....

iii. Calcutta Boys' School.
⇨ ....

iv. Yes, I am a teacher.
⇨ ....

v. I teach maths and science.
⇨ ....

5. Strike off the incorrect forms of the verbs:

i. I <u>believe/am believing</u> in God.
ii. I <u>love/am loving</u> my mother.
iii. I <u>don't understand/am not understanding</u> your point.
iv. You <u>don't do/aren't doing</u> the right thing.
v. Professor Habib <u>is teaching/teaches</u> at Delhi University.
vi. Shops in our locality <u>close/are closing</u> at 8 PM.

6. Guess the professions:

1.	Bhawani doesn't go to office every day. She goes around and observes interesting places, people, and events. She writes about them in several newspapers.	Bhawani is a
2.	Rani is attached to a hospital. She advises patients about what they should eat and what they shouldn't.	Rani is a
3.	Whenever Rajeev is on duty, he is on his feet. As part of his work, he travels from one end of the city to the other. He issues tickets and stops and starts a vehicle.	Rajeev
4.	Mani sits at the front desk of a bank. She accepts and pays cash, and updates records on the bank's computer.	Mani

7. Fill in the blanks:

Durga: It was a (a) _____ of fortune that I met you after 40 years, Lisa. You still look young, although you have a few (b) _____ of grey hair. And you haven't put on any weight.

Lisa: Last year, I had a (c) _____ of jaundice. Since then, I've lost some weight.

Durga: Shall I make (d) _____ tea for you?

Lisa: Yes, please. But please don't put (e) _____ milk in my tea.

Durga: And sugar?

Lisa: Just a (f) s _____ l.

8. There are two blanks in each of the following sentences. Fill one of them with the appropriate group noun. Fill in the other with the correct form of the verb given within brackets:

i. The .... of directors .... (decides/decide) about bonus every year.
ii. A .... of elephants .... (is playing/are playing) among themselves.
iii. A .... of puppies .... (is/are) suckling at their mother's breast.
iv. Walmart .... (has/have) a .... of retail stores all over the world.

9. Write 10 sentences (approximately 100 words) about what you do on a Sunday.

....
....
....
....
....
....
....
....
....
....
....
....
....
....

10. Write a paragraph (approximately 200 words) about the jobs and occupations of your family members.

....
....
....
....
....
....
....
....
....
....
....
....
....
....
....
....
....
....
....
....

PART 3

TO THE PAST, ON A TIME MACHINE

16 Ordinary Verbs, Helping Verbs

Learning Objectives: In English, a verb often consists of two or more words, for example, *am going.* If you wish to be fluent in English, you must understand the relationship between the two/three words that form a verb. Check this important aspect here.

16.1 ORDINARY VERBS, HELPING VERBS

Rohan has just had a bout of flu. His aunt is talking to him over the phone:

Aunt: Hello Rohan, how <u>are</u> you today?

Rohan: I <u>am</u> fine, auntie, thanks. I <u>have checked</u> my temperature just now. It's normal.

Aunt: What <u>are</u> you <u>doing</u> now?

Rohan: I <u>have</u> an engineering set, I'<u>m building</u> a bike. I <u>have</u> lots of homework, but I <u>don't want</u> to study.

I have highlighted the verbs in this dialogue. Consider the following:

- ✓ I <u>am</u> fine.
- ✓ I <u>am building</u> a bridge.

The verb *am* functions differently in these sentences. In the first sentence, Rohan is talking about his condition. The verb *am* is the main (and the only) verb here. We will call it an ***ordinary verb.*** But in the second sentence, the main idea is <u>building</u>. Here, *am* plays a supporting role. It has been used to form the verb <u>am building</u> (present continuous tense). Let's call the second *am* a ***helping verb.*** (Some books call it the *auxiliary verb,* but let's use a simpler name.)

The verb **be** can have dual functions. It is used as an <u>ordinary verb</u>, and also as a <u>helping verb</u> to form sentences in continuous tenses.

[We have studied sentences in *the present continuous* in Chapter 14].

A few other verbs too have dual functions. Of them, **do** and **have** are used most often. Read the following sentences and note the different roles these verbs play in different situations:

	Used as an Ordinary Verb	Used as a Helping Verb
be	✓ How <u>are</u> you now? ✓ I <u>am</u> fine. ✓ I <u>was</u> ill. ✓ Rohan will <u>be</u> 13 tomorrow.	✓ What <u>are</u> you doing now? ✓ I'<u>m</u> building a bridge. ✓ I <u>was</u> preparing for my exams. ✓ I'<u>ll</u> be going to school tomorrow.
do	✓ <u>Do</u> your homework now. ✓ Rohan's father, Ravi, was the secretary of the Robotics Club at college. He was also a champion athlete and a fine actor. He <u>did</u> lots of things.	✓ <u>Do</u> you have a pen? ✓ <u>Did</u> Radhika live in Mumbai?
have	✓ I <u>have</u> a set of building blocks. ✓ We <u>have</u> an engineering set.	✓ What <u>have</u> you made with the building blocks? ✓ I'<u>ve</u> just checked my temperature.

Have you noticed? When a verb such as *be, do,* or *have* functions <u>as an ordinary verb, it is often alone</u>. However, when the same <u>verb plays a helping role, it always goes with another verb</u>.

Please note: In many languages, there are no helping verbs. To frame sentences in different tenses, speakers of these languages change the verbs themselves. *If you too do not use helping verbs in your mother tongue, it will be good to get a clear idea about the role of helping verbs in English.*

- The helping verb **be** is used to frame sentences in continuous tenses: *I'm reading a chapter on helping verbs.*
- To frame sentences in perfect tenses, we bring in the helping verb **have**: *We **have read** the first 15 chapters of this book.*
- We frame the negative statements and questions by bringing in the helping verb **do**: *They **do** not **know**. **Do** you **know** how important helping verbs are in English?*

ACTIVITY 1

In the table below, I have highlighted **am, are, is, does, did,** and **has.** Strike off the incorrect options with a pencil. Check your answers with the key below. If you haven't got them all, erase your answers and try again. It is important that you get them right.

→ I **am** a student of the English language.	Ordinary verb	~~Helping verb~~
→ We **are** studying English now.	~~Ordinary verb~~	Helping verb

1. Rohan **is** writing a letter.	Ordinary verb	Helping verb
2. He **is** a lovely child.	Ordinary verb	Helping verb
3. **Does** Rohan go to school?	Ordinary verb	Helping verb
4. **Did** Aunt Leela come yesterday?	Ordinary verb	Helping verb
5. Rohan **does** exercises every day.	Ordinary verb	Helping verb
6. He **doesn't** open his school bag on Sunday.	Ordinary verb	Helping verb
7. Ravi **has** a copy of *The Old Man and the Sea.*	Ordinary verb	Helping verb
8. He **has** read it several times.	Ordinary verb	Helping verb

16.2 NEGATIVES AND QUESTIONS

- **Rules for framing negatives:**

  1. If the sentence has a helping verb, add **not** or **n't** between the helping verb and the main verb. For example:

     ✓ *Rohan **is building** a bridge.* ⇨ *Rohan **isn't/is not building** a bridge.*
     ✓ *He **has gone** to school today.* ⇨ *He **hasn't/has not gone** ….*

  2. If the sentence has no helping verb, 'create' a helping verb **do.** Place this helping verb to the left of the main verb and then add **not** or **n't** between **do** and the main verb:

     ✓ *Rohan **loves** mangoes.* ⇨ *Rohan **doesn't/does not love** ….*
     ✓ *Rohan and Rani **play** video games.* ⇨ *Rohan and Rani **don'tplay** ….*

- **Rules for framing questions:**

  1. If the sentence has a helping verb, move it to the left of the subject:

     ✓ *Rohan **is watching** TV.* ⇨ ***Is** Rohan **watching** TV?*
     ✓ *Rohan **has built** a bike.* ⇨ ***Has** Rohan **built** a bike?*

  2. If there is no helping verb, 'create' a helping verb **do** and then move it to the left of the subject:

     ✓ *Rohan **loves** ice cream.* ⇨ ***Does** Rohan **love** ice cream?*
     ✓ *Rohan **read** a story to Rani* ⇨ ***Did** Rohan **read** a story to Rani?*

- **Framing questions with question words such as *what, when,* and so on.**

  1. If there is a question word (*who, what, when,* and so on), it is placed in the first position (left-most) in the sentence:

     ✓ ***What does** Rohan **like** to eat?*
     ✓ ***What has** Rohan **built**?*
     ✓ ***When did** Aunt Leela **telephone** him?*

ACTIVITY 2

Convert the sentences following the instructions given in the second column:

→ I am a student of history.	Make it negative	I am not a student of history.
→ She goes swimming every day.	Ask a question	Does she go swimming every day?
→ We are watching a film on TV.	Ask a question with **what**	What are you watching/doing?
1. Rohan has 11 toy cars.	Make it negative	
2. Rohan has a sister.	Ask a question	
3. The play together all the time.	Make it negative	
4. Rohan isn't fond of milk.	Make it positive	
5. Rani loves chocolate.	Ask a question with **what**	
6. Rohan goes to school by bus.	Ask a question with **how**	
7. Mom has given Rani a toy car on her birthday.	Make it negative	
8. Rohan wants to become a pilot when he grows up.	Make it negative	
9. Rohan wants to become a scientist when he grows up.	Ask a question with **what**	
10. Rohan is reading.	Make it negative	
11. Rohan is reading a Harry Potter story.	Ask a question with **what**	
12. Rani asks a lot of questions.	Ask a question	

◼ KEY TO ACTIVITIES

Activity 1: 1. helping verb 2. ordinary verb 3. helping verb 4. helping verb 5. ordinary verb 6. helping verb 7. ordinary verb 8. helping verb

Activity 2: 1. Rohan doesn't/does not have 11 toy cars. 2. Does Rohan have a sister? 3. They don't/do not play all the time. 4. Rohan is fond of milk. 5. Rani doesn't love chocolate. 6. How does Rohan go to school? 7. Mom hasn't given Rani a toy car on her birthday. 8. Rohan doesn't want to become a pilot when he grows up. 9. What does Rohan want to become when he grows up? 10. Rohan isn't/is not reading. 11. What is Rohan reading? 12. Does Rani ask many (or a lot of) questions?

Three Forms of Verbs

17.1 THE THREE FORMS

Last night, I saw a man killing a beautiful wild goose.[1] When he was about to cut off the bird's head, I froze in terror. I pleaded with him not to kill it but he shouted at me. A small girl came forward and knelt down before him. She begged for the bird's life. Another man, who looked like a lawyer and wore a black coat and a tie, said that killing wild geese was forbidden under the Indian Wildlife Protection Act. Despite this, the cruel man slit open the bird's stomach. A stream of blood flowed along the road. He then skinned the bird, lit a fire, ground[2] some powder, and threw it into the fire.

TV reporters and cameramen telecast the incident live. A reporter said, 'The government is doing nothing to protect wildlife. And when will people arise[3] against cruelty to animals?' She held a microphone before the small girl and asked, 'Now that the bird has been killed, how do you feel?' The girl cried bitterly. The lawyer said, 'Violence breeds[4] more violence.' Suddenly, a huge goose flew down towards us and shut out the sun. Its wings spanned more than a kilometre. Soon the place turned dark. The cameramen complained about poor light. The big man knew that the huge bird was coming at him. He started running. He ran for his life. The bird chased him.

This story is about something that happened yesterday. The verbs in this story are in the *past tense*. To frame sentences in the past tense, we use the *past form of verbs*. A verb has two other forms.

A verb has three forms: *the base*, the *past*, and the *past participle*. For example: *go–went–gone*.

We divide verbs into two groups: ***regular*** *verbs* and ***irregular*** *verbs*. Regular verbs follow certain rules to form the past and the past participle. Table 17.1 shows how to form the ***past*** and the ***past participle*** forms of regular verbs:

---

[1] **goose:** (noun) a large duck with a long neck.

[2] **ground:** past form of *grind*, which means to crush something into fine particles (*grind–ground–ground*).

[3] **arise:** (against something) to come together and protest against something (*arise–arose–arisen*).

[4] **breed:** to be the cause of something (*breed–bred–bred*).

TABLE 17.1   Regular Verbs in Base and Past Forms

	Base Form	Rule for Past and Past Participle	Past Form	Past Participle Form
Verbs ending with -e	move	Add -d at the end	moved	moved
For most verbs	miss, start	Add -ed at the end	missed, started	missed, started
For short verbs ending with a vowel + a consonant	plan, stop	Repeat the last consonant and add -ed	planned, stopped	planned, stopped
verbs ending with a consonant + y	fry, try	Replace -y with -ied	fried, tried	fried, tried
verbs ending with -c	panic, picnic	Add -ked	panicked, picnicked	panicked, picnicked
For some verbs	cast	No change	cast	cast

Note: As you can see in the above table, there is no difference between the past and the past participle forms of regular verbs.

However, irregular verbs don't follow any rule. Some frequently used irregular verbs are shown in Table 17.2.

TABLE 17.2   Some Commonly Used Irregular Verbs

Base Form	Present Forms	Past Form(s)	Past Participle Form
be	am/is/are	was/were	been
do	do/does	did	done
have	have/has	had	had
flow	flow/flows	flowed	flowed
fly	fly/flies	flew	flown
freeze	freeze/freezes	froze	frozen
hold	hold/holds	held	held
say	say/says	said	said
telecast	telecast/telecasts	telecast	telecast

A list of irregular verbs has been given in Appendix A at the end of this book.

ACTIVITY 1

Read the above story and underline the verbs which are in the simple past tense. Refer to Appendix A at the back of the book and note the *base*, *past*, and *past participle* forms of these verbs.

PRACTICE

1. In the following grid, find nine verbs used in the story. Search across and down. (You will find only past forms here.)

T	A	C	E	P	G	H	J
B	D	K	I	L	L	E	D
F	R	O	Z	E	L	L	N
F	H	J	S	A	I	D	K
J	F	H	G	D	E	C	N
F	L	O	W	E	D	D	E
R	E	S	T	D	Q	W	L
R	W	O	R	E	T	Y	T

2. Complete the following table:

Present	Past	Past Participle
beg		
breed	bred	
come		come
cry		
fly	flew	
		flowed
forbid	forbade	
	froze	frozen
	held	
kill		
	knew	
plead		
	said	
see		seen
shout		
	told	
wear		

KEY TO THE ACTIVITY

Last night, I <u>saw</u> a man killing a beautiful wild goose. When he <u>was</u> about to cut off the bird's head, I <u>froze</u> in terror. I <u>pleaded</u> with him not to kill it but he <u>shouted</u> at me. A small girl <u>came forward</u> and <u>knelt</u> down before him. She <u>begged</u> for the bird's life. Another man, who <u>looked</u> like a lawyer, and <u>wore</u> a black coat and a tie, <u>said</u> that killing wild geese was forbidden under the Indian Wildlife Protection Act. Despite this, the cruel man <u>slit open</u> the bird's stomach. A stream of blood <u>flowed</u> along the road. He then <u>skinned</u> the bird, lit a fire, <u>ground</u> some powder, and <u>threw it</u> into the fire. TV reporters and cameramen <u>telecast</u> the incident live. A reporter <u>said</u>, 'The government is doing nothing to protect wildlife. And when will people arise against cruelty to animals?' She <u>held</u> a microphone before the small girl and <u>asked</u>, 'Now that the bird has been killed, how do you feel?' The girl just <u>cried</u> bitterly. The lawyer <u>said</u>, 'Violence <u>breeds</u> more violence.' Suddenly, a huge goose <u>flew</u> down towards us and <u>shut out</u> the sun. Its wings spanned more than a kilometre. Soon the place <u>turned</u> dark. The cameramen <u>complained</u> about poor light. The big man <u>knew</u> that the huge bird was coming at him. He <u>started</u> running. He <u>ran</u> for his life. The bird <u>chased</u> him.

18

The Film Has Already Started

18.1 RAVI HAS JUST GOT ONTO A BUS

Radhika is in front of a cinema, waiting for Ravi. As usual, Ravi is late. Their conversation begins over the phone in the following manner:

Radhika: Where are you? I'm waiting outside the cinema. The film **has** already **started**.

Ravi: Sorry, I am a little late. I**'ve** just **got** onto a bus.

Radhika: And where is your bus?

Ravi: Well, it**'s crossed** M.G. Road.

Radhika: In that case, you are not a little late, but extremely late. You will reach only after the interval!

When we talk about things that happened a little earlier, we use sentences such as *the film has started* and *I have got onto a bus*. We often use words such as *just, already,* and *recently* in statements such as these. These sentences are in the ***present perfect tense.***

This is how you frame sentences in the present perfect:

1. I/We/You/They + **have** (or **'ve**) + **past participle form of the main verb**
2. He/She/It + **has** (or **'s**) + **past participle form of the main verb**

ACTIVITY 1

Complete the following sentences based on the two models given below. Use the verbs: **escape, finish, go, leave, lose,** and **start.**

→   I have just had my breakfast.
→   I've read the newspaper.
1.   The children .... to bed.
2.   Sorry, I'...... already .... the potato chips.
3.   Dr Ram? He'...... .... for hospital a minute ago.
4.   Savitri .... an earring in the bus.
5.   A dangerous criminal .... from prison.
6.   The police .... an investigation.

ACTIVITY 2

Police detective Bhola Singh is following a dangerous criminal, who is staying in a hotel at Colaba, Mumbai. It's 9 AM. Detective Singh is shadowing[1] the criminal's movements and reporting to his boss over the phone. To complete the story, frame complete sentences based on the hints, following this model: <u>The man/just/come out/of the hotel</u> ⇨ <u>The man has just come out of the hotel.</u>

<u>The man/just/come out/of the hotel</u>. He's of fair complexion … and yes, he has a mole on his right cheek. He's in a red shirt and black trousers. … Yes, he's carrying a black briefcase. (1) <u>He/take/a taxi</u>. The number is MH-01-B2258. I am following him in my car. Yes, sir, I have three constables with me …. (2) <u>The man/ light/a cigarette</u>. No, sir, I can't see the brand of the cigarette. (3) <u>Now he/start/ reading a newspaper</u>. … *Times of India*…. We are on S.V. Road now.

(4) <u>We/just/go past/Shivaji Park</u>. (5) <u>The taxi/stop/in</u> front of a travel agency. (6) <u>The man/get off</u>, but the taxi is waiting. (7) <u>He/go/into the travel agency</u>. Maybe, he has to pick up an air ticket. Yes, sir, I'll arrest him as soon as he comes out. (8) <u>I/take out/my gun</u>. … What did you ask? His height? He's about five feet two inches. Oh! The real criminal is six feet four inches! I am extremely sorry, sir. (9) <u>I/make/a mistake</u>.

Detective Bhola Singh

---

[1] **shadow:** (verb) to follow and watch someone, often secretly.

(1) He/take/a taxi ⇨ ....
(2) The man/light/a cigarette ⇨ ....
(3) Now he/start/reading a newspaper ⇨ ....
(4) We/just/go past/Shivaji Park ⇨ ....
(5) The taxi/stop/in front of a travel agency ⇨ ....
(6) The man/get off .... ⇨ ....
(7) He/go/into the travel agency ⇨ ....
(8) I/take out/my gun ⇨ ....
(9) I/make/a mistake ⇨ ....

18.2 WHEN DO WE USE THE PRESENT PERFECT?

1. We use this form to talk about events that happened a little earlier. In general, we use this form to talk about *past events which have a connection with the present*.
2. An action that began earlier and continued to the present time:
   ✓ We'**ve lived** in this house for 20 years.
   ✓ The young author **has written** two novels (The author is still active. Compare with: *Leo Tolstoy wrote some of the greatest novels of all times.* We use the past tense for an author who is no more.)
   We often use phrases with *for* and *since* in sentences like these. [See Section 33.3 for *since* and *for*]
   ✓ Raghu **has been ill** for a week. He **hasn't eaten** anything since yesterday.
3. A past event, the effect of which is still continuing:
   ✓ I **have fractured** my leg. (⇨ My fracture hasn't healed yet.)

ACTIVITY 3

You'll find two sentences in the first column of the following table. Combine them and express the idea in one sentence following the model answer:

→ Professor Irfan Habib joined this university long ago. He is still teaching.	Professor Irfan Habib has taught in this university for a long time.
1. The municipality was constructing this bridge over two years. The bridge is ready now.	
2. Mr and Mrs Ray moved into this house 20 years ago. They still live here.	
3. The police filed a case against Professor Muralidhar. It is yet to be settled.	
4. I misplaced my purse. I am yet to find it.	
5. My car broke down. It is yet to be repaired.	
6. Radhika was doing a course in Spanish. The course was over recently.	

4. A past event with an unspecified time of occurrence:
  ✓ You **haven't done** the right thing.
  ✓ '**Have** you ever **gone** abroad?'—'Yes, I **have**. I **have visited** Pakistan and Nepal.'

18.3 HAVE YOU TALKED WITH RADHIKA YESTERDAY?

- Generally, words or phrases relating to the past (*yesterday, last month,* and the like) *are not used with the present perfect.* You don't say:
  I **have talked** with Radhika ~~yesterday~~. ✗ Or: We **have bought** this house ~~last year~~. ✗
- When you want to specify the time of occurrence, you use the simple past:
  ✓ I **talked** with Radhika **yesterday**.
  ✓ We **bought** this TV last **year.**

18.4 NEGATIVE SENTENCES AND QUESTIONS

- The negative forms of the present perfect are:
  ✓ I/We/You/They + **have not** (or **haven't**) + **past participle form of the verb.**
  ✓ He/She/It + **has not** (or **hasn't**) + **past participle form of the verb.**
- Questions in the present perfect:
  ✓ **Have** + I/we/you/they + **past participle form of the verb**?
  ✓ **Has** + he/she/it + **past participle form of the verb**?

When we speak, we often don't answer a question fully. For example, if you ask me, *Have you seen the latest film of Tom Cruise?*
I <u>don't</u> say:
  Yes, I have seen the latest film of Tom Cruise.
Or
  No, I haven't seen the latest film of Tom Cruise.
I <u>say</u> either:
  Yes, I have.
Or
  No, I haven't.
Note how the present perfect is used when we speak:

Giving and Taking an Exam

Kuttan says: *I haven't **done** the test.*

- *Exam* is the usual word for a written, spoken, or practical test at school, college, or university.
- *Examination* is a very formal word.
- A *test* is something that students might be given in addition to regular exams, to check how much they have learnt. We also say: *driving test, blood test,* and so on.

Please keep in mind that you

✓ **take** an exam,
✓ **do** an exam, or
✓ **sit** an exam.

As a student, you DO NOT

- write an exam ✗
- give an exam ✗

We Indians make this mistake often. However, *you **take** an exam* when your teacher ***gives*** *you an exam.*

Father: **Have** you **completed** your driving lessons?
Kuttan: Yes, dad, I **have**.
Father: But **have** you **learnt** driving?
Kuttan: To be honest, I **haven't**.
Father: Be careful, the traffic is heavy these days. The number of vehicles **has gone up** considerably.
            How many kilometres **have you driven**?
Kuttan: Well, I **have logged**[2] about 300 km.
Father: **Have** you **got** your driving licence?
Kuttan: I **haven't,** yet. **I've passed** the test. I expect to get the licence next week.

ACTIVITY 4

Write down the positive and negative answers you are likely to give orally:

Question		Answer
1. Have you had your breakfast?	✔	Yes, I have.
	✔	No, I haven't.
2. Have you had your bath?	✔	....
	✔	....
3. Has your brother got up?	✔	....
	✔	....
4. Have your parents gone out?	✔	....
	✔	....

PRACTICE

1. George and Ravi are talking over the phone. Complete the dialogue with the appropriate form of the verb given within brackets:

George: Howdy, Ravi! .... you .... the latest film of Aamir Khan? (see)
Ravi: No, I .... (...)
George: Why? You are such a big fan of Aamir?
Ravi: I'......... .... down with a bout of influenza. (be)
George: Oh! Since when?
Ravi: Since last week. I .... to office for the last two days. (not go)
George: Get well soon, buddy.
Ravi: Thanks, ... you .... the film? (see)
George: Yes, I .... It's a brilliant film. (...)

---

[2] *To log* is to write records of events. Kuttan means that his driving log book shows he has driven 300 km.

2. In the first column of the following table, there are sets of two sentences. You have to combine them and express the idea in one sentence, as shown in the model answer:

→ I was doing my homework. It's just over.	I've just done my homework.
a. My friend was doing PhD. The work is complete.	....
b. He was also making a film on the slums in Mumbai. The film is ready now.	....
c. The slums in Mumbai were bad. Now they are worse.	....
d. 'You made a documentary film. It is interesting.'	....

3. Correct the following sentences:

   a. I have read *Crime and Punishment* when I was in college.
   b. My car has broken down yesterday.
   c. I have fractured my leg last month.
   d. I have seen Sachin Tendulkar at Dhaka airport in 2010.

4. Write down the missing sentences:

   Positive sentence: 1. You've done the right thing.
   Negative sentence: 2. ....
   Question: 3. ....

   Positive sentence: 4. You have forgotten your promise.
   Negative sentence: 5. ....
   Question: 6. ....

   Positive sentence: 7. ....
   Negative sentence: 8. They haven't lived in this city for many years.
   Question: 9. How long ....

   Positive sentence: 10. ....
   Negative sentence: 11. ....
   Question: 12. Have prices gone up sharply in recent years?

5. Write 10 sentences on what you have done today.

   ....
   ....
   ....
   ....
   ....
   ....
   ....

6. What has happened to your country and state in the last seven days? Write down 10 sentences based on newspaper reports.

....
....
....
....
....
....
....

KEY TO ACTIVITIES

Activity 1: 1. The children have gone to bed. 2. Sorry, I've already finished the potato chips. 3. Dr Ram? He's left for hospital a minute ago. 4. Savitri has lost an earring in the bus. 5. A dangerous criminal has escaped from prison. 6. The police have started an investigation.

Activity 2: (1) He has taken a taxi. (2) The man has lit a cigarette. (3) Now he has started reading a newspaper. (4) We have just passed Shivaji Park. (5) The taxi has stopped in front of a travel agency. (6) The man has got off, but the taxi is waiting. (7) He has gone into the travel agency. (8) I have taken out my gun. (9) I've made a mistake.

Activity 3: 1. The municipality has constructed this bridge recently. 2. Mr and Mrs Ray have lived in this house for 20 years. 3. The police have filed a case against Professor Muralidhar. 4. I have misplaced or lost my purse. 5. My car has broken down. 6. Radhika has done a Spanish course recently.

19

We've Been Studying English

Learning Objective: In this chapter, we are going to discuss the present perfect continuous form.

19.1 RADHIKA HAS WAITED? OR SHE HAS BEEN WAITING?

In the previous chapter, we said that the present perfect tense is used to talk about *past events that have a connection with the present.* For example: I *have read the book Gandhi Before India.*

If we wish to emphasize[1] that a recent event *has continued for some time up to now,* we use sentences like:

- ✓ Radhika **has been waiting** at the bus stop (⇨ She is waiting even now.)
- ✓ It **has been raining** since Sunday (⇨ The rain hasn't stopped yet.)
- ✓ We**'ve been studying** English for three months.

We often use time phrases (*for an hour, since Sunday,* and so on) in expressions like these. These sentences are in the *present perfect continuous* tense.

When we wish to emphasize that a recent event has continued up to now, we use the **present perfect continuous**. The forms are:

- • Positive:
    - ✓ I/We/You/They + **have/'ve been** + **+ing form of the main verb.**
    - ✓ He/She/It + **has/'s been** + **+ing form of the main verb.**

- • Negative:
    - ✓ I/We/You/They + **haven't been/have not been** + **+ing form of the main verb.**
    - ✓ He/She/It + **hasn't been/has not been** + **+ing form of the main verb.**

---

[1] **emphasize** (verb): to give special importance to something, HIGHLIGHT.

- Question:
  - ✓ **Have** + I/we/you/they + **been** + **+ing form of the main verb?**
  - ✓ **Has** + he/she/it + **been**+ **+ing form of the main verb?**

19.2 IS THE ACTION OVER?

As seen in Table 19.1, the choice between the *present perfect* and the *present perfect continuous* <u>usually</u> depends on whether the past action is complete or not.

TABLE 19.1 The Present Perfect and the Present Perfect Continuous

Incomplete Action	Completed Action
Mother <u>has been knitting</u> a sweater for me.	*Mother <u>has knitted</u> a sweater for me.*
↑	↑
She is still knitting it. The sweater isn't ready yet.	The sweater is ready. I can wear it now.
The police <u>have been searching</u> for a prisoner who has escaped from prison.	*The police have been searching for a prisoner <u>who has escaped</u> from prison.*
'have been searching' as the action of searching isn't over yet	'has escaped' as the action of escaping is complete

There are two exceptions to this pattern: the verbs ***live*** and ***work*** (as in *she works in an office*). They convey the same thing in the present perfect and the present perfect continuous.

- ✓ We**'ve lived** in this city for 20 years. = We**'ve been living** in this city for 20 years.
- ✓ Raghu **has worked** (= has had a job) in this company since 2016. = Raghu **has been working** in this company since 2016.

19.3 WHEN DO WE USE THIS FORM?

We use this form in the following situations:

Situation	Example
1. We want to emphasize that a recent event has continued up to now.	Mother **has been knitting** a sweater for me.
2. We talk about repetitive actions up to now.	Bobby D'Souza **has been driving** a taxi in Panaji since he was 18.
3. We talk about an action that happened over a period and has ended a short while ago.	Why do you look so tired?—Oh! I **have been running around** all day.

ACTIVITY 1

Complete the sentences following the given models. Use the verbs given within brackets:

→ I <u>have been reading</u> this book since yesterday.
→ My father has <u>been building a house</u>.
1. My mother .... (knit) a sweater for me. I am eagerly waiting for it.
2. Raghu .... (repair) his scooter since morning. It will take some more time.
3. Rani .... because she has lost her kitten. (cry)
4. Since last year, Detective Bhola Singh .... (look for) Bullet Singh, a dangerous criminal. But Bhola has no idea where Bullet Singh is.
5. My pet panda .... kung fu since she was a baby. (learn)

19.4 STATE VERBS AND ACTION VERBS

In Section 14.6, we saw that state verbs (*be, believe, know,* and the like) are not normally used in continuous tenses. We do NOT say: *I am believing in God.* ✗ We say: *I believe in God.* ✓

This holds for the present perfect continuous too:

• I ~~have been believing~~ in God since childhood. ✗ I have believed in God since .... ✓
• She ~~has been hating~~ her husband since that day. ✗ She's hated her husband since .... ✓

ACTIVITY 2

Fill in the blanks using the verbs given within brackets:

1. Kuttan ....n't .... (study), he .... (play) computer games since morning.
2. Why are your clothes wet?—I'....................................... (dance) in the rain.
3. I am tired, I'....................................... (work) in the garden since morning.
4. I .... (do) homework since morning, but I have a long way to go.
5. How long .... you .... (study) Spanish?
6. I' .... (study) the language for two years.
7. Raghu .... (be) ill for a week.
8. I .... (know) her since I was a child.

PRACTICE

1. Strike off the incorrect sentences in the following table:

A	B
I have sent six emails today.	I have been sending six emails today.
He is playing cricket since morning.	He has been playing cricket since morning.
I have changed buses twice to reach here.	I have been changing buses twice to reach here.
The movie has started.	The movie has been starting.

2. Correct the following:

   a. I have been liking her performance. ⇨ ....
   b. I have been knowing this secret all along. ⇨ ....
   c. We have been having this car since 2011. ⇨ ....
   d. Ravi and Radhika have been knowing each other since college. ⇨ ....

3. Complete the dialogue using the verbs given within brackets. Use the present perfect and the present perfect continuous:

   Mother: _____ you _____ (do) your homework?
   Boogie: Yes, Amma, I'_____ since morning (study). I am tired.
   Mother: Which subjects _____ you _____ (study) today?
   Boogie: Maths and English.
   Mother: What _____ you _____ (do) in maths?
   Boogie: I'___ _____ (solve) 20 arithmetic problems.
   Mother: And what _____ you _____ (learn) in English?
   Boogie: Framing sentences in the present perfect tense.
   Mother: What is the present perfect tense?
   Boogie: We use this tense to describe recent events. You and I _____ _____ _____ (talk)
              in the present perfect tense.
   Mother: Good. Now, please get your geography book.
   Boogie: No! I'___ _____ (do) enough for today.

KEY TO ACTIVITIES

Activity 1: 1. My mother has been knitting a sweater for me. … 2. Raghu has been repairing his scooter since morning. 3. Rani has been crying because …. 4. … Detective Bhola Singh has been looking for Bullet Singh …. 5. My pet panda has been learning kung fu since she was a baby.

Activity 2: 1. Kuttan hasn't been studying, he has been playing computer games since morning. 2. … I've been dancing in the rain. 3. I am tired, I've been working in the garden …. 4. I have been doing homework since morning …. 5. How long have you been studying Spanish? 6. I've been studying the language for two years. 7. Raghu has been ill for a week. 8. I have known her since I was a child.

To the Past, on a Time Machine

Learning Objectives: This chapter covers the language we use to describe events and regular activities in the past.

20.1 AN OLD WOMAN WHO LIVED LONG AGO

There was an old woman, who lived in a shoe,
She had so many children she didn't know what to do.
She gave them some broth[1] without any bread,
And whipped them all soundly and put them to bed.

She lived long ago. So all the verbs in this rhyme are in the simple past tense.

In Chapter 17, we discussed three forms of a verb: *the base form, the past form,* and *the past participle form.* The simple past form is:

I/We/You/He/She/It/They + **the past form of verb** + other words

---

ACTIVITY 1

The first column of the table below has sentences in the simple present tense. Rewrite them in the simple past. Follow the models given:

---

[1] **broth:** (noun) a thick soup made with boiled meat or fish and vegetables; a poor man's food.

Present Tense	Past Tense
→ These days, I have a Maruti car.	Those days, I had a Maruti car.
1. On Sundays, we go out on long drives.	
2. Mr and Mrs Iyer often accompany us.	
3. You drive carefully.	
4. Our dog, Dogendran, loves these outings.	
5. He puts his head outside the window.	
Note: ***This*** in the present becomes ***that*** in the past. Similarly, ***these*** becomes ***those.***	

ACTIVITY 2

Here is a newspaper report about a bank robbery in Vishakhapatnam. Complete the report by filling in the blanks with past forms of the verbs given within brackets:

Yesterday, three men .... (enter) the Diamond Park branch of the Bank of Prosperity[2] at 11 am. One of them .... (take) out a pistol and .... (hold) it at the bank manager's head. The second person .... (disconnect) the telephone lines and .... (get) hold of everyone's mobiles. The third person, who .... (have) another gun, ... (take) position at the gate. Then the first two men .... (force) the manager and the cashier to open the vault.[3]

They .... (remove) currency notes and .... (put) them into three plastic bags. The bank employees were stunned; they neither .... (move) nor .... (say) anything. While leaving, one of the robbers .... (notice) that a lady employee was wearing a substantial[4] gold necklace. He .... (try) to snatch it. At this, the lady .... (start) to shout and .... (bite) the robber in his shoulder. The man .... (jump up) in pain and in the process, his pistol .... (fly off).

Fortunately, at that moment, Inspector Bhola Singh .... (walk into) the bank to draw his salary. Seeing a policeman in uniform, the robbers .... (panic). They .... (drop) the plastic bags and .... (start) running. The robber bitten by the lady was easily overpowered by Inspector Bhola and the bank employees, although the other two .... (manage) to escape.

The lady bank employee who .... (bite) the robber will receive a gallantry award from the police commissioner.

---

[2] **prosperity***:* (noun) the state of being rich and successful, AFFLUENCE.

[3] **vault***:* (noun) a strong room where valuables are kept, as in a bank.

[4] **substantial***:* (adjective) with some amount of substance, HEAVY.

20.2 WHEN DO WE USE THIS FORM?

From Activities 1 and 2, we see that the simple past is used to describe: (a) habitual or regular actions in the past and (b) stand-alone completed events and actions. Let me explain.

Regular Activities in the Past	Completed Actions/Events
On Sundays, we went out for long drives. (We went out on Sundays regularly.)	Yesterday, three men went to a bank.
Mr and Mrs Iyer often accompanied us. (They accompanied us on many occasions.)	They disconnected the telephones and removed bundles of currency notes.
Dogendran loved those rides. (Normal behaviour in the past)	A lady employee bit one of the robbers in his shoulder.

20.3 NEGATIVE STATEMENTS

Consider the sentences:

✓ We didn't/did not go on long drives.
✓ Mr and Mrs Iyer didn't/did not accompany us.

The form for negative sentences is:

I/We/You/He/She/It/They + **didn't/did not + the base form of verb**

We don't use a past form after *didn't/did not*. We don't say:

✗ We did not ~~went~~ for long drives. Dogendran didn't ~~loved~~ those outings.

ACTIVITY 3

Transform the following into negative sentences:

Positive Sentence	Negative Sentence
→ I had a Maruti.	I didn't/did not have a Maruti.
1. We went out on long drives.	
2. Mr and Mrs Iyer accompanied us.	
3. You drove carefully.	
4. Dogendran loved these outings.	
5. He enjoyed the rushing wind.	

20.4 A MORE FORCEFUL NO!

Mr and Mrs Iyer didn't accompany us. If you wish to say it more forcefully, you say: *Mr and Mrs Iyer never accompanied us.* A few more examples:

Negative Statement	More Forcefully Negative
I didn't like her.	I <u>never liked</u> her. (= I didn't like her at any time.)
I didn't live in Mumbai.	I <u>never lived</u> in Mumbai.
You didn't say anything like that.	You <u>never said</u> anything like that.

20.5 NEITHER/NOR

To show that a positive statement is true for any one of two things, we use *either/or*:

- ✓ At school, <u>either Ravi or George</u> came at the top of the class.
- ✓ You can take <u>either the red shirt or the white</u>.
- ✓ <u>Either return the book now or pay a fine</u>.

To show that a negative statement is true for two situations, we use *neither/nor*:

- ✓ <u>Neither Ravi nor George</u> played hockey.
- ✓ I liked <u>neither the red shirt nor the white</u>.
- ✓ He <u>neither returned the book nor paid a fine</u>.
- ✓ Not a wasted word did he speak, <u>not</u> a friend, <u>neither</u> man, woman, <u>nor</u> beast, did he have. [From John le Carré's *The Spy Who Came in from the Cold*]

20.6 ASKING QUESTIONS ABOUT THE PAST

The form for asking questions in the simple past is:

Did	I/we/you/he/she/it/they	play hockey in school? eat banana chips last night? visit Varanasi?

ACTIVITY 4

You went to Varanasi last month. Given below is a conversation you had with your friend after your return. Complete the questions using the verbs given within brackets:

→ Where did you go in your holiday?	We went to Varanasi.
1. How long ...... you .... there? (stay)	We were there for a week.
2. ...... you ...... the place? (like)	Yes, we did. We liked the place very much.
3. Where ....? (stay)*	In a tourist lodge.
4. What places .... there? (visit)	We went to the Kashi Viswanath Temple and the Benares Hindu University campus.
5. And what else ....? (do)	Well, we bathed in the Ganga every day.
6. ....? (return)	We returned last Sunday.

20.7 DID THEY HAVE A CAR?

In Section 11.5, we learned the use of *have* and *have got*. Let's recall that to describe possession of ownership, we say:

✓ She <u>has</u> a dog. Or: She <u>has got</u> a dog.
✓ She <u>has</u> a husband. Or: She <u>has got</u> a husband.

When we talk about the past, we normally don't use *had got*. In the past tense, *had* is used in positive statements. In negatives and questions, we use *did not have*.

> ### * Stay and Live
>
> **To stay** is to spend a short period of time at a place: ➢ *We stayed in a tourist lodge in Varanasi.*
>
> **To live** is to have a home at a place. ➢ *I've been living in Kolkata for a year. Earlier, I lived in Kerala.*

Positive Statement	**Negative Statement**	**Question**
I <u>had</u> a pink sweater.	I <u>didn't have</u> a pink sweater.	<u>Did</u> you <u>have</u> a pink sweater?
Tania <u>had</u> a boyfriend.	Tania <u>didn't have</u> a boyfriend.	<u>Did</u> Tania <u>have</u> a boyfriend?

PRACTICE

1. This is how a small boy spends his days. If he writes about his daily routine say, 20 years later, how will he express them?

→ I study at a boarding school.	I studied at a boarding school.
A. We go to the prayer room by 5.30.	
B. We hate prayers, particularly in winter.	
C. Our school ends at 4 in the afternoon.	
D. We play football after school.	

2. Write the negatives of these sentences:

A. I studied at a boarding school.	

B. At school, we participated in many extracurricular activities.	
C. We had an electronics club in our school.	
D. I became interested in electronic gadgets early in my life.	

3. Underline the mistakes in the following sentences:

   When I was in high school, I never study. I play from morning to evening. And I didn't listened to my parents. Once I bunked off school and go to see a film. A friend of my father see me in the cinema. But I didn't knew that he see me. And when I came home ….

4. Frame questions for these answers and the clues given within brackets:

   A. **Rabindranath Tagore** (the first Asian to win the Nobel Prize)
      Who was the first Asian to win the Nobel Prize?

   B. **1945** (the end of the Second World War)

   C. **1947** (India's freedom from the British rule)

   D. **Sheikh Mujibur Rahman** (the first President of Bangladesh)

   E. **1996** (Sri Lanka's first Cricket World Cup victory)

5. Fill in the blanks with **never, neither,** or **nor:**

   A. I didn't know him. As a matter of fact, I _____ met him.
   B. My friend Ram studied 24×7, he _____ went out to play.
   C. I didn't learn music; _____ did I have an ear for music.
   D Rajani _____ knew _____ cared to know if Rajesh was interested in her.
   E. Those trousers fit me very well. They were _____ tight _____ loose.

6. Think of a special day in your childhood. Write 10 sentences on what happened on that day.

   ....
   ....
   ....
   ....
   ....
   ....
   ....
   ....
   ....
   ....
   ....
   ....
   ....
   ....

KEY TO ACTIVITIES

Activity 1: 1. On Sundays, we went out on long drives. 2. Mr and Mrs Iyer often accompanied us. 3. You drove carefully. 4. Our dog, Dogendran, loved those outings. 5. He put his head outside the window.

Activity 2: Yesterday, three men entered the Diamond Park branch of the Bank of Prosperity .... One of them took out a pistol and held it at the bank manager's head. The second person disconnected the telephone lines and got hold of everyone's mobiles. The third person, ... took position at the gate. Then the first two men forced the manager and the cashier to open the vault.

They removed currency notes and put them into ... bags. The bank employees ... neither moved nor said anything. ... one of the robbers noticed that a lady employee was wearing a substantial gold necklace. He tried to snatch it. At this, the lady started to shout and bit the robber in his shoulder. The man jumped up in pain and in the process, his pistol flew off.

... Inspector Bhola Singh walked into the bank to draw his salary. Seeing a policeman in uniform, the robbers panicked. They dropped the ... bags and started running. The robber bitten by the lady was easily overpowered by Inspector Bhola and the bank employees, although the other two managed to escape.

The lady bank employee who bit the robber will receive a gallantry award ....

Activity 3: 1. We didn't go out on long drives. 2. Mr and Mrs Iyer didn't accompany us. 3. You didn't drive carefully. 4. Dogendran didn't love those outings. 5. He didn't enjoy the rushing wind.

Activity 4: 1. How long did you stay there? 2. Did you like the place? 3. Where did you stay? 4. What places did you visit there? 5. And what else did you do? 6. When did you return?

21

I Was in Hyderabad

21.1 FRUITS IN THE MARKET, FRUITS ON THE FIELD

Read the passage below and underline the sentences that talk about the *state, location, existence,* or *condition* of something in the past. (I have underlined the first.)

Long ago, I worked in Hyderabad. <u>I was newly married then</u>. My office was near Mozam Jahi Market, which was the largest fruit market in the city. In the mango, grape, and custard apple seasons, the market spilled over to roads; the entire area was flooded with fruits. There were many custard apple orchards[1] around the city. There is even a railway station nearby called *Seetaphal Mandi*. (*Seetaphal* is custard apple in Urdu, and *mandi* is market.) When my wife and I first went to the city, we stayed with our friends, Uma Sankar and Indrani. Their house was on the outskirts,[2] in a barren area dotted with small hillocks. Although the fields around were not cultivated, they had lots of custard apple trees. During August and September, the trees used to be laden with fruits. At weekends, we used to climb to the top of a hillock in front of Uma Sankar's house, hoist our handkerchiefs as flags, and eat custard apples gathered from under the trees.

In this passage, all the sentences are in the ***simple past*** except one: *There is a railway station by the name Seetaphal Mandi.* It has been written in the present tense because the station exists even now.

The following sentences, which have the past forms of the *be* verb, talk about the *state, quality, location, existence,* or *condition* of someone/something in the past:

✓ I *was* newly married then.	⇨ my state with reference to marriage
✓ My office *was* near Mozam Jahi Market.	⇨ the location of my office
✓ It *was* the largest market in the city.	⇨ the quality/size of the market
✓ There *were* lots of custard apple orchards around the city.	⇨ existence of something
✓ His house *was* on the outskirts of the city.	⇨ location
✓ Although the fields around his house *were* not cultivated, ….	⇨ state/condition

---

[1] **orchard:** (noun) a piece of land on which fruit trees are grown.
[2] **outskirts:** (noun) an area far away from the centre of a city.

- In the past tense, the conjugation for the *be* verb is:

> ✓ I/He/She/It + **was** + complement
> ✓ We/You/They + **were** + complement

ACTIVITY 1

Dr Ram, Rohan's grandfather, has written these lines in his memoir[3] about a time in Rohan's childhood. I have removed most of the verbs from the passage.

Fill in the blanks to complete the passage in the past tense. Use the following verbs: *be* (× 10), *not express, feel, know* (× 2), and *suffer.*

Rohan's parents were delighted. Rohan had just joined a good school. But little Rohan ……… not happy. He ……… scared of big buildings and crowds. He f………… secure in his house, in his small room, surrounded by his toys. He ……… extremely fond of his mother. He could not think of staying without her even for a few minutes. Naturally, he ……… worried. But even at that tender age—he ……… only four years then—Rohan ……… too proud to admit that he ……… scared. So he ………………………………… his feelings. He ……………… in silence. But his parents …………… nothing about his anxiety. Although I ……… 60 years older than Rohan, I ………… a friend of his. I ………… he ………… deeply disturbed.

21.2 NEGATIVES

For negative sentences with the *be* verb in the simple past, the form is:

> ✓ I/He/ She/It + **was not/wasn't** + complement
> ✓ We/You/They + **were not/weren't** + complement

ACTIVITY 2

In the following table, transform the sentences into negative:

Affirmative	Negative
→ I was determined to do it.	I was not/wasn't determined to do it.
→ It was a hasty decision.	It was not a hasty decision.
1. I was sorry for my hasty action.	
2. You were angry with me.	

---

[3] **memoir:** (noun) a written account of personal memories.

3. And mother was hurt.	
4. But my parents were very affectionate.	
5. Ultimately, they forgave me.	

21.3 QUESTIONS

For asking questions in the past tense, the syntax is:

✓ **Was** + I/he/she/it + complement?
✓ **Were** + we/you/they + complement?

ACTIVITY 3

In the following table, a few questions are given in the present tense. Rewrite them in the past in the second column:

The Simple Present Tense	The Simple Past
→ Are you sure of what you are doing?	Were you sure of what you were doing?
1. Are we doing the right thing?	
2. Are you tired?	
3. Are you happy with your new job?	
4. Is it all right?	
5. Is he the right kind of person for you?	
→ Are the workers happy?	Were the workers happy?
6. Are they determined to go on strike?	

ACTIVITY 4

Complete the questions in the following table:

Questions	Answers
→ How was your holiday in Mexico?	It was fantastic.
→ Was there any problem?	The only problem was that we couldn't speak Spanish.
1. How .... in Mexico?	The people were very polite and warm.

2. And ....?	The weather was fine. It was pleasant in Mexico City, but slightly hot near the sea.
3. .... the flight from New York to Mexico City?	Oh! The flight was long and tiring.
→ What places did you visit?	Mexico City, Cancun, and Chichen Itza.
4. .... Mexico City?	It was crowded, but beautiful!
5. And ....?	Cancun too was crowded, but it is a lovely sea resort.
6. Which ....?	The best place we visited was the Pyramid of Kukulkan, which is one of the seven wonders of the world.

21.4 REGULAR ACTIVITIES IN THE PAST?

In the passage at the beginning of this chapter, I wrote: *At weekends, we **used to climb** to the top of a hillock in front of Uma Sankar's house.*

This form is known as **the habitual past form**. It is used to describe things that we did regularly in the past. For example:

- ✓ On Sundays my friend and I went for walks. = On Sundays, my friend and I used to go ….
- ✓ We played chess under a tree. = We used to play chess under a tree.
- ✓ We also ate custard apples. = We also used to eat custard apples.

Note that this form is not normally used for negative sentences.

ACTIVITY 5

Complete the conversation between Kuttan and his parents with the **used to** form:

(Kuttan is from Kerala and *achchan* means *dad* in Malayalam.)

Kuttan: Achchan, is it true that you didn't have TVs when you were a child?

Dad: Yes, it is. We didn't have televisions when I was your age.

Kuttan: How did you live without TVs?

Dad: (1) We _____ to _____ (watch) films on Sundays. (2) They _____ _____ _____ (show) films in tents in our village.

Kuttan: Films? You mean those TVs with big screens? What else did you do?

Dad: (3) We _____ _____ _____ (play) football in summer.

Kuttan: Did you play any other sport?

Dad:	(4) We _____ _____ _____ (play) cricket too.
Kuttan:	Were you a good student?
Dad:	(5) Yes, I was. I _____ _____ _____ _____ (get up) at 5.00 in the morning and walk to school.
Kuttan:	You mean you didn't have school buses?
Dad:	There were no roads, so there was no question of buses.
Kuttan:	How big was your school?
Dad:	It was small. (6) But we _____ _____ _____ (study) real hard.
Kuttan's mom:	You should also tell him how mischievous you were.
Dad:	Mischief and me? Ha!
Mom:	(6) Then who _____ _____ _____ (steal) mangoes from our garden?

▌ PRACTICE

1. Rewrite this paragraph in the past tense:

    My father is a doctor and my mother is a dietician. My older brother is a freelance reporter. He works for some TV channels. My sister is a beautician. We live near the railway station. It is a crowded place. There are five cinemas near our house. They show Hindi films, but one of them shows English films on Sundays. On Sundays, we go out to see films, after which we eat ice cream.

2. Write negatives of the following sentences:

    a. I enjoyed my days in college.
    b. You were the best singer in our college.
    c. Raju was the badminton champion.
    d. His uncle was a professor in our college.

3. Frame questions for the following answers:

    a. .... as a child?—You were lovely and active as a child.
    b. .... my sister?—She was lovely too.
    c. Were ....…................—No, you were not naughty.
    d. ....—Not at all, you both were very talkative.

4. Complete the following email from Radhika to her mother. Use appropriate forms of the verbs given within brackets. *Don't use the past tense for things that are always true.*

    Hi Mom,

    I am writing from Kasargod, a small town in North Kerala. We _____ (come) to Kerala a few days ago. We _____ (take) a plane from Chennai to Thiruvananthapuram. The aircraft _____ _____ (take off) at 7:00 in the morning and _____ (reach) Thiruvananthapuram in one hour. The flight _____ (be) fantastic. We _____ (fly) low over a green carpet of coconut trees. Before landing, the plane _____ (take) a turn over the famed Kovalam beach. The view from above _____ (be) breathtaking.

    We _____ (spend) two days at Kovalam, which _____ (be) 16 km away from Thiruvananthapuram. After Kovalam, we _____ (go) to Thekkady. Thekkady _____ (be) a lovely wildlife reserve beside the Periyar Lake. We _____ (see) a herd of elephants frolicking in the lake. This morning, we _____ _____ (arrive) at Kasargod. It has been a fantastic vacation so far. I wish you were here with us.

Love,
Radhika

5. Given below are some historical facts about three famous Indian companies. Using your imagination, write a paragraph on each of these companies with the help of the points given below. Use the verbs given within brackets. The first one has been done as a model for you.

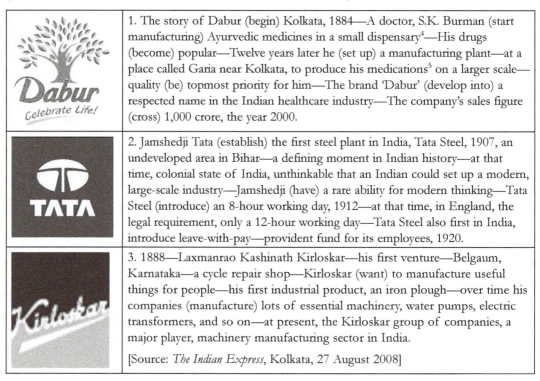

Dabur Celebrate Life!	1. The story of Dabur (begin) Kolkata, 1884—A doctor, S.K. Burman (start manufacturing) Ayurvedic medicines in a small dispensary[4]—His drugs (become) popular—Twelve years later he (set up) a manufacturing plant—at a place called Garia near Kolkata, to produce his medications[5] on a larger scale—quality (be) topmost priority for him—The brand 'Dabur' (develop into) a respected name in the Indian healthcare industry—The company's sales figure (cross) 1,000 crore, the year 2000.
TATA	2. Jamshedji Tata (establish) the first steel plant in India, Tata Steel, 1907, an undeveloped area in Bihar—a defining moment in Indian history—at that time, colonial state of India, unthinkable that an Indian could set up a modern, large-scale industry—Jamshedji (have) a rare ability for modern thinking—Tata Steel (introduce) an 8-hour working day, 1912—at that time, in England, the legal requirement, only a 12-hour working day—Tata Steel also first in India, introduce leave-with-pay—provident fund for its employees, 1920.
Kirloskar	3. 1888—Laxmanrao Kashinath Kirloskar—his first venture—Belgaum, Karnataka—a cycle repair shop—Kirloskar (want) to manufacture useful things for people—his first industrial product, an iron plough—over time his companies (manufacture) lots of essential machinery, water pumps, electric transformers, and so on—at present, the Kirloskar group of companies, a major player, machinery manufacturing sector in India. [Source: *The Indian Express*, Kolkata, 27 August 2008]

1   The story of Dabur began in Kolkata in 1884, when a doctor, S.K. Burman, started manufacturing Ayurvedic medicines in his small dispensary. His drugs became popular and 12 years later, he set up a manufacturing plant at Garia, near Kolkata, to produce his medications on a larger scale. For Dr Burman, quality was always the topmost priority. Over time, the brand 'Dabur' developed into a respected name in the Indian healthcare industry. The company's sales figure crossed 1,000 crore in the year 2000.

2.   ....

....

....

....

---

[4] **dispensary:** (noun) a place where medicines are prepared for patients.
[5] **medication:** (noun) MEDICINE.

3. ....

KEY TO ACTIVITIES

Activity 1: … But little Rohan was not happy. He was scared of big buildings and crowds. He felt secure in his house …. He was extremely fond of his mother. … Naturally, he was worried. But even at that tender age—he was only four years then—Rohan was too proud to admit that he was scared. So he did not express his feelings. He suffered in silence. But his parents knew nothing about his anxiety. Although I was 60 years older than Rohan, I was a friend of his. I knew he was deeply disturbed.

Activity 2: 1. I was not/wasn't sorry …. 2. You were not angry …. 3. And mother wasn't/was not hurt. 4. But my parents were not very affectionate. 5. Ultimately, they didn't/did not forgive me.

Activity 3: 1. Were you doing the right thing? 2. Were you tired? 3. Were you happy with your new job? 4. Was it all right? 5. Was he the right kind of person for you? 6. Were they determined to go on strike?

Activity 4: 1. How were the people in Mexico? 2. How was the weather? 3. How was the flight from New York to Mexico City? 4. How was Mexico City? 5. And how was Cancun? 6. Which was the best place that you visited?

Activity 5: (1) We used to watch films on Sundays. (2) They used to show films in tents in our village. (3) We used to play football in summer. (4) We also used to play cricket. (5) Yes, I was. I used to get up at 5.00 in the morning and walk to school. (6) But we used to study real hard. (7) Then who used to steal mangoes from our garden?

22

I Was Sleeping When My Boss Walked In

Learning Objectives: In this chapter, we are discussing the grammatical form used for talking about incomplete actions in the past, that is, the past continuous tense.

22.1 WHILE SOMETHING WAS IN PROGRESS

We <u>were driving</u> from North Goa to Panaji. It <u>was raining</u>. The road was slushy and the car skidded a couple of times. I <u>was driving</u> and found it difficult to control the vehicle. My wife was tense but our little son <u>was sleeping</u> peacefully on the rear seat.

The highlighted verbs talk about a time when we were in the middle of an action. These verbs are in the *past continuous* (some books call it the *past progressive*):

✓ We <u>were driving</u> from North Goa to Panaji.
✓ It <u>was raining</u>.
✓ I <u>was driving</u>.
✓ Our son <u>was sleeping</u> ….

But we use the *simple past* to describe states or conditions, or when we use state verbs.

The road <u>was</u> *slushy, my wife* <u>was</u> *tense.*

We also use the simple past for actions or events that were completed:

The car <u>skidded</u> *once, I* <u>found</u> *it difficult to control the vehicle.*

• The syntax for the past continuous is:

Positive statements:

✓ I/He/She/It + **was** + **+ing form of the main verb.**
✓ We/You /They + **were** + **+ing form of the main verb.**

Negative statements:

✓ I/He/She + **was not/wasn't** + **+ing form of the main verb.**
✓ You/They + **were not/weren't** + **+ing form of the main verb.**

Questions:

✓ **Was** + I/he/she + **+ing form of the main verb?**
✓ **Were** + you/they + **+ing form of the main verb?**

ACTIVITY 1

Rewrite the following sentences in the negative form and frame questions following the given model:

→ I was sleeping in my office.	Negative: I wasn't/was not sleeping in my office
	Question: Were you sleeping in your office?
1. I was reading a newspaper.	Negative:
	Question: Were you
2. We were jogging in Shivaji Park.	Negative:
	Question:
3. You were talking over the phone.	Negative:
	Question: Was I
4. My grandpa was playing kabaddi.	Negative:
	Question:
5. The boys were fighting.	Negative:
	Question:

22.2 SIMPLE PAST OR PAST CONTINUOUS?

In the following paragraph, underline the verbs in the simple past and put a border around the verbs in the past continuous. Note the situations in which the two forms are used:

We were travelling from Panaji to Mumbai on a ship named *MV Akbar*. As we were sailing along the Konkan coast, we saw many fishing boats. Some of them were carrying heaps of fish that looked like molten silver from a distance. At the time, our son was two years old. While he was running around with unsteady steps, my wife and I were worried that he might fall overboard![1] After a while, he actually vanished. We looked everywhere but couldn't find him. In the end, we climbed on to the bridge[2] to talk to the captain. And what did we see? The little fellow was talking excitedly with the captain!

---

[1] **overboard:** (adverb) over the side of a ship or boat into water.
[2] **bridge:** (noun) a small cabin, usually at the highest level of a ship, from where the captain controls the ship.

Let's put the two forms in two columns:

Simple Past	Past Continuous
… we <u>saw</u> many fishing boats	We <u>were travelling</u> from Goa to Mumbai …
… (the fish) <u>looked</u> like molten silver …	As we <u>were sailing</u> along the Konkan coast …
… our son <u>was</u> two years old	While he <u>was running</u> around …
… my wife and I <u>were</u> scared …	Some of the boats <u>were carrying</u> heaps of fish …
… he actually <u>vanished</u>	The little fellow <u>was talking</u> excitedly …
We <u>looked</u> for him everywhere …	
… but (we) <u>couldn't find</u> him anywhere	
… we <u>climbed</u> on to the bridge …	
And what <u>did</u> we <u>see</u>?	

From these sentences, we note the following:

1. We use the *past continuous* to describe an action that we were in the middle of:
   - ✓ We <u>were travelling</u> from Goa to Mumbai.
   - ✓ The child <u>was running</u> around.

2. For state verbs, we use the simple past, not the past continuous:
   - ✓ The fish <u>looked</u> like molten silver. Not: The fish ~~were looking like~~ ….
   - ✓ … my wife and I <u>felt</u> scared. Not: … my wife and I ~~were feeling scared~~. ✗

▌ 22.3 I WAS SLEEPING WHEN MY BOSS WALKED IN

We may have to describe two actions that happened during the same time in the past, of which one took a longer time.

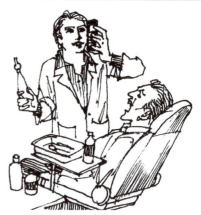

- ✓ Dr Dantwalla <u>was extracting</u> a tooth when his girlfriend <u>telephoned</u>.

The action of extracting a tooth took some time (the verb is in the *past continuous*: *was extracting*), and over a shorter duration during that period, the doctor's girlfriend phoned in. (This verb is in the *simple past*: *telephoned*.)

Each of the following sentences talks about two events. As you will see, a second event took place while the underlined event was happening.

- ✓ When my boss walked in, I <u>was sleeping</u> in my chair.
- ✓ A fire broke out in the astrologer's home when he <u>was preparing</u> Raghu's horoscope.

ACTIVITY 2

Insert the past continuous forms of the verbs given within brackets, then match the parts, and write down complete sentences:

→ Grandpa . . . . (climb) a coconut tree	1. when Ramachandra attacked Lanka
A. I . . . . (get off) the train	2. when a burglar broke into our flat
B. The minister . . . . (deliver) a speech	3. when her father died
C. He . . . . (wait) for his girlfriend,	4. when someone pushed me from behind
D. Kumbhakarna . . . . (sleep)	→ when a coconut fell on his head
E. We . . . . (sleep)	5. when I saw a dolphin
F. You didn't hear the doorbell Because	6. when someone threw an egg at him
G. I . . . . (swim) in the Chilika	7. but instead, her father walked in
H. She . . . . (prepare) for her final exams	8. you . . . . (talk) over the phone

→	→	Grandpa was climbing a coconut tree when a coconut fell on his head.
A.		
B.		
C.		
D.		
E.		
F.		
G.		
H.		

22.4 BACKGROUND INFORMATION

We often use the past continuous to describe what is happening in the background:

- ✓ It was raining. A storm <u>was raging</u> outside. The trees around our tent <u>were swaying</u>.
- ✓ Later, after it stopped raining, water <u>was dripping</u> from the leaves. The night became clear, stars <u>were twinkling</u>.
- ✓ 'The river between us and the village <u>was rippling</u> to a light breeze and <u>shining</u> like cut-glass in the afternoon sun.' [From Nirad C. Chaudhuri's *Autobiography of an Unknown Indian*]

PRACTICE

1. In the first column, there are some situations where we use the past continuous, whereas in the second column, there are some sentences in the past continuous form. Match the rules with the sentences:

1. We use the *past continuous* to describe a past action that we were in the middle of.	A. It was the evening rush hour. Streams of cars, buses, and motor bikes were rushing past our hotel.
2. If we are talking about a situation in the past when a shorter event happened while a longer event was happening at the same time, then we use the past continuous to describe the longer event.	B. I was sleeping in my hotel room when some-one knocked at the door.
3. We use the past continuous to describe back-ground information.	C. The phone was ringing.

2. Complete the captions:

A.	B.	C.	D.
Raghu was .... when his boss .... in.	I .... the newspaper when the phone	The cat .... my food while I .... the entrance.	A fire broke out at the astrologer's house when he .... Raghu's horoscope.

3. How will you complete these sentences? Use the verbs: **blow in, splash, snow,** and **twinkle.**

   a. The water was not calm. Waves after waves .... on our boat.
   b. We sat on the balcony. A pleasant breeze .... from the north.
   c. When we reached, it .... in Manali, all the roads were closed.
   d. It was a clear night. Stars ....

4. A new chief minister has been elected recently. A special inspector appointed by him made a sudden inspection of a government department yesterday. Complete the inspector's report based on the hints given below. I have solved the first two for you.

   → The departmental head was away for a meeting. But no one knew/where the meeting/take place. ⇨ But no one knew where the meeting was taking place.
   → His deputy/solve/a crossword puzzle ⇨ His deputy was solving a crossword puzzle.

   i. The head clerk/tell/a visitor/to come back after a week

   ....

ii.   Four employees/play cards/in the lunchroom

   ....

iii. An employee/read/a newspaper

   ....

iv.   Two employees/discuss/the unexpected election results

   ....

v.   A lady typist/type/a memorandum

   ....

vi.   A record-keeper/file/papers/in the records room

   ....

vii. Two employees/plan/their next vacation

   ....

viii. Two lady employees/knit/sweaters

   ....

KEY TO ACTIVITIES

Activity 1: 1. I wasn't/was not reading a newspaper. Were you reading a newspaper? 2. We were not jogging in Shivaji Park. Were we jogging in Shivaji Park? 3. You weren't/were not talking over the phone. Was I talking over the phone? 4. My grandpa wasn't/was not playing kabaddi. Was my grandpa playing kabaddi? 5. The boys weren't/were not fighting. Were the boys fighting?

Activity 2: A-4: I was getting off the train when someone pushed me from behind. B-6: The minister was delivering a speech when someone threw an egg at him. C-7: He was waiting for his girlfriend, but instead, her father walked in. D-1: Kumbhakarna was sleeping when Ramachandra attacked Lanka. E-2: We were sleeping when a burglar broke into our flat. F-8: You didn't hear the doorbell because you were talking over phone. G-5: I was swimming in the Chilika when I saw a dolphin. H-3: She was preparing for her final exams when her father died.

23

The Runaway Bride

Learning Objective: In this chapter, we are going to study the grammatical form called 'the past perfect' which is used to express an action prior to a point of time in the past.

23.1 AN UNFORTUNATE INCIDENT

Recently, I was at a wedding reception. Everything was fine: lights, flowers, and arrangements for a feast. The shehnai was playing in the background. It was early evening and guests were yet to arrive. The bride **had gone** to a beauty parlour for her bridal make-up. She **hadn't returned** yet. A little later, a lady rushed in and said that the bride **had run away** with another boy. When the groom arrived, he found that his future wife **had vanished.** Naturally, there was a big commotion[1] at the place. And sadly, I had to leave without having dinner!

Let's look at this unfortunate incident from the point of view of English grammar. Read the text again, focusing on the sentences in which the verbs have been highlighted. These verbs are in the ***past perfect tense.*** Let's see when we use sentences like these.

When (1) <u>we are talking about the past</u> and (2) <u>go back in time to describe an earlier event</u>, we use these sentences.

✓ A lady	**said**	that the bride **had run away**
✓ The groom	**found**	his future wife **had vanished**
	↑	↑
We're talking about this event		An earlier event
	(the simple past)	*(the past perfect)*

---

[1] **commotion:** (noun) a situation where there is a lot of confusion and noise.

We do not say:

- ✘ A lady said the bride just ~~ran away~~. Or
- ✘ A lady said the bride ~~has run away~~. Or
- ✘ A lady said the bride ~~was run away~~.

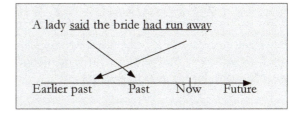

- The past perfect form:

⊞	Subject +	'd/had +	the past participle form of the verb +	other words
⊟	Subject +	hadn't/had not +	the past participle form of the verb +	other words
?	Had +	subject +	the past participle form of the verb +	other words

In sentences like these, we often use *time markers,* that is, expressions such as *by the time, when,* and the like: *When / By the time the groom arrived, the bride had run away.*

ACTIVITY 1

The table below has sentences describing two past events that occurred one after the other. Combine the two to form one new sentence. (Use the simple past for the later event and the past perfect for the earlier.)

Earlier Event	Later Event	The Combined Sentence
→ The bride's mother fainted.	When I went in, I saw it.	When I **went** in, I **saw** (that) the bride's mother **had fainted**.
A. The bride left behind a note.	Someone found it in her room.	Someone found a note which the bride .... in her room.
B. An uncle of the bride saw her with a boy at the airport.	He phoned in to inform.	An uncle of the bride ....
C. She boarded a flight.	Her father reached the airport.	When ....
D. She always knew something like this would happen.	A neighbour told the guests	.... something like this would happen.
E. The girl crossed the borders of her country.	The guests returned home.	By the time ....

Check your answers with the key. Even if some of them are incorrect, don't worry. You might make a few mistakes in the beginning. Try again. You'll surely get them right!

23.2 *I MET/HAD MET MY WIFE*

When you describe only *one* completed event or action from the past, *do not use the past perfect*. People often say: *I ~~had met~~ my wife at college.* This is not quite all right. Say: *I met my wife ….* Use the past perfect <u>only when you talk about two events from the past</u>.

Don't Say	Say
My neighbour ~~had been~~ awake.	My neighbour was awake.
I'd ~~worked~~ on a project on robotics at college.	I worked on a project on robotics ….
I ~~had~~ first ~~seen~~ the sea when I was 10.	I first saw the sea when I was 10.

ACTIVITY 2

Correct the <u>errors</u>. (I have underlined them.)

A.   After reaching home I realized I <u>lost</u> my key.
B.   I called my sister. She <u>hadn't answered</u> the phone as she <u>was</u> asleep.
C.   Luckily, my next-door neighbour <u>had been</u> awake.
D.   I told him what <u>has happened</u>.

23.3 PRESENT PERFECT OR PAST PERFECT?

We use the present perfect when we talk about a non-specific time before now. We use the past perfect when we talk about a time before a past event:

Present Perfect (Before Now)	Past Perfect (Before an Earlier Event)
I feel the shopkeeper **has cheated** me.	I felt the shopkeeper **had cheated** me.
The book is with Ravi. You **haven't lost** it.	The book was with Ravi, you **hadn't lost** it.
You look different. **Have** you **changed** your glasses?[2]	You looked different at the party. **Had** you **changed** your glasses?

23.4 WHEN WE DON'T USE THE PAST PERFECT

If you describe two past events in the chronological order, that is, in the order in which they happened, *do not use the past perfect for the earlier event*. Use *the simple past for both the verbs*. For example:

---

[2] **glasses:** (pair noun) SPECTACLES or SPECS.

✓ The train **left** at 4.25 and we **reached** the station after half four.[3]
✓ After she **finished** her supper, she **read** a story book for an hour.
✓ My father **died** before I **was born**. [From Charles Dickens's *David Copperfield*]

We don't use the past perfect for the earlier event in these sentences because *we are not going back in time*. We are describing events in the sequence in which they occurred.

ACTIVITY 3

Fill in the blanks with the appropriate forms of the verbs given within brackets:

(a) My friend Mohan .... (set up) the tea stall in 2005 and .... it ....
(close down) two years later.

(b) He .... (take up) a job and a year later, he .... (marry) his girlfriend
Karishma.

(c) Their first child .... (arrive) a year later and three years after that, they ....
(have) their second child. By that time, Mohan .... (purchase) a flat.

ACTIVITY 4

Correct the following. If a sentence is okay, put a ✓ next to it. (Three of them are correct.)

A.   India had become independent in 1947.
B.   I had participated in the Bengaluru Midnight Marathon last year.
C.   Jim Corbett shot the Man-Eater of Rudraprayag in 1926. Over eight years before that, the leopard killed 125 people.
D.   Spain won the football World Cup for the first time in 2010; Italy had won the previous championship in 2006.
E.   The computer didn't start because I forgot to turn on the power.
F.   I joined college last year and soon met Archana, who is my best friend.
G.   I had got caught in a traffic jam and reached the cinema late.
H.   Ravi and Radhika had announced their engagement last March. They got married in April.
I.   When Radhika got married, she had almost completed her PhD.
J.   Radhika had met her future husband at university.

PRACTICE

1.   What are the tenses of the underlined verbs? Write *simple past*, *the present perfect*, or *the past perfect* in the second column:

---

[3] **half four:** it is a way of saying 'half past four' or 4.30.

Sentence	Tense	Matches with
i. By the time Raju graduated, he <u>had found</u> a job through campus placement.		
ii. Raju <u>graduated</u> last month.		
iii. Raju <u>has</u> just <u>joined</u> a software company.		
iv. Raju <u>graduated</u> and <u>started</u> working soon.		

Match the above sentences with A, B, C, or D from the table below:

A. Describes a completed event in the past	B. Describes a recent event
C. Describes two events from the past in the chronological order	
D. Describes a past event, and from there looks back at an earlier event	

2. Which forms will be appropriate? The simple past or the past perfect? Complete the following sentences with the appropriate forms of the verbs given within brackets:

A. The traffic signal turned green, but our bus .... (not move).

B. She .... (pass) secondary exams in 2005, but didn't take higher secondary in 2007.

C. Radhika .... (switch off) the light and .... (go) to bed.

D. Two athletes were disqualified as they .... (fail) the drug test.

E. He .... (buy) a flat only when he .... (save) enough money.

F. We reached the station late as we .... (get) stuck in a traffic jam.

G. My wife .... (tell) me that she .... (not see) the man before.

H. Before he .... (lose) the 2006 elections, he .... (be) an MLA for 10 years.

I. Sania .... (defeat) Mary Pierce in the semi-final but .... (lose) to Sharapova in the final.

J. He was an old man who fished alone in a skiff in the Gulf Stream and .... (go) eighty-four days now without taking a fish. [This is the first sentence in Ernest Hemingway's *The Old Man and the Sea*, one of the finest novels in world literature.]

3. Fill in the blanks with the appropriate forms of the verbs given within brackets:

Three monkeys, who [1]........................ (live) on the ground floor of a two-storey building, [2]..................... (came) to the city in search of jobs. On the first floor of the building [3]..................... (live) a young couple, who [4]..................... just .... (get) married. The wife [5]..................... (be) exceedingly beautiful.

On a Sunday morning, the monkeys [6]..................... (wake up) and [7]........................ (hear) the couple fighting. It [8].................. (be) a noisy argument. The leader monkey [9].................. (send) the youngest one to check what [10]..................... (go wrong) upstairs.

As the little monkey [11]........................ (not return) after a long time, the senior [12]........................ (send) the second monkey to enquire. He too [13]............................... (not come back).

After some time, the leader himself [14]........................ (go up). He [15]........................ (find) the two younger monkeys sitting on the parapet[4] of the balcony and nodding their heads, saying: 'We have a chance .... Yes, of course, we have a chance!'

---

[4] **parapet:** (noun) a low wall on the edge of a balcony, roof, or bridge.

Inside the flat, the wife [16]....................... (shout) at her husband: 'If I had known you were so useless, I would have married a monkey. Indeed, I should have married a monkey.'

[I do not know who originally wrote this story. I heard it from someone.—Author]

KEY TO ACTIVITIES

Activity 1: A. Someone found a note which the bride had left behind in her room. B. An uncle of the bride phoned in to inform that he had (just) seen her at the airport. C. When her father reached the airport, she had boarded a flight. D. A neighbour told the guests (that) she had always known something like this would happen. E. By the time the guests returned home, the girl had crossed the borders of her country.

Activity 2: A. After reaching home, I realized I had lost my key. B. She didn't answer the phone as she had been asleep. C. Luckily, my next-door neighbour was awake. D. I told him what had happened.

Activity 3: (a) My friend Mohan set up a tea stall in 2005 and closed it down two years later. (b) Then he took up a job and a year later, he married his girlfriend Karishma. (c) Their first child arrived a year later and three years after that, they had their second child. By that time, Mohan had purchased a flat.

Activity 4: A. India became independent in 1947. B. I participated in the Bengaluru Midnight Marathon last year. C. . Over eight years before that, the leopard had killed 125 people. D. ✓; E. The computer didn't start because I had forgotten to turn on the power. F. ✓; G. I got caught in a traffic jam and reached the cinema late. H. Ravi and Radhika announced their engagement in March last year. The got married in April. I. ✓; J. Radhika met her future husband at university.

He Had Been Saving All His Life

24

Learning Objectives: Continuing with our discussion on the past tenses, in this chapter, we will cover the past perfect continuous.

24.1 HE'D BEEN SAVING ALL HIS LIFE

In the last unit, we discussed the structure of sentences like:

When <u>we reached Kolkata</u>, <u>it had started raining</u>. Or
By the time <u>he was 80,</u> <u>he had bought 10 houses</u>.

Each of these sentences describes <u>two completed events in the past</u>. Let's now move on to a slightly different situation. Imagine that:

(a) you are talking about an event in the past and
(b) you go back in time to describe another event *which happened over a period of time before* the event you are describing.

Let me tell you a story to explain the point. It is about my Uncle Skinflint,[1] who bought his 10th house last month, on his 80th birthday. As he stands before the house, he suddenly starts thinking. He never had any friend. And now, with his wife dead and family drifted away, he lives alone in a big house, in the company of cats and constipation. With a deep sense of sadness, he suddenly realizes that all his life he did nothing but running after money.

Look at the chart below and complete the sentence using the verb *run after* and the time phrase *all his life*. (Better use a pencil.)

---

[1] **skinflint:** (noun) a person who hates spending money, a MISER.

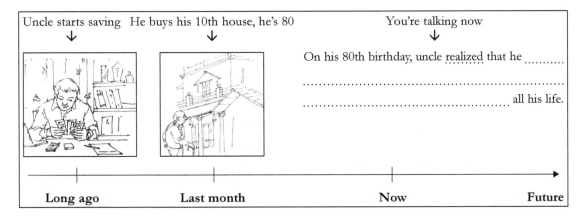

If you have written '*On this 80th birthday, uncle realized that he had been running after money all his life*', you can choose to skip this chapter. However, you can do the exercises to become more confident about handling this grammatical form.

If you haven't got it right, read on! Compare the sentences below and jot down the difference between the first two sentences and the last:

1. When Ravi arrived at the restaurant, Radhika was furious. She <u>had been waiting</u> for an hour.
2. As they sat down, Ravi took out a small packet he <u>had been hiding</u> under his shirt.
3. Radhika's anger turned into a smile, she <u>hadn't expected</u> such a lovely gift.

Each of these sentences describes two past events. However, in the first two, besides describing two events, the focus is on <u>the duration or extent of the earlier event</u> (*She had been waiting <u>for an hour</u> …, he <u>had been hiding</u>* …). The underlined verbs in the first two sentences are in the ***past perfect continuous*** tense.

We use this form when we are talking about a past event (or action) and go back in time to describe <u>the period over which an earlier event (or action) had taken place</u>.

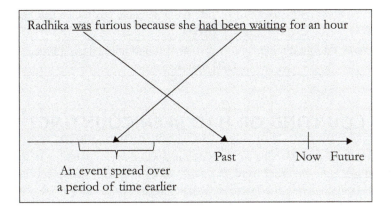

Here are some more examples. The ⟨later event⟩ has been circled and the <u>earlier event</u>, underlined:

- I ⟨suffered⟩ a cramp because I <u>had been swimming</u> for hours.
- At last, I ⟨found⟩ my yellow socks. I'<u>d been looking</u> for them for days.

- The *past perfect continuous* form is:

⊞	Subject +	'd/had been +	the past participle form of the verb +	other words
⊟	Subject +	hadn't/had not been +	the past participle form of the verb +	other words
?	Had +	subject + been +	the past participle form of the verb +	other words

Note: You will *not* use this structure in negative sentences or questions often.

Also, in sentences like these, we often use a time phrase to indicate the length of time for which the event had been happening, such as *for an hour* or *all his life.*

ACTIVITY 1

Fill in the gaps with the *past perfect continuous form* of the verb given within brackets:

A. I was tired because I .... the whole day. (run around)
B. My eyes hurt because I .... the computer for 10 hours. (work on)
C. I was angry with my girlfriend because I .... for an hour. (wait)
D. Finally, I managed to find the bug[2] in my program. I .... on it for hours. (work on)

24.2 HAD SAVED OR HAD BEEN SAVING?

We use *the past perfect* for two <u>completed events or actions</u>. We use *the past perfect continuous* to describe <u>events that happened over a period.</u>

Completed Action: Had Done	Over a Period: Had Been + +ing
When uncle was 40, he <u>had saved</u> enough to buy his first house.	By the time uncle was 80, he <u>had been saving</u> for 50 years.
When I moved to Pune, I'<u>d found</u> a job.	At last I found one! I'<u>d been looking for</u> a job for six months.

24.3 WAS COUNTING OR HAD BEEN COUNTING?

The past perfect continuous is used to describe an event that happened over a period, <u>but which ended before a point of time in the past.</u> On the other hand, the *past continuous* describes an event that happened over a period, <u>but which was not complete at a point of time in the past.</u> Let's compare the two forms:

---

[2] **bug:** (noun) an error in a computer system or program.

The Past Perfect Continuous	The Past Continuous
When Mr Dindayal had a heart attack, he <u>had been counting</u> cash for two hours.	Mr Dindayal <u>was counting</u> cash when a robber broke in. Dindayal said, 'Wait! Let me complete my work', and went on.
↑ Counting of cash was interrupted.	↑ Counting continued.
Sachin <u>had been batting</u> on 196 when the captain declared. (= Sachin's innings came to an end with the declaration)	Saurabh was batting on 196 when the ball was changed. (= Saurabh continued to bat after the change of the ball)
It <u>had been raining</u> when we reached the station. (= it wasn't raining when we reached)	It <u>was raining</u> when we reached the station. (= the rain continued after we reached)

ACTIVITY 2

In the second column, write <u>Completed</u> if the action described by the underlined verb was complete. Otherwise, write <u>Not completed</u>:

A. Mumbai was flooded because it <u>had been raining</u> for days.		
B. When we reached Mumbai, it <u>was raining</u>.		
C. When I went to my sister's home, <u>they had just had</u> breakfast.		
D. When I went to my sister's home, they <u>were having</u> breakfast.		
E. When we reached the top of the Tiger Hill, the sun <u>was rising</u>.		
F. At last, we reached the top of the Tiger Hill. <u>We'd been climbing</u> for three hours.		

Write down the tense of the underlined verbs in the third column: *past continuous*, *past perfect*, or *the past perfect continuous*.

24.4 WHEN THE PAST PERFECT CONTINUOUS IS NOT USED

In Section 14.6, we saw that we do not use continuous tenses for the **state verbs** such as *be, believe, have, know, like, dislike, remember,* and so on, even if these verbs talk about a continuing event. This is true for the past perfect continuous too.

✓ When they got married, they had known each other for a week. (NOT They ~~had been knowing~~ each other ✗)

✓ My uncle sold his car last month. He had had it for 15 years. (NOT He ~~had been having~~ it for 15 years. ✗)

✓ The cinema was knocked down last month. It had stood there for 50 years. (NOT It ~~had been standing~~ .... ✗)

ACTIVITY 3

Strike off the incorrect options:

1. My boss walked in when I **had been/was sleeping.** I don't wish to say what followed.
2. When the car broke down, George **had been/was driving** for 10 hours.
3. I couldn't answer the phone because I **had been/was taking** a shower.
4. Prasad's book came out last month. He **had been/was writing** it for two years.
5. I slept through the film. I **had been/was running around** throughout the day.
6. I told her that I **had loved/had been loving** her for many years.
7. I became an atheist[3] in my teens. Before that, I **had believed/had been believing** in god.
8. Till the last day at college, Aneesh never managed to talk to Ayesha, although he **had liked/had been liking** her a lot.

PRACTICE

1. Write the sentences in the past perfect or the past perfect continuous using the clues given. Follow the model answer:

    ➔ I joined office after a week, but I felt weak because I - **take** - strong antibiotics. ➢ I joined office after a week, but I felt weak because I **had been taking** strong antibiotics ....

    a. At last, I found the book in a College Street bookshop. I - **search** - for it for months. ➢
        ....

    b. My uncle was delighted when the court ruled in his favour; for several years, he - **fight** - a legal battle - to get his flat back. ➢...
        ....

    c. We repaired the roof. Rainwater - **seep in** - for some time. ➢.................................
        ....

    d. The workers - **repair** - the boiler when the accident occurred. ➢ ....
        ....

    e. I felt sleepy; because I - **not (be) able** - to sleep the previous night. ➢.......................
        ....

    f. Amla - **bat** - brilliantly when he was injured. ➢...
        ....

2. Correct the following:

    A. He'd been loving her for years, but didn't have the courage to tell her.
    B. I agreed when they asked me to join them; I had been liking their work.
    C. Sorry, I had been doubting your intentions when I didn't have all the facts.
    D. I had been seeing the point even before you explained it to me.

---

[3] **atheist:** (noun) a person who doesn't believe in the existence of god. An **agnostic** is a person who believes no one can know or prove whether god exists.

3. Match the two parts and write a complete sentence. Follow the model given:

This happened earlier	*This happened later*
→ It was raining nonstop for 20 days	A. Radhika was delighted to see it.
1. It rained for hours.	B. Radhika was angry.
2. Radhika waited for an hour.	→ We reached Cherrapunji.
3. Ravi worked on the computer for 10 hours.	C. Ravi's eyes were red.
4. Ravi hid a gold chain under his jacket.	D. Ravi met Radhika at a restaurant.

→ → When we reached Cherrapunji, it had been raining for 20 days.

☐ ☐ When Ravi ....
....

☐ ☐ Radhika ....
....

☐ ☐ Radhika was delighted ....
....

▍ KEY TO ACTIVITIES

Activity 1: A. I was tired because I <u>had been running around</u> the whole day. 2. My eyes hurt because I'<u>d been</u> or <u>had been working on</u> the computer for 10 hours. C. I was angry with my girlfriend because I'<u>d been</u> or <u>had been waiting</u> for an hour. D. ... I <u>had been working on</u> it for hours.

Activity 2: A. Completed, past perfect continuous; B. Not completed, past continuous. C. Completed, past perfect; D. Not completed, past continuous; E. Not completed, past continuous; F. Completed, past perfect continuous

Activity 3: 1. My boss walked in when I ~~had been~~/**was sleeping**. 2. When the car broke down, George **had been**/~~was~~ **driving** for 10 hours. 3. I couldn't answer the phone because I ~~had been~~/**was taking** a shower. 4. Prasad's book came out last month. He **had been**/~~was~~ **writing** it for two years. 5. ... I **had been**/~~was~~ **running around** throughout the day. 6. I told her I **had loved**/~~had been loving~~ her for many years. 7. ... Before that, I **had believed**/~~had been believing~~ in god. 8. Till the last day at college, Aneesh never managed to talk to Ayesha, although he **had liked**/~~had been liking~~ her a lot.

The Great Plains, the Grand Canyon

Learning Objective: This chapter covers vocabulary around travel and tourism, besides some idiomatic expressions. It also reviews the past tenses.

25.1 EVERYONE LOVES HOLIDAYS

As you read the passage below, focus on the words in bold:

Everyone loves **holidays** or (in North American English) **vacations.** That is, everybody loves to spend time away from home, travelling. I guess you too do? How do you travel? Do you tour independently, maybe, with the assistance of a **travel agent** who books your tickets and so on? Or do you buy a **package tour** from a **tour operator?**

When you travel alone (or with friends), you have a lot of freedom. You can move at your own pace and visit the **tourist attractions** that **catch your fancy**. You can also plan your trip to suit your pocket. You can even be a **backpack traveller** and **hitch-hike,** saving on transport. However, to travel on your own, you have to do lots of things, such as getting travel documents (a **passport** if you are going abroad, and a **visa**, which you need to enter many countries), besides **booking** hotels and air/train/bus tickets.

On the other hand, if you go on a **package holiday,** someone else takes care of everything. You just report at a railway station, or go to an airport and get your **boarding pass** (or **boarding card**). When you reach your destination, there is someone to take you to a hotel. There is even a **tour guide** so that you can go **sightseeing** without hassles. Often, the tour operator arranges a **coach** for tourists to go around. In short, package holidays help you travel without **breaking sweat.**[1]

---

[1] **(to) break sweat:** (verb) to exert yourself physically.

ACTIVITY 1

Fill in the squares following the clues given below. You will use some of the words highlighted in the above passage. Also, I have given the first letters for three of the solutions to make the task a little easier. [Use a dictionary if you have to.]

1. A TOUR _ _ _ _ _ _ _ _ is a person who specializes in organizing holiday packages, which include transport, accommodation, and so on.
2. A document with your name, photograph, address, and so on, which you require if you wish to leave your country. (8)
3. TOURIST _ _ _ _ _ _ _ _ _ _ are places frequently visited by travellers.
4. If you are a _ _ _ _ _ _ _ _ TRAVELLER, you carry very little luggage, which you carry it on your back.
5. A document required to enter many countries other than your own. Typically, it is stamped on a blank page of your passport. (4)
6. A TRAVEL _ _ _ _ _ is a person who makes arrangement for travellers.
7. If you travel by getting free lifts in vehicles, you are called a HITCH-_ _ _ _ _.
8. The activity of going around and seeing interesting places during holiday. (11)
9. A large comfortable single-decker bus that doesn't run on a fixed route. (5)
10. A TOUR _ _ _ _ _ is someone whose job is to show you around places of interest.
11. A _ _ _ _ _ _ _ _ PASS/CARD allows you to get on to an aircraft.

Master clue (vertical): A trip in which tourists travel in a group, and everything is arranged by an individual or company.

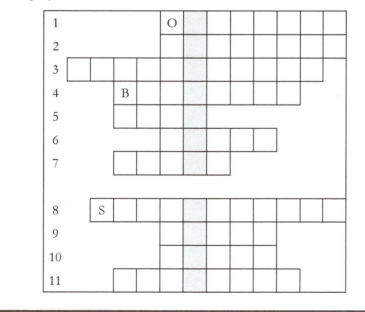

25.2 THE GRAND CANYON

[As you read the passage below, fill in the blanks using words and phrases you have just come across. If you cannot fill in some of them, read on and try to understand the message, ignoring the blank spaces.]

In Spanish, *Las Vegas* means grassy plains, but actually, it is a bustling city with lots of tourist _____. Part of our _____ in Vegas and the Grand Canyon was arranged by ourselves. The rest was a _____ ____. We b_____ air tickets and **reserved** hotels in Vegas online beforehand. After spending a few blissful days in Las Vegas, we took a **day trip** to the Grand Canyon.

Our journey began at an office of the Grand Canyon Tour Company, where we **got onto** a comfortable c_____ along with 30 other tourists. We drove through a vast plain; there were neither trees, nor any **habitation.**[2] On the horizon were low flat hills under a cloudless blue sky. The Great Plains of America, read in books, were in front of my eyes.

We passed some hillocks with beautiful **bungalows** on their slopes. Ron, our driver-cum-tour _____, said that some Hollywood **celebrities** lived there: 'That pink bungalow belongs to Barbara Streisand … the one there on your right now … is Brad Pitt and Angelina Jolie's … and that house with three palm trees … it belongs to my girlfriend, Nicole Kidman.'

Like many Americans, Ron took the business of **cracking jokes** seriously. As we approach the Hoover Dam, he announced: 'Ladies and Gentlemen, we are going to stop at a **checkpoint**. Please be seated. A police officer will come on board and check for guns and explosives. His name is Jack. You can greet him. You can say, "Good morning, Jack!" or "How are you, Jack?" or "Have a good day Jack!" … but please, … please don't say "Hi Jack!"'

The land turned sandy. We had just crossed the Hoover Dam when a group of h____-_____ carrying large b_____ asked for a lift. We ignored them and drove on.

Soon, we were driving through the Mojave (MO'**HAA**VI) Desert. The only t_____ attraction there seemed to be Joshua trees, which have short, stout trunks with clusters of **spiky** leaves. Ron talked **eloquently** about the plants, birds, lizards, and snakes of the Mojave Desert. For example, he told us quite cheerfully how long we would **survive** if bitten by different species of snakes.

On a serious note, I had never come across a more **knowledgeable** _____ guide. Ron had been driving tourists for five years. During lunch, I asked him if everyone in his line took the trouble to learn so much about the **environment**. He smiled an embarrassed smile, but with a **touch of pride**. And added that he read about the desert every evening after going home.

[If you haven't been able to fill in all the blanks, try again, using the following words: attractions, backpacks, booked, coach, guide, hitch-hikers, holiday, package tour or package holiday, tour, and tourist.]

ACTIVITY 2

Read the passage again focusing on the following words or phrases in bold and match the words with their meanings given below:

---

[2] **habitation:** a place where people live.

backpack	bungalow	celebrity	without breaking sweat
checkpoint	coach (noun)	day trip	eloquently
environment	to get on to	habitation	knowledgeable
to reserve	spiky	to survive	a touch of pride

1. a little bit of pride   ⇨ ....
2. a bag that you carry on your back   ⇨ ....
3. a barricade, typically at a border, where policemen check
   if travellers are carrying anything illegal   ⇨ ....
4. (to) board a bus, train, aircraft, and so on   ⇨ ....
5. (to) book (hotel rooms and such others)   ⇨ ....
6. a comfortable bus that often runs over long distances   ⇨ ....
7. (to) continue to live, despite dangers   ⇨ ....
8. an excursion that is over in a day   ⇨ ....
9. a famous person, especially in sports or performing arts   ⇨ ....
10. (to talk) fluently, in an impressive manner   ⇨ ....
11. the natural surroundings and conditions in which we all live   ⇨ ....
12. a one-storey building that mostly serves as a home   ⇨ ....
13. a place where humans live   ⇨ ....
14. someone who knows a lot about a particular subject   ⇨ ....
15. with sharp edges, thorny   ⇨ ....
16. without any physical effort   ⇨ ....

ACTIVITY 3

Fill in the blanks with appropriate forms of the following verbs. In this activity too, I have given parts of some of the words.

be	not be	be thrilled	book	push/come	change
come across	create	cross	drive	drop	fall
forget	form	make	wear		

After a satisfying lunch at an eatery called the Grand Depot Café, where waiters served us _____ing hats, belts, fake guns, and high boots, we _____ on the last leg of our journey to the Grand Canyon. As we were _____ along Route 66, we cr_____ a small township that looked straight out of a Western movie. I almost f_____ off my seat when I saw Clint Eastwood riding a horse, with a Stetson[3] hanging low over his eyes. Then I realized that I ___ _____ a mistake. It ___n't Clint Eastwood in flesh and blood, but a lifelike statue of him.

---

[3] **stetson:** a hat with a very wide brim, which cowboys used to wear.

The journey was so enjoyable that we almost _____ about the destination. However, we _____ when Ron _____ us on the South Rim of the Grand Canyon. And we started walking along what is known as the Kaibab Trail.

We looked at the canyon below. The layers of earth we saw on the canyon had been f_____ under sea. Around 65 million years ago, this plateau ___ ____ ____ up 1,500 to 3,000 m after a massive earthquake. But the River Colorado kept flowing, undaunted. The waters of the mighty river together with wind and rain erosion c_____ an intricate pattern of layered earth.

The earth and the rocks were of different colours and textures. With the sun going behind and coming out of clouds, the sunlight _____ continuously, and the landscape altered every minute. I felt we were watching a movie projected from another world.

We also ____ _____ a mule trail. We wanted to hire a mule ride and go down to the bottom of the valley, but we couldn't. The mule rides ___ ____ ____ a year before.

A visit to the Grand Canyon is a humbling experience. Here, you come face to face with the enormity of Nature. You return after a feast for your eyes, with thoughts in your mind.

ACTIVITY 4

Change the sentences following instructions given:

A. In the shop selling Native Indian artefacts,[4] I liked a replica of a puma.	*Use an idiom containing* 'fancy'	In the shop selling Native Indian artefacts, a replica of a puma ....
B. We didn't have to put in any effort; a travel agent organized everything.	*Begin this way:*	We didn't have to break ....
C. Americans are fond of telling jokes.	*Change the verb* 'tell'	....
D. 'Yes', the old soldier said somewhat proudly, 'I fought in the Liberation War.'	*Replace* 'somewhat proudly' *with a phrase containing* 'touch'	....
E. She spoke fluently, in an impressive manner.	*Replace* 'fluently, … manner' *with one word*	....
F. To board an aircraft, you have to first get a document that allows you to get on to the aircraft.	*Replace* 'document that allows you to get on to the aircraft' *with two words*	....

---

[4] **artefact:** (noun) a hand-made object that is typically of historical or cultural interest.

KEY TO ACTIVITIES

Activity 1:

1					O	**P**	E	R	A	T	O	R
2					P	**A**	S	S	P	O	R	T
3	A	T	T	R	A	**C**	T	I	O	N	S	
4			B	A	C	**K**	P	A	C	K		
5			V	I	S	**A**						
6					A	**G**	E	N	T			
7			H	I	K	**E**	R					
8		S	I	G	H	**T**	S	E	E	I	N	G
9					C	**O**	A	C	H			
10					G	**U**	I	D	E			
11			B	O	A	**R**	D	I	N	G		

Activity 2: 1. a touch of pride; 2. backpack; 3. checkpoint; 4. (to) get on to; 5. (to) reserve; 6. coach; 7. (to) survive; 8. day trip; 9. celebrity; 10. eloquently; 11. environment; 12. bungalow; 13. habitat; 14. knowledgeable; 15. spiky; 16. without breaking sweat

Activity 3:
After a satisfying lunch at an eatery called the Grand Depot Café, where waiters served us wearing hats, belts, fake guns, and high boots, we were on the last leg of our journey .... As we were driving along Route 66, we crossed a small township .... I almost fell off my seat when I saw Clint Eastwood riding a horse .... Then I realized that I had made a mistake. It wasn't Clint Eastwood ....

The journey was so enjoyable that we almost forgot about the destination. However, we were thrilled when Ron dropped us on the South Rim of the Grand Canyon. ...

... The layers of earth we saw on the canyon had been formed under sea. Around 65 million years ago, this plateau had been pushed up .... But the River Colorado kept flowing, undaunted. The waters of the mighty river together with wind and rain erosion created a most intricate pattern ....

... With the sun going behind and coming out of clouds, the sunlight changed continuously, and the landscape altered every minute ....

We also came across a mule trail .... The mule rides had been booked a year before.

... Here, you come face to face with the enormity of Nature. You return after a feast for your eyes, with thoughts in your mind.

Activity 4:
A. ... a replica of a puma caught my fancy. B. We didn't have to break sweat as .... C. Americans are fond of cracking jokes. D. 'Yes', the old soldier said with a touch of pride .... E. She spoke eloquently. F. To board an aircraft, you have to first get a boarding pass/card.

PRACTICE

Write a paragraph on a holiday you have had.

....
....
....
....
....
....
....
....
....
....
....
....
....
....
....
....
....
....
....
....

Test 3:
The Blast That Wasn't
(A Test on Describing the Past)

1. The solutions to this crossword puzzle are verbs (base form, past, or past participle).

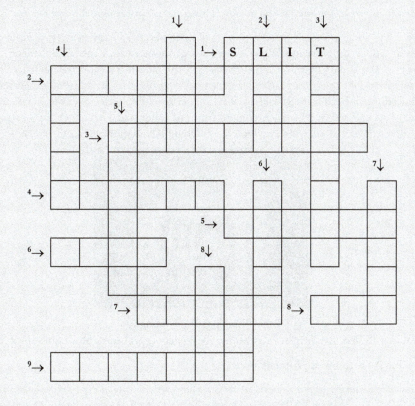

Clues:

Across	Down
1→ The cruel man .... open the stomach of the bird with a knife.	1↓ Please talk loudly, I can't .... you.
2→ The past participle form of CHOOSE	2↓ The past/past participle form of this verb is LED

3→ Hunting animals is .... in India.

3↓ Last Sunday, the DD Sports channel .... the match live.

4→ The past/past participle form of GRIND

4↓ The past form of the verb CLING

5→ The past participle form of ARISE

5↓ Much water has .... under the bridge since then.

6→ Our plane ....over the Shivalik hills.

6↓ The past form of 5→

7→ She has .... her sufferings with great dignity. (the base form of this verb is BEAR)

7↓ The past/past participle form of KNEEL

8→ Past/past participle form of CUT

8↓ The past /past participle form of BREED

9→ Past form of FORBID

2. Strike off the errors in the following passage. There are 12 errors and all of them are about verbs:

Yesterday, I had some work in Kharagpur, a small town about 130 km away from Kolkata. I start from my house at 6.00 in the morning. While I drive along Alipur Road, I saw an old friend, Tausif. He was wait for a bus. Tausif didn't saw me, but fortunately, I saw him. It is a happy coincidence; Tausif too went to Kharagpur. So he get into my car and we start chatting. We had breakfast at a roadside eatery. Tausif didn't allowed me to pay for the breakfast. While we crossed the bridge over the Rupnarayan River, a car just ahead of us collided with a vehicle coming from the other side. Fortunately, no one is hurt. But there was a massive traffic jam after the accident. We reaching Kharagpur only in the evening.

Main Building, IIT Kharagpur
Source: CC BY 2.5, https://commons.wikimedia.org/w/index.php?curid=1760532

3. Fill in the blanks with the appropriate options:

   i. It has been raining heavily since last week. The dam .... (1) bursts (2) has burst
   ii. We .... in New Delhi from 2005 to 2006. (1) lived (2) have lived (3) were living
   iii. .... News from all corners of the country .... bad. (1) was (2) were
   iv. .... (1) The luggages were (2) The luggage was heavy.
   v. The police .... for a dangerous criminal. (1) were searching (2) was searching
   vi. Those days, I .... to office by bus. (1) was going (2) used to go
   vii. Mr Mohanty .... the hotel just a while ago. (1) had left (2) has left (3) is leaving

    viii. We saw a meteor when we ………… the field. (1) had crossed (2) crossed (3) were crossing

    ix. We missed the train because we ………… stuck in a traffic jam. (1) were (2) had been (3) have been

    x. I was tired as I ………… for three hours. (1) played (2) 'd played (3) 'd been playing

4. Rita had an interview for a job. Here are some of the questions the interviewers asked her. Write down the possible answers based on the following information:

Rita was born in Lucknow. When she was five, her family moved to New Delhi where she studied at a Kendriya Vidyalaya. She is a BTech in computer science and technology from IIT Kanpur.

Interviewer:	Good morning, Rita. What are your educational qualifications?
Rita:	A. Good morning, sir. I ....
	....
Interviewer:	From which university?
Rita:	B ....
	....
Interviewer:	What was your specialization in BTech?
Rita:	C ....
Interviewer:	Tell us something about your childhood.
Rita:	D ....
	....
	....
	....

5. Write down the questions for the following answers:

    i. Where …………… you ……………… ? I was born in Lucknow.

    ii. At which school ………………………… ? I studied at a Kendriya Vidyalaya in New Delhi.

    iii. When/In which year ………………… ? I did my higher secondary in 2002.

    iv. …………………………………… ? I studied Hindi, English, maths, physics, and chemistry.

    v. …………………………………… ? I scored 84% in higher secondary.

    vi. …………………………………… ? I did my BTech at IIT Kanpur.

6. Fill in the blanks with the verbs given within brackets. This story is about an incident that took place in 2006. Naturally, you have to use past forms: *the simple past, the past continuous, the past perfect, and the past perfect continuous.* There may be more than one correct answer for some of the blanks:

Chhatrapati Shivaji Terminus

Source: CC BY-SA 3.0, https://commons.wikimedia.org/w/index.php?curid=21159792

It .... (happen) in 2006. I was to visit Gwalior on a holiday. While I .... (go) to the station, our bus .... (have) an accident. I just .... (manage) to reach the Chhatrapati Shivaji station in time. It .... (rain) when I reached the station. And then, I suddenly .... (realize) that I .... (leave) the ticket behind at home.

I .... (telephone) home. But no one .... (pick up) the phone. Actually, my mother and father .... (watch) TV and so .... (not hear) the phone.

Fortunately, after some time, my father left the drawing room to make tea and .... (hear) the phone ringing. He immediately rushed to the station, but .... (cannot) reach in time.

In the normal course, the train should have left by then, but a strange thing .... (happen) in the meantime. Shortly before the train was to leave, someone .... (notice) an abandoned bag in a compartment.

A few months earlier, there .... (be) a series of bomb blasts in some local trains in Mumbai. Over 200 innocent people .... (lose) their lives that day. The memory of that tragedy .... (be) still fresh in people's minds. Naturally, the passengers .... (panic) and .... (get off) the train. Policemen immediately .... (come in) with sniffer dogs. They cordoned off the platform and .... (search) the bag carefully.

Fortunately, they .... (find) only two coconuts. That .... (delay) the train and I could travel that day.

7. In about 250 words, describe when and where you went on your last vacation, who accompanied you, how you travelled, how the journey was, whether you liked the places you visited, and so on.

8. Think of an interesting incident in your life and write it down within approximately 250 words.

PART

4

THE FUTURE AND A LITTLE MORE

Talking About the Future

Learning Objective: In this chapter, we will check the different grammatical forms we use to talk about the future.

26.1 THE FUTURE IS UNCERTAIN

Until now, we have been discussing the past and the present times. Some of the forms that we have learnt so far are given below:

When We Talk About	We Use	For Example
A habitual action in the present	The simple present	I study English. / I go to office by bus.
An action that is not over yet	The present continuous	I'm reading a book on learning English.
Something that has happened recently	The present perfect	I've just done a test on tenses.
The past in general	The simple past	I didn't study English at college.
A past event	–do–	I saw a film last night.
An incomplete action in the past	The past continuous	I was reading when the phone rang.
A habitual action in the past	The *used to* form	I used to go to school by bus.
An earlier past	The past perfect	When I went to bed last night, I had completed Chapter 25.
An earlier past event spread over some time	The past perfect continuous	I was tired as I had been reading continuously for six hours.

As we can see, the rules regarding the forms of verbs for the present and past are clear and straightforward. However, when we talk about the future, there are quite a few variations. You will see the variations in this passage from Ravi's diary. (As you read, underline the verbs that talk about the future.)

Friday, 16 February 2018: At last, my leave has been sanctioned. We are going to spend a week in Santiniketan. We'll be visiting Dubrajpur too. We are starting tomorrow and our train leaves at 6. Oh! It's already 10 PM! I'll reserve a hotel room over the Internet.

Rohan will be 4 next Monday. We are going to have a small party after we return. Next year, we will celebrate his birthday in a big way.

I look forward to a great holiday. But there are two problems. First, the weather forecast says it might rain during the next few days. But weather forecasts are often wrong. Let's hope the weather will be fine. Second, the prime minister is to visit Shantiniketan next week. The place will be crowded with policemen, and we may not be able to move around freely. Anyway, we'll cross the bridge when we get to it.

The highlighted verbs talk about the future. As you can see, Ravi has used several forms to talk about the future, and not many of the sentences are in the simple future tense:

Form	Examples	We Use This to Talk About
The **be going to** form	✓ We <u>are going to spend</u> a week in Santiniketan. ✓ We <u>are going to have</u> a small party.	Planned future actions. We **do not** use *will* here.
The **present continuous**	✓ We <u>are starting</u> tomorrow.	Planned future actions by individuals
The **will be doing** form	✓ <u>We'll be visiting</u> Dubrajpur too.	Things that are likely to happen in course of events
The **simple present**	✓ Our train <u>leaves</u> at 6.00 in the morning.	Future events that are part of a time table
The **simple future**	✓ Next year, we <u>will celebrate</u> his birthday in a big way. ✓ Let's hope the weather will be fine. ✓ We'll cross the bridge when we get to it.	1. Our hopes and expectations[1]
	✓ Rohan will be four next Monday. ✓ The place will be crowded.	2. Things over which we have no control; neutral statements about the future
	✓ It's 7 PM now, I'll reserve a hotel room over the Internet.	3. Instant decisions
May and **might**	✓ It might rain during the next few days. ✓ We may not be able to move around freely.	Possibilities (We'll discuss this later.)
be to + base form of the verb	✓ The prime minister is to visit Shantiniketan next week.	Official plans and arrangements

As you can see, when we talk about the future, we use verbs in different forms. Remember that two structures may express the same idea.

---

[1] **expectation:** (noun) a hope that something good will happen.

26.2 THE SIMPLE FUTURE: FORMS

Verbs conjugate in the *simple future* tense in the following way:

✓ Positive: I/We/You/He/She/It/They + **will** + base form of verb.
✓ Negative: I/We/You/He/She/It/They + **will not/won't** + base form of verb.
✓ Questions:

   1. Seeking permission and offering suggestions:

      Shall + I/we/you/he/she/it/they + the base form of the verb

   2. In all other situations:

      Will + I/we/you/he/she/it/they + the base form of the verb

26.3 WHEN DO WE USE THE SIMPLE FUTURE?

As we have seen above, we use the **simple future tense** when we talk about:

1. Our expectations and predictions
2. The future in a neutral manner, or things over which we have no control
3. Instant decisions

ACTIVITY 1

The Earth in the Year 2100

Scientists say that about four billion (4,000,000,000) years from now, the sun will expand into a massive red star and destroy the earth. But our earth may be destroyed much earlier if we continue to play with its environment. Here are some of the predictions about the earth in the year 2100. Match the three parts and write down the predictions in complete sentences:

1. Earth's surface	will rise	completely
2. The North Pole	will be	any ice during summer
3. The mean sea level	will melt	by 50 to 100 centimetres
4. Rising sea waters	won't have	island like the Maldives
→ Himalayan snow caps	will submerge	warmer by 3 centigrade degrees compared to 1900
5. Perennial[2] rivers like the Ganga	will be able	in floods, storms and forest fires
6. Doctors	will drink	dry
7. But millions or people	will become	to cure cancer and AIDS
8. People	will die	desalinated sea water[3]

---

[2] **perennial:** (adjective) continuing for a very long time.
[3] **desalinated sea water:** sea water from which salt has been removed.

1. ....
2. ....
3. ....
4. ....

→ Himalyan snow caps will melt completely.

5. ....
6. ....
7. ....
8. ....

26.4 INSTANT DECISIONS/PLANNED ACTIONS

When we decide something <u>all of a sudden</u>, we use the **simple future tense**:

✓ Grandpa has fallen off the coconut tree. <u>I'll telephone</u> our family physician. Oh! It's 11 PM now. <u>I won't call</u> the doctor, <u>I'll go</u> to his house and since it's raining, <u>I'll take</u> an umbrella.

Compare these with a sentence that talks about a <u>planned future action</u>:

✓ Next week <u>I am going to take</u> grandpa to a hospital for medical check-up.

Table 26.1 explains the difference between the *simple future* and the *be going to* form.

TABLE 26.1 Difference Between the Simple Future and the 'Be Going To' Form

Simple Future		Be Going to Form	
Okay, I'll telephone Raghu.	← I decided to phone Raghu while I was talking to you	I am going to telephone Raghu.	← I decided to phone Raghu before talking to you
I'll take grandpa to a doctor.	← Something has happened suddenly. An instant decision	I am going to take grandpa for a check-up.	← A planned future action
No, we won't accept the proposal.	← We've heard about it just now. An instant reaction	We are going to reject the proposal.	← A considered decision

Note: Both the following forms are used to talk about a planned action by individuals: *I am going to buy* a car/*I am buying* a car. These forms are often interchanged. When we talk about plans made by individuals.

ACTIVITY 2

I Will … or I Am Going To …?

Delete the incorrect options:

1. Someone is knocking. **I'll open/I am going to open** the door.
2. The food is done, **I'll turn off/'m going to turn off** the gas.
3. I **will spend/am going to spend** a week in Goa. (Arrangements have been made.)
4. Grandma has fallen down. I'll **call/am going to call** a doctor.
5. I have an exam next Monday. I **will study/am going to study** hard during the weekend.

26.5 IT'S GOING TO RAIN

In Activity 1, you framed sentences about some scientific predictions. These are in the *simple future tense*. However, when we predict an event based on some evidence, we often use *be going to* form:

✓ The sky is overcast. It <u>is going to</u> rain.
✓ From the president's speech, it is clear that the USA <u>is going to</u> veto the proposal at the UN.

26.6 THE SIMPLE PRESENT TENSE TO TALK ABOUT THE FUTURE

We use the *simple present* form to express a future event that is a part of a timetable:

✓ Our train <u>leaves</u> at 10 AM tomorrow.
✓ The school <u>reopens</u> the day after tomorrow.

26.7 THE PRESENT CONTINUOUS TO TALK ABOUT THE FUTURE

We also use the *present continuous* to talk about things we have planned to do in the future: (As

---

Millions **and** *Billions*

A million is 1,000,000. A billion is one thousand million or 1,000,000,000. And a trillion is 1 followed by 12 zeros.

We say *10 or 20 thousand* without a final *s*. But when we don't specify the exact number, we say: ***thousands*** *of people*.

Similarly, we say *one million, two billion or six trillion*, without a final *s*: *There are **six billion** people in the world.*

But when we don't specify a figure and only wish to express the idea of a very large number, we say: ***millions*** *of people,* ***trillions*** *of stars*.

Will **or** *Shall?*

At school, many of us learned that in British English, ***shall*** was used with *I* or *we*, and ***will*** with *you, he, she, it,* or *they*.

➤ I shall be back before dinner./She will be late./Some friends will join us.

While expressing a strong desire or instruction, traditional rule was that ***will*** was used with *I* and *we*, while ***shall*** was used with *you, he, she, it,* or *they*.

➤ I will not tolerate this. Or: I won't tolerate this.

already mentioned, there is little difference between this and the *be going to* form.)

✓ I am meeting my girlfriend tomorrow. She is joining a university next July. We are getting married next year.

However, this is valid only for plans made by individuals. If the subject of the sentence is an organisation, we use the 'be going to' form alone.

✓ SriLankan Airlines are going to buy IO aircraft.
✗ SriLankan Airlines ~~are buying~~ IO aircraft.

➤ You shall not see that film.

English has changed. These rules are no longer valid outside law courts. In modern English, ***shall*** and ***will*** are used more or less interchangeably in statements (both positive and negative). Also, ***shall*** is used less frequently of late. We usually say: *I will look into these points.*

In questions, we use ***shall*** <u>only</u> to seek permissions or to offer suggestions:

➤ <u>Shall</u> I go now? (seeking permission)/ <u>Shall</u> I make some tea? (a suggestion)

But in all other questions, we use ***will***:

➤ When I was just a little girl/I asked my mother, 'What <u>will</u> I be? <u>Will</u> I be pretty, <u>will</u> I be rich?' …

ACTIVITY 3

Fill in the blanks with the correct form of the verbs given within brackets:

1. Twenty MLAs have resigned. The government _____. (fall)
2. There is a deep depression over the Arabian Sea. It _____ in Mumbai. (rain)
3. The policeman doesn't even listen to me. He _____ us. (not help)
4. The meeting _____ at 9.00 in the morning. (begin)
5. The chief minister _____ the trade fair tomorrow. (inaugurate)
6. I _____ a university next month. (join)

▰ PRACTICE

1. Complete the rules by filling in the blanks with one of these: the **simple present**/the **simple future**/ the **be going to** form/the **will be doing.**

   a. We use _____ to talk about planned future actions.
   b. To talk about things that are going to happen in course of events, we use _____ form.
   c. When we talk about future events that are part of a timetable, we often use _____ form.
   d. When we talk about likely future events over which we have no control, we use _____ form.

2. Here are some sentences about the future. Complete them using one of these forms: *simple present, present continuous, simple future,* and *be going to.* Use the verbs given within brackets:

   a. The fortune teller says Tania _____ a doctor. (become)

b. The sun _____ into a giant red star after four billion years. (turn)

c. I think East Bengal _____ the National Football League this year. (win)

d. The film _____ at 6.30. (begin)

e. We _____ Agra next Sunday. (visit)

f. A message? Please hold the line for a moment, I' _____ a pen and paper. (get)

g. The farmers are angry and desperate. There' _____ trouble in the village. (be)

h. The Venezuelan prime minister _____ India next month. (visit)

i. I think Mandira _____ the Indian women's cricket team someday. (lead)

j. The sky is overcast. It _____. (rain)

k. The storm has passed. It' _____ a sunny day. (be)

l. The room is stuffy. I' _____ the window. (open)

3. Here is a list of things that have been planned. Rewrite the plans following the example given below:

→ Raju   join   college   next month   → Raju is joining college next month.

a) I   buy   a flat   next year   → ....
b) Our club   organize   a picnic   on 1 Jan   → ....
c) Abhishek   act   next film   of Karan Johar   → ....
d) Coca-Cola launch   a new soft drink   → ....

4. It's an hour before your train departs. You are at the enquiry counter of the Jaipur railway station, trying to get some information. Complete the dialogue. You may or may not use these verbs: *travel, be, be, arrive, have, check, tell, be, be, receive, check,* and *come.*

You: Good evening, I .... to Ahmedabad by the Ashram Express tonight. .... the train on time?

Railway official: Yes, it ....

You: On which platform .... the train ....?

Railway official: Platform no. 1.

You: I .... an unconfirmed ticket .... you please .... the present status?

Railway official: Yes, of course. Please .... me your PNR number.

You: It's 450-3522494.

Railway official: Your reservation .... confirmed, sir. Coach S-10, berth 72.

You: Thank you. Where exactly .... coach S-10?

Railway official: We ....n't .... the position of the coaches yet. I'll be able to tell you only after some time.

You: At what time .... I .... with you again?

Railway official: Please .... back around 7.30.

5. Write down five things that you *have planned to do* in the next 12 months.

....
....
....
....
....
....
....

....
....
....
....
....
....
....
....
....
....
....

KEY TO ACTIVITIES

Activity 1: 1. Earth's surface will be warmer by 3 centigrade degrees. 2. The North Pole won't have any ice during summer. 3. The mean sea level will rise by 50 to 100 cm. 4. Rising sea waters will submerge islands like the Maldives. 5. Perennial rivers like the Ganga will become dry. 6. Doctors will be able to cure cancer and AIDS. 7. But millions of people will die in floods, storms, and forest fires. 8. People will drink desalinated sea water.

Activity 2: 1. Someone is knocking, I'll open the door. 2. The food is done, I'll turn off the gas. 3. I am going to spend a week in Goa. 4. Grandma has fallen down. I'll call a doctor. 5. I have an exam next Monday. I am going to study hard during the weekend.

Activity 3: 1. Twenty MLAs have resigned. The government is going to fall. 2. There is a deep depression over the Arabian Sea. It is going to rain in Mumbai. 3. The policeman doesn't even listen to me. He is not going to help us. 4. The meeting begins at 9.00 in the morning. 5. The chief minister is to inaugurate the trade fair tomorrow. 6. I am going to join (or am joining) a university next month.

27

I'll Be Travelling Next Saturday

Learning Objective: This chapter discusses the grammatical form we use to talk about an incomplete event in the future.

27.1 INTRODUCTION

Read this dialogue between two friends and underline the verbs:

Tania: We are going to demonstrate in front of the principal's office tomorrow. Would you join us?
Alverin: Sorry, Tania. I'll be travelling tomorrow.
Tania: Where are you going?
Alverin: To my home in Shillong. I'll be spending a week there. What are you demonstrating against?
Tania: Don't you know? The principal says we can't come to college in jeans.
Alverin: What a shame!

Let's focus on the following sentences that talk about the future:

1. We are going to demonstrate ....   → We use this form to talk about planned actions [Chapter 26]
2. I will be travelling tomorrow.   → We are going to discuss this form in this chapter
3. I'll be spending a week in Shillong.

The last two sentences are in the future continuous. And the form is:

I/We/You/He/She/They	**will be/'ll be**	**travelling/spending** a week in Shillong/**sleeping**

We use this form in two situations:

- ✓ To talk about future actions in progress
- ✓ To talk about events which are likely to happen during the course of other actions [See Section 26.1]

27.2 ACTIONS THAT WILL BE IN PROGRESS IN THE FUTURE

We use the future continuous to talk about a future situation when we will be in the middle of an action:

- ✓ Alverin will be travelling tomorrow.
- ✓ The students will be demonstrating when the principal arrives tomorrow.

Compare these sentences:

1. The students will demonstrate tomorrow. → A neutral statement about the future
2. The students will demonstrate when the principal arrives tomorrow. → The students will start demonstrating **after** the principal arrives.
3. The students will be demonstrating when the principal arrives tomorrow. → Describing the course of a future event. The students' demonstration will start **before** the principal arrives and will continue **thereafter**.

Here is a comparison of the continuous tense in the past, present, and future:

Past Continuous	Present Continuous	Future Continuous
The students were demonstrating when the principal arrived.	The students are demonstrating outside the principal's office now.	The students will be demonstrating when the principal arrives tomorrow.
Raghu was sleeping when I went to his house.	Raghu is sleeping at the moment.	Raghu will be working this weekend.

ACTIVITY 1

Will Do or Will Be Doing?

Select the right option:

1. Forty fighter aircraft will fly past/will be flying past during the Republic Day parade.
2. An army band will play/will be playing when the defence minister arrives.
3. Our anti-aircraft guns will fire/will be firing if enemy aircraft attack us.
4. Hundreds of army tanks will move/will be moving towards the battlefield through the night.

27.3 A FUTURE ACTION IN THE COURSE OF DOING SOMETHING ELSE

We also use the present continuous tense when we talk about events that are likely to happen in the course of another action or things in general. [We have already seen this in Chapter 26.]

✓ Alverin is going to Shillong, she will also be visiting Guwahati. → The second action will happen in the course of the first action.
✓ I am going to join a Spanish course. I'll also be buying a tutorial[1] on the Spanish language.
✓ I am taking my grandpa for a check-up tomorrow. He'll be undergoing an MRI[2] scan.

ACTIVITY 2

Given below are some incomplete sentences. Complete them using the hints given within brackets:

a. I'm going to buy a second-hand car. And I' _____ (give) it a fresh coat of paint.
b. Next week, we are driving down to Puri in my 'new' car. We'll also _____ (visit) Konark.
c. We are visiting the Chilika Lake too. We' _____ (watch) dolphins in the lake.
d. We _____ (return) on the 20th of December.

PRACTICE

1. Fill in the blanks with the appropriate forms of one of these verbs: *play, take on,* and *watch*.

Ravi: George, would you like to join us for dinner tomorrow?
George: Sorry, Ravi. Tausif and I .... be .... a football match tomorrow evening.
Ravi: What match?
George: Don't you know? Lionel Messi .... in Kolkata.
Ravi: Messi?
George: Yes, Messi. Argentina .... Venezuela in a friendly match here.

2. Fill in the blanks with appropriate forms of the verbs given within brackets:

(i) It's sad that you can't come to the party. We' .... you. (miss)
(ii) I will be in Lucknow for a week. I guess I' .... biriyani every day. (eat)
(iii) I am going to buy a DVD player next month. And I' .... as many Charlie Chaplin films as possible. (buy)
(iv) We are .... a week in Delhi. We' .... also .... to Agra. (spend/go)
(v) 'I .... at Paris for a day on my way to New York.' —'............ you .... the Louvre?' (stop/visit)
(vi) Grandpa will be admitted to hospital tomorrow. He .... an MRI scan. (undergo)

KEY TO ACTIVITIES

Activity 1: 1. Forty fighter aircraft will fly past during the ... parade. (The duration of the fly past will be less than the duration of the parade.) 2. An army band will play/will be playing when the defence minister

---

[1] **tutorial:** (noun) a short book or computer program that gives information on a particular subject.

[2] *MRI* or *magnetic resonance imaging* is a medical imaging technique used to visualize detailed internal structures of patients.

arrives. (Both possible: 'will play' if the band starts playing when the defence minister arrives. 'Will be playing' if the band starts playing before he arrives, and continues thereafter.) 3. Our anti-aircraft guns will fire if enemy aircraft attack us. 4. Hundreds of army tanks will be moving … through the night.

Activity 2: a. And I'll be giving it a fresh coat of paint. b. We'll also be visiting Konark. c. We'll be watching dolphins in the lake. d. We will be returning on the 20th of December.

28

The Future Is Perfect

Learning Objective: What kind of language do you use to talk about completion of an event at a future time? We are going to check it in this chapter.

28.1 I WILL HAVE REACHED JAIPUR BY TOMORROW AFTERNOON

What is the difference between these statements?

- I'll reach Jaipur at 6:00 in the morning tomorrow.
- I will have reached Jaipur by 6 AM tomorrow. Can you please arrange a taxi?

The first sentence is about a likely future event: about reaching Jaipur at a particular time. In the second, the emphasis is on the completion of the journey. We use the latter form *when we talk about completing an action in the future*. It is known as the **future perfect tense**. The form is:

I/We/You/He/She/It /They + **will have** + **the past participle form of the verb.**

28.2 A HOUSE UNDER CONSTRUCTION

Lucky Singh is a contractor who is building a house for Kartar Singh. The house is almost ready. One day, they are discussing the progress of the work:

Kartar Singh: When can I move into my new house, Lucky Singh?
Lucky Singh: Well, the plumbers will have fitted the bathroom fixtures by Monday. The painters also will have finished by then. The carpenters will have made the cupboards by next Thursday. I'll hand over the house to you before the end of next week.

Kartar Singh: But Lucky Singh, didn't you say the same thing last week, and the week before?

Lucky Singh: Yes, sir, I did. But you know, everything is in god's hands.

Kartar Singh: I hope god <u>will have completed</u> the work before the next weekend, even if you don't.

Note: We often use phrases such as *by midnight, by then,* and *before the weekend* with this form.

Let me give you another example. Once you have read this book and completed the exercises:

- ✓ You will have learned how to write proper English sentences.
- ✓ To a lesser extent, you will have learned how to speak in English.
- ✓ Your vocabulary will have improved significantly.

ACTIVITY 1

Answer the following questions, taking a cue from the model given:

→ An aircraft has taken off from the Bagdogra airport at 10 AM. If the flight takes 45 minutes, by what time will it have reached Kolkata?	The aircraft will have reached Kolkata by/ at quarter to 11:00.
1. Aju is an upholsterer. He has an order for stitching 12 cushions. It's 10 AM now. If Aju takes 30 minutes to stitch one cushion, by what time will he have completed the work?	He will have ....
2. And how many cushions will he have stitched by 11 AM?	....
3. Dr Ram, an eye surgeon, has started an operation at 8.00 in the morning. If the surgery takes one hour, by what time will he have completed it?	.... in the morning.
4 It's Saturday morning. We have just commenced a journey from Kolkata to Delhi. The distance is 1,500 km. If we drive 750 km every day and rest at night, when will we reach Delhi?	You .... by Sunday evening.

28.3 THE PRESENT PERFECT, THE PAST PERFECT, AND THE FUTURE PERFECT

Here is a comparison:

Present perfect: I have just done my homework.

Past perfect: When my tutor arrived, I had done my homework.

Future perfect: I will have my done my homework by tomorrow morning.

PRACTICE

Here are some predictions made by scientists about what the world will be like in 2100. Rewrite these following the model given. (Note: 'in the year 2100' is replaced by 'by the year 2100' in the second column.)

→ In the year 2100, the earth's surface will be warmer by 3°C compared to what it was in 1900.	By the year 2100, the earth's surface will have become warmer by 3°C compared to what it was in 1900.
1. In the year 2100, the mean sea level will rise by 50 to 100 cm.	By 2100, the mean sea level will have ....
2. In the year 2100, the snow caps of the Himalayas will melt completely.	....
3. In the year 2100, perennial rivers like the Ganga will become dry.	....
4. By 2100, rising sea waters will submerge many islands like the Maldives.	....
5. By 2100, many low-lying coastal regions will go under water.	....
6. By 2100, doctors will invent medicines to cure cancer and AIDS.	....
7. But millions of people will die in floods, storms, and forest fires.	....
8. By 2100, the energy problem of the world will be solved.	....
9. In 2100, scientists will be able to produce electricity from water.	....
10. In 2100, human beings will set up colonies on the moon.	....

KEY TO ACTIVITY

Activity 1:

1. Aju will have completed the work by 4 PM. 2. He will have stitched two cushions by 11 AM. 3. Dr Ram will have completed the operation by 9.00 in the morning. 4. You will have reached Delhi by Sunday evening.

29

Academic Language

Learning Objective: In this chapter, we will discuss the vocabulary relating to higher education.

29.1 A STUDENT AND HER PROFESSOR

Academic means 'connected to education'. Read this conversation between a student and her professor and note the highlighted words, which are commonly used in a university. Try to guess the meanings of the unknown words from their contexts. Look up a dictionary only if you have to.

Professor	Good morning, Zemima. Have you written your **dissertation**[1]? The **deadline** isn't far off.
Zemima	Yes, sir. Actually, I **submitted** it online last night.
Professor	Sorry, haven't checked my mail this morning. Good! You're ahead of **schedule**.
Zemima	In fact, I could have **handed it in** even earlier. I **typed up** the **first draft** last week. But wasn't happy with it. So, I **revised** it thoroughly. Also, sir, I have some good news to share. I've been selected for a PhD programme.
Professor	That's wonderful. Congratulations! What will be your **area of research**?
Zemima	I don't know yet, but I think I will select a topic around Pakistani novelists in English.
Professor	That should be interesting. What university are you going to?
Zemima	Professor Linda Jackson of North American University has agreed to be my **research guide**. They have a track for **transcultural studies** and I think my research interests should fit in there. But it's a **provisional offer**. I can **enrol** only if I get a band score of 8 or above in the IELTS exam. Sir, could you please give me some tips on how to do well in IELTS[2]?
Professor	Well, you really don't have to worry about your language competency. But I would suggest you do some **mock tests**.

---

[1] **dissertation:** a long essay you write as part of your work for a degree.
[2] **IELTS:** the International English Language Testing System.

Zemima	Thank you. I will. And sir, I must thank you. I know that your **reference** has been a great help.
Professor	It might have been, but you've been selected because of your academic records and the impressive **SOP**[3] you wrote. When are you leaving?
Zemima	I think I'll leave in early September; before the **fall semester**[4] begins.
Professor	How will you **fund** your studies? Have you got a **scholarship**?
Zemima	No, but I've got **funding** from the university. They are giving me a **teaching assistantship**. I've also got an **award** for **coming at the top of my class** last semester. That should cover my airfare and the preliminary expenses.
Professor	That is wonderful. What will be your role as a **teaching assistant**?
Zemima	I am not quite sure, sir, but I guess I'll have to work as a **tutor** for **undergrad** students. And I might have to check exam papers too.
Professor	Where will you stay?
Zemima	From what I see on the Internet, the university has a beautiful **campus**. And they offer **accommodation** to students. I guess it shouldn't be a problem.
Professor	Of course, it won't be. Wish you all the best.
Zemima	Thank you, sir.

ACTIVITY 1

Solve the crossword with words you have read in the above conversation:

A1	The _____ DRAFT: A report or essay initially prepared, likely to be revised (5)
A3 & D6	A letter from a university saying they would admit you if you fulfil certain conditions (11, 5)
A4	A junior faculty member who supervises small groups of students; in the USA, an assistant lecturer at a college or university (5)
D1	Your _ _ _ _ of research is the field of your study, often for a PhD
D2	Money provided by a university or government to you for higher studies (7)
D3	The date by which you have to submit an assignment to your teacher (8)
D4	All the buildings and the area of a university (6)
D5 & A2	Not real, but you take them before an exam to prepare for the real one (4, 4)

---

[3] **SOP:** *Statement of Purpose* is a written account which you may have to submit while applying for admission at a university. Typically, it should cover your educational background and goals, and also, your interests in the field.

[4] **fall semester:** a **semester** is a half-year academic term in a university or college typically for 15-18 weeks. In America, the **fall semester** refers to the semester that begins in autumn, usually in September.

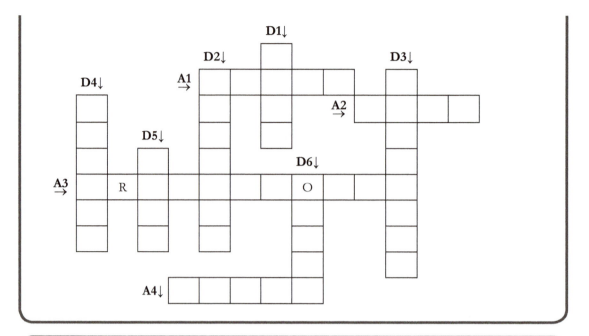

ACTIVITY 2

Read the dialogue in Section 29.1 again and write down the terms for the definitions given:

A. A long essay on a topic, which you submit as a part of your work for a degree (12 letters)	
B. To personally submit an assignment[5] to your teacher (4, 2)	(to)
C. When you key in any text in a computer or similar device, you are said to do this (4, 2)	(to)
D. Another word for a TIMETABLE (8)	
E. To go through what you have written in order to make it better (6)	(to)
F. A professor or senior teacher at a university who supervises your independent studies (8, 5)	
G. A letter from a teacher (or an employer) testifying someone's qualities and reliability (9)	

ACTIVITY 3

A. Write down the nouns for the verbs below:

1. renovate ⇨ renovation........................   2. accommodate ⇨ ....

---

[5] **assignment:** a task given to you as part of your course of study (or job).

3. assess	⇨	6. study	⇨ ....
4. refer	⇨	7. submit	⇨ ....
5. revise	⇨		

B. Fill in the blanks using *campus, deadline, dissertation, semester, tutor,* and your answers in Activity 3A:

I have a problem. My landlord wants my room back because he thinks his house needs urgent (1) .... I have to look for another apartment. I'll try for some (2) .... in the (3) .... It might be possible now because a new (4) .... begins next month, and a lot of (5) ....s will leave. But the problem is that the (6) .... for (7) .... of my .... is just 10 days away, and I have a lot of catching up to do. Also, I am a (8) .... for five undergrad students and I am compiling an (9) .... of their progress.

29.2 FALLING IN LOVE

This is how an Indian student studying in the USA talks about his recently developed interest in a new academic field. Strike off the incorrect option as you read:

Hi! I am Sendil from Chennai, India. I am doing my [1]**master's/post-graduation** in geology. At our university, every student has to study a subject from a different [2]**field/topic** each semester. This time, I have [3]**enrolled in/admitted to** a [4]**course/class** on the history of human civilization. A senior [5]**professor/lecturer** from Israel, Dr David Gelfand, is [6]**teaching/giving** the course. He is an authority on the subject. He also gives [7]**talks/speeches** at a local radio station every Sunday. In the university, it is fascinating to attend Dr Gelfand's [8]**lectures/talks**. For this course, there won't be an [9]**exam/assessment** at the end of the [10]**semester/year**. All we have to do is to summarize what we have learned and submit a short [11]**essay/thesis**. But I have fallen in love with the [12]**subject/topic** and I tend to spend more time on it than on geology. Next month, Dr Gelfand's department is organizing a series of [13]**seminars/symposiums** on genetic markers for small groups of students. I have volunteered to join and I look forward to the experience. On a longer timescale, I am seriously considering if I should move on to [14]**studying/learning** how geology shaped human history. Yes, that is going to be my [15]**subject/area** of research!

Key: [1]*master's (post-graduation* is a word used for a second degree only in South Asia. It is not incorrect, but in Standard International English, you say *master's degree* or *master's)*; [2]*field*; [3]*enrolled in*; [4]*course*; [5]*professor* (a *lecturer* is a junior teacher in a college or university); [6]*teaching*; [7]*talks*; [8]*lectures*; [9]*exam*; [10]*semester*; [11]*essay* (A *thesis* is a long essay which involves personal research.); [12]*subject*; [13]*seminar* (A *seminar* is a class at a university in which a teacher and a small group of students discuss a topic. *Seminar* also means a conference to discuss a topic on a larger scale.); [14]*studying* (*learning* is used in a more general sense, it does not refer to a course of study at a school or university.); [15]*subject*

ACTIVITY 4

What is the difference? In the first column of each textbox below, you will see some related terms. Write down what you understand by each of them. Follow the model given for 1 to 4:

1. article	A short write-up you often read in newspapers or magazines
2. essay	A composition in prose on a particular subject, which is analytical or interpretative.
3. dissertation	A long essay you write on a particular topic as part of obtaining a degree
4. thesis	A long essay which includes results of personal research, which has to be submitted to obtain a PhD

5. professor	
6. lecturer	
7. tutor	

8. university	
9. campus	

10. funding	
11. scholarship	

12. course	
13. lecture	
14. talk	

15. bibliography	
16. footnote/ endnote	
17. deadline	
18. target date	

19. class	
20. seminar	
21. (to) hand in	
22. (to) hand out	

KEY TO ACTIVITIES

Activity 1:

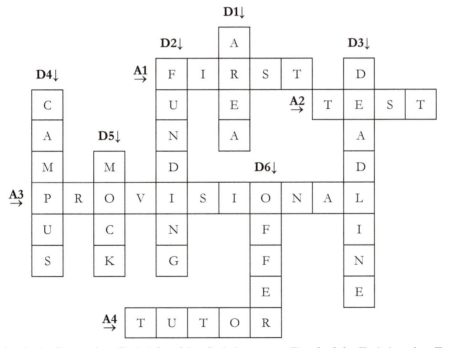

Activity 2: A. dissertation; B. (to) hand in; C. (to) type up; D. schedule; E. (to) revise; F. research guide; G. reference

Activity 3A: 2. accommodation; 3. assessment; 4. reference; 5. revision; 6. student; 7. submission

Activity 3B: (1) renovation; (2) accommodation; (3) campus; (4) semester; (5) students; (6) deadline; (7) submission; (8) tutor; (9) assessment

Activity 4:

5–7: Professor, lecturer, and **tutor:** In a university, a *professor* is a teacher of the highest rank; a *lecturer* too is a teacher, but he/she is relatively junior. In the USA, a tutor is an assistant lecturer in a university/college; however, elsewhere, a tutor is a teacher who personally supervises small groups of students.

8–9: University and **campus:** A university is a high-level academic institution which offers degrees. It runs courses and conducts research. All the buildings and grounds of a university or college is known as its *campus*. (You do not use *campus* for anything else. Don't say: ~~school campus~~ ✗; say: school compound.)

10–11: Funding and **scholarship:** *Funding* is money given by a government or any other body for a project or activity, not necessarily for an academic purpose. *Scholarship* is funding given by a university or some other organization to a student for his/her studies.

12–14: Course, lecture, and **talk:** A *course* is a programme of lessons on a particular area of study: *a course on evolutionary biology*. A *lecture* is an educational talk given to a class of students at university or college. A *talk* is an informal speech; it may or may not be in an academic context.

15–16: Bibliography and **footnote/endnote:** *Bibliography* is a list of books you have consulted for your research. You put it at the end of an essay, dissertation, thesis, or book. A *footnote* is a brief explanation of, or reference to, a point and it comes at the bottom of a page. (We have given meanings of difficult words as footnotes in this book.) An *endnote* is similar to footnote, but it comes at the end of an essay or a chapter in a book.

17–18: Deadline and **target date:** *Deadline* is the date by which a student has to submit an assignment or essay to a teacher. *Target date* too is a date by which you are expected to complete a task, but it may or may not be imposed by anyone from outside. You can set your own target date for completing a piece of work.

19–20: Class and **seminar:** A *class* is a group of students taught together. (Or a time when a teacher teaches some students, that is, a LESSON). A *seminar* is a class at a university in which a teacher and a small group of students discuss a topic. *Seminar* can also be an academic conference to discuss a topic on a larger scale.

21–22: Handing in and **handing out:** When a student completes a task, they *hand* it *in* to their teacher. On the other hand, a teacher *hands out* supplementary study material to students.

Test 4:
Can We Review[1] the Future?

1. Put these sentences in appropriate categories given below:

   A. I am going to join a university next year.
   B. I might join a university next year.
   C. It's hot. I'll open the window.
   D. Your train leaves at 6 AM tomorrow.
   E. The sky has turned cloudy. It's going to rain.
   F. Grandpa will turn 80 next June.
   G. Just seen an ad for a job. It seems good. I'll respond.
   H. I am going to upload my CV on a job portal.[2]
   I. The school reopens on the 1st of January.
   J. Rani's grandparents are arriving tomorrow.

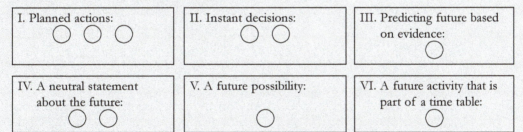

I. Planned actions: ○ ○ ○	II. Instant decisions: ○ ○	III. Predicting future based on evidence: ○
IV. A neutral statement about the future: ○ ○	V. A future possibility: ○	VI. A future activity that is part of a time table: ○

2. Correct the following sentences if there is any mistake. If a sentence is correct, put a ✓ next to it:

   a. I think Rita goes to college tomorrow.
   b. Her college reopens tomorrow after the winter vacation.
   c. Rita and I have booked tickets for the latest Vidya Balan film. We will see it next Saturday.
   d. Oh! I haven't signed the letter? Sorry, I am going to sign it in a moment.
   e. Thanks for your letter. I'm going to pass it on to my manager.

---

[1] **review**: (verb) to carefully examine or consider something again, especially to check if it is necessary to make changes.

[2] **job portal** : (compound noun) a website that collects information about jobseekers and places them with prospective employers. A portal is a website that serves specific purposes: *a business portal, a news portal,* and so on.

f.   The sky is dark, it's going to rain.
g.   I will have reach Jaipur by 4 PM tomorrow.
h.   I certainly might change my job next year.

3.   Fill in the blanks with the appropriate forms of the verbs given within brackets:

Rani's grandparents (a) .... (arrive) in Kolkata next week. Their train (b) .... (reach) Howrah station tomorrow at 3 pm. They (c) .... (come) to celebrate Rani's birthday. Rani (d) .... (be) 13 next Friday. Her parents (e) .... (organize) a birthday party. Many of Rani's friends (f) .... (attend) the party. If it doesn't rain, they (g) .... (have) the party in their garden.

4.   Given below are some planned actions, expectations, and possibilities about my future:

•   Planned actions: to retire next year/to build a new house in my village before I retire
•   My expectations, for which there are no definite plans: to visit Egypt and see the pyramids sometime after retirement/(hopefully) to read the complete works of Rabindranath Tagore after I retire/learn how to play the sitar/settle down in my quiet village with lots of books and a good music system/ no TV in my new house
•   Things that may or may not happen: putting my only son in a boarding school/visiting China

Imagine that you are on the verge of retirement. Write a paragraph about your plans, expectations, and possible scenarios based on the points given above.

I am going to retire next year. Before that ....
....
....
....
....
....
....
....
....
....
....
....
....
....
....

5.   Where do you see yourself after 10 years? What are your goals and how will you achieve them? Write 10 sentences about your dreams and plans.

....
....
....
....
....
....
....
....

....
....
....
....
....
....

PART
5

WHEN VERBS ARE NOT ALONE

Rani Loves Dancing

30.1 THEY LOOK LIKE VERBS BUT ACT LIKE NOUNS

We know that the +ing form of a verb is used in continuous tenses. For example: *Who is walking in the garden?* The +ing form can also be used as a *noun* or an *adjective*:

- ✓ <u>Walking</u> is good for health. (*Walking* is used as a noun here.)
- ✓ A <u>walking</u> doll. (*Walking* is an adjective here.)

> When the **+ing form of a verb** is used as a noun, it is called a ***gerund*** or ***verbal noun***.

In this book, we will call them gerunds.

30.2 GERUNDS AS OBJECTS OR COMPLEMENTS

Do you remember Rani, the daughter of Ravi and Radhika? Here are three things she loves.

1. Rani loves <u>chocolates</u>.
2. She loves <u>dancing</u>.
3. Her favourite pastime[1] is <u>reading</u>.

In the first sentence, I have used a **noun** to tell you what Rani loves *(chocolates)*. In the second, I have used a **gerund** *(dancing)* to say what she loves. Here, *dancing* is an object of the verb *loves*, just like the noun *chocolate* in the previous sentence. Remember that *a gerund is used like any other noun*. And in the third sentence, the gerund, *reading*, is used as a complement. [If necessary, please check the terms *object* and *complement* in Section 6.4.]

---

[1] **pastime:** (noun) something you enjoy doing in your free time, HOBBY.

We have seen that gerunds come after the verb *love*. But it is important to bear in mind that *they don't come after all verbs*. Table 30.1 lists some common verbs that are normally followed by gerunds:

TABLE 30.1   Verbs Frequently Used Before Gerunds

admit	avoid	burst out (crying/laughing)	(can't) help
consider	delay	deny	dislike
enjoy	face	fancy	feel like
finish	forgive	give up	imagine
keep, keep on	like, love, hate	mind	postpone, put off
practise	resist	stop	suggest

Read the following paragraph, and underline the verbs that are followed by gerunds:

Ravi used to smoke earlier and often suffered from cough and cold. One day, Radhika told him that unless he stopped smoking, she would walk out on him. After that, Ravi gave up smoking. Ravi is much healthier now and loves running, swimming, and other outdoor sports. Perhaps I have told you, Ravi also enjoys working with tools. He has just finished repairing his scooter.

ACTIVITY 1

Find out what Rani loves, dislikes, enjoys, and hates. Look at the pictures. carefully and complete the sentences with verbs and/or gerunds. (The first one has been done for you.)

→   Rani loves <u>chatting with</u> her friends.
1.   She l............ eating bread and jam.
2.   She enjoys l.............. t... music.
3.   She doesn't like w..................... for the school bus.
4.   She doesn't .... homework.
5.   And she h.............................. to school on Mondays.

| 1 | 2 | 3 |

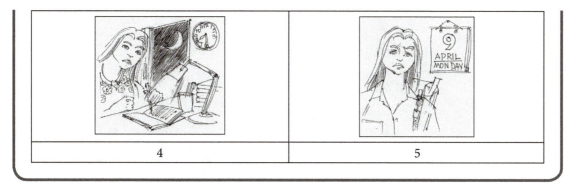

4	5

ACTIVITY 2

Read the sentences on the left and on the basis of them use a gerund to complete the sentence on the right:

Ravi used to smoke earlier.	a. Ravi has given up ....
He doesn't smoke any more.	
Ravi: What do we have for dinner?	b. Radhika suggested ....
Radhika: Nothing much. Let's eat out.	
Ravi: Do you want to go for Chinese food?	c. Radhika didn't fancy .... Chinese food.
Radhika: No, not really. I don't care much for Chinese.	
Ravi: Can you please wait for half an hour?	d. Radhika didn't mind .... for half an hour.
Radhika: No problem.	

30.3 MORE USES OF GERUNDS

Some nouns and adjectives can be followed by gerunds. In the following examples, the *nouns/adjectives* are connected to *gerunds* through *of* or *at:*

- ✓ The <u>idea of connecting people</u> is at the core of the Internet.
- ✓ The government has to tackle the <u>problem of rising prices</u>.
- ✓ I am <u>tired of reading</u> news about wars and disasters.
- ✓ Rani is <u>good at solving puzzles</u>.

Gerunds are also used to explain the purpose of an activity. Once, I went camping with Ravi, Radhika, and their friends in Bandipur. Here is a sample of the conversation that I heard shortly after reaching the camp site:

- ✓ I need a hammer <u>for fixing</u> the tent.
- ✓ Can you give me a knife <u>for cutting</u> vegetables?
- ✓ Do you have anything <u>for keeping</u> the vegetables?

[You can also say: I need a hammer to fix the tent. ... a knife to cut vegetables? Or ... have anything to keep the vegetables?]

ACTIVITY 3

Construct sentences with the following words. Add punctuation marks if necessary:

→   writing/stop/children
     ⇨ Children! Stop writing. (Your teacher never said, 'Children, stop to write.')

a.   writing/you/finished/have/the letter?
     ⇨ Have ....

b.   don't mind/I/extra work/doing
     ⇨ ....

c.   Rohan/good/solving/SUDOKU[2]'s/ at/is
     ⇨ ....

d.   I/of/boiled potatoes/tired/'m /eating
     ⇨ ....

e.   has/he/a habit/comments/unnecessary/making/of
     ⇨ ....

---

[2] **SUDOKU:** a number puzzle that originated in Japan; it has become popular all over the world.

f. me/please give/taking down the address/a pen/for
⇨ ....
g. reheating food/we/use/the microwave/for
⇨ ....
h. for/have you got/from clothes?/anything/removing/stain
⇨ ....

30.4 GERUNDS AS SUBJECTS

So far, we have used gerunds as objects or complements of verbs. They can also be the subject of a sentence:

✓ <u>Swimming</u> is good exercise.
✓ <u>Smoking</u> causes cancer.

In each of the following sentences, the subject is a gerund in combination with other words:

✓ <u>Waiting</u> for a bus makes me fidgety.[3]
✓ <u>Doing</u> exercise is good for health.

ACTIVITY 4

Make gerunds with these verbs and fill in the blanks: **drink, drive, eat, read, travel,** and **watch, watch.**

a. R.................... is perhaps the best pastime.
b. T...................... makes us wiser.
c. .... television has made us lazy.
d. .... television makes us better informed.
e. .... fried food is not good for health.
f. D.................... and d........................ don't go together.

30.5 I LOOK FORWARD TO MEETING YOU

When we expect something positive, we say: *I look forward to your reply.* Or: *I look forward to your phone call.*
   We also use a gerund after 'look forward to'. A common mistake is: *I look forward to meet you.* ✘
The correct form is: *I look forward to meeting you.* ✓
Here is a list of phrasal verbs that are followed by gerunds:

✓ look forward to (= think with pleasure about something you want to happen)
✓ get down to (= find the time to do something)

---

[3] **fidgety:** (adjective) (of a person) unable to remain still or quiet; RESTLESS.

✓ get round to (the same as *get down to*)
✓ object to
✓ (be) used to (= be familiar with)

For example:

✓ Sorry, I couldn't <u>get round to</u> writing the letter.
✓ I <u>objected to travelling</u> so frequently on office work.
✓ I <u>am not used</u> to typing.

30.6 YOU CANNOT USE GERUNDS AFTER CERTAIN VERBS

You do not use gerunds after some verbs such as *attempt, decide, forget,* and *plan.* It would be incorrect to say:

✗ She attempted ~~cooking~~ a curry without oil.
✗ He planned ~~telling~~ his son about his cancer.
✗ Do you want ~~going~~ to the toilet?

In the next chapter, we will discuss these verbs. Meanwhile, try to correct the above sentences.

PRACTICE

1. Do you like the activities shown in the pictures on next page? Write true sentences beginning with: **I love/I enjoy/I don't like/I hate/I don't care much for** (You can use these expressions more than once.)

A.

B.

C.

D.

E.

F.    G.

→ I hate riding a bike in cities. ....

A. ....

B. ....

C. ....

D. ....

E. ....

F. ....

G. ....

2. Kuttan's father, who is a school teacher, had the following conversation with him. Complete each sentence using one of the following verbs:

~~Check~~ close hear keep listen to make play sing sing spoil

Father: Last night, I couldn't finish checking the exam papers. Could you please stop .... so much noise?

Kuttan: I wasn't making noise, dad. I was singing. You know that I love ....

Father: You were singing? How could you play so many instruments?

Kuttan: The new music system that amma gave me has karaoke.[4] It is a system for .... the music as you sing along yourself. Now, whenever I feel like ...., I turn on the music too.

Father: That is most unfortunate, son. Your mother should stop .... you. And how can we avoid h.................... the noise?

Kuttan: OK, if you wish to deny yourself the pleasure of .... the finest of modern music, it's your problem! I won't sing when you are at home.

Father: No, not at all son. I only suggest k............................ the volume a bit low. And one more thing, would you mind .... the door when you sing?

Kuttan: Not at all, dad.

3. Think of someone close to you: a good friend, your husband/wife, or your child. Write a short passage about what he/she likes, loves, enjoys, or hates doing.

....

....

---

[4] **karaoke:** (noun) a machine that plays only the music of popular songs so that people can sing the lyrics along with the music; pronounced as KA-RI-**OU**-KI.

....
....
....
....
....
....

KEY TO ACTIVITIES

Activity 1: 1. loves eating; 2. enjoys listening to; 3. doesn't like waiting; 4. enjoy doing; 5. hates going

Activity 2: a. Ravi has given up smoking. b. Radhika suggested eating out. c. Radhika didn't fancy eating/ going for Chinese food. d. Radhika didn't mind waiting for half an hour.

Activity 3: a. Have you finished writing the letter? b. I don't mind doing extra work. c. Rohan is good at solving SUDOKUs. d. I am tired of eating boiled potatoes. e. He has a habit of making unnecessary comments. f. Please give me a pen for taking down the address. g. We use the microwave for reheating food. h. Have you got anything for removing stain from clothes?

Activity 4: a. Reading; b. Travelling; c. Watching; d. Watching; e. Eating; f. Driving, drinking

31

In Japanese, Ikiru Means to Live

31.1 IKIRU

Akira Kurosawa's *Ikiru* is one of the finest films I have seen. In Japanese, *ikiru* means *to live*. In English, phrases such as *to live* and *to die* are used as nouns. They are called *infinitives*.

- 'To' followed by the base form of a verb is known as the ***infinitive*** or the ***to infinitive***: *to live, to die, to say,* and so on. An infinitive may also stand alone (the ***zero infinitive***: *live, die,* and the like).
- Like gerunds, infinitives too behave like nouns.

31.2 THEY COME AFTER NOUNS, ADJECTIVES, AND SOME VERBS

Kanji Watanabe is a middle-aged man who has worked in the same boring bureaucratic position for decades. After learning he has stomach cancer and has less than a year **to live**, Watanabe attempts **to come** to terms with his impending death. He plans **to tell** his son about the cancer, but decides against it when his son doesn't pay attention to him. He then tries **to find** escape in the pleasures of Tokyo's nightlife, but after one night, he realizes it is not the answer. [*Source of information:* Wikipedia]

In the above passage, infinitives follow *year* (a noun) and the verbs *attempt*, *plan*, and *try*.

Remember that the infinitive follows nouns, adjectives, and only *some* verbs. The table below has a list of the common verbs that are followed by infinitives:

afford	agree	allow
arrange	ask	attempt
decide	fail	forget
hope	manage	mean
learn	need	offer
plan	promise	refuse
threaten	want	wish

You do not use gerunds *coming, calling, telling,* and the like [Chapter 30] after any of the above verbs. You do not say: *Watanabe attempts coming to terms* ✘ *… He plans telling his son about the cancer.* ✘ *… He tries finding escape in ….* ✘

If a verb has a direct object, the infinitive comes after the object.

1. Ravi's boss **allowed him to leave** early.
2. Radhika **asked Rohan to put** on the sweater.

There can be two negative forms of the second sentence, meaning different things.

1. Radhika **didn't ask** Rohan **to put** on the sweater.
2. Radhika **asked** Rohan **not to put on** the sweater.

31.3 GERUNDS OR INFINITIVES?

Gerunds and infinitives are used in similar ways. *A few* adjectives and nouns are followed by both gerunds and infinitives.

- ✓ It was nice meeting you. Also, ✓ It was nice to meet you.
- ✓ Give me a knife for cutting the cake. Also, ✓ Give me a knife to cut the cake.

The verbs given below are followed by both *gerunds* and *adjectives:*

begin	bother	continue
go	hate	intend
like	love	prefer
start		

And importantly, the meaning doesn't change whether you use a gerund or an infinitive after these verbs:

- ✓ I love <u>eating</u> mangoes. Also, ✓ I love <u>to eat</u> mangoes. (especially North American English)
- ✓ I didn't bother <u>telling</u> you. Also, ✓ I didn't bother <u>to tell</u> you.
- ✓ It started <u>raining</u>. Also, ✓ It started <u>to rain</u>.
- ✓ I prefer <u>eating</u> with a fork. Also, ✓ I prefer <u>to eat</u> with a fork.

Normally we don't use gerunds after verbs that already have an -ing.

- ✓ It was beginning <u>to rain</u>. Not: It was beginning raining. ✘

There are some verbs that are followed by both gerunds and infinitives, but they convey different meanings. For example:

- ✓ The children stopped <u>gathering</u> flowers when they saw a man coming.
- ✓ The children stopped <u>to gather</u> flowers. (= They stopped doing what they were doing to gather flowers.)

But for most verbs, adjectives, and nouns, you can either use gerunds or infinitives but not both. This is illustrated in the table below:

Gerunds **Follow Certain Verbs and Adjectives**	*Infinitives* **Follow Certain Verbs and Adjectives**
I <u>don't mind cooking</u> once in a while. (You don't say: I <s>don't mind to cook</s>….)	I <u>attempted to cook</u> a curry without oil (You don't say: I attempted <s>cooking</s>….)
He <u>considered telling</u> his son about his cancer.	He <u>planned to tell</u> his son about his cancer.
You have to <u>stop using</u> the library until you renew your membership.	Do you <u>want to use</u> the toilet?
This book <u>is</u> all <u>about learning</u> English.	I <u>will try to learn</u> English.

Unfortunately, there is no easy way to find out which verbs, adjectives, and nouns are followed by infinitives and which are followed by gerunds. You can only look up a good dictionary.

ACTIVITY 1

Fill in the blanks with 'to infinitives'. Use the following verbs: *book, select, disagree, go, go, lend, take,* and *visit.*

Ravi and his friends were planning to go on an excursion. Ravi wanted (a)…………… to Matheran, but George wanted (b)………………… Lonavla. George also said that he had a friend there and he could arrange (c)………………… rooms straight away. Another friend, Kartar Singh, fancied a trip to Goa. He even offered (d)……………… his minibus for the trip. But Anirudh said he couldn't afford (e)………………… leave. In the end, they agreed (f)………………… and decided (g)………………… a place by drawing lots.[1]

31.4 IS YOUR COFFEE TOO HOT TO DRINK?

We also use infinitives after some adjectives such as happy, pleased, and sad:

- ✓ I'm <u>pleased to meet</u> you.
- ✓ I was <u>surprised to see</u> our headmaster dancing at the disco.
- ✓ (I'm) <u>sad to say,</u> I'm on my way/Won't be back in many a day. [A Caribbean song]

To infinitives are often used after phrases such as *too hot, too cold,* and *too tired:*

- ✓ The coffee is <u>too hot to drink.</u>
- ✓ The water was <u>too cold to swim in.</u>

---

[1] **draw lots:** to decide something by randomly picking a card, number, or name.

To infinitives are also used after an adjective + enough:

- ✓ Grandpa is **strong enough to carry** two suitcases.
- ✓ She is **young enough to be** his daughter.

ACTIVITY 2

Fill in the blanks with 'to infinitives'. Use the following: *enter, fall, find, see, see,* and *suspend.*

The boss was very angry (a) t......f......... Raghu sleeping at his desk, but he said nothing. When Raghu woke up, he was surprised (b)…….............. his boss sitting quietly in front of him. The boss said, 'Raghu, I am disappointed (c)…….............. that there is no change in you. I am forced (d)…….............. you. You won't be allowed (e)…….............. the office for a week and you won't get salary for the period.' Raghu said, 'Sir, please believe me. When I was a child, I was once bitten by a snake. Since then, I tend (f)…….............. asleep in the afternoon.'

ACTIVITY 3

From the given hints, write complete sentences in the simple present. You have to add either **too… to** or **enough to** at the right place. Follow the models given:

→ The dog/tired/wag its tail   ⇨ The dog is **too tired to wag** its tail.
→ Grandma/smart/travel alone   ⇨ Grandma is **smart enough to travel** alone.
1. She/exhausted/talk   ⇨ ....
2. Raju/strong/defend himself   ⇨ ....
3. Raghu/nervous/do well in the interview ⇨ ....
4. Your car/big/carry six people   ⇨ ....
5. Ravi/smart/operate any machine   ⇨ ....

31.5 TALKING ABOUT PURPOSE

We also use infinitives after nouns to indicate the idea of purpose:

- ✓ Kanji Watanbe learnt that he had stomach cancer and had less than a **year to live.**
- ✓ George brought his **car to take** Ravi to the railway station. Ravi took a **book to read** on the train. The train was usually crowded. He also carried a folding **stool to sit on.**

ACTIVITY 4

In the following table, the first column describes some actions and the second gives the purpose for the action. Match the columns and write complete sentences following the model given:

→ Please give me a knife	gather news
1. The robbers used a hammer	jot down your message
2. Please hold on for a second. I'll get a pen	→ cut the cake
3. I often use the Internet	take us to the airport
4. Please use a sharpener	break open the door
5. My friend is bringing his car	sharpen your pencil

→ Please give me a knife to cut the cake.

1. ....
2. ....
3. ....
4. ....
5. ....

31.6 THE ZERO INFINITIVE

The infinitives are not preceded by *to* if they come after some special verbs such as *feel, hear, see, help, let, make,* and *watch*. They are also referred to as *zero infinitives*.

✓ My boss **let** me **leave** early. (Compare with: My boss **allowed** me **to leave** early.)
✓ Ravi **helped** Radhika **fill in** the income tax return.

PRACTICE

1. Write 'T' in the box if the statement is true or 'F' if it is false:

   a. In a sentence, both gerunds and infinitives behave like nouns.
   b. All verbs can be followed by gerunds and infinitives.
   c. There are a few verbs that can be followed by either gerunds or infinitives.
   d. Only infinitives follow the verbs *forget, hope,* and *want*.

2. Correct the sentences if there is any mistake. If there is no error, put a ✓ next to it:

   a. Radhika has to attend a meeting at 9 AM. She needs leaving early.
   b. It's easy learning English.

   c. Rajiv has gone to the post office collect a parcel.

   d. I don't mind waiting for a short while.

   e. I was disappointed not seeing my name in the list.

   f. My boss let me to leave early.

   g. She was too exhausted for talking.

   h. I'm always happy to help.

3. Fill in the blanks with an appropriate infinitive. Use the verbs: *act, eat, eat, eat, entertain, extract, play, see, sit,* and ***bring.***

     Grandpa was going to his dentist (a) .... a painful tooth. On the way, he stopped at a restaurant (b) .... something. He was shocked (c) .... two tigers in the restaurant. It seemed the tigers wanted (d) .... some soup and pizza. One tiger asked his companion, 'Do you like the food?' His companion replied, 'The pizza is good, but the soup is too hot (e) ....' Grandpa is a brave man. He is also fit enough (f) .... kabaddi with young boys. But he was scared (g) .... in a restaurant along with two tigers. When the waiter came to take orders, grandpa told a white lie. He said, 'Sorry, I forgot (h) .... my wallet. I must go back.' The waiter said, 'Sir, please don't worry. They are not real tigers. They are employees of an amusement park. They are paid (i) .... like tigers. Their job is (j) .... children.'

▌KEY TO ACTIVITIES

Activity 1: (a) to go; (b) to visit; (c) to book; (d) to lend; (e) to take; (f) to disagree; (g) to select

Activity 2: (a) to find, (b) to see, (c) to see, (d) to suspend, (e) to enter, (f) to fall

Activity 3: 1. She is too exhausted to talk. 2. Raju is strong enough to defend himself. 3. Raghu is too nervous to do well in the interview. 4. Your car is big enough to carry six people. 5. Ravi is smart enough to operate any machine.

Activity 4: 1. The robbers used a hammer to break open the door. 2. I'll get a pen to jot down the message. 3. I often use the Internet to gather news. 4. Please use a sharpener to sharpen your pencil. 5. My friend is bringing his car to take us to the airport.

Verbs + Prepositions: Were You Waiting for This Book?

Learning Objectives: Often, verbs are combined with prepositions to describe specific actions. In this chapter, we are going to discuss these combinations or *prepositional verbs*.

32.1 VERB + PREPOSITIONS

As you are in Chapter 32, you must have gone through several chapters of this book. I am happy that you have come this far. And I would be happier if somewhere on the way, you thought, '*Ah! I was **waiting for** this book!*

We've seen that in many situations, a verb alone is pretty much useless. You need other words to give shape to your thoughts, like *wait for*. In this chapter, we are going to discuss *verbs* with *prepositions*. The first point to note is:

A preposition comes after a verb only if it has an object. If there is no object, the verb stands alone.

[What is an object? See Section 6.4.]

- ✓ *Please **wait for me*** (Not: *Please wait me*. ✗). However: *Please **wait**. (Not: *Please wait for*. ✗) Similarly,
- ✓ ***Listen to me!*** (Not: *Listen me*. ✗) Or: ***Do** you **listen to** Sufi music?* But you say, *I hear a strange sound. Please **listen**.*

In questions too, if there is an object, you put a preposition after the main verb:

- ✓ *What kind of music **do** you **listen to**?* (Here, **what** is the object of the verb **listen**. So, we add **to**.)
- ✓ *The office won't open today. What **are** you **waiting for**?* However: *The office won't open today. Why **are** you **waiting**?* (The verb **waiting** has no object.)

In English, a verb is usually followed by one or more specific prepositions:

- ✓ *You **write to** a friend and **go to** a meeting.* But
- ✓ *You **arrive at** a meeting.* And
- ✓ *You **arrive in** a city or country.* Recently I read this:
- ✓ *Roger Federer **arrived on** the world tennis scene in 1999.*

Therefore, the verb **go** is followed by **to,** and **arrive** can take three prepositions: **at, in,** and **on** to convey the same meaning in different contexts. Before we go into details, please read a passage from my diary. Focus on the verbs, and the prepositions that follow them.

My friend Volker[1] and his wife Linda <u>have come from</u> Germany on holiday. They <u>arrived in</u> New Delhi last night. Volker <u>phoned me</u> to say their flight <u>had been delayed by</u> six hours. They <u>reached</u> hotel after midnight. Tomorrow they <u>are driving to</u> Hardwar. They <u>are also visiting</u> Mukteshwar. They <u>are not going to</u> Agra because they <u>visited</u> the Taj last time. This Sunday, they <u>are coming to</u> our place. (I must not forget: They <u>are travelling by</u> the Rajdhani Express, which <u>reaches Kolkata</u> at 10:00 in the morning.) After spending a week with us they <u>will leave</u> Kolkata for Goa. They are <u>travelling to</u> different parts of India, and then <u>returning</u> home, that is, Munich, after three weeks.

This passage tells us a few things about combining verbs and prepositions.

1. When we talk about movement from one place to another, that is, *going, coming, travelling, driving, flying,* or *returning,* the verb is most often followed by **to:**

   ✓ They <u>are driving to</u> Hardwar. They <u>are not going to</u> Agra. They are <u>travelling to</u> different parts of India ….

2. But we **don't use** a preposition if we are *going home, abroad, somewhere, anywhere, here,* or *there:*

   ✓ They <u>will return home</u> after three weeks. Or: <u>Come home</u> for dinner.
   ✓ <u>I'm going abroad</u> next week on a business trip. (Not ~~going to abroad~~ ✗)
   ✓ Let's <u>go somewhere</u>. (Not Let's ~~go to somewhere~~ ✗)

3. The verbs *come* and *go* take quite a few prepositions other than *to:*

   ✓ They <u>have come from</u> Germany.
   ✓ They <u>have come on</u> a holiday. Also: They <u>are going on</u> a holiday.
   ✓ They <u>are going/coming by</u> the Rajdhani Express.

4. We use *by* after the verb *delay:*

   ✓ Their flight <u>was delayed by</u> six hours.

5. Between the verb *leave* and the place you are leaving, there is no preposition. Also, you leave a place *for* another place:

   ✓ They <u>will leave Kolkata for Goa.</u>

6. The verbs *call, phone, reach,* and *visit* do not take a preposition:

   ✓ Volker <u>phoned</u> me (Not phoned ~~to~~ me✗) You also say: he <u>called</u> me ….
   ✓ The train <u>reaches</u> Kolkata at 9 AM.
   ✓ They <u>will be visiting</u> Mukteshwar. (Not visiting ~~to~~ Mukteshwar ✗) …

---

[1] Pronounced FOLKAR.

To check what prepositions a verb combines with, that is, to check the *collocation* [Section 6.3] regarding prepositional verbs, you can check an online collocation dictionary.[2]

ACTIVITY 1

Nandini has sent this email from Hyderabad to her aunt in New Delhi. I have removed some of the prepositions from her mail. Put them back. Some of the blanks do not need any preposition. Put a '–' in them.

Dear Auntie,

I am writing this to tell you about my British friends, Vicky and Ann, who I met during a tournament in Colombo. They have come .... India .... holiday. They arrived .... Hyderabad last Sunday and are staying .... me now. They are visiting .... different places in India and are keen to see the Taj. They're also visiting .... New Delhi. Afterwards, they'll go .... Hardwar to watch .... Ganga Aarti there.

From Hyderabad, they are leaving .... New Delhi .... Golkonda Express next Saturday. They should reach .... New Delhi on Sunday morning. They are going to stay .... the International Youth Hostel in Naya Marg, Chanakyapuri. I've given your phone number .... them and asked them to call .... you after reaching .... Delhi. They are smart enough to take care of themselves, but just in case they needed anything, could you please help them? Love —Nandini

---

ACTIVITY 2: YOU KNOW QUITE A BIT, DON'T YOU?

Fill in the blanks with prepositions. If no preposition is required, put a dash:

My sister is suffering [1]............ kidney stone. Doctors are going to operate [2]............ her in a few hours. I am driving [3]............ the hospital, but I don't know when I will reach. It depends [4]............ the traffic. But I believe [5]............ God. I know that He will take care [6]............ all my problems. Oh! A procession is crossing [7]............ the junction. Can't see where it ends. I'll be late, but who can I complain [8]............?

32.2 A VERB TAKES SEVERAL PREPOSITIONS

As we have seen with *arrive*, a verb can take several prepositions to form different prepositional verbs (*arrive at, arrive in, arrive on*). Here are a few more:

- ✓ You **agree with** a person **on/about** something: *I agree with you about the need to change our approach.*
- ✓ You **agree to** a proposal or suggestion.
- ✓ You **ask about** something; you **ask for** something. You often begin official letters like this: *I am writing to ask for information about ….*

---

[2] For example: http://www.freecollocation.com/

✓ When you **apply for** a job, you **apply to** someone.

✓ That person **decides about** your application. I hope he/she will not **decide against** (= reject) you. Also: *We ~~decided against~~ moving to another house.*

✓ You **get off** a bus/tram/train/aircraft. And you **get on to** them.
Don't say: *I ~~got down from~~ the bus.* ✘   Say: *I got off the bus.*
Similarly: *I got onto the train, but couldn't find a seat.* (Not *~~into~~ a train.* ✘)

✓ Rather strangely, the form is different for taxis and cars: *You **get into** a taxi and **get out of** it.*

✓ When you **go into** something, it means you are examining it in detail: *Let me go into the sequence of events carefully.* **Going into** also means describing something in detail: *Just give me an overview, you don't have to go into details.*

✓ If you **go on** doing something, or if you **go on** with something, it means you continue to do it: *He went on solving old test papers.*

✓ You **know** a lot of things (generally); but you **know of/about** specific matters: *Do you know about Irfan's new job?* Or: *He knows a lot about music.*

✓ You also **pay** your employees and **pay** your rent and bills. However, you **pay for** a cup of tea; you also **pay for** your mistakes. You **pay by** cash or card.

Let's *look at* some more high-frequency[3] prepositional verbs:

✓ **apologize for:** *The hospital must apologize for their mistake.*

✓ **apologize to:** *The hospital must apologize to the patient.*

✓ **care for** (something) is commonly used to mean LIKE: *I love coffee, but I don't care much for tea.* Also: *Would you care for a discussion with Niki to understand the problems?*

✓ In a formal context, **care for** (someone) is also used to talk about helping others: *Ours is a voluntary organization. We care for elderly people.*

✓ **care about** (someone or something) = to worry or think about: *There's no point in **appealing to** this manager. I don't think he cares about employees.*

✓ **feel like** = want: *Do you feel like a cup of tea? —Yes, I do.*

✓ **look at** (something): *Look at the strange traffic light. It's pink!*

✓ **look for** (somebody or something) = try to find something, SEARCH FOR: *I am **looking for** my keys. Have you seen them?*

✓ You **study at** a college or university and you **study for** a particular degree or exam: *Tania studies at Cotton College. And at home she's studying for the IAS.*

✓ You **work for** a company, **work in** a place, and **work with** some people: *Sonal works for a primary school; she works with small children. She works in Karachi.*

ACTIVITY 3

Add *about, against, at, by, for, in, of, on, to,* and *with* to the verbs to form prepositional verbs you have come across in this chapter:

agree	1. agree with	2. agree to		know	1.	2.
apply	1.	2.		look	1.	2.

---

[3] **high-frequency:** (adjective) Something that is seen often.

care	1.	2.	pay	1.	2.
decide	1.	2.	wait	1.	

32.3 VERBS THAT DON'T TAKE PREPOSITIONS

In Section 32.1, we saw that the verbs *leave, phone, reach,* and *visit* are not followed by prepositions. We do not normally use prepositions after the following verbs either:

answer	approach	control	demand
discuss	enter	expect	request

- ✓ You **answer** the phone, not ~~answer to~~ the phone ✗
- ✓ You **discuss** an issue, not ~~discuss on / about~~ an issue ✗
- ✓ You **expect** a pay hike, not ~~expect of~~… ✗
- ✓ To work with us, **request** an application pack. Not ~~request for~~ an… ✗

ACTIVITY 4

Complete the conversation below using appropriate forms of the following verbs:

agree with	apply to	apply for	ask for	care about	decide about
decide against	kill by	look for	pay by	pay for	know about

Irfan: Raju said he would come to college. Have you seen him? I've been [f   ] him since morning. The exam fees are to be [   ] today. Tania just told me Raju hasn't paid yet.

Ramesh: I [k   ] the problem. Raju has [applied   ] a fee waiver.[4]

Irfan: Oh! I didn't know that.

Ramesh: Yes, he's [   ] to the principal.

Irfan: Has the principal [   ] about it?

Ramesh: Not yet, he has [a   ] Raju's mother's income certificate. But I am sure the principal will help. He [   ] about us.

Irfan: I am sure he does. Since Raju's dad was [   ] a drunk driver, his family has been struggling.

Ramesh: Yes. In fact, Raju is [   ] someone else's mistake.

Irfan: I completely [   ] you. And if unfortunately the principal [   ] [   ] helping Raju, we must do something quickly.

---

[4] a request for a *fee waiver:* An appeal to someone not to charge fees.

ACTIVITY 5

Correct the following. If a sentence is all right, put a ✓ next to it:

A.   I am expecting a call.
B.   In India, students stand up when a teacher enters into the classroom.
C.   The workers are demanding for a pay hike.
D.   After reaching New Delhi, my friend Volkar telephoned to me.
E.   When our train was approaching Patna, it started raining.
F.   We are discussing about a serious matter.
G.   I am going to ask you a question. Please listen me carefully.
H.   Can you hear a sound? Please listen to.
I.   'Is the train late?' — 'Yes, it is. Please wait for.'
J.   I requested for a copy of their brochure.

PRACTICE

1.   Put prepositions required in three sentences among the following and '–' in the others:

    i. Please answer............ my question.
    ii. We must approach............ the problem with an open mind.
    iii. We demand............ justice.
    iv. We do not enter............ a temple wearing shoes.
    v. I requested............ a day's leave.
    vi. There was a fire, but we managed to control............ it in minutes.
    vii. Do you still believe............ communism?
    viii. Let us discuss............ the problem of water shortage.
    ix. Please state the main points alone. Don't go............ details at this stage.
    x. He doesn't know when to stop. He just went............ and on.

2.   Select the correct preposition or no preposition (–):

    i. 'I am not done. Please wait <u>to/ – /for</u> me.
    ii. Sorry, I can't wait <u>to/ – /for</u> you.
    iii. The train is slowing down. We have to get <u>down/off</u> at this station.
    iv. Sonia got <u>onto/into/in/ – /within</u> the taxi.
    v. She asked <u>to/ –</u> the driver <u>to/ –</u> drive fast.
    vi. I love classical music, but I don't care much <u>in/ – /for</u> film songs.
    vii. Look <u>to/ – /at</u> me.
    viii. I apologize <u>about/for</u> the delay in getting back <u>at/to</u> you.
    ix. 'You are making a big mistake.' — 'I don't agree <u>for/ – /with</u> you.'
    x. 'You don't have to agree <u>to/ – /with</u>.
    xi. I have asked <u>– /on/for</u> a copy of their booklist.
    xii. I have requested <u>for/ – /about</u> a copy of their booklist.

3. Write sentences based on the hints given. You may have to add one of the following: *at, by, from, to,* and *with.*

→ Raju/has come/his hometown/Mumbai	
	→ Raju has come from his hometown to Mumbai.
A. He/is going/abroad/next week.	
B. He/arrived/Dadar/last night	
C. He came/his hometown, Durg	
D. His train was delayed/an hour	
E. Tomorrow/he is flying/Barcelona/Air India	

▍ KEY TO ACTIVITIES

Activity 1: They have come <u>to</u> India <u>on</u> holiday. They arrived <u>in</u> Hyderabad… and are staying <u>with</u> me now. They are visiting <u>=</u> different places in India…. They're also visiting <u>=</u> New Delhi. Afterwards, they'll go <u>to</u> Hardwar to watch <u>=</u> Ganga Aarti there. / From Hyderabad, they are leaving <u>for</u> New Delhi <u>by</u> Golkonda Express next Saturday. They should reach <u>=</u> New Delhi on…. They are going to stay <u>in/at</u> the International Youth Hostel…. I've given your phone number <u>to</u> them and asked them to call <u>=</u> you after reaching <u>=</u> Delhi.

Activity 2: 1. from; 2. on/upon; 3. to; 4. on; 5. in; 6. of; 7. –; 8. to

Activity 3: apply for, apply to; care about, care for; decide about, decide against; know of, know about; look at, look for; pay for, pay by; wait for

Activity 4:

Irfan:	… I've been looking for him ……. fees are to be paid by today.
Ramesh:	I know about the problem. Raju has applied for a….
Irfan:	Oh! I didn't know that.
Ramesh:	Yes, he's applied to the ….
Irfan:	Has the … decided about it?
Ramesh:	Not yet, he has asked for Raju's mother's income certificate. … He cares about us.
Irfan:	… Since Raju's dad was killed by a drunk driver ….
Ramesh:	… Raju is paying for someone else's mistake.
Irfan:	I completely agree with you. And if the principal decides against helping Raju….

Activity 5: A. ✔ B. … students stand up when a teacher enters ~~into~~ the classroom. C. The workers are demanding ~~for~~ a pay hike. D. After reaching New Delhi, my friend Volkar telephoned ~~to~~ me. E. ✔ F. We are discussing ~~about~~ a serious matter. G.…. Please listen **to** me carefully. H.… Please listen ~~to~~. I.…?—'Yes, it is. Please wait ~~for~~.' J. I requested ~~for~~ a copy of their brochure.

Phrasal Verbs: Don't Drop Off as You Read This

Learning Objectives: In this chapter, we are discussing phrasal verbs. These are often *idiomatic* and make your language sound *natural*.

33.1 PHRASAL VERBS, IDIOMATIC VERBS

In the two columns below, the same story has been told in two different styles. Which one is more natural, particularly when you speak?

I <u>fell asleep</u> as I was watching a test match on TV. When the telephone rang, I <u>awoke</u> with a jerk. It was Aunt Annie.	I <u>dropped off</u> as I was watching a test match on TV. When the telephone rang, I <u>got up</u> with a start. It was Aunt Annie.
'Hi Auntie, how are you?'	'Hi Auntie, what's new?'[1]
'Please <u>speak loudly</u>. Can't hear a word of what you're saying!'	'Please <u>speak up</u>! Can't hear a word of what you're saying!'
Well, it was an old problem. I said, 'Auntie, can you please <u>increase</u> the volume of your phone?'	Well, it was an old problem. I said, 'Auntie, can you please <u>turn up</u> the volume of your phone?'
She seemed confused, 'Increase the volume? A phone is not a radio, is it?'	She seemed confused, 'Turn up the phone? A phone is not a radio, is it?'
I <u>decided not to pursue the matter</u>. And shouted, 'It's OK. How are you?'	I <u>gave up</u>. And shouted, 'It's OK. How are you?'
'Wait, the water is boiling. Let me <u>deactivate</u> the oven …. And <u>your voice is getting interrupted</u>! Can you <u>return</u> my call in an hour?	'<u>Hang on</u>, the water is boiling. Let me <u>turn off</u> the gas …. And you're <u>breaking up</u>! Can you call me back in an hour?
She <u>disconnected</u>.	She <u>cut</u> me <u>off</u>.

---

[1] When you meet a friend or relative, you often ask, *How are you?* You can also say: *What's up?*, *What's new?*, *How's life?*, *How's everything?*, or *What's going on?*

Compare the underlined verbs in Column 1 and their equivalents in Column 2. The first column is written in formal language, while the second shows the language we use in informal speech. When you speak informally, you don't say, *I decided not to pursue the matter.* Instead, you often use **phrasal verbs**, like *I gave up.*

> A **phrasal verb** is a combination of a *verb* and *a small word, called an adverb particle*, such as *drop off, speak up, call back,* and *cut off.*

[In Chapter 32, we discussed *prepositional verbs*, which look very similar to *phrasal verbs*. The difference between the two is technical, and we won't go into it. Our focus is on using the language!]

Let's check some more phrasal verbs *in the context of telephone conversations*:

- ✓ **call up** = *I called up Inspector Bhola to thank him.*
- ✓ **call on** (someone) = to visit a person: *I called on Inspector Bhola to thank him.*
- ✓ **call at** = to visit a place: *I called at the police station last night.*
- ✓ **get through** = to connect with someone over the phone: *I've been calling the police station, but can't get through.*
- ✓ **hold on** = wait
- ✓ **put** (someone) **through** = to connect a caller with someone: *Can you hold on for a second? I'll put you through to Inspector Bhola.*

Some phrasal verbs are understood easily: *decide on/upon, fight with, go away,* and so on. However, most of them are **idiomatic**. They have a meaning different from the literal meaning of the words:

- ✓ **call off** = to cancel something: *Hardly any tickets were sold; the show was called off.*
- ✓ **come across** = find something or meet someone by chance: *Try to remember phrasal verbs when you come across them.*
- ✓ **look on** = to watch something without getting involved. *The policemen looked on as the ruffians harassed the elderly man.*
- ✓ **look out** = WATCH OUT: *Look out! That truck is turning right.*
- ✓ **look after** (someone or something) = to supervise or manage: *When Ravi and Radhika are away, a nanny looks after their children.*
- ✓ **look into** (something) = EXAMINE: *The manager should look into our complaint.*

If you use phrasal verbs while speaking, your language sounds natural.

ACTIVITY 1

Here are some sentences from conversations. Fill in the blanks with one of the following: **back, off, on, through,** and **up.**

i. Did you call ☐ the pharmacy?

ii. I tried to call, but couldn't get ☐.

iii. I could connect, but someone cut me ☐.

   iv. Could you put me [＿＿＿＿＿] to Dr Ram?
    v. Please hold [＿＿＿], I'll transfer the call in a moment.
   vi. Sorry, Dr Ram is in the surgery. Could you ring [＿＿＿＿] in an hour?
  vii. I can't hear anything. Can you please speak [＿＿＿＿]?
 viii. Neither can I hear you. You are breaking [＿＿＿＿].

33.2 MULTIPLE MEANINGS

Here are some phrasal verbs which have two or more meanings:

- ✓ **look up** = (1) to improve: *The economy has been <u>looking up</u> since the new finance minister <u>took over</u>.* (2) to check for something in a list, book, and the like: *What is a phrasal verb? <u>Hang on</u>, let me <u>look up</u> in a dictionary.*
- ✓ **drop off** = (1) to fall asleep: *I often <u>drop off</u> when I try to read serious stuff, but please don't <u>drop off</u> as you read this!* (2) to go down: *Our profit <u>dropped off</u> after the new tax was introduced.*
- ✓ **take off** = (1) (for an aircraft) to leave ground and begin to fly: *Our flight <u>took off</u> on time.* (2) (for a product or idea) to become successful quickly: *The new travel and tourism magazine TNT <u>has taken off</u> in no time.*
- ✓ **take (someone) apart** = to defeat someone in a big way in sport and the like: *Sindhu <u>took</u> her young opponent <u>apart</u>. The game was over in just 20 minutes.* Also: *They <u>took apart</u> the old machinery and sold it as scrap.*

Some more phrasal verbs with *take*:

- ✓ **take over** = to begin controlling something: *After the elections, a new government took over as expected. In traditional Indian family-owned businesses, when the head of the family dies, the senior-most male member takes over.*
- ✓ **take after** (someone) = look or behave like someone older in family, particularly parents: *Your sister looks like your mom, but you've taken after your dad.*
- ✓ **take (someone) out** = to go to a restaurant, cinema, and the like with someone you have invited: *I was nervous when I took my girlfriend out the first time.*

Collins Cobuild Dictionary explains phrasal verbs beautifully and gives lots of illustrative sentences.[2]

ACTIVITY 2

Fill in the blanks with one word:

   i. Sashi is a brilliant debater. She regularly takes [＿＿＿] her opponents.
  ii. The machine is too big; to transport it, we must take it [＿＿＿].

---

[2] To check phrasal verbs, visit: https://www.collinsdictionary.com/dictionary/english

iii. Our aircraft took ⬚ late, but otherwise, the flight was comfortable.
iv. Akbar took ⬚ as the chief editor after his boss retired.
v. What new expressions have you come ⬚ in this chapter?
vi. She was a topper in school. But at college, her grades dropped ⬚.

ACTIVITY 3

Guess the meanings of the phrasal verbs given in the box and match them with the words below:

blow up	call (something) off	find out	go into
go away	go on	hold on	leave out
make up	think over	throw away	turn down

1. cancel		7. exclude	
2. consider		8. explode	
3. continue		9. invent	
4. discard/remove		10. leave	
5. discover		11. refuse/reject	
6. examine		12. wait	

ACTIVITY 4

Fill in the blanks with phrasal verbs you have come across in this chapter:

i. The speech was unbearable; half way through, I .... to a snooze.[3]
ii. I c .... a restaurant and reserved a table for the party.
iii. 'The phone line isn't good; you are ....ing ....'
iv. 'There's a problem with my phone, can't hear anything. Please ....'
v. 'Could you please h .... for a moment? I'll check if a room is available.'
vi. It was the first time I was ....ing......... my girlfriend. I put on my best shirt.
vii. 'You saw the accident?'—'There was no accident, I just .... it ....'

---

[3] **snooze:** (noun) a brief sleep; NAP. It is a verb too.

PRACTICE

1. Complete the phrasal verbs with a word. Then match their meanings:

   1. blow up
   2. call............. (some place)
   3. call.............
   4. look...........
   5. take........ (someone)
   6. take........

   A.   to visit a place
   B.   to visit a person
   C.   to explode
   D.   to get the control of (something)
   E.   to improve
   F.   to look/behave like someone

2. Replace the underlined words with <u>a phrasal verb</u>:

   → How could the selectors omit Shami from the team?   leave out ....
   A. As a manager, I don't <u>examine</u> every minor detail.   g..................................
   B. Should we <u>continue</u> repeating our mistakes?   ....
   C. I have <u>discovered</u> an easier way to do the sum.   ....
   D. 'What's the name of the David Lean film in which British POWs[4] <u>exploded</u> a bridge in Burma?'   ....
   E. Could you <u>wait</u> for a minute?   ....
   F. You <u>meet</u> lots of bright people in the IT industry.   ....

3. Fill in the blanks with <u>one word</u> to complete the sentences:

   A. The main speaker had an upset stomach. So they .... off the meeting.
   B. Don't use your phone while charging it. It might .... up.
   C. 'What's the capital of Albania?'—'Don't know. Look .... the Wikipedia.'
   D. Our company's fortunes have been .... up since the new MD joined.
   E. Rani is as sweet as her mom. Clearly, she has taken .... her mamma.
   F. Radhika was a nice boss. She took me .... for dinner shortly after I joined.
   G. I'm sleepy. Will you please turn .... the TV? And the light?
   H. I .... across some wonderful people at my new workplace.

4. Rewrite the sentences by changing the underlined words. Follow the model answer and use the verb given in brackets:

   → She <u>disconnected my telephone call</u>. (cut)
   She cut me off. ....
   A. I <u>telephoned</u> the bank. (call)
   ....
   B. I'll <u>transfer your call</u> to Dr Ram in a moment. (put)
   ....
   C. The minister <u>went to</u> the hospital to see the accident victims. (call)
   ....
   D. Do you really need a bigger house? Please <u>consider</u>. (think)
   ....

---

[4] **POW:** short form for prisoner of war.

E. We're sorry, we had to <u>cancel</u> the function because of bad weather. (call)

....

F. Your proposal seems good. Give me some time, I will <u>consider</u> it carefully. (go)

....

KEY TO ACTIVITIES

Activity 1: i. up; ii. through; iii. off; iv. through; v. on; vi. back; vii. up; viii. up

Activity 2: i. apart; ii. apart; iii. off; iv. over; v. across; vi. off

Activity 3: 1. cancel = call (something) off; 2. consider = think over; 3. continue = go on; 4. discard/remove = throw away; 5. discover = find out; 6. examine = go into; 7. exclude = leave out; 8. explode = blow up; 9. invent = make up; 10. leave = go away; 11. refuse/reject = turn down; 12. wait = hold on

Activity 4: i. dropped off (also, dozed off); ii. called up; iii. breaking up; iv. speak up; v. hold on; vi. taking out; vii. made/up

More Phrasal Verbs

34

Learning Objectives: Continuing from where we left in Chapter 33, in this chapter, we will look at more phrasal verbs with *check*, *get*, *give*, *put*, and *turn*.

34.1 HOW MUCH DO YOU KNOW ALREADY?

Long before televisions, laptops, and mobiles came, we were a group of young men who had just started their career together in a small town. The townsfolk were warm and friendly; we [A]**got on** with them easily. The only problem was that most of us were unmarried, and no house owner would [B]**let out** houses to bachelors. So some of us had to [C]**go on** staying in hotels for months. However, when one of us got married, the situation [D]**looked up** for him immediately. Many a time, prospective landlords [E]**turned us away** the moment we [F]**gave away** our marital status. But we wouldn't [G]**give up.** We used to [H]**call up** estate agents[1] regularly, and every Sunday, we [I]**put on** white full-sleeve shirts and **go out,** [J]**looking for** houses.

ACTIVITY 1

Match the meanings below with the phrasal verbs that have been numbered in the passage above:

1. continue (C)	6. rent out (B)
2. did not entertain (E)	7. searching for (J)
3. had a friendly relationship (A)	8. revealed (F)
4. improved (D)	9. telephone (H)
5. lose hope and stop (G)	10. wear (I)

---

[1] **estate agent:** a person whose job involves buying, selling, and renting land and building.

34.2 PHRASAL VERBS WITH CHECK, GET, AND GIVE

check off	1. to put a tick next to something; 2. to count and match things with reference to a list	1. *Check off the correct sentences.* 2. *Before you sign the receipt, check off the items.*
check into	enter a hotel/hospital for the purpose of staying	*The place was crowded. We checked into a shabby hotel.*
check out (of)	to pay your bill and leave a hotel, lodge, guest house, and so on.	*Hurry up, we have to check out (of the hotel) by 12 noon.*
get across	You *get across* a bridge. When an idea *gets across*, or when you *get* an idea *across*, it is communicated successfully.	*In the presentation, you got across your points, but you should have given more evidence to support them.*
get along/ on	If you get along/get on with someone, you have a friendly relationship with them.	*She has a high EQ.[2] She gets along/gets on with people easily.*
get ahead	to be successful; the opposite is *fall behind*	*We should get ahead in career, but career isn't everything.*
get away	When you are able to leave a place or a person, you *get away*.	*She wanted a divorce, she wanted to get away from the failed marriage.*
get down	to lower your body until you are sitting, kneeling, or lying down	*Get down, quick! Someone is shooting!*
get down to	to begin doing something important	*OK, the break is over, now, let's get down to work.*
give away	1. If you *give away* something, you give it for free, rather than selling it; 2. If you are disclosing information that you shouldn't, you are *giving away* information; 3. To give someone or something away means to reveal their true identity.	1. *He gave away all his books to a library.* 2. *He lost his job because he gave away company information.* 3. *He was pretending to be an American, but his accent gave him away.*
give back	to return	*I'm going to the library to give back a book.*
give in (to someone/ something)	to accept defeat, to be overcome by something	*The easiest way to fight temptation is to give in.*
give up	to abandon an attempt	*After the snowstorm, the mountaineers gave up.*
give out	to distribute things	*As we approached the rally, a man was giving out leaflets.*

ACTIVITY 2

Complete the sentences by adding: *ahead, away (2), back, down (2), on, into,* and *out (4).*

A.   Bullet Singh disguised himself as a beggar, but his mobile gave him [   ].

---

[2] **EQ:** Short form for *emotional quotient.* If you have strong interpersonal and communication skills, you are said to have high EQ. Compare EQ with IQ.

B. After checking [ ] an expensive hotel in Hyderabad, Inspector Bhola Singh went [ ] for a stroll on the Tank Bund.

C. Someone picked his pocket. Later at the hotel, when he went to check [ ], he found [ ], he had neither cash nor card.

D. An angry Bhola muttered, 'Hang [ ], Bullet Singh! I will give it [ ] to you, with interest.'

E. Inspector Bhola barked, 'Get [ ], everybody! Someone is shooting!'

F. Inspector Bhola nearly lost his job. Last month, the dreaded criminal Bullet Singh managed to get [ ] when Bhola had fallen asleep.

G. But otherwise, Bhola has a perfect track record. I am sure ultimately he will get [ ] in his career.

H. As we approached the town, someone was giving [ ] a handbill. It had the photo of a criminal on the run.

I. Sorry, I just couldn't get [ ] to writing the report on Bullet Singh.

34.3 PUT AND TURN

put aside	to leave something for a short time, to be dealt with later	Let's *put aside* the complex issues for now. Let's tackle the easier ones first.
put (something) **across**	to convey your ideas clearly	I've read your article. You've *put across* your points beautifully.
put on (something)	to dress yourself in something	It was freezing; she *put* her overcoat *on*.
	to switch on something	It is getting dark, please *put on* the light.
	to pretend to have a particular feeling or quality	Don't *put on* any accent, speak naturally.
	to play a record, CD, and the like	Please *put on* this CD.
put (something) **off**	to delay or postpone something Compare with **call off**	As we couldn't find a hall, we had to *put the function off*.
put off by someone	if you are *put off* by someone, you dislike him/her	I *was put off* by her rudeness.
put up (with someone)	to tolerate	Our new boss *cannot put up with* lazy people.

turn around	1. move something so that it faces in the opposite direction; 2. if a situation turns around, or if you turn it around, it means it has become successful after a period of failure	1. I can't read what's written. Please *turn the paper around*. 2. The company didn't make profit for years. The new CEO[3] has *turned it around*.
turn (someone) **away**	if you turn someone away, you don't allow them to enter your place	It would be inhuman to *turn* the refugees *away*.
turn (something) **on/off**	to start/shut down an electrical gadget	Please *turn off* the fan. Our neighbour *turns* the radio *on* by 5.00 in the morning.

---
[3] **CEO:** short form for chief executive officer, who often is the head of a company.

turn something **up** or **down**	to increase/reduce (the speed or volume of a device)	*A: Can you please <u>turn down</u> the TV?* *B: Turn down? I must <u>turn</u> it <u>up</u>. Can't hear a thing!*
turn up	When someone turns up, he/she arrives, often unexpectedly, or after a long wait	*The big surprise at the party was Ravi. No one expected him to <u>turn up</u>.*

ACTIVITY 3

Follow the given model and restate the sentences twice:

→   I turned off the TV

1. *I turned the TV off.*   2. *I turned it off.*

A. She tried on the new pair of jeans.

1.   2.

B. I threw away the empty can.

1.   2.

C. The cinema turned away Rina. (She looked much younger than her age.)

1. *The cinema*   2.

D. I turned around the Scrabble board.

1.   2.

E. She didn't give away her real purpose.

1.   2.

F. I gave back the pen drive to Ravi.

1.   2.

ACTIVITY 4

These are sentences from conversations. Fill in the blanks with appropriate forms of *get, give, put,* and *turn:*

A.   Do you think the new policies can _____ the economy around?

B.   Guess who _____ up at the meeting? It was Shahrukh Khan!

C.   I tried to fix the computer, but couldn't. I _____ up after two hours.

D.   I will have to buy a house, can't _____ it off any longer.

E.   It's stuffy. Can you please _____ up the fan?

F.   Our college is run by a charity. We don't _____ away applicants because they can't pay.

G.   The break is over, folks. Let's _____ down to business.

H.   The hotel was cold and dirty. We _____ up with everything because there was no choice.

34.4 TAILPIECE

We were rather astonished when one Sunday, a prospective landlord, Mr Vignesh, agreed to give my friend Dinu a house on rent. He didn't even quiz Dinu about his marital status. We thought something was wrong, but we **put aside** our niggling worries. Mr Vignesh seemed to have **fallen for** Dinu.

As we were talking in Mr Vignesh's drawing room, a 20-something girl, tall, slim, and pretty, **walked in,** saying, 'Dad!....' Seeing us, she stopped abruptly and left, much to our regret. Her father said, 'It's settled then, let me get the car keys. You can **look up** the house straightaway.'

I thought it would be better if Dinu's wife too saw the place, and **barged in,** 'Sir, wouldn't it be better if Mrs Menon also saw the house?'

'Who is Mrs Menon?'

Pointing at Dinu, I said, 'His wife.'

I thought the elderly man had had a sudden bout of colic pain. Nothing else would explain why he turned so pale. At length, he **turned towards** Dinu and asked through his suffering, 'Are you married?'

PRACTICE

1. Think about the meanings of these phrasal verbs and use them to fill in the blanks below. Use the simple present tense unless instructed otherwise:

check into	check off	get across	get away
give back	give out	give in	turn off

    A. An excellent public speaker, Sashi always .... her ideas .... clearly.
    B. At the entrance of the Louvre Museum, a man .... a map of the museum. (Past continuous)
    C. Can I borrow your cycle? I' .... it............. after an hour. (Simple future)
    D. I hated my last job. I just wanted to ....
    E. OK, I .... How do you solve this puzzle?
    F. Raghu, the storekeeper, ... long lists of goods every day.
    G. She pulled the car to the side and .... the engine. (Simple past)
    H. We reached Dhaka by 11.00 and .... a hotel by midday.

2. Rewrite the sentences by changing the underlined words. Follow the model answer and use the verb given in brackets:

    →   I was upset by her rudeness. (put)
    I was put off by her rudeness. Or: Her rudeness put me off...

    A. Can you please <u>increase the volume of</u> the radio? (turn)
    ....

    B. A. I've just reached Pune. —B. Have you <u>taken a room in</u> a hotel? (check)
    ....

    C. At what time do we <u>leave the hotel</u>? (check)
    ....

D. I joined a karate class. But I <u>discontinued</u> after three months. (give)

....

E. Can you <u>move the table lamp in the opposite direction</u>? (turn)

....

F. All the seats have been filled; the <u>college has been sending back</u> new applicants. (turn)

....

G. I <u>stop thinking</u> when I return from office. (switch)

....

H. She usually <u>conveys her ideas</u> easily. (get)

....

KEY TO ACTIVITIES

Activity 1: 1. (C); 2. (E); 3. (A); 4. (D); 5. (G); 6. (B); 7. (J); 8. (F); 9. (H); 10. (I)

Activity 2: A. away, B. into, out; C. out, out; D. on; back; E. down; F. away; G. ahead; H. out; I. down

Activity 3: A. 1. She tried the new pair of jeans on. 2. She tried it on. B. 1. I threw the empty can away. 2. I threw it away. C. 1. The cinema turned Rina away. 2. The cinema turned her away. D. 1. I turned the Scrabble board around. 2. I turned it around. E. 1. She didn't give her real purpose away. 2. She didn't give it away. F. 1. I gave the pen drive back to Ravi. 2. I gave it back to Ravi.

Activity 4: A. turn; B. turned; C. gave; D. put; E. turn; F. turn; G. get; H. put

Test 5:
Joe Was Shocked to Find His Wallet Empty

1 Write 'T' if the statement is true, and 'F' if it is false:

A. In a sentence, both a gerund (verb + ing) and an infinitive (to + verb) behave like nouns. ☐
B. You cannot use a gerund after the verbs *avoid, consider,* and *enjoy.* ☐
C. An infinitive comes after the verbs *allow, ask, decide,* and *plan.* ☐
D. Either a gerund or an infinitive may follow the verbs *begin, continue, love,* or *hate.* ☐

2. Underline the mistake in the following sentences. If a sentence is correct, put a ✓ next to it:

A. The teacher said, 'Children, stop to make noise!'
B. Radhika asked Rohan put on a sweater.
C. My boss allowed me leaving early.
D. To acting on stage is not easy.
E. It was nice meeting you.
F. It was nice to meet you.

3 Fill in the blanks with gerunds or infinitives using the verbs given below. For some blanks, the first letter has been given:

accompany	accept	be	chirp	climb	dance
set	join	lie down	reach	~~trek~~	walk × 3

I love <u>trekking</u>. On a Sunday, I decided .... c............ to the top of the hill near our village. I asked my friend Gautam, 'Would you like .... j............ me for a short trek?'

He said, 'Generally, I hate .... unless there is a strong reason, but for a change, I don't mind .... you today.'

On the way, we saw thousands of butterflies .... around flowers. We also heard birds ...., but we didn't see them. It was a very hot day, and after three hours, we found it difficult .... Gautam sat down under a tree and said, 'You seem strong enough .... r................. the top, but I am too tired .... even one more step. It was a mistake .... your crazy idea.'

I pretended .... hurt, but actually, I was relieved to hear what Gautam said. We had our lunch and decided .... under a tree. When we woke up, the sun was about .... on the horizon.

4. Fill in the blanks with infinitives. Use the following verbs: ~~attend~~, **bail (someone) out, do, find, have, pay, pray,** and **walk.**

    1. It happened sometime in the 1980s, long before credit or debit cards arrived on the scene. My friend Joe was in Mumbai to attend a meeting.
    ☐ He didn't know what ....
    ☐ When he took out his wallet .... the bill, he was shocked .... it empty.
    ☐ And he appealed to God .... him .... of the awkward situation.
    ☐ After the meeting, he went to an expensive restaurant .... dinner.
    ☐ For the first time after growing up, he decided .... to God.
    ☐ And God appeared in the shape of an old friend, Madhusudan Rao, who happened .... into the restaurant at that precise moment.

5. Number the above sentences in the order they happened. Then, without looking at them, write down the story from memory:

    It happened sometime in the 1980s, long before credit or debit cards arrived on the scene. My friend Joe was in Mumbai to attend a meeting..
    ....
    ....
    ....
    ....
    ....
    ....
    ....
    ....
    ....
    ....
    ....
    ....

6. Correct the sentences:

    A. Volker and Linda arrived New Delhi this morning, shortly after midnight.
    B. Tomorrow, they are leaving at Kolkata from New Delhi.
    C. Volker phoned to me say they had arrived. (There are two mistakes in this sentence.)
    D. I needn't worry about Volker and Linda. They can look about themselves.

7. Fill in the blanks with one word:

    A. The match was called .... because of bad weather.
    B. The meeting has been put .... to next Monday.
    C. Do you still believe .... communism?
    D. Which university did you study ....?

8. Complete the sentences by combining the appropriate forms of the verbs given within brackets with one of these prepositions: *at, for, into, off, on, out, to, with,* and *up.*

   A. We have invested a lot of money in the project. We cannot .... at this stage. (give)
   B. The police .... the complaint. (look)
   C. 'What are you doing?' —'I've misplaced my keys. I' .... them.' (look)
   D. I .... Raghu's office yesterday; he was not in office. (call)
   E. Listen carefully, they .... the names. (call)
   F. The room is stuffy. Please .... the fan. (put)
   G. He speaks English fluently, but .... a strange accent. (put)
   H. I left early because I was .... by her rudeness. (put)
   I. I .... the problem.................. the headmaster, but he refused to see my point. (explain)
   J. I .... coffee .... tea. (prefer)
   K. Why is the train stuck here? I don't know, I'll .... the station manager. (check)
   L. I've reached Chennai and have just .... Hotel Savera. (check)

9. Fill in the blanks with gerunds, infinitives, phrasal verbs, or prepositions. The first letter has been given in a few places to help you. But you may ignore it and use any other appropriate word. There can be more than one correct answer for some of the blanks:

   Once George and I were t .... t............ New Delhi .... train for a job interview. We had decided .... p .... for the interview during the journey. After we settled down in the train, I suggested, 'Let's .... a game of chess. Then we'll open the books.'

   But unfortunately, we didn't stop p .... until late night. The next morning, I realized I had forgotten .... my toothbrush and paste. My friend had brought his toothbrush, but he too didn't have toothpaste. So George decided .... g.................. o.................. at Patna t............. .... toothpaste. As I anxiously waited for him .... r ...., the train began .... m..............

   After some time, the train stopped at Danapur. And I was pleasantly surprised .... George w........................ in with a broad smile on his face and a toothpaste tube in his shirt pocket. Said he, 'When the train left, I decided .... a taxi. Fortunately, there was a problem at the level crossing near Danapur. So here I am!'

PART

NUTS AND BOLTS OF THE ENGLISH LANGUAGE

A, An, or The?

Learning Objectives: In this chapter, we are going to check how to use *a, an,* and *the,* and when not to use them.

35.1 DEFINITE, INDEFINITE

The determiners *a, an,* and ***the,*** commonly known as ***articles,*** are three of the most frequently used words in English. They come before nouns or noun phrases and point at them. Non-native speakers of English are often confused about them. However, it's easy to learn how to use them, and also, equally importantly, when *not to use them.* And with that, we will be able to eliminate lots of errors.

A and *an* are called indefinite articles. We use them when we aren't talking about any particular thing. *The* is a definite article; it refers to a specific thing.

When I tell you: *You must see a doctor,* I mean you should consult a doctor, any doctor. But if I say: *You must see the doctor,* I will be talking about a specific doctor, someone who both you and I know.

ACTIVITY 1

Fill in the blanks with ***a, an,*** or ***the:***

It was …… cloudy evening. Nandini was going to her uncle's home along …… desolate road. There was no one else on …… road. …… place was absolutely still, not even …… bird was chirping. Suddenly,……… man appeared before her from nowhere. He was in ill-fitting clothes and had …… evil glint in his eyes. He took out …… leather pouch that he had been hiding under his shirt. Pointing at it, he said, 'I have …… diamond studded necklace. Would you buy it?' By then …… evening had turned almost dark and …… road looked even more desolate. …… evil glint in the man's eyes had turned into …… mocking smile.

Before you proceed further, compare your answer with the key at the end of this chapter and note how the articles are used.

> When we mention something for the first time in speech or writing, whether a *cloudy evening*, a *desolate road*, or a *man*, we use the indefinite article *a* or *an.* But when we refer to the same thing again, we use *the*, because by then it has become a definite reference.

35.2 A OR AN?

> The choice between *a* and *an* depends on the <u>pronunciation</u> of the word that follows. We use *a* before words beginning with a consonant sound and *an* before words beginning with a vowel sound:

✓ an angry man	✓ an eagle	✓ an experiment	✓ an Indian
✓ an honest man	✓ an heir[1]	✓ an hour	✓ to do an MA

All these nouns begin with a vowel sound. Although *honest, heir,*[1] and *hour* are spelled with the consonant *h*, when you speak, you begin these words with a vowel sound; *h* is silent. And you pronounce MA as **EM**-EI. Here are some nouns beginning with consonant sounds:

✓ a Bangladeshi	✓ a tiger	✓ a zoo	✓ a city
✓ a European	✓ a young man	✓ a one-rupee coin	✓ a university

The words *European, young,* and *university* are pronounced with the consonant sound *y.* Similarly, one-rupee note begins with the consonant sound *w.* Therefore, we use *a* before them.

ACTIVITY 2

Which of the following expressions are correct? Put a ✓ if an expression is correct or a ✖ if it isn't:

1. an university ☐	2. an horse ☐	3. a flying horse ☐
4. a one-storey building ☐	5. an useful thing ☐	6. a hotel ☐

---

[1] **heir:** (pronounced AIR) a person who will legally receive the property of someone when they die.

35.3 WE USE THE BEFORE...

We use *the* before nouns in the following cases:

1. When we talk about a particular person or thing:

    ✓ The girl in red? She's Fatima's sister.
    ✓ The 15th of August.
    ✓ Long live the Revolution! (A specific revolution, our revolution, not every one of them!)

2. Before words such as *best, worst, first, second, last, highest, lowest,* and *fastest*:

    ✓ Fatima is the best footballer in our school.
    ✓ Currently, the train between Shanghai airport and the city centre is the fastest train in the world.
    ✓ And as of now, the tallest building in the world is the Burj Khalifa in Dubai.

3. When a singular noun represents a whole class:

    ✓ The dog is a loyal pet (You can also say: A dog is a loyal pet.)
    ✓ The pen is mightier than the sword.
    ✓ Uneasy lies the head that wears the crown.[2]

4. Before names of celestial bodies and natural elements: rivers, deserts, islands, mountains, canals, and so on:

    ✓ The sky, the sun, the moon, the Andromeda Galaxy, but you don't put *the* before formal names of constellations: Orion, Ursa Major, Cygnus, and so on
    ✓ The Indian Ocean, the Ganga, the Himalayas, the Maldives

5. Before names of books and other man-made objects that are *unique*. This includes:

    ✓ Names of unique structures: *The Taj, the Suez Canal, the Burj Khalifa*
    ✓ Names of books known to everyone: *The Gita, the Bible, the Five Books of Moses,* and so on...
    ✓ Before names of famous paintings: *the Mona Lisa, the Starry Nights,* and so on...

6. Before musical instruments:

    ✓ the sitar, the flute, the piano, the drum, and the like

7. Before an adjective where the noun is understood:

    ✓ The poor are with our party. (The poor = the poor people)
    ✓ When the going gets tough, the tough gets going.
    ✓ After the earthquake, thousands are living in the open.

8. Before names of countries which are also organisations of states, such as:

    ✓ The United Arab Emirates, the United States of America, the USA, the UK

---

[2] This line from Shakespeare's *Henry IV* (1597) has become a proverb in English. It says the head that wears the crown is uneasy, that is, people who have immense responsibility are often unhappy.

9. Before a name that is in plural:

- ✓ The Netherlands, the West Indies

10. Before names of institutions if they don't begin with the name of a person or place:

- ✓ The State Bank of India
- ✓ The Life Insurance Corporation of India
- ✓ The University of Delhi

11. However, if the name of an institution begins with the name, don't put *the:*

- ✓ Delhi University
- ✓ Tata Steel

35.4 WHEN DO WE OMIT ARTICLES?

While it is important that we know where to use the indefinite article *the*, it is perhaps more important to understand *when we don't* use an article before a noun.

We don't use articles:

1. Before names of people, places, films, and so on:

- ✓ Ravi lives in Mumbai now.
- ✓ Amitabh Bachchan and Dharmendra acted in *Sholey*.
- ✓ Where is Leelavati?

2. Before uncountable nouns used in a general sense:

- ✓ <u>Money</u> makes the world go round.
- ✓ <u>Plastic</u> (polymer) is used to print currency notes in Australia.
- ✓ <u>Time</u> and <u>tide</u> wait for none.

3. Before plural countable nouns used in a general sense:

- ✓ The price of <u>computers</u> has fallen drastically in recent years.
- ✓ <u>Mobile phones</u> have changed our lives.

However, when you refer to a particular thing that is either an uncountable noun or a plural countable noun, use *the:*

- ✓ Please pass me <u>the salt</u>.
- ✓ <u>The computers</u> in our office are quite old.

> A friend of mine from Bengaluru told this story:
>
> 'Some people have a tendency to use *the* before people's names. We have one such person in our office. He was enquiring about the whereabouts of one of our managers, Leelavati (Leela for short). He asked a colleague, "Where is the Leela?"
>
> The colleague promptly (and quite innocently) replied, "In the Old Airport Road."
>
> (That is where the Leela, a well-known hotel, is located in Bengaluru!)'

4. Before names of relations such as *father, mother, aunt,* and the like:

    ✓ <u>Dad</u> is taking his Sunday-morning nap.
    ✓ <u>Grandpa</u> is playing kabaddi.

5. Before school, college, church, prison, and so on, when these places are visited in the usual course:

    ✓ We learn Spanish at <u>school</u>. (Not <s>at the school</s>)
    ✓ Dr Ram doesn't go to <u>hospital</u> on Sundays.

    But if we use the same words as specific destinations or places, we put *the:*

    ✓ <u>The school</u> isn't far from our house.
    ✓ I'm going to <u>the hospital</u> to see grandma.

PRACTICE

1. The passage below is from a story 'Shiladitya' by Abanindranath Tagore. Fill in the blanks with *a, an,* and *the* to complete the story. If no article is needed, put a '–' in the blank space:

    Before Shiladitya was born, during (A) .... rule of the last king of (B) .... Kanakasena dynasty, there was (C) .... sacred water tank, Suryakund, in Ballabhipur. In a gigantic Sun Temple beside the tank lived (D) .... very old priest. He had neither family nor friends. The water in the vast Suryakund was blue, like (E) .... blue of (F) .... sky. And beside it, (G) .... old priest and sun worshipper was as lonely and solitary as (H) .... sun in (I) .... endless sky. He had no follower, no assistant, and not even one disciple. Every day, (J) .... frail old man lifted (K) .... heavy brass lamp and performed (L) .... *aarti*[3] of (M) .... Sun God.

2. Complete the following sentences with *a, an,* or a '–':

    (i)   Rice is .... staple food in Bangladesh and Myanmar. Myanmar has .... petroleum, Bangladesh has an abundant supply of .... natural gas.
    (ii) Mount Everest is .... highest point in the world .... *Challenger Deep* in .... Pacific Ocean is......... deepest point in the earth's seabed.
    (iii) Raju has been selected for a course in .... university in Germany. He will join .... university next month.
    (iv) For Hindus, ... Ganga is .... sacred river, just as .... Jordan is for .... Jews and Christians.

3. Rewrite the sentences using articles where necessary. Check (✓) the correct sentences:

    (i)   Sun rises in east. _____
    (ii) Doctor says it is hopeless case. _____
    (iii) Musician was as ancient as his tanpura. _____

---

[3] **aarti:** a Hindu prayer performed while holding a lighted lamp or a metallic bell.

(iv)   Have you seen tiger in open? _____

(v)   Flimsy, wooden bridge joined two sides of river. _____

(vi)   We started late in the afternoon. _____

(vii)   Dr Reddy is headmaster of our school. _____

(viii)   Project failed because of shortage of funds. _____

4.   There are six extra words in the passage below. Strike them off:

The computers have changed our lives. The information is easily available these days. For example, take the case of the Irfan, one day, he was searching the Internet to gather information on the Commonwealth Games. He stumbled upon a site about the scholarships available to students of the Commonwealth countries. And would you believe it? Next summer, Irfan is going to the Auckland University of Technology to do masters in the Artificial Intelligence.

KEY TO ACTIVITIES

Activity 1: It was **a** cloudy evening. Nandini was going… along **a** desolate road. There was no one else on **the** road. **The** place was absolutely still, not even **a** bird was chirping. Suddenly, **a** man appeared before her from nowhere. He… had **an** evil glint in his eyes. He took out **a** leather pouch…. Pointing at it, he said, 'I have **a** diamond studded necklace. Would you buy it?' By then **the** evening had turned almost dark and **the** road looked even more desolate. **The** evil glint in the man's eyes had turned into **a** mocking smile.

Activity 2: 1. ✗; 2. ✗; 3. ✓; 4. ✓; 5. ✗; 6. ✓

Nuts and Bolts of the English Language

Learning Objectives: In this chapter, we are going to discuss the use of prepositions, that is, words such as *in*, *on*, *at* in general and the prepositions of places in particular.

36.1 WE ARE GOING FOR A CIVIL MARRIAGE[1]

Radhika is talking to Catherine over the phone:

Radhika: Hi Catherine!

Catherine: Hi Radhika, how are you?

Radhika: I'm fine, Cathy, thanks. I'll give you some good news. Ravi and I are getting married next Sunday.

Catherine: Wow! Congrats, Radhika! I am delighted! Will the *dulha*[1] come riding a horse, with a band playing Hindi songs?

Radhika: Nothing *of* that sort. You know us. We aren't fond *of* showing off. We're going *for* a simple civil marriage.[2] It will be at the banquet hall *of* the Hotel Star, ***in*** the evening. Only 50 *of* our closest friends would be present. You and Joseph must come.

Catherine: Of course, we will. We'd love to be there. See you on Sunday.

Read the highlighted sentences carefully. In these sentences:

- ✓ *of joins* nothing (pronoun) with *that sort* (noun)
- ✓ *of* joins *fond* (an adjective) with *display* (a noun)
- ✓ *for* connects *'re going* (a verb) with *civil marriage* (a noun phrase)
- ✓ *of* connects *banquet hall* with *Hotel Star*, that is, two nouns
- ✓ *in* joins *will be* with *the evening*
- ✓ *of* connects *50* (a determiner) with *our closest friends* (a noun phrase)

---

[1] **dulha:** bridegroom in Hindi.

[2] **civil marriage:** a marriage performed by a government official, not a priest.

Words such as *of, for,* and *in* are called *prepositions.*

> A preposition usually comes before a noun or a pronoun and establishes its relationship with some-
> one or something else.

One of my teachers in school described prepositions as nuts and bolts that join nouns (and pronouns) with other words. But you should also keep in mind that some verbs are *not* followed by prepositions. And in some cases, you can either use a preposition or omit it. For example:

- ✓ I'll give you some good news. (Not: I'll give ~~to~~ you some good news.✗)
- ✓ Ravi and I are getting married next Sunday. (You don't normally say, *on next Sunday.*)
- ✓ Will the *dulha* come <u>riding a horse</u>? (You can also say: *riding on a horse.*)

36.2 WHERE IS THE CAT?

Can you draw the last three pictures to match the captions?

The cat is on the table.

The cat is under the table.

The cat is beside the table.

The cat is behind the table.

The cat is before the table.

The cat is near the table.

As you can see, these prepositions change the picture that we draw with words. These are called prepositions of place. In this unit, we are going to discuss these prepositions.

36.3 ENGLISH HAS QUITE A FEW OF THEM

In English, you find many more prepositions compared to South Asian languages. Let's compare a few Hindi prepositions with their English equivalents:

> *upar* → on, over, above
> *neeche* → under, below, beneath, underneath
> *andar* → in, into, inside, within

As you can see, whereas just one word like *upar* serves the purpose in Hindi (and in many other languages), English has three words for it. And more importantly, each of them has specific uses; you may not be able to substitute one with another. As we are not familiar with this variation in our languages, we often use English prepositions incorrectly.

Please remember: English prepositions don't follow any rule. We have to remember how they are used.

36.4 ON/OVER/ABOVE, AND UNDER/BELOW

We will now discuss how some common prepositions (given in Table 36.1) are used:
Likewise, *under*, *below*, *underneath*, and *beneath* mean similar yet different things.

TABLE 36.1 Common Prepositions and Their Usage

Preposition	Meaning	Usage
on	in or into a position covering, touching, or forming a surface	✓ There is a stain *on* your shirt. We use on to denote a line: ✓ Kolkata is *on* the river Hooghly. ✓ Which is the next town *on* this road? We also use on **+ floor**: ✓ Kartar Singh lives on the first floor. (A common mistake is: ~~in~~ the first floor)
above/over	used to describe a position higher than something	✓ His office is *above/over* the restaurant. ✓ There's no floor *above/over* our flat.
over	when we mean movement from one side to the other	✓ Look, Rani is jumping *over* a hedge. ✓ *One Flew over the Cuckoo's Nest*
	over also refers to covering	✓ She put a blanket *over* the child.
	over also means more than; it is used in relation to number, age, money, and time	✓ Dr Ram is *over* 80. ✓ We waited for *over* two hours.
above	*above* also means more than, but it is used in relation to a fixed level or point	✓ This shirt costs *over* ₹2,000. ✓ Darjeeling is 7,000 ft *above* sea level. ✓ We saw no animals *above* the snowline.[3]

---
[3] **snowline:** the level on a mountain above which snow never melts completely.

under	In, to, or through a position that is at a lower level than something; also, covered by something	✓ The trunk is *under* the cot. ✓ Raju is *under* the blanket. ✓ After the rains, the roads are *under* water.
	Less than; *under* is an antonym of *over*	✓ Buy a shirt *under* ₹200. ✓ You use *under* (not *below*) to talk about movement from one side to another. ✓ Our boat passed *under* the bridge.
below	At a lower level than something, someone, or some standard or rank; *below* is the opposite of *above*	✓ Please sign *below* this line. ✓ Mr Singh lives *on* the floor *below*. ✓ Her English is much *below* the expected level.
underneath	*Underneath* can be used when you wish to say that something is being covered or hidden by another thing.	✓ The notepad is *under*/*underneath* the dictionary. ✓ Underneath the top layer, I found another layer of chocolates.
beneath	Another word for underneath is *beneath*. It is used only in literature or in formal language.	✓ Beneath our feet was a carpet of leaves. ✓ His behaviour is beneath contempt.

These pictures will tell you more about some prepositions of place:

There is a stain on your shirt.

The boat is on the river.

Kartar lives on the first floor.

The children are on the bus.

The cat is on the table.

An aircraft above clouds.

A plane flying over hills.

The ship is under the bridge.

ACTIVITY 1

Fill in the blanks with any one of **over, above, under, below,** and **underneath:**

1. Since the rains, the river has been flowing _____ the danger mark.
2. This restaurant is expensive. A meal here costs _____ ₹500.
3. Our plane flew _____ the Shivalik Hills.
4. We built a floor _____ our garage.
5. Cigarettes are not sold to people _____ 18.
6. Officers _____ the rank of major are not eligible for foreign posting.
7. The rumour is that there is a secret chamber _____ the building.
8. She hid her sorrows _____ a smiling face.
9. Almost half the world's population earn _____ two dollars a day.
10. Which is the next town _____ this road?

36.5 SOME MORE PREPOSITIONS OF PLACE

We will now discuss some frequently used (and misused) prepositions. If you get them right, you will eliminate a large percentage of errors.

In and *at:* We use *in* when something is surrounded on all sides.

- ✓ You'll find the book in the second bookcase.
- ✓ The girl in red (= the girl in the red dress) is my cousin Nandini.
- ✓ Don't go out in the rain.

We use *at* when we refer to a point:

- ✓ The post office is at the crossing of two roads.
- ✓ Mr Ismail? He's at the last table.

We also use *in* before names of countries, cities, towns, and villages. But when we refer to a specific place within that area, we use *at.* Compare the following sentences:

- ✓ I'll be in Patna for a month.
- ✓ Meet me at the Patna railway station tomorrow.
- ✓ We lived in Vizag for 10 years.
- ✓ We stopped at Vizag on our way to Chennai.

We use *in* before names of streets and *at* when we give the house number:

- ✓ He lives in Sukia Street.

But we say:

- ✓ He lives at 30 Sukia Street.

We use *at* to refer to group activities and workplaces:

- ✓ I didn't see you <u>at</u> the party.
- ✓ He works <u>at</u> the Quality Control Department.

In and *into:* We use *into* when there is movement from outside to inside something.

- ✓ He fell <u>into</u> the ditch. You can also say: He fell <u>in</u> the ditch.
- ✓ We jumped <u>into</u> the swimming pool. Also: We jumped in the swimming pool.

Nests <u>in</u> a tree.   The cat is <u>in</u> the room.   Putting coins <u>into</u> a piggy bank.   The baby is <u>in</u> the pram.

Round and *around* mean surrounding something:

- ✓ There was a lovely garden <u>around</u> our hotel in Loleygaon.
- ✓ There was jam all <u>around</u> Rohan's mouth.

Around also means on, to, or from the other side of something:

- ✓ We have almost reached. The monastery is just <u>around</u> the corner.

Beside and *besides: Beside* means *by the side of; besides* means *in addition to.*

- ✓ She was <u>beside</u> her father when he died.
- ✓ Someone picked my pocket. <u>Besides</u> losing ₹500, I lost my driving licence.

Between, from … to, opposite:

Between means in or through the space that separates two things. For example: *Bharatpur is <u>between</u> Agra and Jaipur.*

From … to: *You come across Bharatpur when you drive <u>from</u> Agra <u>to</u> Jaipur.*

When two things are facing each other, we say one is **opposite** the other: *My house is opposite the bank.* (Not *opposite to the bank.*)

A patient <u>on</u> a bed. His medicines <u>beside</u> him.   Raghu <u>at</u> his desk.   He sits <u>between</u> two lady colleagues.   A visitor sitting <u>opposite</u> Raghu.

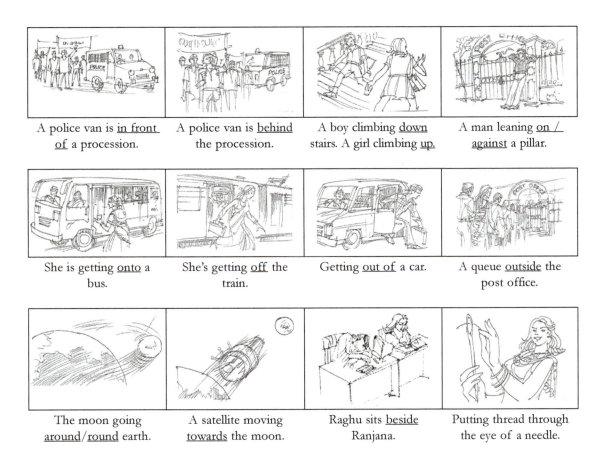

A police van is <u>in front of</u> a procession.	A police van is <u>behind</u> the procession.	A boy climbing <u>down</u> stairs. A girl climbing <u>up</u>.	A man leaning <u>on / against</u> a pillar.
She is getting <u>onto</u> a bus.	She's getting <u>off</u> the train.	Getting <u>out of</u> a car.	A queue <u>outside</u> the post office.
The moon going <u>around/round</u> earth.	A satellite moving <u>towards</u> the moon.	Raghu sits <u>beside</u> Ranjana.	Putting thread through the eye of a needle.

The following passage has a few prepositions that we haven't discussed so far. Can you see the situation in your mind?

A man was walking <u>across</u> the road <u>along</u> which the queen was passing in her limousine.[4] The queen's chauffer didn't see the man because he was <u>around</u> a sharp bend. He pressed the brake and stopped just <u>before</u> hitting the man. The queen got <u>off</u> her car and said, 'I apologize. Are you hurt?'

The man was shaken. He leaned <u>against</u> a post and tried to regain his breath. Then he said slowly, 'Your Majesty, I am proud to be a citizen <u>of</u> a country where the queen apologizes to a common man. I am fine, thank you.'

He slowly walked <u>past</u> the royal palace <u>towards</u> the railway station.

---

[4] **limousine:** (noun) a big luxurious car in which a glass partition separates the driver from the Passengers.

ACTIVITY 2

Strike off the incorrect options:

1. There are three banks **in/at/on** this town.
2. The Prosperity Bank? It's **in/at/on** the crossing of M.G. Road and J.N. Road.
3. The meeting took place **in/into/at** Hotel Windsor Manor **in/at/on** Bangalore.
4. After a long walk we were delighted to see the river. We jumped **into/at/on** its cool water without wasting time.
5. There is a stain **in/on/over** your jacket.
6. A man is pasting posters **at/on/over** the wall.
7. Which is the next town **at/on** this road?
8. Mr Kartar Singh lives **in/on** the first floor.
9. Nandini met her future husband **in/at/on** a party.
10. Did you hear the bell? I think someone's **in/into/at/on** the door.

'I beg your pardon', said the mole, pulling himself together with an effort. 'You must think me very rude; but all this is so new to me. So-this-is-a-River!' 'The River', corrected the rat.

'And you really live by the river? What a jolly life!'

By it and with it and on it and in it', said the rat.

[From Kenneth Graham's *The Wind in the Willows*]

ACTIVITY 3

In the following lines, I have tried to draw a picture of a lake near my village. But I have left out the prepositions. Can you fill in the blanks and see the lake with your mind's eyes?

There is a beautiful lake near my village. There are trees all _____ it. Thousands of birds have built their nests _____ those trees. Birds fly _____ the water; kingfishers snatch up fish _____ the lake. Children of the village swim and make merry _____ its cool waters. Men sit _____ it for hours to catch fish. In the evening, elderly men sit and chat ___ the cemented ghats _____ the lake _____ the lengthening shadows. The ghat is old and has many cracks _____ it. _____ the side _____ the lake is a huge acacia tree. There is a rumour that a pot of gold is buried _____ the tree.

▮ PRACTICE

1. Fill in the blanks:

   (i) The man jumped _____ the fence and ran away.
   (ii) It was very cold yesterday. The temperature was 5° _____ normal.

(iii)   The nurse pulled a blanket _____ the patient.
(iv)   As you climbed the mountain, did you see any trees _____ the snowline?
(v)   Since then, much water has flowed _____ the bridge.
(vi)   I was _____ my grandfather when he passed away.
(vii)   This is our station. We'll get _____ here.
(viii)   The Lake Titicaca is _____ Peru and Bolivia.
(ix)   In our school, there were four big buildings _____ a central playground.
(x)   As we drove _____ the royal palace, we caught a glimpse of the queen.
(xi)   Raghu and her girlfriend were walking _____ the river when it started raining.
(xii)   The earth goes _____ the sun.

2.   Complete these sentences by using prepositions at the appropriate places. You will require more than one in some sentences:

(i)   We stopped Dubai for three hours our way London.
(ii)   Our boat was the river Godavari.
(iii)   London is the river Thames.
(iv)   Darjeeling is 7,000 ft the sea level.
(v)   He put the letter an envelope and affixed a stamp it.
(vi)   He dived the water.
(vii)   When we were going Delhi, we bought some wooden toys the Varanasi station.
(viii)   There were not many people the rally.
(ix)   I didn't see you the party.
(x)   She hid his letter the cupboard some clothes.
(xi)   Our train went a tunnel on the way to Araku Valley.
(xii)   Mr Ismail sits the last desk.

KEY TO ACTIVITIES

Activity 1: 1. Since the rains, the river has been flowing <u>above</u> the danger mark. 2. A meal at this restaurant costs over ₹500. 3. Our plane flew <u>over</u> the Shivalik Hills. 4. We built a floor <u>over/above</u> our garage. 5. Cigarettes are not sold to people <u>under</u> 18. 6. Officers <u>below</u> the rank of major are not eligible for foreign posting. 7. The rumour is that there is a secret chamber <u>under/underneath</u> the building. 8. She hid her sorrows <u>beneath</u> a smiling face. 9. Almost half the world's population earn <u>under</u> two dollars a day. 10. Which is the next town <u>on</u> this road?

Activity 2: 1. in; 2. at; 3. at, in; 4. into; 5. on; 6. on; 7. on; 8. on; 9. at; 10. at.

Activity 3: There is a beautiful lake near my village. There are trees all <u>around</u> it. Thousands of birds have built their nests <u>in</u> those trees. Birds fly <u>over</u> the water; kingfishers snatch up fish <u>from</u> the lake. Children of the village swim and make merry <u>in</u> its cool waters. Men sit <u>beside</u> it for hours to catch fish. In the evening, elderly men sit and chat <u>on</u> the cemented ghats <u>of</u> the lake <u>in</u> the lengthening shadows. The ghat is old and has many cracks <u>in</u> it. By the side <u>of</u> the lake is a huge acacia tree. There is a rumour that a pot of gold is buried <u>beneath/underneath</u> the tree.

37

Talking About Time

37.1 *IN*, *ON*, AND *AT*

In Chapter 36, we discussed the prepositions used when we talk about places. In this chapter, we are going to study the prepositions of time. The general rule is:

We use *in* before a period of time such as a year, season, month, or week. We use *on* before days and dates. Before a specific point in time, we use *at*.

Follow this chart to talk about time:

In before year/month/season	Ravi is going to attend a conference <u>in</u> March. Radhika and Ravi got married <u>in</u> 2015.
On before day/date	They got married <u>on</u> 29 November 2015. They go to a Spanish class <u>on</u> Friday. I don't feel like going to Spanish class <u>on</u> a day like this. (=I don't want to….)
At before a specific point in time	The class starts <u>at</u> 6 PM. <u>At</u> the beginning of the class, the teacher announced a test. <u>At</u> dinner (time)/<u>at</u> the end of the test/<u>at</u> that moment We sleep <u>at</u> night. (= We sleep when it is night.)

Also:

In before part of the day	<u>In</u> the morning/<u>in</u> the evening/<u>in</u> the night of 27/28 July He heard a strange sound <u>in</u> the night (= sometime <u>in</u> the night).
On before day plus part of the day	It happened <u>on</u> Monday night. The meeting will be held <u>on</u> Friday morning.
At before a period of two or three days	<u>at</u> the weekend

Note: Indian newspapers often use the expression *'in the wee hours'* to mean early morning. This is a North American expression. Better use ***the small hours*** to convey <u>early in the morning</u>, soon after midnight. *We started from Ranchi after an early dinner and reached Kolkata in the small hours.*

37.2 MORE PREPOSITIONS OF TIME: *WITHIN, DURING* ...

The following conversation shows the use of some more prepositions of time:

Project manager: We have to complete the project <u>within</u> six months.

Assistant: Yes, I know. We have to lay the foundation <u>during</u> January. And the pillars have to be raised <u>before</u> the end of March.

Project manager: Right. And we have to complete the rest of the work <u>between</u> April and June. But as we've fallen <u>behind</u> schedule, can we work longer hours?

Assistant: Sir, we already have a long day. We reach office <u>by</u> 8.00 in the morning and work <u>through</u> the day <u>till</u> 8.00 in the evening. We even work <u>during</u> our lunch break.

Notes:
1. ***Between … and:*** A common mistake: *Our office is open between 4 PM ~~to~~ 8 PM.* ✗ You should say:
    ✓ Our office is open <u>between</u> 10 AM and 5 PM. Or
    ✓ Our office is open <u>from</u> 10 AM <u>to</u> 5 PM.
2. ***Till*** and ***until*** mean the same thing, but ***until*** is preferred at the beginning of a sentence.

37.3 *SINCE* AND *FOR*

Since means *from that time till now.* *For* is used to refer to a period of time.

Since	For
I've been waiting <u>since</u> 6 o' clock.	I've been waiting <u>for</u> an hour.
It hasn't rained <u>since</u> last October.	It hasn't rained <u>for</u> six months.
He has been working here <u>since</u> 2006…	I waited <u>for</u> two hours./He'll be away <u>for</u> a month. He had been working here <u>for</u> 10 years before he resigned.
We use *since* only with the present perfect to talk about something that started in the past and has continued till now.	We use *for* with the present perfect, simple past, past perfect, and also when we talk about the future.

We often confuse between *since* and *for*. Avoid mistakes like: *He has been sick ~~since~~ 20 days.* ✗

ACTIVITY 1

Fill in the blanks with *a, an, the,* and *as, of, for, at, on, to, in, against, with,* and *by*

Mohandas Karamchand Gandhi, popularly known _____ Mahatma Gandhi or Gandhiji, was _____ tallest leader _____ our struggle _____ independence. He was born _____ Porbandar, Gujarat, _____ the 2nd _____ October 1869. ___ barrister trained in England, Gandhi was not successful as _____ lawyer ___ a lower court _____ Porbandar initially. _____ 1893, ___ rich Gujarati businessman requested him _____ work as his lawyer _____ South Africa. The visit _____ South Africa proved to be _____ turning point _____ Gandhiji's life. _____ South Africa, he participated _____ many struggles _____ racial discrimination.[1] He returned _____ India _____ 1915 and became the undisputed leader _____ our freedom struggle. He was one leader who could carry the masses _____ our country _____ him. He was killed _____ a Hindu fanatic[2] _____ 30 January 1948.

37.4 *AGO, BEFORE,* AND *EARLIER*

We use the adverb *ago* when we talk about a past time with reference to the present:

- ✓ Long <u>ago</u>, there lived a king.
- ✓ I applied for a passport three months <u>ago</u>; I am yet to receive it.

We use *before* or *earlier* with the past perfect tense:

- ✓ Ramu got a job only last month. He had completed his studies two years <u>before</u>/<u>earlier</u>.

---
[1] **racial discrimination:** treating people badly because of the colour of their skin.
[2] **fanatic:** (noun) a person who holds extreme or dangerous opinions.

37.5 *DURING* OR *WHILE?*

During is a preposition like *in, on,* or *at.*

- ✓ It means all through a period of time. (*There will be special trains _during_ the summer.*)
- ✓ It also means at some point in a period of time. (*Sister phoned _during_ the lunch break.*)

Compare *during* with *while:*

- ✓ My sister phoned <u>while</u> I was having lunch.
- ✓ Did anyone call <u>while</u> I was away?

While is a linking word like *when.* It is used before a clause like *I was having lunch.*
You don't remember what a clause is? Please turn back to Section 4.3 and check the definition.

PRACTICE

1. Fill in the blanks with one word:

   A. You use .... only with the present perfect to talk about something that started in the past and has continued till now.
   B. We use .... with the present perfect, the simple past, the past perfect, and also when we talk about the future to describe a period of time.

2. Correct the following sentences. (You have to change only one word in each sentence.)

   A. I have been waiting since two hours.
   B. He gets up early at the morning.
   C. I have to attend a meeting in Monday.
   D. We admit children between 4 to 5 years.
   E. I passed higher secondary exams long before.
   F. Finally, I received the passport for which I had applied six months since.

3. Fill in the blanks:

   A. I am tired. I've been waiting _____ more than an hour!
   B. I am tired. I've been waiting _____ morning!
   C. Durga Puja will be held _____ September this year.
   D. George and Rini married last year. They had met five years _____.
   E. A band played music _____ the half-time of the match.
   F. A troop of dancers entertained the spectators _____ the players were having lunch.

4. Complete the sentences by adding prepositions:

   A. We stopped/Dubai/three hours/our way/London.
   B. I am going/a short trip/Goa/the weekend.
   C. My grandfather goes/a walk/the morning.
   D. We will issue admission forms/4th July/9th July.
   E. The Nilgiri's Kurinji flowers bloom once/12 years.
   F. I'll be attending a short course/baking /the summer vacation.

5. I have removed the prepositions of time from the following paragraph. Put them back to complete it.
    Use **ago, at, before, behind, for, in,** and **on.**

    Next month, I am going abroad three years. that, I have to do a lot of work. I applied for visa two weeks, but I haven't received it yet. I must telephone my travel agent again Monday. I had to submit a report in my present office last week, but I couldn't. I fell schedule because of various reasons. But today I will leave the office sharp 5 PM because I have to go to my friend Ravi's house the evening.

◼ KEY TO ACTIVITY

Activity 1: Mohandas Karamchand Gandhi, popularly known <u>as</u> Mahatma Gandhi and also Gandhiji, was <u>the</u> tallest leader of our struggle for independence. He was born <u>at</u> Porbandar, Gujarat, on <u>the</u> 2nd <u>of</u> October 1869. <u>A</u> barrister trained in England, Gandhiji was not successful as a lawyer at a lower court in Porbandar initially. <u>In</u> 1893, <u>a</u> rich Gujarati businessman requested him <u>to</u> work as his lawyer <u>in</u> South Africa. The visit <u>to</u> South Africa proved to be <u>a</u> turning point <u>in</u> Gandhiji's life. <u>In</u> South Africa, he participated <u>in</u> many struggles <u>against</u> racial discrimination. He returned <u>to</u> India <u>in</u> 1915 and became the undisputed leader <u>of</u> our freedom struggle. He was one leader who could carry the masses <u>of</u> our country <u>with</u> him. He was killed <u>by</u> a Hindu fanatic <u>on</u> 30 January 1948.

38 More on Prepositions

Learning Objectives: After covering the prepositions of place and time in the previous two chapters, we will check some other prepositions now.

38.1 OTHER PREPOSITIONS

In the last two chapters, we discussed how we combine prepositions with nouns or pronouns to indicate the place or the time of an event. They also come in when we talk about how something happened, the cause of an event, and so on. Underline the prepositions in the following passage:

> Charandas Chor, a thief, works **with** sincerity. One day, he came to know from a source that the Sharmas were on vacation and there were lots of valuables in their house. He broke into the house **by** cutting a grille **with** a hacksaw. Unfortunately, the street dogs started barking and Charandas was caught **by** Mr Sharma's neighbours.
>
> Although Charandas got caught, he was not sorry **for** what he had done. But he was sorry that **for** all his expertise in burglary, he had failed once again. When Mr Sharma came back, he thanked the neighbours profusely **for** what they had done.

- We use *with* to talk about the manner or means of doing something:
    - ✓ Charandas works <u>with</u> sincerity. (manner)
    - ✓ He cut a grille <u>with</u> a hacksaw. (means)
- We use *by* before what causes something:
    - ✓ Charandas broke into the house <u>by cutting</u> a grille.
    - ✓ His attempt to burgle the house was foiled <u>by street dogs</u>.
    - ✓ He was caught <u>by Mr Sharma's neighbours</u>.
- *For* is used when we talk about the cause, reason, and purpose of something:
    - ✓ Charandas thought it was a wonderful opportunity <u>for</u> burgling the house. (purpose)
    - ✓ Charandas was (not) sorry <u>for</u> what he had done. (cause)
    - ✓ Mr Sharma thanked his neighbours <u>for</u> what they had done. (reason)

- *For* is used also when we talk about contrast and comparison:
  - ✓ <u>For</u> (= in spite of) all his expertise, Charandas failed once again.
  - ✓ <u>For</u> one enemy, he has a hundred friends.
- For measure, standard, rate, and value, we use the following (let's forget Charandas Chor for a moment):
  - ✓ The bank pays interest <u>at</u> 9%.
  - ✓ This cloth costs ₹550 <u>per</u> metre.
  - ✓ Petrol is sold <u>by</u> litre in India and <u>by</u> gallon in the USA.
- We use *of* to connect adjectives and the nouns that follow them:
  - ✓ I am fond <u>of</u> Chinese food.
  - ✓ I am tired <u>of</u> watching cricket on TV.
- The following prepositions are used when we talk about possession or some other connection:
  - ✓ The girl <u>with</u> red hair is my sister.
  - ✓ Nandini had ₹500 <u>on</u> her.

ACTIVITY 1

On the Internet, I found this letter written by a parent to his/her son's teacher. The author seems to be unknown. I have removed some prepositions from the letter. Fill in the blanks and enjoy the beauty of the language:

He will have to learn, I know, that all men are not just, that all men are not true. But teach him also that (1) .... every villain there is a hero, (2) .... every selfish politician, there is a dedicated leader. Teach him that (3) .... every enemy there is a friend. It will take time, I know, but teach him, if you can, that a dollar earned is (4) ...... far more value (5) .... five found.

Teach him to learn to lose and also to enjoy winning. Steer him away (6) .... envy, if you can, teach him the secret (7) .... quiet laughter. Teach him, if you can, the wonder (8) .... books. But also give him quiet time to ponder[1] the eternal mystery (9)......... birds (10) .... the sky, bees in the sun, and flowers on a green hillside.

In school, teach him it is far more honourable to fail (11) .... to cheat. Teach him to be gentle (12) .... gentle people, and tough (13) .... tough. Try to give my son the strength not to follow the crowd.

Teach him to listen to all men. But teach him also to filter all he hears (14) ...... a screen of truth and take only the good that comes through.

Teach him, if you can, how (15) .... laugh when he is sad. Teach him there is no shame (16) .... tears.

Teach him to close his ears (17) .... a howling mob and to stand and fight, if he thinks he is right. Treat him gently, but do not cuddle him, because only the test (18) .... fire makes fine steel.

Let him have the courage to be impatient, let him have the patience to be brave.

This is a big order, but see what you can do … He is such a fine fellow, my son!

---

[1] **ponder:** (verb) to think about something seriously over a period of time.

38.2 INFERIOR, SUPERIOR, PRIOR, SENIOR, *AND* JUNIOR

Comparative adjectives are usually followed by ***than***: *He is older than me*. But the following adjectives ending with *-or* are followed by ***to:***

- ✓ Ravi was senior <u>to</u> me in college.
- ✓ As a singer, Mukesh is not inferior <u>to</u> Anil.
- ✓ Her marriage happened prior <u>to</u> her sister's.
- ✓ You are junior <u>to</u> me in age, but you are superior <u>to</u> me in other respects.

PRACTICE

1. Strike off the incorrect options:

   a) My friend works **with/by** sincerity.

   b) I came to know **of/from** a friend that a new shopping mall would come up in our city.

   c) For a long time, I had dreamed **of/for** setting up my own store.

   d) We wanted to check with the builders of the shopping mall **for/of** whatever it was worth.

2. Correct the following sentences. If a sentence is correct, put a ✓ next to it:

   a) You should be sorry by what you have done.

   b) Cloth is sold for the metre in India.

   c) 'How much does milk cost?' —'Rs. 20 by litre.'

   d) I am writing with a pen given by my dad.

   e) Ravi was senior than me in office.

   f) I don't think Sony laptops are inferior than Toshiba laptops.

3. Fill in the blanks with appropriate prepositions:

   a) Pujara batted _____ determination, like he always did.

   b) Are you fond _____ Punjabi food?

   c) Mangoes are selling _____ 50 rupees a kg.

   d) I bought 2 kg of mangoes _____ ₹100.

   e) We must not blame others _____ our failure.

   f) My sister is younger _____ me by two years.

   g) Ravi was junior _____ me in office.

   h) If you can speak English fluently, you can face the world _____ confidence.

KEY TO ACTIVITY

Activity 1: (1) for; (2) for; (3) for; (4) of; (5) than; (6) from; (7) of; (8) of; (9) of; (10) in; (11) than; (12) with; (13) with; (14) through; (15) to; (16) in; (17) to; (18) of

Test 6:
New Zealand Burglar with a Conscience

1. Strike off the incorrect options:

   A. We ~~use~~/**do not** use *a*, *an*, or ~~the~~ before names of people or places.
   B. We **use/do not use** *the* before names of oceans, seas, rivers, mountains, and the like.
   C. We **use/do not use** *the* before names of books that are known to everyone.
   D. We **use/do not use** *the* before names of musical instruments.
   E. We **use/do not use** *the* before the name of an institution that begins with the name of a person or place.
   F. If the name of an institution doesn't begin with the name of a person or place, we **use/do not use** *the* before its name.
   G. We **use/do not use** *the* before uncountable nouns used in a general sense.
   H. We **use/do not use** *the* before plural countable nouns used in a general sense.

2. Fill in the blank with *a*, *an*, or *the*:

   A. Uranium is ………. radioactive metal.
   B. I don't think it's ………. honourable proposal.
   C. Hardwar is ………. holy city for Hindus.
   D. This is ………. most expensive dinner I've ever had.
   E. We reached the concert hall ………. hour before the programme.
   F. Sheela is going to join ………. university next month.

3. Fill in the blanks with *a*, *an*, or *the*. If no article is required, put a '–' in the blank:

   A. Rohan is ………. best footballer in his school.
   B. ………. pen is mightier than ………. sword.
   C. Uneasy lies ………. head that wears ………. crown.
   D. ………. Maldives are a lovely archipelago of islands.
   E. When the going gets tough, ………. tough gets going.
   F. Have you visited ………. USA?
   G. The price of ………. computers has fallen drastically in recent years.
   H. ………. computers in our office are very old.

4. Complete the captions:

A. Rani is putting a coin ...... a piggy bank.

B. Birds have built their nests ...... the tree.

C. Mr Singh lives....... the first floor.

D. The kids are ...... the bus.

E. The boat is ...... the river.

F. He is leaning ...... a pillar.

G. Ravi is walking ...... the road.

H. The aircraft is flying ...... the

I. She's putting thread ...... the eye of a needle.

J. George is getting ...... a car.

K. There is a stain ...... your shirt.

L. Raghu is ...... his desk.

5. Complete the dialogue by adding prepositions:

Nisha: Do you know? Aamir Khan's next film will be released .... Friday, the 20th of March.

Rani: That's day after tomorrow. I am a great fan .... Aamir. I'd love .... see the movie. Besides, I haven't seen any film .... the holidays ended.

Nisha: I have two tickets .... the premiere. Why don't you come .... me?

Rani: Wow! The first show of *Taare Zameen Par*? Thanks a heap, Nisha!

Nisha: You're welcome, Rani. The premiere will be .... the Regal Cinema.

Rani: .... what time?

Nisha: The film starts .... 6.00 in the evening.

Rani: And where do we meet?

Nisha: Let's meet in front ………….. the theatre at 5.45.

Rani: That should be fine. But Nisha, I'll pay …………. the tickets.

Nisha: No, you won't. I didn't give you anything …………. your birthday. Treat this as my birthday gift.

Rani: Thanks. By the way, do you know anything …………. the film?

Nisha: Nothing much. I think it's …………. the relationship …………. a child and his teacher.

Rani: I heard that Amir has made the film …………. less than a year.

Nisha: In fact, he wanted to complete it …………. six months. The project was delayed…………. a few months.

6. This is a true story reported in newspapers in 2007. I have removed all the articles and some preposi-tions from the text. Fill in the blanks to complete the text. You will use the following prepositions (some of them more than once): *at, for, from, in, of, on, to, while,* and *with.*

New Zealand Burglar……… a Conscience

Associated Press, Queenstown, New Zealand, 31 August: ……… burglar visited Graeme Glass's home twice ……… one day, first to steal some goods and later to return them along ……… a heartfelt apol-ogy note.

……… thief struck while Glass was ……… work on Tuesday.

……… burglar smashed ……… window to gain entry and made off ……………… laptop computer, ……… camera, and Glass's wallet ……… …… American Express credit card. The thief returned the goods later …… ……… day, along with ……… new basketball and two pairs ……… gloves bought ……………… stolen credit card.

Glass and his wife Shirley discovered ……… loot piled ……… their kitchen table ……… a neat, handwritten full-page note ……… the burglar saying he was sorry ……… 'violating ……… safety and security ……… your home'. The robber also promised ……… leave cash ……… Glass's mailbox ……… pay ……… the smashed window when he had enough money.

'I have never written truer words when I say that I wish that I had never done this ……… you and your family,' ……… note read. '……… the bottom ……… my heart I am sorry.'

PART

7

SOME PRACTICAL AND USEFUL LANGUAGE

39

I Can Speak English Fluently

Learning Objectives: This chapter introduces Modal Verbs and covers the use of the verb 'can' for describing ability.

39.1 A GROUP OF VERBS CALLED *MODALS*

In Chapter 16, we discussed the helping verbs *be (am, is, are, was, were, will be)*, *have,* and *do.* We use these special verbs to frame negative statements, questions, and different tenses. The verbs **can, could, may, might, should, would, must,** and **ought to** belong to another group of helping verbs called **modal verbs** or simply **modals.** They are used before ordinary verbs to convey *ability, permission, possibility, compulsion, obligation, necessity,* and so on. These verbs are different from ordinary verbs. For example:

- We say *he can do it,* or *she might come. We* don't add *-s* or *-es* after them.
- These verbs don't have the *+ing* form or the *past participle* form. They cannot be used in continuous or perfect tenses.

The verb *need* is sometimes used as a modal verb. In Chapters 39 to 45, we are going to discuss some of these special verbs. Let's begin with the modal verb *can.*

39.2 DIFFERENT USES OF *CAN*

In isolation and without a context, the verb *can* usually doesn't tell you anything. It usually comes before another verb.

To talk about someone's **ability** to do something: *Rani can solve the Rubik's Cube.* Or: *'Can you drive?'* — 'Yes, I can.'

The verb *can* is also used in several other contexts. In this unit, we will discuss the use of *can* for talking about **ability** and **knowledge.**

39.3 STRUCTURES WITH *CAN*

The verb *can* has only two forms: **can** (present) and **could** (past). It neither has the *+ing* form nor the *past participle*. The forms in the present and past tenses are:

Positive Sentences:

I/We/You/He/She/It/They	**can/could**	**climb** coconut trees **play** the piano **hear** a noise

Negative sentences:

I/We/You/He/She/It/They	**cannot*** or **can't**/ **could not** or **couldn't**	**eat** 20 rasgullas at a time **swim** **see** anyone on the road

Questions:

Can/ Could	I/we/you/he/she/it/they	**break** three bricks with a karate chop? **cook?**

* Note: You shouldn't write ~~can not~~, it is *cannot*.

39.4 *CAN* AND *BE ABLE TO*

In the present tense, we use either **can** or **be able to.** They convey the same meaning but the second expression is a little more formal:

- ✓ Rani <u>can</u> swim or Rani <u>is able to</u> swim.
- ✓ Rohan is just four. Already, he <u>can/is able to</u> write.

For the future, we do not use ~~will can~~. We use **will be able to:**

- ✓ Take a taxi. <u>You'll be able to</u> reach the station in time.
- ✓ I think Tania <u>will be able to</u> live alone.

39.5 *COULD* AND *WAS/WERE ABLE TO*

For positive sentences in the past tense, we use either **could** or **was able to/managed to,** but they convey different meanings. **Could** is used to express general ability. But when we discuss someone's performance in a specific situation, we use **was able to** or **managed to** (not *could*), as shown in Table 39.1

TABLE 39.1 Use of *Can* in the Past Tense			
Can		**Was Able To/Manage To**	
Rani <u>could swim</u> when she was four years old.	*A past ability*	There was a competition last week. Rani <u>was able to swim</u> across the river.	*A specific performance in the past*
Magician Harry Houdini <u>could escape</u> from locked underwater boxes.	*A past ability*	There was a fire in the cinema. Fortunately, everyone <u>managed to escape</u>.	*A specific performance in the past*

Note: This rule is true for *positive* sentences. For *negative* sentences in the past form, we can use either *could not* or *was not able to*. For example:

✓ The market was closed, I <u>couldn't</u>/<u>wasn't able to</u> buy anything.
✓ Rohan was ill, he <u>couldn't</u>/<u>wasn't able to</u> play yesterday.

ACTIVITY 1

Complete the sentences using **could, was/were able to,** and **the verbs given within brackets:**

→   I <u>could climb</u> coconut trees when I was young. (climb)
→   The test was tough. Only two of us <u>were able to pass</u>. (pass)
1.   Sakuntala Devi long calculations in her head even as a child. (do)
2.   Usha 100 m in 13 sec when she was in school. (run)
3.   There was huge demand for the concert tickets, but I two. (get)
4.   The train was terribly crowded. But we (get in)
5.   The book was long and rather difficult. But I it. (finish)
6.   She _____ when she was a child, but now she sings really well. (not sing)

39.6 *COULD* AND VERBS ABOUT FEELING AND THINKING

Detective Bhola Singh hid himself behind a bush. He <u>could see</u> a gang of armed robbers discussing something in an open space barely 50 m away. He <u>could</u> even <u>smell</u> their cigarettes, but <u>couldn't hear</u> what they were saying. Bhola was scared. He <u>could feel</u> sweat running down his spine and <u>could hear</u> his heart pounding.

As you can see, even in positive sentences in the past tense, we use ***could*** with the sensory verbs such as *feel, hear, see, smell,* and *taste,* and also some state verbs such as *remember and understand* to talk about specific situations. This is an exception to the usage described in Section 39.5.

ACTIVITY 2

Complete these sentences using the following verbs: **smell, see, hear, remember, understand.** Follow the example given below:

The meteor[1] fell 10 miles away from our village, but we the .... explosion.

The meteor fell 10 miles away from our village, but we <u>could hear</u> the explosion.

1.   Radhika gave me the direction to her house. I .... it clearly.
2.   We .... the gorgeous peak of Kanchenjunga from our hotel.
3.   As Calvero entered the building, he .... leaking gas.
4.   I had to telephone Ravi urgently. Luckily, I .... his phone number.

39.7 ROHAN HASN'T BEEN ABLE TO PLAY...

To talk about ability in the present perfect tense, we use *be able to* as shown in the table below.

Present	Past	Present Perfect
Rohan isn't well, he cannot play today.	Rohan was sick, he couldn't/ wasn't able to play yesterday.	Rohan is sick, he hasn't been able to play today.
I can't/cannot put a thread through the eye of a needle.	I wasn't able to put the thread through the eye of a needle.	I've never been able to put thread through the eye of a needle.

PRACTICE

1.   Correct the following sentences if they are wrong. If a sentence is correct, put a ✓ next to it:

   a.   Take a taxi, you will can reach the station in time.
   b.   Tania is going to New York next month for three years. I think she can take care of herself there.
   c.   There was a transport strike in the city yesterday. Ravi could walk to his office.
   d.   I couldn't prepare at all, but I managed to pass the exam.
   e.   It was a difficult book, but I could finish it.
   f.   As our train was crossing the bridge over the Yamuna, we could see the Taj Mahal.

---

[1] **meteor:** (noun) a piece of rock falling from outer space, SHOOTING STAR.

2. Fill in the blanks using the verbs given within brackets and any one of the following:

can	**could**	**managed to**	**was able to**
will be able to	**couldn't**	**hasn't been able to**	

My friend Raju belongs to a very special family. All his family members have some special talents. Let me begin with his grandad, who passed away last year. Grandpa (1) .... (climb) coconut trees even when he was 80. His wife, that is, Raju's grandma too is no more. She (2) .... (speak) 11 languages, (3) .... (teach) us maths, but she (4) .... (not cook) very well. Raju's mother has a fantastic memory, she (5) .... (recite) long verses from the Mahabharata. One of Raju's uncles, Nikhil Das, was a champion swimmer. Once Uncle Nikhil was travelling by a boat on the Ganga, when it capsized.[2] He (6) .... (swim) ashore. Raju himself is a black belt in karate. He (7) .... (break) three bricks with a karate chop. In fact, Raju (8) .... (break) a brick with a karate chop when he was 10 years old. Last year, Raju (9) .... (defeat) the karate champion of his college. Raju (10) .... (participate) in the next inter-university games. As Raju spends a lot of time on karate, unfortunately, he (11) .... (pass) the annual exam this year. Oh! I haven't mentioned Raju's older sister. She is an excellent driver. One day, she drove us to the railway station. There was a massive traffic jam on the way, but thanks to her, we (12) .... (reach) the station just in time.

3. Complete the sentences using appropriate verbs. Make all of them positive sentences. Follow the given model:

The boat capsized in midstream. All the people on board .... ashore.

The boat capsized in midstream. All the people on board <u>managed to swim/was able to swim</u> ashore.

1. There was a solar eclipse yesterday; we .... it from Eastern India.
2. The professor explained a difficult concept, but we .... u .... it clearly.
3. If you start now, you .... Kottayam by sunset.
4. I am still reading the book I borrowed from you last week. I' .... r ....
   it next week.

4. Write about two things that you can do now and two things that you could do 10 years ago. Then write about two things that you cannot do now, but will be able to do in the future.

▌ KEY TO ACTIVITIES

Activity 1: 1. Sakuntala Devi <u>could do</u> long calculations in her head ... . 2. Usha <u>could run</u> 100 m in ... . 3. ... but I <u>was able to get</u> two. 4. ... we <u>were able to</u> get in. 5. ... but <u>I was able to finish</u> it. 6. She <u>couldn't</u> sing .../<u>wasn't able to</u> sing ... .

Activity 2: 1. ... I <u>could understand</u> it clearly. 2. We <u>could see</u> ... . 3. ... he <u>could smell</u> leaking gas. 4. Luckily, I <u>could remember</u> ... .

---

[2] **capsize:** (verb) when something like a boat capsizes, it turns over on its side in water.

Suggestions and Permissions

Learning Objectives: In this chapter, we are going to check the use of 'can' and 'could' for making suggestions and asking for and giving permissions.

40.1 WE CAN TAKE A BUS

In Chapter 39, we discussed the use of the verb **can** for talking about someone's *ability to do* or *knowledge of* something. Let us now check the functional language used for making suggestions and asking for or giving permissions. More specifically, we will cover the areas shown in the Table 40.1.

TABLE 40.1 Expressions for Making Suggestions, Seeking/Denying Permission

Suggestions	1.	To make suggestions	The place is too far to walk. We <u>can take</u> a bus. Or: We <u>could take</u> a bus.
Permissions	2.	To ask for permission	<u>Can I borrow</u> your pen for a minute? Or: <u>Could I borrow</u> your pen for a minute?
	3.	To give/refuse permission	The principal said, 'You <u>can go</u> now.' = The principal said, 'You <u>may go</u> now.'
	4.	To communicate/deny permission on behalf of someone else	You <u>can meet</u> the manager after 3 PM. You are <u>not allowed to enter</u> a temple wearing shoes.

40.2 MAKING SUGGESTIONS: *CAN* AND *COULD*

Sometimes, we also use the verb *can* and *could* to make suggestions:

Radhika: Where are we going for our holidays?
Ravi: We <u>can go</u> to Goa. (Also: We <u>could go</u> to Goa.)

Here, Ravi is making a suggestion. Both *can* and *could* are used for this. The difference between the two forms is that Ravi is *less certain* when he says: *We <u>could</u> go to Goa.* A few more examples:

- ✓ <u>Can</u> I <u>help</u> you with the luggage? (Or: <u>Could</u> I...?)
- ✓ The room is stuffy. <u>Can</u> I open the window? (Or: <u>Could</u> I...?)

ACTIVITY 1

Complete the dialogue using *could* and the keywords given within brackets:

Radhika: What shall we do in the evening?
Ravi: *We could see a movie*. (see a movie)
Radhika: What movie?
Ravi: I. We .... (see *Kahaani* once again)
Radhika: But there is no time for cooking dinner.
Ravi: 2. Well, we .... outside. (eat)
Radhika: And how will we go to the cinema?
Ravi: 3. We .... a taxi. (take)

40.3 ASKING FOR/GIVING PERMISSIONS: *CAN, COULD,* AND *MAY*

1. We can use the verb *can* to ask for and to give permissions:
   - ✓ <u>Can</u> I go in as an opening batsman? —Yes, you <u>can</u>.
   - ✓ <u>Can</u> I read the newspaper? —Yes, please.
2. But when you are asking for permission, it is more polite to use *could:*
   - ✓ <u>Could</u> I go in as an opening batsman? —Yes, you <u>can</u>.
   - ✓ <u>Could</u> I have your pen for a minute? —Yes, you <u>can</u>.
3. *May* is used in formal situations such as during an exam or in an office:
   - ✓ <u>May</u> we start writing now? —Yes, you <u>may</u>.
   - ✓ <u>May</u> I come in, sir? —Please come in.
4. To refuse permissions, you use *can't.* (You don't use *could/couldn't* to give/refuse permission.)
   - ✓ <u>Can</u> I smoke here? —I am sorry, you <u>can't</u>.
   - ✓ I am afraid, you <u>can't</u> take this lift. It's only for patients.

5. To refuse permission, you also use **must not,** which is more forceful than can't:
   ✓ The patient is critically ill. You <u>must not</u> enter the ICU.[1]

ACTIVITY 2

Fill in the blanks with one of the given options:

1. .... I borrow your bicycle for a day?   (Could/Should/Will)
2. .... I give you a little more rice?   (Can/Shall/Should)
3. .... you please hold my bag for a moment?   (Shall/Could/Would)
4. Sir, I've to see a doctor. .... I leave office an hour earlier?   (May/Shall/Will)
5. .... I sit down?   (Will/Should/Can)
6. .... I see the document?   (Will/May/Must)
7. .... you show me the way to the post office?   (Could/Shall/Might)
8. You .... talk during the exam.   (Will not/Cannot)

40.4 MORE ABOUT PERMISSION: *BE ALLOWED TO*

Often, you have to communicate permission on behalf of someone else. For example, if you are a hospital administrator, you may have to write notices for visitors. I saw the following instructions in a hospital recently:

VISITORS *CAN SEE* PATIENTS BETWEEN 5 PM AND 7 PM	VISITORS *ARE NOT ALLOWED TO* ENTER THE ICU
ONE RELATIVE *IS ALLOWED TO STAY* OVERNIGHT WITH CRITICAL PATIENTS	VISITORS *MUST NOT BRING* FOOD FOR PATIENTS

For conveying permission on behalf of someone else, we use *can* or *is/are allowed to.* And as we saw earlier, *must not* is used when you wish to convey something strongly.

---

[1] **ICU:** Acronym for intensive care unit; *ICCU:* Intensive cardiac care unit.

PRACTICE

1. Put a ✓ next to a sentence if it is correct. Put a ✗ if it is not:

   A. Can you please put a little more sugar in my tea?
   B. Would I read the newspaper?
   C. Could I carry your bag?
   D. Will I use your calculator?
   E. You can pay your telephone and electricity bills at this counter.
   F. Tourists are not allowed to take any foodstuff into the USA.

2. Fill in the blanks with the verbs given within brackets and with the following:

can   could   may   must not   are allowed to   are not allowed to

   What shall we do in the evening? —Well, we <u>can/could play</u> cards. (play)

   1. .... I .... the window please? (open)
   2. The museum is far away from here. We .... a taxi. (take)
   3. .... I .... this book for a day? (borrow)
   4. My son is ill .... I .... from home for a week? (work)
   5. You .... your car here. (park)
   6. Employees .... their infants in the crèche run by the office. (leave)
   7. Visitors .... on the lawn. (sit)
   8. Passengers .... only one hand baggage on flight. (carry)
   9. This office is a no-smoking zone. You .... here. (smoke)
   10. There are critically ill patients in this ward. Visitors .... their mobile phones here. (use)

3. What do these signs convey? Write in full sentences:

   A. Smoking .... here.
   B. You are ....
   C. Parking is..................................this side of the road.
   D. ....

KEY TO ACTIVITIES

Activity 1: 1. We <u>could see</u>.... 2.... we <u>could eat</u> outside. 3. We <u>could take</u> a taxi.

Activity 2: 1. Could; 2. Can; 3. Could; 4. May; 5. Can; 6. May; 7. Could; 8. Cannot

Talking About Possible Future Events

41.1 *MAY* AND *MIGHT*

Read this conversation between Ravi and George and note the underlined verbs. If a verb is about a certain future event, put (C) next to it. If it talks about a possibility, put (P):

George: Congrats, Ravi! I'm really happy that <u>you're going</u> to Argentina on an overseas posting[1] (C/P)!
Ravi: Can't say I will go, but I <u>might</u> (C/P).
George: Are you not sure about it?
Ravi: No, I'm not. Actually, our company <u>is setting up</u> a power plant in Argentina (C/P). Next January, they<u>'ll send</u> a team of five engineers there (C/P). That is certain. Our management has drawn up a shortlist[2] of 10 people, and I am one of them. Finally, five of us <u>will be sent</u> (C/P). So right now, you can say I <u>might get</u> an overseas posting (C/P).
George: And how are they going to select?
Ravi: Well, the 10 of us are doing a crash course in Spanish. After a month, we<u>'ll have to take</u> a test in Spanish (C/P). I'll have to pass the test.
George: I am sure you <u>will</u> (C/P).
Ravi: Thanks, George. But I am not too sure. All I can say is that I <u>might pass</u> (C/P).

You would have marked the following sentences as CERTAIN future events:

1. … you<u>'re going to</u> Argentina…. (When George says this, he has no doubt in his mind.)
2. My company <u>is setting up</u> a power plant in Argentina.
3. The company <u>will send</u> a team of five engineers there.
4. Five of us <u>will be</u> finally <u>sent</u>. (3 and 4 are neutral statements about future events.)

---

[1] **posting:** (noun) the act of sending someone to a distant place on work.

[2] **shortlist:** (noun) a small number of people who have been chosen for final selection for a job, prize, posting, and the like. The verb *shortlist* is generally passive: *Salman Rushdie has been shortlisted for the Booker Prize again.*

5. After a month, <u>we'll have to take</u> a test in Spanish. (A future obligation)
6. I am sure that you <u>will</u>. (George is certain that Ravi will pass.)

You learned these forms earlier. The following sentences talk about POSSIBLE events in the future:

1. Can't say I will go, but I <u>might go</u>. (= Perhaps I will go.)
2. I <u>may get</u> an overseas posting. (A possibility)
3. I <u>might pass</u> the test. (Another possibility)

We are going to discuss these forms in this chapter.

41.2 THE STRUCTURE

The structure of sentences with *may/might* is:

I/We/You/He/She/It/They	**may/may not** or **might/might not**	**join** a university next year **go** to the A.R. Rahman concert **watch** a movie at the weekend

---

ACTIVITY 1

Fill in the blanks with one of the following: *be going to, may, or might.*

1. I've got a scholarship. I .... join a postgraduate course next July.
2. I haven't got a scholarship yet, but I am trying. All I can say is that I .... join a post-graduate course.
3. Priyanka has been shortlisted for an interview. She .... get the job.
4. This is not a difficult exam. If you work hard, you .... certainly pass.

41.3 *MAY* OR *MIGHT?*

As we see from the dialogue in Section 37.1, *may* and *might* are interchangeable when we talk about real possibilities. But when we talk about imaginary possibilities, we use *might* (and NOT *may*):

✓ I am really tired. If it was a Sunday, I <u>might sleep</u> through the day.
✓ If the rain stopped, we <u>might</u> go out for a walk.

Might is also used as a past form of *may*, when we report a possibility expressed in the past.

✓ Ravi said he <u>might pass</u> the test. (= Ravi was not sure.)
✓ Smita said she <u>might go</u> to the party.

41.4 POSSIBLE SITUATIONS IN THE PRESENT

We also use *may* or *might* to talk about possible situations in the present time:

- ✓ Ravi <u>may be</u> in office. Or: Ravi <u>might be</u> in office. (= Perhaps Ravi is in office now.)
- ✓ It <u>may be</u> true. Or: It <u>might be</u> true. (= Possibly it is true.)

We will discuss this in detail in the next chapter.

PRACTICE

1. Fill in the blanks with the verbs given within brackets and one of the following: ***am going to***, ***may***, ***might***, ***'ll***, ***won't***.

   1. We have finished our packing. We .... within an hour. (start)
   2. There is a transport strike tomorrow, but I have to go to office. I .... to the office. (walk)
   3. Raghu has just got a big pay hike. He .... his job. (change)
   4. There is a massive traffic jam. We .... not .... the station in time. (reach)
   5. I haven't decided what I'll do after school. I .... computer science. (study)
   6. We haven't decided where to go during the holidays. We .... Goa. (visit)
   7. Do you think Rahul will top his class this year?—I am not sure, he ....
   8. Aamir Khan .... an Oscar this year. (win)
   9. If God gave me a boon, I .... a pair of wings. (ask for)
   10. My boss was not very sure, he said he .... on leave for a week. (go)

2. Think of five things that you would like to do, but you are not certain about. Then write down five sentences with *may or might*. I have written two such sentences:

   → I may join a baking class next month.
   → After retirement, I might travel to China to see the Great Wall.

   A. ....
   B. ....
   C. ....
   D. ....
   E. ....

KEY TO ACTIVITY

Activity 1: 1. am going to; 2. may/might; 3. may/might; 4. 'll/will

Possibilities Now ...

42.1 MAY/MIGHT BE, SHOULD BE/OUGHT TO BE, MUST BE, CAN'T BE

How do you talk about a *possible situation* in the present? Imagine a situation when you are fairly sure that Ravi is in office. It would be grammatically correct if you say:

It is possible that Ravi is in office.

But it wouldn't be natural English. Normally, you say:

- ✓ Ravi may be in the office. Or: Ravi *might* be in the office. (= Perhaps he is in the office.)
- ✓ It <u>may</u> be true. Or: It <u>might</u> be true. (= Perhaps it is true.) While talking about the present, *may* and *might* are interchangeable.

42.2 SHOULD BE/OUGHT TO BE, MUST BE, CAN'T BE

Should or ***ought to*** is used when we talk about something that we think is correct:

- ✓ Ravi should be in the office. Or: Ravi ought to be in the office. (You are more certain now than when you say: Ravi <u>may</u> be in the office.)
- ✓ Shall I put two spoonfuls of salt? —That should/ought to be fine. (The speaker thinks two spoonfuls will be the right quantity.)

Must is similar to ***should/ought to,*** but is stronger or more definite. When you are certain about something, you normally use ***must:***

- ✓ (Ravi left an hour ago. He reaches office in 15 minutes.) Ravi <u>must</u> be in the office now.
- ✓ (Raghu wakes up late on Sundays.) It's only 6.30. Raghu must be sleeping now.

The opposite of ***must be*** is ***can't be:***

- ✓ Ravi left only five minutes ago. He <u>can't</u> be in office now.
- ✓ Raghu has been denied promotion again. He <u>can't</u> be happy.

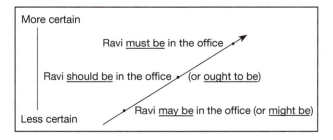

I/We/You/	**must**	**be**	in office/happy/tired/
He/They	**can't**		joking/kidding[1]/sleeping

ACTIVITY 1

Fill in the blanks with **might be, must be,** or **can't be:**

A. Satish expected a 20% bonus. He got 25%. He .... happy.
B. Manish was expecting a 20% bonus. He got only 10%. He ....
    happy.
C. Rohit missed first class by just three marks. He .... upset.
D. You've been running around all day. You .... tired.
E. You've been sleeping all day. You .... tired.
F. Radhika isn't answering her phone? She .... in a meeting.

42.3 ARE YOU SURE IT HAPPENED?

When you talk about a possibility in the past, you use ***might have.*** If you are certain that something actually
happened in the past, you use ***must have.*** And if you think something was impossible, you use ***couldn't
have.***

Case 1: Possibility

✓ Tausif and I grew up in the same town. We <u>might have known</u> each other as kids.
✓ I don't know why the cheque's bounced. I might have forgotten to sign it.

Note: You can't use *may* for the past: I ~~may~~ have forgotten to sign it. ✗

---

[1] **You must be kidding** is an informal way of saying *you must be joking.*

Case 2: Certainty

- ✓ This is a hand-painted silk sari. It <u>must have been</u> expensive?
- ✓ I built a bungalow at Bengaluru. —It <u>must have cost</u> a fortune?

Case 3: Impossibility

- ✓ I <u>couldn't have finished</u> the work in a day.
- ✓ After the floods, the farmers <u>couldn't have repaid</u> the loans even if they wanted to.

The form is:

I/We/You/He/They	**might**	**have**	**been** in the office
	must		**forgotten** to pay the bill
	couldn't		**finished** the work

ACTIVITY 2

Complete the dialogues following the model given:

Dialogue 1 A: I trekked to Manas Sarovar last year.
　　　　　　B: It **must have been** difficult?
Dialogue 2 A: Raghu told me you have been selected for a posting to Paris.
　　　　　　B: Paris? He .... joking.
Dialogue 3 A: In Paris, we had dinner at a restaurant on the second level of the Eiffel Tower.
　　　　　　B: It .... expensive!
Dialogue 4 A: In Australia we climbed the Sydney Harbour Bridge.
　　　　　　B: It .... exciting!

■ PRACTICE

1. Add *one word* to complete the following sentences:

   A. 'Radhika and I went to see the Great Wall of China.' —'It must have .... a great experience?'
   B. Ravi hasn't come to the office. He might .... unwell.
   C. Ravi didn't come to the office the whole of last week. He must have .... ill.
   D. Radhika has been working all day; she must .... tired.
   E. Rohan has just found a big bar of chocolate in the fridge. He must delighted!
   F. Rohan can't play the match because he has a fever. He must .... disappointed.

2. Which of the above sentences talk about the present? And which sentences are about the past?

   Sentences that talk about the present: ☐ ☐ ☐ ☐
   Sentences that talk about the past: ☐ ☐

3. Note the situations and use **must be, must have,** and **couldn't have** to form complete sentences using the hints given:

   —Her face is familiar, but I can't place her.
   I/meet her/somewhere   → I must have met her somewhere.

   A. Raghu sleeps in the office and you say that he works hard.
      You/joke   → ....
   B. He had been driving for 10 hours when the accident occurred.
      He/tired   → ....
   C. George seemed out of sorts[2] at the party last week.
      He/upset   → ....
   D. You didn't answer the phone yesterday afternoon.
      You/sleep   → ....
   E. The letter was mailed only two days ago.
      Radhika/not get it/yesterday   → ....
   F. Rohan has come at the top of his class.
      He/work hard/during the year.   → ....

KEY TO ACTIVITIES

Activity 1: A. must be; B. can't be; C. must be; D. must be; E. can't be; F. might be

Activity 2: Dialogue 2: He must have been joking. Dialogue 3: It must have been expensive? Dialogue 4: It must have been exciting?

---

[2] **out of sorts:** Ill or upset.

We Should, We Must, We've Got to ...

Learning Objectives: In this chapter, we are going to analyse and practise the language we use to talk about (a) our obligations and (b) what we think is proper. We will also learn some verb–noun collocations in the process.

43.1 LIVE WELL, LIVE LONG

A friend of mine once said, 'If a man is good, he's good in everything. He is a good husband, good father, he's responsible towards his parents, works diligently[1] at office, talks politely, and never drives recklessly.'

How true! If we wish to be a good human being and a good citizen, we must follow some rules. What does that mean? We will continue the discussion, but let's take a break for two activities to improve our vocabulary.

ACTIVITY 1

Combine words from the two columns to form meaningful phrases:

1. avoid	carefully
2. be	exercises regularly
3. be	graciously
4. behave	housework
5. do	responsible towards parents
6. do/get/take	punctual
7. drive	overeating

---

[1] **diligent:** (adjective) a person who is careful and hardworking.

8. eat	time with your family
9. go (out)/do	healthy (food)
10. go on/have/take	diligently
11. have	in a small voice
12. pay	a holiday
13. talk	fun
14. spend	shopping
15. work	taxes promptly

Check your answers with the key before moving ahead.

ACTIVITY 2

Here is a passage that talks about good living. Strike off the incorrect options and fill in the blanks with words from the phrases you have framed in Activity 1:

We all want to be successful, and we work hard to achieve our goals. However, in today's world, haven't many of us become 'money-rich-time-poor'? Don't many of us have incomplete family life, suffer from 'lifestyle diseases', and age prematurely? Here is a recipe for living happily and being successful.

For good health, you **should/must/have to eat** .... and .... **overeating**. You **should/must/have to** also d............ e........................ r....................... and be disciplined. Avoid stress and cigarettes, and sleep well. Your mind is a part of your body, and so you **should/have to** .... **fun** once in a way. .... **shopping**, watch films. You **should/must/have to** also try to .... **a holiday** when you can.

To be successful, you **should/must/have to w**......... d...................... You **should/must/have to be p**..................... at office every day and plan ahead to complete work in time.

To have a healthy social life, you **should/must/have to be r**....................... towards your parents, be a good husband/wife and s............ t............ with your children. You **should/must/have to do h**....................... and help your spouse. In general, you **should/must/have to** spend as much time as you can with family. Keep in touch with friends who matter, and b.............. g....................... while dealing with people.

Finally, let's follow the laws of the land. For example, we **should/must/have to** pay our taxes p..................... We **should/must/have to** also follow rules everywhere. So let's d .... c....................... and not cross speed limits, neither on the road nor in life in general.

43.2 SHOULD OR MUST?

Let's move back to our discussion. *What does it mean to be a good human being?*

I think it means you have certain obligations[2] towards the people around you and to the world in general. A good person accepts responsibilities, and a bad person doesn't.

Moving back to the English language, we use ***should*** or ***must*** to talk about

1. obligations and
2. what we think is right.

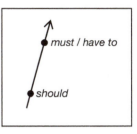

And between the two, *must* is stronger. For example:

1. We <u>must</u> pay our taxes. ++
2. We <u>should</u> reach the station 15 minutes before our train leaves. +
3. You've a cold for two weeks? I think you <u>should</u> see a doctor. +
4. You have a cough for two months? You <u>must</u> see a doctor. ++

Often, the boundary between *must* and *should* depends on your judgement. For example, you can say: *We <u>mustn't</u> eat too much chocolate.* You can also say: *You <u>shouldn't</u> eat too much chocolate.* The two sentences indicate how strongly you feel about the effect of chocolate on health.

Ought to is another way of saying ***should.*** But it is used less often.

- ✓ You <u>should</u> wash your hands before a meal. = You <u>ought</u> to wash ….
- ✓ You <u>shouldn't</u> sleep so little = You <u>ought not to</u> sleep so little.

ACTIVITY 3

Select (✓) the more natural expression:

1. There are a few typos[3] in your report. You **should/must** be more careful.
2. Your answer is completely off-topic. You **should/must** analyse the task first.
3. They would cut off the electricity if I didn't pay the bill by tomorrow. I **should/must** pay it now.
4. This bill is to be paid by next week. I **should/must** pay in a day or two.

43.3 MUST, HAVE TO, OR HAVE GOT TO?

Must, have to, and ***have got to*** are often interchangeable:

- ✓ I <u>must</u> complete my assignment[4] today. = I <u>have (got) to</u> complete ….
- ✓ I <u>have (got) to</u> meet my physics professor regarding the project. = I <u>must</u> meet ….
- ✓ I <u>must</u> form a group to work on the project. = I'<u>ve (got) to</u> form a group ….

---

[2] **obligation:** (noun, uncountable) something you are bound to do, morally or legally, DUTY.

[3] **typo:** (noun) a minor error in typing.

[4] **assignment:** (noun) a task given to you as a part of your job or course of study.

However, there is sometimes a subtle difference between the two. We use *must* more often for moral or internal obligations. On the other hand, *have (got) to* indicates an obligation forced upon us by a law or rule, that is, an external obligation.

- ✓ I <u>must</u> study hard in the new course. ⇨ I would like to ….
- ✓ To take the final exams, I <u>have to</u> attend 80% of the classes. ⇨ It's a rule.

The table below gives more examples:

Have To: External Obligations	**Must:** Internal Obligations/Strong Opinions
In India, you <u>have to</u> pay income tax by 31 July. ⇨ A legal necessity	I <u>must</u> learn to live within budget. ⇨ An internal obligation
You <u>have to</u> drive on the left side of the road in England. ⇨ More natural than ~~You must drive ….~~	You <u>must</u> avoid junk food of all kinds. ⇨ A strong opinion, not ~~You have to avoid junk food….~~

ACTIVITY 4

Beginning with *I, We, You,* or *People*, complete the sentences using the given words. *Make the sentences longer by adding more details from your imagination.*

A. work diligently/office

  ………

B. take a holiday

  ………

C. share housework/your spouse

  ………

D. children/go to bed/10.00 in the night.

  ………

E. be gracious/strangers

  ………

F. watch Aamir Khan's films/important social messages

  ………

43.4 NEGATIVES AND QUESTIONS

The negative forms are ***should not*** (or ***shouldn't***) and ***must not*** (***mustn't***). ***Must not*** is stronger:

- ✓ You <u>shouldn't</u> drive so fast.
- ✓ You <u>mustn't</u> drive so fast. ⇨ Stronger than the previous sentence

The negative of both ***must*** and ***have to*** is ***must not*** or ***mustn't***:

- ✓ You <u>mustn't</u> smoke—it's killing you. ⇨ A strong opinion
- ✓ You <u>mustn't</u> smoke in public places in India. ⇨ A legal restraint

---

ACTIVITY 5

Fill in the blanks with either *have to* or *must:*

➤ At this college, you ¹..................... attend at least 75% classes to be eligible to take university exams. But if you want to do really well, you ²..................... attend all the classes. To enter the college premises, you ³..................... show your ID card.

➤ I ⁴..................... work night shifts every other week and I am tired of working at night. I ⁵..................... look for another job.

However, the negative form ***don't have to*** means something entirely different. It means *you have the freedom not to do something.* Check these sentences:

Mustn't or Must Not	*Don't Have To*
We <u>mustn't</u> wear jeans in our office.	We <u>don't have to wear</u> formals in our office.
You <u>must not</u> feed animals in the zoo.	You <u>don't have to</u> tip taxi drivers here.
↑ We aren't allowed to/ ↓ A very bad idea	You <u>don't have to</u> pay for incoming phone calls in India.
You <u>mustn't</u> irritate animals in a zoo.	↑ It's not necessary, but you can, if you wish.

43.5 SHOULD, MUST, AND HAVE TO IN THE PAST

There are no past forms of the verbs *should* or *must*. If you have to talk about a necessity or obligation in the past, we use this form:

[+] Subject + **should have** + **past participle form of the verb** + other words
[–] Subject + **shouldn't have** + **past participle form of the verb** + other words

We often use this form to express regret:

[+] Lost your keys? You <u>should/ought to have been</u> more careful.
[+] It's too late now. You <u>should have applied</u> for the job a month ago.
[+] I missed the train, I <u>should have started</u> earlier.
[–] George left the job after a tiff with his boss. He <u>shouldn't have been</u> so hasty.
[–] People <u>shouldn't have elected</u> this government to power.

It is easy to express sentences with ***have to*** with reference to the past:

Present: I <u>have to</u> renew my driving licence.
Past: I <u>had to</u> renew my driving licence.
Present: It's a new firm. We <u>don't have to</u> pay any tax this year.
Past: Last year, our company made a tiny profit. We <u>didn't have to</u> pay income tax.

PRACTICE

1. For the words given in the table below, select the opposite from *behind time, diligent, reckless, rude, ungracious, sporadically.*

A. (−) careless ⇨		(+)	B. (+) cautious ⇨		(−)
C. (+) gracious ⇨		(−)	D. (+) polite ⇨		(−)
E. (+) prompt ⇨		(−)	F. (+) regularly ⇨		(−)

2. Use the given clues and with one of the antonyms you have just written in Task 1, frame meaningful sentences:

    A. There are too many mistakes in this essay. [_____]/ be/more/should/you/been/have
        You should have been more diligent. ....

    B. You almost killed all of us. you/have/shouldn't/so/[_____]/been
        ....

    C. I am sorry about my outburst last night. shouldn't/have/been/I/[_____]
        ....

    D. She was kind to you, but you didn't even thank her. shouldn't/been/have/you/[_____]
        ....

    E. Once again, you've submitted the report late. do/month/have/you/be/to/[_____]/every/?/
        ....

3. Fill in the blanks with ***should, must, have to, has to, shouldn't,*** or ***mustn't:***

    *   I [(a)]................. go to bed now. I'll [(b)].................... go to office early tomorrow morning. Ah! I [(c)].................... set an alarm on my phone.
    *   I'd love to spend more time at the party, but I [(d)]............ go now. I [(e)].................... join a conference call with my boss in the USA and our client in China.
    *   Different countries have different rules and cultures. All over the world, you [(f)].................... carry your driving licence while driving.
    *   In Saudi Arabia, every foreigner [(g)]...................... carry their ID card at all times.
    *   Chewing gums are banned in Singapore and any violation invites heavy penalty. You [(h)]........................ chew gums at a public place there.
    *   If you are invited to an Arab home, you [(i)]........................ appreciate a painting on the wall or anything similar. Because if you do, your host might pack it and give it to you as a gift.
    *   When you are in India, you [(j)]........................ touch anything with your feet; people consider it inauspicious.

4. Frame sentences following the model given:

    ➤   You missed the opportunity to learn computers at school.
        You should have learned computers at school.

    A. You missed a deadline because of genuine problems, but didn't explain your difficulties to the boss.
        You .... boss.

    B. Raghu complained against his colleagues. It was not the right thing to do.
        Raghu ....

C. You've just bought some expensive air tickets because you delayed buying them. ....
    .... the tickets earlier.
D. By the time she went to a doctor, her condition had become serious. ....
    .... much earlier.
E. Your telephone line has been disconnected because you forgot to pay the bill. ....
    .... in time.

KEY TO ACTIVITIES

Activity 1: 1. avoid overeating; 2. be punctual; 3. be responsible towards parents; 4. behave graciously; 5. do housework; 6. do/get/take exercises regularly; 7. drive carefully; 8. eat healthy food; 9. go (out)/do shopping; 10. go on/have/take a holiday; 11. have fun; 12. pay taxes promptly; 13. talk in a small voice; 14. spend time with family; 15. work diligently

Activity 2: For good health, you **should** eat **healthily** and **avoid** overeating. You **should** also **do exercises regularly** and be disciplined. Avoid stress and cigarettes, and sleep well. Your mind is a part of your body, and so you **should have fun** once in a way. **Go/Go out shopping**, watch films. You **should** also try to **go on/take/have** a holiday when you can.

To be successful, you **must/should work diligently**. You **should** be **punctual** at office every day and plan ahead to complete your work in time.

To have a healthy social life, you **must** be **responsible** towards your parents**,** be a good husband/wife and **spend time** with your children. You **should** do **housework** and help your spouse. In general, you **must** spend as much time as you can with family. Keep in touch with friends who matter, and **behave graciously** while dealing with people.

Finally, let's follow the laws of the land. For example, we **have to/must** pay our taxes **promptly.** We must also follow the rules everywhere. So let's **drive carefully** and not cross speed limits, neither on the road nor in life in general.

Activity 3: 1. should; 2. must; 3. must; 4. should

Activity 4: *Suggested answers*

A. I/We **must** work diligently at office at all times.
B. We all **should** take a holiday once in a way to destress ourselves.
C. We **must/should** share housework with our spouse because sharing is at the heart of a healthy relationship.
D. Children **should** go to bed by 10.00 in the night because a good night's sleep is essential for development of the brain.
E. We **should** be gracious with strangers.
F. I think you **should** watch Aamir Khan's films, they often carry important social messages.

Activity 5: 1. have to; 2. must; 3. have to; 4. have to; 5. must

The Versatile Would

44.1 *WOULD:* A VERSATILE VERB

We use the verb **would in many different ways. The short form of would is 'd.** In this chapter, we are going to discuss some important uses of the verb. We use it in the following cases:

1. To make polite requests:
   - ✓ <u>Would</u> you close the door behind you?
   - ✓ <u>Would</u> you please show me your ID card?
2. To make offers or invitations:
   - ✓ <u>Would</u> you like to have a cup of coffee?
   - ✓ <u>Would</u> you join us for dinner tomorrow?
3. To talk about the result of an event that you imagine:
   - ✓ She <u>would</u> look better in a sari.
   - ✓ It <u>would</u> be foolish not to accept the job.
4. To convey that you like/love/hate/prefer/enjoy something:
   - ✓ I'<u>d love</u> a cup of hot coffee.
   - ✓ I <u>would</u> prefer a window seat.
5. You also say you **would like to do** or **would like to be** something:
   - ✓ 'What are your plans for the weekend?'—'Nothing. I'd just <u>like to lie down</u> and do nothing.'
   - ✓ I <u>would like to buy</u> a bungalow at Bandra seafront.
   - ✓ I'<u>d be</u> glad to help.
6. When you are giving an opinion that you are not certain about, you use the form: *I **would imagine/ say/think,** or the like (that)....*
   - ✓ I'<u>d say</u> his girlfriend is over five feet eight inches.
   - ✓ I <u>would imagine</u> it will take a week to get the car repaired.
7. We use **would** to talk about regular activities in the past:
   - ✓ On Sundays, we <u>would go out</u> for long drives.
   - ✓ When we were small, we <u>would go</u> to school on foot.

We also use the **used to** form to describe these situations: *We <u>used to go</u> to school on foot.* (= We walked to school every day.)

ACTIVITY 1

Unscramble these questions and statements:

1. Would please you this report check? ....
2. You'd hair better look in short ....
3. have Would like you to cup a of tea? ....
4. I prefer would a seat window ....
5. the I to would go to moon like ....
6. say tall the I'd thief feet is about six ....

44.2 THE NEGATIVE FORM

The negative form is ***would not*** or more commonly ***wouldn't:***

- ✓ I <u>wouldn't like</u> to work in a call centre.
- ✓ The salary offered to me is good, but I <u>wouldn't like</u> to work night shifts.
- ✓ I <u>wouldn't like</u> to talk to Murthy, but unfortunately, he's my boss.

44.3 AN IMAGINARY FUTURE, A POSSIBILITY IN THE PAST

- When we talk about imaginary situations in the *future*, we use the form **would + verb**.
- When we talk about imaginary situations in the *past*, we use the form **would have + past participle form of the verb.**

Would Do (Future)	Would Have Done (Past)
I <u>would go</u> out for a walk, but it's raining.	I <u>would have gone out</u>, but it was raining.
I'd <u>withdraw</u> some cash, but I can't find my ATM card.	I <u>would have withdrawn</u> some cash, but I couldn't find my ATM card.

PRACTICE

1. Would you like doing these things? Complete the sentences with *would, 'd, or wouldn't* depending on your choice, and the verb given within brackets:

   → I .... to meet Vidya Balan. (love)
   → I'd <u>love</u> to meet Vidya Balan.

   A. I .... live in a house without windows. (like)
   B. I .... delighted to watch a play by Naseeruddin Shah. (be)

    C. I .... a visit to New Delhi in the summer. (enjoy)
    D. It .... a good idea to get into a fight with a professional boxer. (be)
    E. Oh! I am awfully tired. I .... to have a shower. (love)

2. Complete the sentences following the given model:

    → I .... a flat. But I don't have any money.
    → I'd like to buy a flat. But I don't have any money.
    A. I .... but I have a sore throat.
    B. I .... Kashmir, but I don't have any leave.
    C. I .... a car, but there is no parking space near my house.
    D. I .... a computer, but there is no electricity in our village.
    E. I .... match, but it's completely sold out.

3. Write the above sentences in the past tense. Follow the model given:

    → I would have liked to buy a flat, but I didn't have any money.

    A. ....
    B. ....
    C. ....
    D. ....
    E. ....

4. What will you say in these situations? Follow the given model answer:

    A. You are requesting your friend to join you for a picnic.
    → Would you join us for a picnic?
    B. You are offering someone a cup of tea.
    → ....
    C. You are in a restaurant with friends. You are yet to decide about the menu. Tell the waiter to come back after a few minutes.
    → ....
    D. You are asking someone to show you his ID card.
    → ....
    E. Ask a shopkeeper to send the goods to your house.
    → ....

KEY TO ACTIVITY

Activity 1: 1. Would you please check this report? 2. You'd look better in short hair. 3. Would you like to have a cup of tea? 4. I would prefer a window seat. 5. I would like to go to the moon. 6. I'd say the thief is about six feet tall.

Wish You Good Luck

45.1 THE VERB *WISH*

We convey our good wishes to people in different ways. And for this, we often use the verb **wish**.

- ✓ **Wish** you good luck. (= I wish you good luck. *I/we* is often silent in sentences like this.)
- ✓ We **wish** you a long and happy married life.
- ✓ My friends **wished** me a pleasant journey.

45.2 *WISH* AND *HOPE*

We wish people good luck or success, but we cannot say: *I wish you'll have a pleasant stay in India.* ✗
Instead, use the verb *hope* in sentences as shown below:

- ✓ Welcome to India. Hope you'll have a pleasant stay in our country. (This is more formal than 'Wish you a….')
- ✓ I hope the weather will be good when you visit Darjeeling.

Some more examples:

Wish	Hope
(I) Wish you a safe journey.	(I) Hope your journey will be safe. (Correct, but rarely used.)
Congrats! Wish you a long and happy married life.	–
We wish the Indian team all success.	We hope the Indian team will win.

45.3 REGRETS

In the last chapter, we saw that we express regrets with *would: I wouldn't like to talk to Murthy, but he's my boss.*
We express this idea a little differently with the verb *wish.*

✓ I <u>wish I didn't have to talk</u> to Murthy, but he's my boss.
✓ I <u>wish I could sleep</u> now. (= I can't sleep now.)
✓ I <u>wish I were</u> rich. (= I am not rich.)
✓ I <u>wish you put</u> on a sweater. (= You refuse to put on a sweater.)

In all the sentences above, you are talking about *something in the present that is not all right*. So to express regrets about things as they are at the present, we use the form:

I+wish+I/we/he/she/it/they+past form of verb+other words

45.4 REGRETS ABOUT THE PAST

When you express regret for something that happened or did not happen in the past, you say:

✓ I <u>wish I hadn't bunked off</u> classes at college so often. (= It's too late now!)
✓ I <u>wish you had</u> set an alarm on your phone; you wouldn't have missed the train.
✓ I <u>wish I had listened</u> to my father then!

Note the difference between these sentences and those given in Section 45.3. The three sentences in this section are about *something that didn't happen*. And when you express regrets about the past, you use the form:

I + wish + I/we/he/she/it/they + past perfect + other words

PRACTICE

1. Fill in the blanks with the appropriate form of *wish* or *hope:*

   A. I .... you every success in life.
   B. I .... you'll find a good job soon.
   C. .... it won't rain during our picnic.
   D. I .... you success in your new job.
   E. I .... you'll come at the top of your class.
   F. I .... income tax rates will be reduced.
   G. My boss .... me good luck for promotion.
   H. I .... my boss was more sensitive.

2. How will you wish a friend in the following situations?

   (a) At the time of her wedding
   ⇨ ....
   (b) When she is about to take an exam
   ⇨ ....
   (c) When she is going abroad
   ⇨ ....

3. If a sentence is about the present, write *present* next to it. If a sentence is about the past, write *past*.

    A. I wish I my friend Joe was here ....

    B. I wish I was not so forgetful ....

    C. I wish I hadn't been so rude with her ....

    D. I wish she kept her words more often ....

    E. I wish I hadn't forgotten my wife's birthday ....

4. What would you say in these situations? Rewrite the sentences beginning with *I wish*:

A. It is my friend's wedding today, but I cannot attend because I have influenza.	I wish ....
B. You are going on a holiday. Your husband forgot to book air tickets. (So you have to spend a lot for the tickets now.)	I wish ....
C. You have to pay a fine because your accountant didn't file your income tax return on time.	I wish ....
D. I am extremely forgetful.	I wish ....
E. I've got an invite to attend a conference in Paris, but I cannot go. I didn't renew my passport.	I wish ....

Test 7:
Modal Verbs

1. Strike off the incorrect options:

   A. **Could/Will** I have a glass of water please?
   B. **Could/Shall/Should** you hold my bag for a moment?
   C. **Will/May/Would** I come in?
   D. **Shall/May/Will** I join the meeting half an hour later?
   E. **Could/Shall/Will** I borrow your bicycle for a day?
   F. **Could/Shall/Will** you please pass the salt?
   G. **Could/Shall/Would** you have a cup of coffee?
   H. We are going to see a film. **Could/Shall/Would** you like to join us?

2. Complete the sentences with one of the following:

can   could × 2   was able to × 2   were able to

   A. Rishi .... run 100 m under 13 sec when he was 14 years old.
   B. Now he .... run 100 m under 12 sec.
   C. Last year, he .... beat the district sprint champion at a sports meet.
   D. It was a difficult exam. Only Raju .... pass.
   E. We .... see Mount Everest from our hotel.
   F. There was a massive traffic jam, but we .... reach the station in time.

3. I work on my computer for many hours every day and often suffer from backache. Once, when I was down with a troublesome back, my sister told me what I should and shouldn't do to avoid back pain. I am giving you some hints. Reconstruct what my sister said using **should, ought to,** or **shouldn't.** You have to add prepositions, adverbs, linking words, and so on to complete the sentences.

   A. use/a firm chair/arms

   ....

   → not bend/the keyboard
   You shouldn't bend down on the keyboard.

   B. not sit/the computer/hours/a stretch

   ....

   C. get up/walk around/a few minutes every hour

      ....

   D. also, do some stretching exercises

      ....

   E. fix/anti-glare screen/your monitor

      ....

   F. splash cold water/your eyes/a few hours

      ....

4. Add two to three words to each of the following sentences to complete them:

   A. You've been travelling all day; you .... tired.
   B. You've been sleeping all day; you .... tired.
   C. 'Yesterday, the coach told Rohan he will play for his school team.'—'He .... delighted?'
   D. I don't know why the cheque bounced. I .... forgotten to sign it.

5. Complete the sentences following the model given:

   → I know her, but I cannot recall who she is. I/meet her/somewhere.
      <u>I must have met her somewhere</u>

   A. Mumbai Indians are second from the bottom. And you're saying they will be the champion. You/joke

      ....

   B. He worked three shifts at a stretch. He/exhausted

      ....

   C. The boss was unusually irritable yesterday. He/upset by something

      ....

   D. I don't see the email to Radhika in my sent email. Radhika/not get it

      ....

6. Complete the sentences with **'ll/will/might:**
   I haven't yet decided what I'... do after secondary exams. I .... visit my uncle in Mumbai. There is only one problem. My uncle .... go to Europe on some work during that time. But I .... still go, my aunt and cousin Arun .... be in Mumbai. My friend Gautam said he .... join me for the trip, but he is not sure. I hope he .... be able to go with me. We .... visit Matheran too, but I am not certain about it.

7. Complete the sentences using any one of *hope, might, must, ought, should, have to, needn't,* and *wish:*

   A. 'Where is Ravi?'—'I am not sure, he .... be in office now.'
   B. It is a Sunday. Irfan doesn't go out on Sundays. He .... be at home.
   C. You have a cough for a week? You .... consult a doctor.
   D. If you wish to go abroad, you .... get a passport first.
   E. As an Indian national, you .... get visa to go to Nepal in advance. You'll get it on arrival.
   F. We .... take care of our elderly parents.
   G. .... you a safe journey.
   H. I .... the weather will be fine when you're in Darjeeling.

8. Rewrite these sentences using **should, shouldn't, must,** and **needn't:**

→ We are late; it is necessary for us to hurry up.
We are late; we should hurry up

A. It is not proper for TV channels to show so much violence.
TV channels..

B. It would be good if the government makes primary education compulsory.
The government..

C. You are not required to reserve a seat in advance for this bus.
You...

D. To work for a call centre, it is essential that you speak English or a foreign language fluently.
To work in a call centre, you..

9. Four of the following sentences are correct and four aren't. Put a ✔ if a sentence is correct and a ✖ if it isn't. If a sentence is incorrect, underline the mistake.

A. Pauls said they may join us for dinner yesterday, but they didn't.
B. You have to cover your head in a Gurudwara, but you needn't in a church.
C. You are suffering from cough. You don't have to smoke.
D. You need not carry inflammable materials such as gas stoves on a train.
E. Wish you a pleasant journey.
F. Sir, may I leave now?
G. No, you couldn't leave before 5 o'clock.
H. My boss said he might not come to office today.

10. What will you say in these circumstances to convey good wishes?

A. Your sister is about to enter an exam hall.
....

B. Your grandma is in hospital. You are talking to her over the phone.
....

C. Your friend is getting married. You have come to attend his wedding.
....

11. What are your plans for the future? What will happen in the normal course? And what are the things that you want to do but are not confident about? Write down a few sentences following the model given below:

→ *I am going to join a university to do research in theoretical physics. After completing my PhD, I will teach at a college or university. My girlfriend and I are getting married next year. We don't like big cities so we will settle down in a small university town somewhere. We might go abroad for further studies.*

....
....
....
....
....
....
....
....

PART

LANGUAGE 'CLEAR AS SUNLIGHT, CRISP AS SAND'

'How Green Was My Valley'

Learning Objectives: In this chapter, we will expand our discussion on adjectives and check where to place them in a sentence. We will also build our vocabulary around adjective–noun collocations in general and global warming in particular.

46.1 DESCRIBING A PERSON, PLACE, OR THING

In Chapter 10, we discussed some basic language to describe people: *Radhika is <u>tall</u> and <u>slim</u>. My boss is <u>strict</u>, but always <u>accessible</u>.* Let's recall:

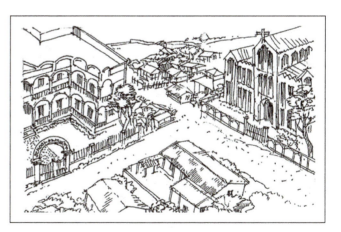

> An adjective is a word that describes a person, or a thing, or an idea.

In order to understand adjectives better, let's do a small task. Cover the text below and tick (✓) the adjectives in these phrases:

black board, free trade, snow white

You would have marked *black, free,* and *white* as adjectives. Now, as you read the passage below, underline all the *adjectives:*

I live in the country.[1] In my village, we have *small, beautiful* cottages and two *large* structures: the school and the church. The *red* school building is *old,* but the pale *yellow* church is even *older.* It is the *tallest*

---

[1] **to live in the country:** to live in a rural area, away from cities.

construction in the entire district. The church spire[2] is *taller* than the *century-old* teak tree in its compound.

The caretaker of the church, Kumar, is the *sole* occupant of the church compound at night. The burial ground behind the church is a *quiet* place full of *tall leafy* gulmohar trees. People say lots of ghosts have their homes there, but Kumar is *fearless*. He says: 'Ghosts? That is *utter* rubbish, sir!'

Kumar is *awake* at night, and *asleep* most of the day. He has a *big brown furry* dog named Kublai. Everyone is *afraid* of Kublai, but he is *fond* of me. Kumar is rather *old*. And these days, he looks *unwell*.

In this passage, all the words in *italics* are adjectives. Note that <u>teak</u> and <u>gulmohar</u> are names of trees, not adjectives. Also, <u>burial ground</u>, <u>school building</u> and <u>church spire</u> are **compound nouns,** that is, a noun phrase which is a combination of two nouns.

ACTIVITY 1

The following passage is an anecdote[3] from my school days. I have highlighted some adjectives and removed the rest of them. Fill in the blanks with the following:

calm	daunting[4]	dazzling	heavy	midday
panicky	scared	small	slushy	unthinkable

The bell announced the end of the (1)............... break, but there was something in the **crystal** sky and the **crisp** autumn sun that made the troop of **muddy** boys defy[5] it. A (2).............. sun had just come out after weeks of (3).............. showers, and almost all the students of our school had gathered on the (4).............. playground during the break. Innumerable football matches were being played on the same pitch at the same time. We kept playing, ignoring the bell. We were no angels, but such indiscipline was (5)...................... even by our standards. After a few minutes, suddenly, there was a **massive** flight.[6] We didn't know what had caused the (6).............. retreat, but we just ran, and the ground became **empty** in minutes. Then we noticed the **familiar dark hefty** figure of our Assistant Headmaster, Umapati Babu, standing beside the playground, doing nothing.

Umapati Babu was a (7).............. **unhurried** man who spoke in a (8).............. voice, but we were terribly (9).............. of him. Controlling 800-odd young rowdies was his responsibility and he made this (10).............. task look **easy**. He rarely raised his arm to beat an **errant** boy, but his name spelled terror.

---

[2] **spire:** (noun) a tall pointed structure on top of a building, particularly a church or a temple.

[3] **anecdote:** (noun) a short and amusing real-life incident.

[4] **daunting:** (adjective) extremely difficult, something that makes you nervous; INTIMIDATING.

[5] **defy:** (verb) to ignore a lawful instruction.

[6] **flight:** (noun) the act of fleeing.

46.2 WHERE DO WE PLACE THEM?

We place the adjectives *beautiful, old,* and many more either before a noun or after a state verb like *be* or *seem*:

- ✓ I live in a <u>beautiful</u> village. ◊ My village is <u>beautiful</u>.
- ✓ Kumar is an <u>old</u> man. ◊ Kumar is <u>old</u>.

When an adjective comes before a noun, it is called an ***attributive adjective.*** When it comes after a state verb, it is known as ***predicative adjective.*** (Don't worry too much about these scary names, but the concept is important!)

Most adjectives come either before a noun or after a state verb. However, there are some that ***never come before nouns.*** You put them only after a state verb (e.g., *be, look,* or *seem*):

- ✓ Everyone is <u>*afraid*</u> of Kublai, but he <u>is *fond*</u> of me.
- ✓ Kumar <u>is *awake*</u> at night, and <u>*asleep*</u> most of the day. These days, he <u>looks *unwell*</u>.

Here are some common adjectives that come only after a state verb:

afraid	afloat	alike	alive	alone
ashamed	asleep	awake	glad	ill
ready	sorry	sure	well	unwell

<u>Don't say</u>	**<u>Instead, use these expressions</u>**
An ~~asleep Kumar~~ ✖	Kumar is *asleep*; or a *sleeping* Kumar
An ~~afraid man~~ ✖	The man is/was *afraid*; or a *frightened* man

A good dictionary labels these adjectives with ***not before nouns, usually not before nouns,*** or ***only predicative.***

On the other hand, a few adjectives are used ***only before a noun:***

- ✓ Kumar is the <u>sole</u> occupant of the church compound in the night.
- ✓ It's <u>utter</u> rubbish.

Here are some adjectives that come only before nouns:

chief	main	only	inner	outer	latter	sheer

A good dictionary tells you which adjectives are used ***only before nouns*** or ***usually before nouns,*** or are ***only attributive.***

Attributive Adjectives

Attributive adjectives usually come before a noun: *strong man, quiet place,* and so on. But in a few situations, they come after the noun they describe.

➤ After words such as *no one, someone, anywhere,* and *somewhere*: *For this job, we need <u>someone mentally tough</u>.*

➤ In a few fixed expressions such as *snow <u>white</u>, secretary <u>general</u>,* and *court <u>martial</u>.*

ACTIVITY 2

Put a ✓ next to a statement if it is correct. If not, put a ✖:

1. The adjectives *inner* and *outer* come only before nouns.

2. We use the adjective *awake* before nouns, for example, an *awake man*.
3. *Beautiful* and *attractive* come both before nouns and after state verbs.
4. The adjectives *alone, afraid, ill,* and *unwell* are used only after state verbs.

ACTIVITY 3

Given below are sets of words that have a noun/noun phrase and an adjective. Combine them to form meaningful phrases. For three of them, you will have to add *am, is*, or *lives.* The first two have been solved.

→	option/my/only	My only option
→	the/awake/child	The child is awake
1.	the constable/head	....
2.	the Ring Road/Outer	....
3.	He/naughty	....
4.	I/ashamed	....
5.	my/alone/grandpa	....
6.	girlfriend/former/Ravi's	....

46.3 COMBINING ADJECTIVES WITH NOUNS

In Section 6.3, we discussed the concept of *collocation,* that is, accepted combinations of two or more words. There are fixed combinations for adjectives and nouns, as we have seen: *global warming, central heating,* and so on.

In the following activity, you will come across more adjective–noun collocations:

ACTIVITY 4

1. Read the following passage quickly and write 'T' if the statement is true. Write 'F' if it is false:

A. The passage discusses some of the effects of **deforestation** and increasing use of **fossil fuels**. ☐

B. The passage indicates that global warming can be controlled. ☐

Global warming refers to the increase in the earth's surface temperature since the late 19th century, and its effects on the environment. Between 1900 and 2010, the average surface temperature of the earth went up by approximately 0.8°C.

Almost all scientists believe that global warming has been happening because of the **greenhouse effect.** Let's recall here that a **greenhouse** is a glass/plastic structure that traps sunlight, increasing the temperature within. It is used for growing plants in cold regions by creating an artificially warm environment (without consuming energy). Unfortunately, the modern man has been burning far too much of fossil fuel, that is, coal, petroleum, and natural gases, which discharges into the atmosphere a lot of carbon dioxide (CO_2) and other **greenhouse gases** that trap heat waves received from the sun. Also, forests have been shrinking[7] as millions of trees are felled every year to make room for a growing human population. When a tree is cut down, it **discharges** its stored carbon into the atmosphere, which adds to the greenhouse gases. Consequently, our atmosphere has become a gigantic greenhouse, resulting in steady increase in temperature.

In 2007, the Intergovernmental Panel on Climate Change (IPCC), a United Nations body, calculated that over the 21st century, global surface temperature is likely to rise further by 1.1–2.9°C in the **best-case scenario**, and 2.4–6.4°C in the **worst-case scenario.**

An increase in global temperature will cause **sea levels** to rise, **submerging** many islands and coastal areas. It will change **rainfall patterns. Subtropical deserts** will possibly expand. Other likely effects of global warming are retreat of **polar ice** and melting of the Himalayan and other **glaciers**, extreme weather events such as **heat waves** and **droughts** (pronounced DRAUTS), or a long period of low rainfall. Many life forms will become **extinct** and crop yields will fall. If the global average temperature increases beyond 4°C above the pre-industrial level, the human race may not survive.

The clock is ticking. We don't have much time left. Governments must enforce deep cuts in **emission** of greenhouse gases and embrace **sustainable development** to save humankind.
[*Source of information:* Wikipedia]

ACTIVITY 5

Complete the crossword with words from the above passage. (Refer to a dictionary if you wish.)

A1	a glass/plastic structure that creates artificial warming	D1	the act of cutting down a large number of trees
A2	a synonym of DISCHARGE (noun)	D2	_ _ _ _ _ _ FUEL, natural fuel like coal formed in the past from the remains of living organisms
A3	_ _ _ _ _ _ _ _ _ _ DEVELOPMENT is progress without harming the environment	D3	H E A T _ _ _ _ _ (plural) are prolonged periods of abnormally hot weather
A4	a river of ice on mountains or poles that moves slowly	D4	a prolonged period of little or no rain
A5	the B E S T-C A S E _ _ _ _ _ _ _ _ is the best among many possibilities	D5	S U B T R O P I C A L _ _ _ _ _ _ _ are waterless areas with little or no plants around the tropics
A6	R A I N F A L L _ _ _ _ _ _ _ _ are the overall sequence and duration of rainfall every year		

---

[7] **shrink:** (verb) to become smaller.

46.4 VOCABULARY BUILDING: MORE ADJECTIVE-NOUN COLLOCATIONS

Try to remember these. You will often find an opportunity to use them.

✓ **circumstantial evidence** = evidence that indicates something, but doesn't prove it
✓ **crowning glory** = the most impressive achievement: *The World Cup victory was the crowning glory of Kapil Dev's career.*
✓ **generation gap** = the differences in attitudes of older and younger people
✓ a **white lie** = a harmless little lie, especially one told to avoid hurting someone

✓ **a fair-weather friend** = a 'friend' who isn't seen in difficult times		
✓ **resounding success**	✓ **a close friend**	an **arch enemy**
✓ **a narrow victory**	✓ **a slender lead** = a small lead	✓ **a slim chance**
✓ **a decisive victory**	✓ **a dark horse** = an unexpected winner	
✓ **mutual respect**	✓ the **hour hand/minute hand** (of a clock)	
✓ **narrow escape**	✓ **notorious criminal**	✓ **unwritten law**

PRACTICE

1. Form pairs:

   A. broad   benefit
   B. circumstantial   lead
   C. close   information
   D. crowning   lie
   E. slender   glory
   F. definite   friend
   G. mutual   evidence
   H. white   daylight

2. Given below is a newspaper report. Fill in the blanks with adjectives from the list below. (Use an adjective only once.)

broad	circumstantial	close	definite	former
ghastly	middle-aged	notorious	slim	unwritten

   Mumbai, 25 August: A (1) .... man was murdered in (2) .... daylight in Malad today. An eye witness said three gangsters shot the man from a close range after he had got off a bus at Sundar Nagar. An inspector of the Malad police station, Bhola Singh told reporters that there was no (3) .... information about the killers. However, there was (4) .... evidence that a (5) .... criminal, Bullet Singh, was behind the (6) .... murder. If it was true, there might only be a (7) .... chance of catching the killers. The police have never been able to arrest Bullet Singh.

   Inspector Bhola also said that the murdered man was Bhaiya Giri, a (8) .... assistant and (9) .... friend of Bullet Singh, who fell out with the latter some time ago. It is an (10) .... law in the Mumbai underworld that gang members who challenge the authority of their bosses are eliminated.

3. Correct the following sentences:

   A. Look at the asleep man.
   B. The doctor says the unwell woman will recover soon.
   C. No one came to pick her up. A teacher took the afraid girl to her home.

4. Write down the opposites:

   a. asleep   ....
   b. leafy tree   ....

c. fashionable ....
d. tight ....
e. daunting ....
f. old-fashioned ....
g. partial ....
h. happy ....

5. Use four of the answers from Task 2 to complete the captions:

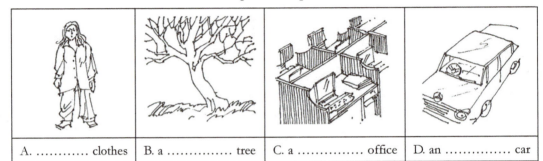

| A. .... clothes | B. a .... tree | C. a .... office | D. an .... car |

6. Write sentences with the words/phrases below:

A. global warming: ....
....

B. greenhouse effect: ....
....

C. sustainable development: ....
....

D. subtropical deserts: ....
....

E. Himalayan glaciers: ....
....

KEY TO ACTIVITIES

Activity 1: midday; 2. dazzling; 3. heavy; 4. slushy; 5. unthinkable; 6. panicky; 7. calm; 8. small; 9. scared; 10. daunting

Activity 2: 1. ✓; 2. ✗; 3. ✓; 4. ✓

Activity 3: 1. The head constable; 2. the Outer Ring Road; 3. He is naughty; 4. I am ashamed; 5. My grandpa lives alone. 6. Ravi's former girlfriend.

Activity 4: A – T; B – T

Activity 5: A1: GREENHOUSE; A2: EMISSION; A3: SUSTAINABLE; A4: GLACIER; A5: SCENARIO; A6: PATTERNS; D1: DEFORESTATION; D2: FOSSIL; D3: WAVES; D4: DROUGHT; D5: DESERTS

47

A Big Brown Furry Dog

Learning Objectives: In this chapter, we are going to focus on how to handle multiple adjectives and when to hyphenate an adjectival phrase. We are also going to check how one noun creates multiple adjectives.

47.1 A STRING OF ADJECTIVES

When we use two or more adjectives before a noun, there is usually one correct sequence for arranging them. For example, in Chapter 46, we found *Kumar had a big brown furry dog.* You do not say: *'a ~~brown furry big dog~~'*✗. Neither do you say *'a ~~furry big brown dog~~'*✗.

There is only one correct sequence of the adjectives: ***a big brown furry dog.***

> When you use two or more adjectives before a noun, the less argument there can be about an adjective, the closer to the noun it goes.

We say *a big brown furry dog* as there can be hardly any argument about whether a dog is *furry* or not. So *furry* goes nearest to the noun. Of the two other adjectives, there can be less argument about whether the dog is *brown* than whether it is *big.* Therefore, *brown* goes just before *furry* and *big* is placed the farthest from *dog.*

Similarly, we say: *a strong green metal door,* because *strong* is more arguable than *green,* which, in turn, is more *arguable* than whether it is *metal* or not. A few more examples:

- ✓ A <u>well-behaved five-year-old Kashmiri</u> boy
- ✓ A <u>hard-working tall Brazilian</u> footballer
- ✓ A <u>smart woollen dinner</u> jacket
- ✓ A <u>lush green</u> forest

Opinions and facts: Following the same logic, if there are two adjectives of which one gives an opinion and the other gives a fact, the adjective relating to the fact goes nearest to the noun. For example: *an expensive quartz watch.*

If one of the adjectives is approving and the other is disapproving, we often separate them with *but* or *though:*

- ✓ an <u>excellent but overpriced quartz</u> watch
- ✓ an <u>enjoyable though tiring</u> journey[1]

ACTIVITY 1

Write the adjectives in the correct order:

A. a .... trunk (steel, rusty)
B. a/an .... army officer (retired, spritely)
C. a/an .... sari (embroidered, reasonably-priced, silk)
D. a/an .... handbag (beautiful, expensive, leather)
E. a.................................... umbrella (folding, sturdy,[1] black)
F. a/an... office (four-storey, modern, impressive)

47.2 REASONABLY PRICED *OR* REASONABLY-PRICED?

When you write *The sari is reasonably priced,* the compound adjective *reasonably priced* is fine. However, if you use the same words before a noun, it is hyphenated: *a reasonably-priced sari.* Here are some more examples:

- ✓ a <u>fine-toothed</u> comb/the comb is <u>fine toothed</u>
- ✓ a <u>hand-woven</u> shawl/this shawl is <u>hand woven</u>
- ✓ a <u>four-storey</u> building/the building has <u>four storeys</u>
- ✓ a <u>state-of-the art</u> classroom/the classroom is <u>state-of-the-art</u>[2]
- ✓ a <u>five-year-old</u> boy/the boy is <u>five years old</u>

A Common Problem

Often, you read sentences like: *In Delhi, we face traffic jams* ~~everyday~~. ✗

If we have to write down <u>something that happens daily</u> *after a verb*, we use *every day* (two words): *In Delhi, we face traffic jams every day.*

However, before a noun, use *everyday: Traffic jams are an everyday problem in Delhi.*

---

[1] **sturdy:** (adjective) not easily breakable; STRONG.

[2] **state-of-the-art:** (adjective) something that incorporates the latest features of a particular product.

ACTIVITY 2

Rewrite the sentences placing all the adjectives before nouns. Follow the given model:

→ Ravi and Radhika drove down from Mumbai to Vadodara in a car they had purchased recently. It was a small Maruti car.	→ Ravi and Radhika drove down from Mumbai to Vadodara in their recently-purchased small Maruti car.
A. In the trunk[3] of their car, they had a large suitcase with a soft body, and a beautiful leather bag that was hand made.	
B. On the way, they stopped at Silvassa, a small town. The town was quiet and beautiful.	
C. They stayed overnight at a modern hotel that had three storeys. It was a comfortable hotel.	
D. The journey was somewhat tiring. But they enjoyed it too.	D. It was an

47.3 PAIRS OF ADJECTIVES: INTERESTING AND INTERESTED

Kartar Singh is playing computer games.

---

[3] **trunk:** (noun) the luggage space at the back of a car, BOOT. We Indians often call it DICKY.

Let me write two more captions for the above picture:

(1) Computer games are ***interesting***

⇩

Computer games attract people, people often have interest in them. Similarly, activities can be *amazing, thrilling, boring,* and so on.

(2) Kartar is ***interested*** in computer games

⇩

Kartar likes computer games, he has interest in them. Similarly, he may be *amazed, thrilled,* or *bored* by other activities.

The noun *interest* produces a pair of adjectives—*interesting* and *interested*— which have different meanings. Here are some more pairs:

Mohamed Salah scored an *amazing* goal.	I'm *amazed!* How could he do it?
Watching Premier League football is always *thrilling*.	I was *thrilled* to watch a match at the Wembley Stadium in London.
We reached London by train after an *exciting* journey through the tunnel.	I was *excited* to travel under the English Channel.

ACTIVITY 3

Given below are a few pairs of sentences. Follow the model given to complete the other sentence:

→ We got a f<u>a</u>sc<u>i</u>n<u>a</u>ting view of the Himalayas from the train.	→ I was f<u>a</u>sc<u>i</u>n<u>a</u>ted to see the Himalayas.
A. The map was a little *confusing*.	I was a little .... with the map.
B. Climbing up the hill was *exhausting*.	I was .... when I reached the top.
C. The fresh air on the hill was *refreshing*.	I was .... by the fresh air.
D. I find the new video game	I am *puzzled* by the new video game.
E. And I think the game is rather	I am rather *bored* with the new game.
F. Shall we go swimming? It's always	Shall we go swimming? I always find myself *relaxed* after a swim.
G. A .... waterfall	Water *cascaded*[4] down the hill.
H. A vast, *undulating*[5] land	The land .... for as long as we could see.

---

[4] **cascade:** (verb) (of water) Fall rapidly in large quantities.

[5] **undulate:** (verb) (to) go up and down; with *-ing* form (as adjective) often used to describe land that is not plain.

PRACTICE

1. Here is some information I have gathered from the Internet about Dadra and Nagar Haveli. Fill in the blanks using each of the following words once. Refer to a dictionary if necessary.

blue	cascading	green	leafy	lush
meandering[6]	rough	tall	tiny	undulating

    The union territory of Dadra and Nagar Haveli has $^{(1)}$ l......... $^{(2)}$ g........... forests covered with $^{(3)}$.............. $^{(4)}$ l......... trees, $^{(5)}$.................. rivers, $^{(6)}$.............. waterfalls, distant $^{(7)}$............ hills, and a wide variety of *flora and fauna*.[7] This land of only 70 villages is sandwiched between the states of Maharashtra and Gujarat. Silvassa is the tiny capital township of this union territory. It is a beautiful garden town with waterfalls, $^{(8)}$........... stone walls, $^{(9)}$........... stores, and $^{(10)}$.......................... fields with islands of flowers in between.

2. A reporter is interviewing a famous cricketer a few hours after the end of an international match. Complete the conversation using adjectives that have the following roots: ***disappoint, excite, exhaust, relax,*** and ***tire.***

Reporter:	Batting for 50 overs in the hot sun must have been *exhausting?*
Cricketer:	I wasn't................., just a little.................
Reporter:	But right now, you don't look................. Rather, you look relaxed.
Cricketer:	Yeah! A hot water bath at the end of the day is always.................
Reporter:	You couldn't hit the winning shot. How....................... were you?
Cricketer:	Not much, but indeed, it is....................... to get out when you are only two runs short of victory.
Reporter:	You are in the finals. The next match should be....................... How confident is the Bangladesh team?
Cricketer:	Well, we are....................... about the finals. Our chances? I would say it's 60:40.

3. Write a pair of sentences each with the following adjectives: (a) *surprised and surprising;* (b) *shocked and shocking;* (c) *confused and confusing;* (d) *annoyed and annoying.*

4. Think of (a) journey you enjoyed and (b) a person you admire. Write a sentence each on them using three or more adjectives:

    a. It was a/an ....
    .... journey.
    b. ....
    ....

---

[6] **meandering:** (adjective) (particularly of a river) that turns at several places along its course.

[7] **flora and fauna:** plants and animals.

KEY TO ACTIVITIES

Activity 1: A. a rusty steel trunk; B. a spritely retired army officer; C. a reasonably-priced embroidered silk sari; D. a beautiful expensive leather handbag; E. a sturdy black folding umbrella; F. an impressive modern four-storey office

Activity 2: A. In the trunk of their car, they had a <u>large soft-body</u> suitcase and a <u>beautiful hand-made leather</u> bag. B. On the way, they stopped at Silvassa, a <u>quiet and beautiful small</u> town. C. They stayed overnight at a <u>modern, comfortable, three-storey</u> hotel. Or:… at a <u>comfortable, modern, three-storey</u> hotel. It was an <u>enjoyable though somewhat-tiring</u> journey.

Activity 3: A. confused; B. exhausted; C. refreshed; D. puzzling; E. boring; F. relaxing; G. cascading; H. undulates

Comparing Cats with Dogs

48

Learning Objectives: Continuing with adjectives, in this chapter, we are going to discuss how adjectives are used to compare two or more things, people, or ideas.

48.1 COMPARING PEOPLE, ANIMALS, AND THINGS

On Sundays, I take a siesta[1] without fail. Last Sunday, when I got up from bed in the afternoon, I couldn't make out if the time was 4.30 or 6.20. When I looked closely, I realized that the minute hand of our grandfather clock was not longer than the hour hand. Naturally, I couldn't decide which was which! Our Alsatian, Dogendran, and our cat, Billy, were sleeping side by side. But Dogendran, a huge dog, had become much smaller than his normal size. And Billy had grown bigger. Presently, Billy was as big as Dogendran! Looking out of the window, I found the world had changed while I'd been sleeping: Our town had a flat horizon; all the buildings were of the same height! None was taller (or shorter) than others. The TV tower, by far the tallest structure around, had shrunk. It was just as tall as our house.

Can you imagine a world where everything was similar, where everyone looked alike, behaved the same way? Where all ice creams were plain vanilla? Surely, life would be miserable on such a planet! But thankfully, in our world, everything is different in shape, size, colour, and other qualities. And humans are so different from one another that you wouldn't find another person just like you unless you had a twin! And for this reason, we compare things and people all the time. We use three directions of comparison:

A Grandfather Clock

---

[1] **siesta:** (noun) rest or sleep taken in the afternoon. *You take/have a siesta.*

1. Higher:

   a. The minute hand of a clock is **longer** than the hour hand. (comparative)
   b. Billy has grown **bigger** (than what he was earlier). (comparative)
   c. The second hand is the **longest**. (superlative)

2. Same:

   The cat is **as big as** the dog.

3. Lower:

   India is **less populous** than China. (comparative)
   Sikkim is the **least populous** state in India. (superlative)

For the purpose of comparison and contrast, English has three forms or *degrees* of adjectives:

The cat was as big as the dog

Absolute	**Comparative**	**Superlative**
long	→ longer	→ the longest
heavy	→ heavier	→ the heaviest
intelligent	→ more intelligent	→ the most intelligent

We use the comparative form to compare two things (or the same thing at two different times) and the superlative when we contrast something with many others.

Contrasting[2] Two Things	**Comparing One Thing with a Group**
Mount Everest is higher than the Kanchenjunga.	Mount Everest is the highest mountain.
Raju is more intelligent than Dinesh.	Raju is the most intelligent boy in our class.
My dad is stronger than your dad.	My dad is the strongest!

We often use *than* after comparative forms of adjectives.

When you say, *Mount Everest is **the highest** mountain*, everyone knows that you are contrasting it with all the other mountains on earth. However, if you said *My dad is **the strongest** man*, the message would be confusing. Is your dad the strongest man in your family? Or is he the strongest man in the world? You have to specify the group of people among whom he is the strongest. So, better say: *My dad is the strongest man in our neighbourhood.*[3] Also, note that we **always** use ***the*** before words like *strongest* or *highest*.

My dad is the strongest man in town

---

[2] **contrast:** (verb) to compare two things in order to show the differences between the two.

[3] **neighbourhood:** (noun) the area around your house, and the people who live there.

48.2 COMPARATIVE AND SUPERLATIVE FORMS

This is how the comparative and the superlative forms of adjectives are constructed:

1. For all long adjectives and for any adjective that ends with *-ed*, we add **more** and **most** before the word to get the comparative and superlative forms:

   ➢ Long adjectives:
   ✓ surprising   → more surprising   → the most surprising
   ➢ Adjectives ending with *-ed*:
   ✓ interested   → more interested   → the most interested

2. For short adjectives (other than those that end with *-ed*):

   ➢ Most short adjectives form the comparative by adding *-er* and the superlative by adding *-est*:
   ✓ smart   → smarter   → the smartest
   ➢ If an adjective ends with *-e*, add *-r* and *-st*:
   ✓ fine   → finer   → the finest
   ➢ For adjectives that have a *consonant* and *y* as their last letters, replace *-y* by *-ier* and *-iest*:
   ✓ easy   → easier   → the easiest
   ✓ noisy   → noisier   → the noisiest
   ➢ For adjectives ending with *a vowel + consonant*, repeat the last consonant and add *-er* and *-est*:
   ✓ red   → redder   → the reddest
   ✓ big   → bigger   → the biggest
   ➢ For many adjectives, there is no rule, you have to remember them:
   ✓ bad, ill   → worse   → the worst
   ✓ good   → better   → the best
   ✓ far   → farther or further   → the farthest or furthest[4]
   ✓ late   → later and latter   → the latest and the last
   ✓ little   → less and lesser   → the least
   ✓ many   → more   → the most
   ✓ much   → more   → the most
   ✓ well   → better   → the best
   ✓ old   → older/elder*   → the oldest

* Note that *elder* and *eldest* are used only before nouns and, that too, for family members alone. Therefore, you don't say: *one of my ~~elder~~ friends* ✗. Nor: *My brother is ~~elder~~ than me.* ✗ You say: *one of my older friends* and *My brother is older than me.* See Section 48.3 for more details.

---

[4] When you talk about distances, you can use either further/furthest or farther/farthest. Further also means MORE. For example, we say: *There has been no further development in the matter.* You cannot use *farther* here.

A Word of Caution

Do NOT use two comparative or two superlative words together. Don't say:

➢ John is ~~less stronger~~ than Abraham. (Say: John is less strong than Abraham ✓)
➢ Vaijayanti is ~~more~~ prettier than Mala.
➢ Ramu is the ~~most~~ strongest boxer in Bhagalpur.

ACTIVITY 1

The States in India

There are 28 states and 7 union territories in India. As per the Census Report 2011, the largest states in terms of population are shown in the table below:

State	Population in Millions	Area in km²)	Population/km²
Uttar Pradesh	196	238,566	828
Maharashtra	112	307,713	365
Bihar	103	93,466	1,102
West Bengal	91	88,752	1,029
Andhra Pradesh	89	275,068	308
Tamil Nadu	72	130,058	555
Madhya Pradesh	73	308,144	236
Rajasthan	69	342,236	201

Using the information given in the table above, complete the sentences below. You will have to use the comparative and superlative forms of the adjectives given within brackets. In some cases, you have to use expressions such as 'second highest' and 'third most populous'.

1. Uttar Pradesh is by far the .... state in India. (populous)
2. Uttar Pradesh has .... people than Bihar and West Bengal put together. (many)
3. Maharashtra is the s........................ m .... state. (populous)
4. In terms of area, Rajasthan is the .... state in India. (large)
5. Among the eight large states, Rajasthan has the .... population. (little)
6. .... people live in Tamil Nadu than in West Bengal. But Tamil Nadu has .... area compared to West Bengal. (few, much)
7. The population density is the .... in Bihar and s................. .... in West Bengal. (high, high)

48.3 WORDS OFTEN CONFUSED

Less and *lesser:*

➤ **Less** = **a smaller amount** of something. It is used with uncountable nouns: *less sugar* or *less time: If you wish to lose weight, you should eat less carbohydrate and fat.*

➤ **Less** is also an adverb which means **to a smaller degree**; not so much: *less expensive, less populous, less intelligent,* and so on: *The shirt is less expensive than what you think.*

➤ When you refer to a countable thing, use **fewer**, not **less**: *There are fewer students in my class than in my sister's.*

➤ **Lesser** = not as great in importance or size in comparison with another or the rest. It is used only before a noun: *people of lesser importance, children of lesser gods,* and the like. The idiom *the lesser evil* means *the less unpleasant of two bad options.*

Later, latest and *latter, last:*

➤ **Later** and **latest** refer to time:
  ✓ I'll talk to you <u>later</u>.
  ✓ The latest fashion. What is the <u>latest</u> position in the match?
➤ **Latter** and **last** refer to position:
  ✓ The <u>latter</u> half of the film was interesting.
  ✓ The <u>latter</u> chapters of the book have been written carelessly.
  ✓ The <u>last</u> chapter of a book, the <u>last</u> song on a CD

Elder, older; eldest, oldest:

➤ **Older** and **oldest** are used for comparing ages of people, animals, and things:
  ✓ Fatima is <u>older</u> than her brother.
  ✓ Jit Sen is the <u>oldest</u> member of Bengal Club, the <u>oldest</u> club in Kolkata.
➤ **Elder** and **eldest** are used only with reference to a family:
  ✓ Anand is the eldest of the famous Amritraj brothers.
  ✓ Anand is Vijay's elder brother.
➤ The words **elder** and **eldest** are not common in spoken English now. Also, *elder* is used only before nouns:
  ✓ Ruby is my <u>elder</u> sister (Not: Ruby is elder than me. ✗)
  ✓ Ruby is <u>older</u> than me.

ACTIVITY 2

Complete the sentences by filling in the blanks with the comparative or superlative forms of the following adjectives:

big	congested	crowded	high	long
old	quiet	short	small	young

1. My father was the ………… of two brothers. My uncle was five years younger than him.
2. I am ……………….. among all my cousins. Some of my cousins are 10 years older than me.
3. Darjeeling would be chock-a-block with tourists now. Gangtok might be better, it would be ………………….
4. This restaurant is too noisy. Let's go to a …………… place.
5. Take the Outer Ring Road. It would be ………………………..
6. The Great Wall of China is ………………… man-made structure on earth. It can be seen even from the moon.
7. The Nile, which is 6,650 km long, is ………………… river in the world. The second longest river, the Amazon, is 250 km ………… than the Nile.
8. At an altitude of 3,810 m, Lake Titicaca is ………………… navigable[5] lake in the world.
9. The Taklamakan Desert in Central Asia is slightly …………… than Germany.

---

[5] **navigable:** (adjective of rivers, lakes, etc.) wide and deep enough for ships and books to sail on.

48.4 AS GOOD AS/NOT AS GOOD AS

This form is used for saying that something is equal to something else:

- ✓ The cat is <u>as big as</u> the dog.
- ✓ My dad is <u>as strong as</u> your dad.

If we want to say that something is not equal to something else, we say:

- ✓ The cat is <u>not as big as</u> the dog.
- ✓ Your dad is <u>not as strong as</u> my dad.

PRACTICE

1. Correct the following:

   A. She has scored low marks this time compared to the last exam.
   B. John is not less richer than Abraham.
   C. The minister claimed it was the most grandest rally of all times.
   D. Virat Kohli is elder than Kuldeep Yadav.
   E. Lesser students passed secondary exams this year compared to the last year.
   F. The last position of the test match? India needs seven to win, with one wicket in hand.

2. Fill in the blanks with the superlative forms of **active, big, beautiful, cold, great, hot, populous:**

   → The Louvre in Paris is possibly the <u>greatest</u> museum in the world.
   A. The Taj Mahal is .... monument in India.
   B. Mount Etna in Italy is one of .... volcanoes on earth.
   C. Jupiter is .... planet in the solar system.
   D. Mumbai is the .... city in India.
   E. Antarctica is the .... place on earth.
   F. .... place on earth is the Sahara Desert in Africa.

3. Complete the proverbs:

   A. Attack is .... form of defence.
   B. Facts are .... than fiction.
   C. Imitation is .... form of flattery.
   D. The pen is ....
   E. Prevention is...................................
   F. Grass is....................... on the other side of the fence.

4. Rewrite the following sentences using the comparative form of an adjective. Follow the model given:

→	I am looking for something **that costs less**.	I am looking for something cheaper.
1	I want to go to a place **where there is less noise**.	I want to go to a .... place.

2	(My car breaks down every now and then.) I wish I had a car that **I could depend upon more**.	I wish I had a m .... d .... car.
3	(It is difficult to drive on city roads.) I wish the roads **had fewer vehicles.**	I wish the roads were ....
4	Anil is rich, but his younger brother Mukesh **has more wealth.**	....
5	Have you seen the Aamir Khan's most **recently released film?**	....
6	Flats **cost more** in Mumbai than in Kolkata.	....

5. Change these sentences using the form **as ... as** or **not as ... as:**

→ Ma and her friend Charu are of the same age.	Mother is as old as her friend Charu.
Papayas are less tasty than mangoes.	→ ....
Abhishek and Ritwik are of the same height.	→ ....
Govind is shorter than Abhishek.	→ ....
Rakhi is not less beautiful than Rekha.	→ ....

KEY TO ACTIVITIES

Activity 1: 1. most populous; 2. more; 3. second most populous; 4. largest; 5. least; 6. Fewer, more; 7. highest, second highest

Activity 2: 1. older; 2. the youngest; 3. less crowded; 4. quieter; 5. less congested; 6. the biggest; 7. the longest, shorter; 8. the highest; 9. smaller

Unfortunately, Bullet Singh Slipped Away

Learning Objectives: In this chapter, we are discussing how adverbs can add clarity and precision to our descriptions. We will also check where to place adverbs in a sentence and how adverbs are used to compare two actions.

49.1 ADVERBS MAKE YOUR LANGUAGE SHARPER

Police Detective Bhola Singh was chasing a dangerous criminal yesterday when he had an accident. Unfortunately, the criminal slipped away. Bhola's boss was furious and called for an explanation. This is how Bhola described the car crash to his boss:

I was chasing the dangerous criminal Bullet Singh. Bullet was driving a new Toyota, but I was in my old Maruti 800. Driving along Rashbehari Avenue, as I approached the Chetla Bridge, I noticed a blue Honda parked on the left. I could see the driver. When my car was about to cross the stationary vehicle, the driver opened the door and started getting out. There was another car close to my right. So I could not turn to avoid hitting the Maruti. I jammed the brake, but it was late. I crashed on the open door of the car. The driver had seen me in time and got in.

Nothing happened to him. But his car was damaged. My vehicle too was damaged, the front mudguard was bent. However, I lost track of Bullet Singh because of this unfortunate incident.

Inspector Bhola has an admirable quality. He is not easily satisfied with what he writes. When he read his report, he felt he could improve it by adding a few details, emphasizing a few points, and moderating a few others. If you were Inspector Bhola, what changes would you make? Please add words in the passage above before reading on.

This is how Bhola modified his language:

I was chasing the dangerous criminal Bullet Singh **yesterday**. Bullet was driving a **brand-new** Toyota, but **unfortunately**, I was in my old Maruti 800. Driving **at a furious speed** along Rashbehari Avenue, as I approached the Chetla Bridge, I noticed a **dark** blue Honda parked on the left. I could **even** see the driver. When my car was about to cross the stationary vehicle, the driver **suddenly** opened the door and started getting out. There was another car close to my right. So I could not turn **right** to avoid hitting the Maruti. I jammed the brake, but it was **too** late. I crashed on the open door of the blue Maruti. **Fortunately,** the driver had seen me **just** in time and got in quickly.

Nothing happened to him. But his car was damaged **badly**. My vehicle too was damaged **slightly**; the front mudguard was bent **just a little**. However, I lost track of Bullet Singh because of this unfortunate incident.

Don't you think the modified passage reads better? All the words that Bhola added—the words in bold types—are adverbs.

An adverb makes our language sharper and clearer, by (A) qualifying a verb, that is, adding more information (such as the place, time, and manner) about a verb, (B) qualifying an adjective, (C) qualifying another adverb. Sometimes, an adverb gives more information about the entire sentence of which it is a part.

If you think the definition given above is too long and complicated, relax. Table 49.1 should make the ideas clear:

TABLE 49.1 Different Functions of Adverbs

1. An adverb qualifies a verb, that is, adds more information about place, time, frequency, manner, cause, or degree to a verb.	✓ I was chasing a criminal <u>yesterday</u>. (*time*) ✓ Driving <u>at a furious speed</u> …. (*manner of driving*) ✓ <u>When</u> my car was about to cross …. (*time*) ✓ I could <u>even</u> see the driver. (*emphasis*) ✓ The man <u>suddenly</u> opened the door. (*manner*)
2. An adverb qualifies or gives more information about an adjective.	✓ a <u>brand</u>-new Toyota ✓ a <u>dark</u> blue car ✓ my car was damaged <u>badly</u>/<u>slightly</u>
3. It qualifies another adverb.	✓ <u>just</u> in time ✓ It was <u>too</u> late
4. Sometimes, an adverb changes the meaning or emphasis of the entire sentence, * rather than any particular word or phrase.	✓ <u>Unfortunately</u>, I was in my old Maruti. ✓ <u>Sadly</u>, Bhola missed a promotion because of this incident.

* If Bhola says: *I was in my old Maruti 800,* he is merely stating a fact. But when he says, <u>*Unfortunately*</u>, *I was in my old Maruti 800,* he also says how he feels about the fact. Therefore, the adverb *unfortunately* adds something to the sentence. Similarly, ***evidently, gradually, obviously, perhaps, possibly, probably, strangely,*** and the like may change the meaning or emphasis of entire sentences. They usually come at the beginning.

49.2 FORMING ADVERBS FROM ADJECTIVES: THE *-LY* ENDING

Adverbs are often formed by adding *-ly* to an adjective: *bravely, cleverly, fluently, immediately, wisely,* and so on. *True → truly* is an exception. The following adverbs follow different rules:

1. For adjectives ending with *-le*, the final *-le* is replaced with *-ly*: *able → ably, possible → possibly, responsible → responsibly*. Exception: *whole → wholly*
2. For adjectives ending with a consonant +y, *-y* is replaced with *-ily*: *angry → angrily, easy → easily, happy → happily, ready → readily*
3. For some adjectives ending with a vowel + a consonant, the final consonant is repeated: *additional → additionally, careful → carefully, occasional → occasionally*
4. Here are some adverbs that end with *-ally*: *dramatic → dramatically, energetic → energetically, genetic → genetically, magnetic → magnetically*. Exception: *public → publicly*
5. Some adverbs are the same as their adjective forms: *fast → fast, early → early: Grandpa wakes up early; late → late: The train arrived late.*

ACTIVITY 1

Write down the adjective/adverb forms to complete the table:

Noun	Verb	Adjective	Adverb
1. absolute		absolute	
2. experience	experience		
3. loudness		loud	
4. profession			
5. reliance	rely		
6. temptation	tempt		
7. quickness		quick	

ACTIVITY 2

Improve the story by putting adjectives and adverbs in the blanks. Use **the adjectives/adverbs from Activity 1** and **the following:**

after that	almost	as silently as he could	
at all times	only	long	rather × 2
to his surprise		unfortunately	utter

An .... and hard-working thief, Charandas Chor was .... out of work for months. The new police chief in town, Inspector Bhola Singh, had made life difficult for Charandas and his friends. So, one day, when a .... source informed Charandas that the Mehras were away on a .... holiday, he was delighted. The source also informed him there was a night-watchman who went in **only** at 10 PM. But during the day, the house was .... empty.

So, one day after sunset, Charandas cut the grille in a rear window of the bungalow .... and got into Mehras' bungalow.

The effort exhausted Charandas and he felt .... thirsty. When he opened the fridge, ..., he found a bottle of red wine and a plate of .... biriyani. Charandas drank the wine and ate the biriyani ...., he felt sleepy. He still had two hours left, so he set an alarm on his mobile for 9 PM and went to sleep on Mehras' bed.

When the watchman came in, to his .... surprise, he heard someone snoring .... in the master bedroom ...., Charandas's mobile battery had run out of charge. What followed was .... sad, let's not go into it.

The moral of the story is that one must keep one's mobile phone charged ...., particularly if one is a .... thief.

49.3 ADJECTIVES AND ADVERBS

Often, you can use an adverb to express what is conveyed by an adjective. But the structures of the sentences would be different, as you can see below:

Describing with an Adjective	Expressing the Idea with an Adverb
The opening batsmen made a <u>slow</u> start.	The opening batsmen started <u>slowly</u>.
The pitch was <u>bad</u>.	The pitch behaved <u>badly</u>.
Sourav Ganguli was a <u>good</u> captain.	Sourav Ganguli <u>captained</u> his team well.

Note: **Well** is the adverb equivalent of **good.** For **bad**, the adverb is **badly.**

Adjectives or **Adverbs?** Most adverbs end with -*ly*. But the following words are adjectives, not adverbs: *elderly, friendly, likely, lonely, lively, lovely, miserly,* and **sprightly** (= full of spirit and energy, used especially for elderly people).

Some adverbs have two forms—one that ends with -*ly* and one that is the same as the adjective:

✓ Brett Lee bowls <u>quick</u>. = Brett Lee bowls <u>quickly</u>.
✓ He works <u>real</u> hard. = He works <u>really</u> hard.
✓ Why are you playing the music so <u>loud</u>? = Why are you playing the music so <u>loudly</u>?

In the sentences above, the -*ly* ending doesn't change the meaning of the adverb. But for some adverbs, the meanings of the two forms are different:

   ✓ He works <u>hard</u>. ⇨ He <u>hardly</u> works. (= does almost no work)
   ✓ I was <u>near</u> the rail station. ⇨ I <u>nearly</u> (= almost) missed the train.
   ✓ He comes <u>late</u> every day ⇨ He has been acting big <u>lately</u>. (= recently)

ACTIVITY 3

Use adverbs instead of adjectives to rewrite these sentences. Follow the model given:

→ Brett is a <u>fast</u> bowler.	→ Brett bowls fast.
A. Rani has a <u>beautiful</u> handwriting.	Rani writes ....
B. She is also a <u>good</u> singer.	She also ....
C. Nandini talks in a <u>soft</u> voice.	....
D. Ravi is <u>calm</u> in difficult situations.	Ravi handles ....
E.	Raju plays football <u>well</u>.

49.4 POSITIONS OF ADVERBS

An adverb may come at the beginning, in the middle, or at end of a sentence. But you cannot place them just anywhere; you have to follow certain rules.

I suggest that you learn the rules by practice. As you read good language, *note* and *remember* where adverbs come in a sentence. Here are a few simple rules you can follow:

1. When an adverb qualifies an adjective or another adverb, it usually comes before he word it qualifies:
    ✓ *a <u>dark</u> blue car,* ✓ *a <u>rather</u> boring film*
2. If a verb has an object, the verb and the object normally go together. We do not put a word between them:
    ✓ I was chasing a dangerous criminal <u>yesterday</u>.
          ↑   ↑   ↑
        verb   object   adverb
    ✓ You can also say: <u>*Yesterday,*</u> *I was chasing*….
      But you don't say: *I was chasing yesterday a dangerous criminal.* ✗
3. If there is a helping verb, the adverb comes in between the helping verb and the main verb:
    ✓ I have often seen her riding a bike.
    ✓ I don't ever miss an opportunity to ride a bike.
4. If a verb is followed by a ***place word*** and a ***time word,*** then the time word comes *after* the place word:
    ✓ We are going to Mumbai next week. Not: *We are ~~next week going to Mumbai~~.* ✗
5. The ***adverbs of manner,*** that is, words such as *slowly, fast,* and *efficiently* usually come after the verb at the end of a sentence:
    ✓ *Grandma drives very <u>slowly</u>.*

49.5 COMPARISON OF ADVERBS

Some adverbs have three degrees of comparison, like adjectives. For short adverbs, comparative degrees are formed by adding *-er* and *-est*, like it is done for adjectives. The other rules like changing the last letter *y* into *-ier* and *–iest* hold good too:

- ✓ fast → faster → fastest
- ✓ late → later → latest
- ✓ early → earlier → earliest

For longer adverbs, we add *more* and *most* before adverbs:

- ✓ swiftly → more swiftly → most swiftly
- ✓ fortunately → more fortunately → most fortunately

But like adjectives, certain adverbs don't follow any rules:

- ✓ ill, badly → worse → worst
- ✓ well → better → best

You will not use the comparative and the superlative degrees of adverbs as frequently as you use them for adjectives.

> ## *Possibly* and *Probably*
>
> ➢ ***Possibly*** is used to say that something might exist, happen, or be true, but you are not certain about it. It means PERHAPS. *He is possibly the best singer in college.*
> ➢ ***Probably*** is used to say that something is likely to happen or be true. *You are probably right. He will probably win the election.*

PRACTICE

1. True or false? Mark the sentences as 'T' if they are true. Mark as 'F' if they are false:

A. An adverb often adds more information about place, time, frequency, manner, cause, or degree to a verb.	
B. Some adverbs give more information about adjectives.	
C. Most adverbs end with *-ly*. But all words ending with *-ly* are not adverbs.	
D. The following sentences mean the same thing: (a) *He works hard.* (b) *He hardly works.*	
E. Many adverbs are formed by adding *-ly* to an adjective.	
F. Adverbs can be placed anywhere in a sentence.	

2. Rewrite the sentences by putting in the adverbs given within brackets. Change *a* to *an* (and *an* to *a*) and make other changes where necessary. Together, these sentences tell you a folk tale of the Oraons of Central and Eastern India.

   1. An Oraon woman gave birth to a beautiful baby girl. (once, exceedingly)
   2. As the little girl grew up, she became more beautiful. (even)
   3. People wondered if such a lovely girl had come to the world before. (ever)
   4. But one day, two soldiers came and announced that the girl was the daughter of the snake-king Nagaraj, who lived under water. (actually)

5. The Nagaraj had ordered them to take the girl back. The Oraon villagers cried. (helplessly)

6. They went to the Nagaraj and begged him not to take the girl. (Then, away)

7. The king did not agree. (Initially,)

8. But he felt sorry for the villagers. (later)

9. He decided that the girl would live in our world for six months. (Finally, every year)

10. For the rest of the year, she would live under water.

11. It has been like that since. (ever)

12. When the girl comes up to our world, trees grow new leaves, flowers bloom, and birds chirp. The fields are filled with golden harvest.

13. But when she goes, trees become barren, birds stop chirping, a great sadness comes down on earth. (away, totally)

    1. <u>Once</u>, an Oraon woman gave birth to an <u>exceedingly</u> beautiful baby girl.

    2. ....

    3. ....

    4. ....

    5. ....

    6. ....

    7. ....

    8. ....

    9. ....

    10. For the rest of the year, she would live under water.

    11. ....

    12. When the beautiful girl comes up to our world, trees grow new leaves and flowers bloom, and birds chirp. The fields are filled with golden harvest.

    13. ....

3. Fill in the blanks with *badly, highly, very, carefully,* and *unfortunately*:

- George drove the (1)................ damaged car (2)................ slowly.
- You must deal with the (3)................ temperamental dog Kublai (4)................. You never know what he might do.
- (5)................ bank employees are on strike today. I couldn't deposit my salary cheque.

4. Correct the following sentences:

A. Tania saw suddenly her old friend Catherine on a bus.   ....

B. Tania came last month from Nagaland.   ....

C. She met by chance Catherine.   ....

D. She met after 10 long years Catherine.   ....

5. Place the adverbs in their correct positions. There might be more than one correct answer.

(A) Raghu brushes his teeth every day. (almost)	
(B) Brett bowls fast. (real)	
(C) Gandhiji could write well with either hand. (equally)	
(D) The fridge is empty. (quite)	
(E) You are right. (probably)	

(F)	Raju is intelligent, he is hard-working. (too)	
(G)	Sriram eats fish. (never)	
(H)	Sonia doesn't eat fish. (often)	

KEY TO ACTIVITIES

Activity 1: 1. absolutely; 2. experienced; 3. loudly; 4. professional, professionally; 5. reliable, reliably; 6. tempting; 7. quickly

Activity 2:

An **experienced** and hard-working thief, Charandas Chor was **almost** out of work for months.... So, one day, when a **reliable** source informed Charandas that the Mehras were away on a **long** holiday, he was delighted. The source also informed him there was a night-watchman who went in **only** at 10 PM. But during the day, the house was **absolutely** empty.

So, one day after sunset, Charandas cut the grille in a rear window of the bungalow **as silently as he could** and entered Mehras' bungalow.

The effort exhausted Charandas and he felt **rather** thirsty. When he opened the fridge, **to his surprise**, he found a bottle of red wine and a plate of **tempting** biriyani. Charandas drank the wine and ate the biriyani **quickly. After that,** he felt sleepy....

When the watchman came in, to his **utter** surprise, he heard someone snoring **loudly** in the master bedroom. **Unfortunately,** Charandas's mobile battery had run out of charge. What followed was **rather** sad, let's not go into it.

The moral of the story is that one must keep one's mobile phone charged **at all times,** particularly if one is a **professional** thief.

Activity 3: A. Rani writes beautifully. B. She also sings well. C. Nandini talks softly. D. Ravi handles difficult situations calmly. E. Raju is a good footballer.

How Hot Is Your Tea?

Learning Objectives: We use adverbs to make our statements stronger or more moderate. In this chapter, we will see how to do this.

50.1 VERY HOT/QUITE HOT/RATHER HOT

When you say *the tea is hot or cold*, you often wish to convey the *degree* of hotness or coldness too. So you use expressions such as *very hot*, *quite hot*, or *rather cold*. If you say someone drives fast/slow, you often use the phrases: *really fast* or *rather slow*.

Very, *quite*, and *rather* are three **adverbs of degree.** Adverbs of degree modify an adjective (like *hot*), an adverb (*fast*), or a verb in three ways:

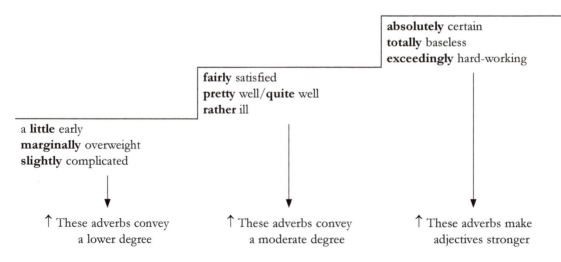

Adverbs of degrees modify verbs too. For example, you can modify the sentence *Yasmin enjoys shopping* in several ways:

✓ Yasmin <u>quite</u> enjoys shopping.
✓ Yasmin enjoys shopping <u>very much</u>.

After watching a film, we often say *it was really enjoyable* or *it was rather boring.* We will now combine *enjoyable* and *boring* with the adverbs *really, very, terribly, awfully, quite, rather, fairly, somewhat, to some extent,* and *slightly* to check the three degrees of modification. I have done the work partly. Complete the following table with the unused adverbs:

Shopping and *Marketing*

I've heard many people say: *I went ~~marketing~~ for my sister's wedding.* ✗

If you are buying something at a market (or shop), you are *shopping, not ~~marketing~~.* The verb *shop* means to buy something at shops/stores. For example, *Yasmin enjoys shopping.*

To *go shopping* means to go around shops and look for things to buy:

➢ *Where is Yasmin? —She's gone shopping.*

Marketing is the activity of presenting, advertising, and delivering a company's products in an attractive manner. The person in charge of this function is often called the *marketing manager.*

	Low Degree	**Moderate Degree**	**High Degree**
enjoyable	1. to some extent enjoyable	2. quite enjoyable	4. …………………
		3. …………………	5. …………………
boring	6. …………………	8. rather boring	10. terribly boring
	7. …………………	9. quite boring	11. …………………

Key: 3. fairly enjoyable, 4. very enjoyable, 5. really enjoyable, 6. somewhat boring, 7. slightly boring, 11. awfully boring

Notes:

1. You use *quite* while making approving comments like *quite enjoyable.* When you are expressing slight criticism or disappointment, you use *rather: rather boring.* But you don't say: *The film was <u>rather</u> enjoyable.* ✗ *Quite* also means entirely or completely. In this sense, it is used as *quite absurd, quite obvious, quite empty, quite enough,* and so on: *The fridge was <u>quite</u> empty. I am <u>quite</u> certain about it.*

2. Certain adverbs such as *terribly* and *awfully* go only with negative comments. You don't say: *The film was ~~terribly enjoyable~~.* ✗

ACTIVITY 1

Make the statements stronger, moderate, or weaker following the instructions. Use *very much, quite, certainly, strongly:*

1. Hritik loves dancing. (Make the statement stronger) …………………………………
2. The students protested against the fee hike. (Make it stronger) …………………………………
3. I'll support you at the meeting. (Say this with more certainty) …………………………………
4. Yasmin speaks English fluently. (Make it moderate) …………………………………

50.2 ALREADY VERSUS YET

Already and *yet* are *time markers,* like *yesterday* or *after a week.* *Already* means (1) before now, particularly if something has happened earlier than expected, and (2) before a particular time in the past. We use it in *positive statements* and *questions.*

In statements, if there is a helping verb, *already* usually comes between the helping verb and the main verb:

- ✓ The film has <u>already</u> started.
- ✓ We are only 10 minutes into the game and Brazil has <u>already</u> scored twice.
- ✓ Sorry! I've <u>already</u> finished the potato chips.

Already is used in questions to show surprise, and it usually comes at the end:

- ✓ Oh Dear! Is it 10 o'clock <u>already</u>?
- ✓ You started reading the book an hour ago. And you've finished it <u>already</u>?

Yet means (1) until now and (2) by that time. We use it in *negative statements* and *questions:*

- ✓ We reached the office at 9 AM. It hadn't opened <u>yet</u>.
- ✓ Aren't you ready <u>yet</u>?

In some constructions, it comes in the middle. For example, the first sentence above can be rewritten as:

- ✓ The reservation office was <u>yet</u> to open.
- ✓ We rushed to the cinema. But the movie was <u>yet</u> to begin.

> ### *Already* and *Yet*
>
> Both these adverbs tell us whether an action is over or not by or before a particular time.
>
> *Already,* used in positive statements, emphasizes that something has happened earlier than expected:
>
> ➤ We're going to Srinagar next month. We've already booked a hotel room.
>
> We use *yet* only in negative sentences and questions:
>
> ➤ We are going to Srinagar next week, but I haven't booked a hotel room yet.
>
> In questions, *already* is used to show surprise and *yet* in the ordinary sense.

50.3 STILL

Still means up to and including a particular point of time:

- ✓ It's <u>still</u> raining.
- ✓ Do you <u>still</u> live in Mumbai?

NOTE: *Still* usually comes in the middle of a sentence. In questions, it comes immediately after the subject.

50.4 NO LONGER AND NOT... ANY MORE

We use *no longer* to say that an activity is over:

- ✓ 'Please give me a box of CDs.'—'Sorry, we <u>no longer</u> sell CDs.'
- ✓ You can't buy a new Bajaj scooter. They <u>no longer</u> manufacture scooters.

There is another, *more informal* way of saying the same thing:

- ✓ Sorry, we do<u>n't</u> sell CDs <u>any more</u>.
- ✓ They do<u>n't</u> manufacture scooters <u>any more</u>.

ACTIVITY 2

Rewrite the sentences by putting the words given within brackets at the right place:

1. Sorry, I've finished the potato chips. (already)
2. Oh, you've done all the 10 sums? (already)
3. I paid for a new phone last week, but haven't got the connection. (yet)
4. I paid for a new phone three months ago, I've not got the connection. (still)
5. I've been selected. But I haven't received the offer letter. (yet)

50.5 ALMOST, NEARLY, AND HARDLY

Almost and *nearly* are used to modify positive sentences:

- ✓ It's been raining for <u>almost/nearly</u> two months at a stretch.
- ✓ We were caught in a traffic jam and <u>almost/nearly</u> missed the flight.

Hardly reverses the meaning of a positive sentence. For example, consider the statements:

- ✓ We could <u>clearly</u> see the mountain from our hotel room.
- ✓ We could <u>hardly</u> see the mountain from our hotel room.

The second sentence means *we almost couldn't see the mountain*. Here are two more contrasting sentences:

- ✓ Yasmin enjoys shopping <u>very much</u>.
- ✓ But her husband <u>hardly</u> enjoys shopping.

Hardly + a positive statement is usually preferred to *almost/ nearly + a negative statement*:

- ✗ You don't say: The sky was cloudy; we <u>almost couldn't see</u> the mountain.
- ✓ You say: The sky was cloudy; we <u>could hardly see</u> the mountain.

PRACTICE

1. Fill in the blanks using *already, yet, still, almost, hardly,* and *not… any more*:

    i. Mr and Mrs Iyer didn't join us for dinner. They'd ………… eaten.
    ii. The year isn't over ………… And we've………… had two governments.
    iii. Radhika hasn't returned. She's ………… in office.
    iv. The train hasn't arrived …………
    v. Haven't you finished …………?

    vi. Do you .... believe in communism?

   vii. Sorry, Dr John doesn't work at this hospital ....

  viii. I'm .... reading *Crime and Punishment*. I haven't finished it ....

    ix. These modern paintings are strange! I can .... make any sense.

     x. We telephoned the police almost an hour ago; they haven't arrived ....

2. Put the words within brackets at the right place:

    i. Hritik loves dancing. (very much) ....

   ii. Your blood pressure is high. (marginally) ....

  iii. I've finished the work. (already) ....

   iv. Haven't you done your homework? (yet) ....

    v. The booking counter hasn't opened. (yet) ....

   vi. I am struggling with my homework. (still) ....

  vii. Please phone him at office. He's there. (still) ....

 viii. It's a dangerous drug. They manufacture it. (no longer) ....

   ix. I don't play computer games. (any more) ....

    x. My car had a fog light. I could see the road. (clearly) ....

3. Rewrite this paragraph by putting the words within sentences in the right order:
driving/enjoys/Yasmin/quite. the night/but/was/dark/very. she/the road/hardly/could/see. the road/and/was/bad/awfully. was/she/slowly/driving/very. driven/already/two hours/for/she/had. but/hardly/covered/46 km/she had. rather/she/tense/was. her/by her side/husband/sleeping/peacefully/was. was/she/annoyed/exceedingly/with him.

....

....

....

....

....

....

....

....

....

....

....

■ KEY TO ACTIVITIES

Activity 1: 1. Hritik loves dancing **very much**. 2. The students **strongly** protested against the fee hike. 3. I'll **certainly** support you at the meeting. 4. Yasmin speaks English **quite** fluently.

Activity 2: 1. Sorry, I've **already** finished the potato chips. 2. Oh, you've done all the 10 sums **already?** 3. I paid for a new phone last week, but haven't got the connection **yet**. 4. I paid for a new phone three months ago, I've **still** not got the connection. 5. ... I haven't received the offer letter **yet**.

Speaking: She, Her, Herself, Hers

Learning Objectives: The points discussed here, that is, different uses of pronouns, are relevant to both writing and speaking. However, as you work through this chapter, you will see that the illustrations given here are used more frequently when we speak.

51.1 PERSONAL PRONOUNS AND GENDER (MALE/FEMALE)

A pronoun is a word that takes the place of a noun in sentences. It is used to avoid repetition of nouns. You don't say: *My friend said my friend is going abroad.* You say: *My friend said **she** is going abroad.*

Personal pronouns are words *(he, his, him,* and so on*)* that come in for a person or thing mentioned earlier. Personal pronouns also include *I, we,* and *you.*

Michael Swan says, 'English does not have many problems of grammatical gender. Usually people are *he* or *she* and things are *it*.'[1] Let's focus on a few points of deviation.

For **countries**, people used *she/her* earlier, but in modern English, *it* is more common. Indians often connect the image of a mother with their country and for India, they use *she/her: India must have friendly relationship with <u>her</u> neighbours.* (You can also say:... *with <u>its</u> neighbours.*)

It is used for **animals in general,** but for **pet animals** such as dogs, cats, goats, or cows we often use *he* or *she:*

✓ Radhika and Ravi's dog, Dogendran, believes <u>he</u> is the head of the family. <u>He</u> is protective about Radhika's son Rohan, who <u>he</u> considers small and helpless.

If **the sex of a person is not known**, in modern English, we often use *they* as a unisex pronoun:

✓ Who has left behind <u>their</u> umbrella?
✓ Travellers must carry <u>their</u> photo ID when travelling by train or air.

---

[1] Michael Swan, *Practical English Usage* (3rd ed.) (New Delhi: Oxford University Press, 2005), Entry no. 222.

51.2 PRONOUNS AS SUBJECTS PRONOUNS AS OBJECTS

A personal pronoun can be the *subject* or *object* in a sentence. [To review the terms *subject* and *object*, refer Section 6.4] The following sentences have *pronouns as subjects* (underlined), which are called **subject pronouns**:

✓ I am an English teacher at this school. The gentleman who's delivering the speech, he's our principal, Biresh Babu. It's an interesting speech, isn't it?

The following have *pronouns as objects* (underlined). They are called **object pronouns:**

✓ Dad gave me a book yesterday. He bought it online.

In these sentences, the subject and the object are different persons or things. However, if they refer to the same person/thing, we get sentences as follows:

✓ I hurt myself. (= no one else hurt me)
✓ They should solve the problem themselves. (= no one else should)
✓ This is an automatic toaster. It switches itself off when the toast is ready.

The words **myself, themselves,** and **itself** are called *reflexive pronouns.*

✓ If the object pronoun of a sentence is the same as the subject, the former (i.e., the object) is called a *reflexive pronoun.*

Subject Pronouns, Object Pronouns, and Reflexive Pronouns

	Singular			Plural		
	Subject	**Object**	**Reflexive**	**Subject**	**Object**	**Reflexive**
1st person	I	me	myself	we	us	ourselves
2nd person	you	you	yourself	you	you	yourselves
3rd person	he/she/it	his/her/it	himself/herself/itself	they	them	themselves

ACTIVITY 1

Fill in the blanks with a personal pronoun **(it × 2, me, she,** and **herself)**. Also, identify the type of pronoun by putting a ✓ next to the correct option:

→ Grandma gave **me** a CD yesterday. (subject/object ✓/reflexive pronoun)
A. .... is a music CD. (subject/object /reflexive pronoun)
B. She bought........ from Music World. (subject/object/reflexive pronoun)
C. Where's grandma now?.........'s in her bedroom. (subject/object/reflexive)
D. She is looking at.............. in a mirror. (subject/object/reflexive)

51.3 REFLEXIVE OR EMPHATIC?

The headmaster of our school, Biresh Babu, was basically a chemistry teacher. He also taught English brilliantly. Once he said: *I taught **myself** English.* He meant he hadn't studied English at college or university but had learnt it on his own. As we have just seen, in this sense, *myself, yourself,* and the like are ***reflexive pronouns.***

But what exactly did he mean when he said, *I **myself** teach English in the 10th standard?*

In this sentence, the emphasis is on the fact that he, *and no other teacher,* taught English in that class. Here, *myself* is an ***emphatic pronoun.*** A few more examples:

✓ Once I wrote a letter to the famous film director Satyajit Ray. I didn't mail the letter, I delivered it **myself.** When I rang the bell at his home, Ray **himself** opened the door.

51.4 POSSESSION/ CONNECTION

To indicate that something belongs to or has a connection with someone, we use an apostrophe: *This is Radhika's house.* Also: *This house is Radhika's.* [Check the text box for more on apostrophes.]

In the table below, the first column shows more natural (and more commonly used) expressions with ***my, your, his, her,*** and ***their.*** These are ***determiners,*** although they look like pronouns.

My and *Mine*

This is <u>my</u> pen.	⇨ This pen is <u>mine</u>.
That is <u>your</u> pen.	⇨ That pen is <u>yours</u>.
This is <u>his</u> eraser.	⇨ This eraser is <u>his</u>.
That is <u>her</u> book.	⇨ That book is <u>hers</u>.
These are <u>their</u> notebooks.	⇨ These notebooks are <u>theirs</u>.

The *Apostrophe* (')

A noun followed by the apostrophe + an *s* shows possession:

✓ **Rani's** cat, the **cat's** tail
✓ **Denis's** toys
✓ **children's** bedroom

If a plural noun ends with *s,* the apostrophe comes at the end. (We don't put another *s.*)

✓ my **parents'** home

An apostrophe is used **only for living things and organizations.**

✓ *Twenty dedicated teachers are behind the **school's** success.*

We don't use them for **non-living things.** We don't say:

✗ the ~~table's~~ legs
✗ the ~~chair's~~ arms

The apostrophe also establishes connections other than possession. For example, *Parkinson's Disease* isn't something that Dr Parkinson had. It's the disease he explained scientifically. Also,

✓ a **girls'** school (a school which admits only girls)
✓ **Charles Dickens's** novels (novels written by Dickens)

Here are more uses of the apostrophe:

✓ A day's leave
✓ Ten minutes' walk

The underlined words in the second column are **possessive pronouns.** We use them in constructions such as:

✓ It was your fault, not **mine.**
✓ Q: 'Is this Radhika's umbrella?' A: 'Yes it's **hers.**'

Complete List of Possessive Pronouns

	Singular		Plural	
	Subject	**Possessive Pronouns**	**Subject**	**Possessive Pronouns**
1st person	I	mine	we	ours
2nd person	you	yours	you	yours
3rd person	he/she/it	his/hers/its	they	theirs

ACTIVITY 2

In the table below, the two sentences in each row mean the same thing. Complete the table by writing down the missing words. Use reflexive pronouns:

→	This is my bike.	This bike is **mine.**
A.	Is this your bag?	Is this bag ....?
B.	This is her umbrella.	....
C.	Is that your pen or my pen?	Is this your pen or ....?
D.	It was my fault, it was not your fault.	....

A Question of Manners

If you have to use, *you, he/she/they,* and *I* in the same sentence, you should use them in the following order: *you* (2nd person), *he/she/they* (3rd person), and *I* (1st person). Remember the formula 2–3–1.

✗ You don't say: ~~I, she, and you~~ *will go to the party.*
✓ You say: *You, she, and I will go to the party.*

PRACTICE

1. Complete the table below:

Singular				Plural			
Subject	**Object**	**Reflexive Pronouns**	**Possessive Pronouns**	**Subject**	**Object**	**Reflexive Pronouns**	**Possessive Pronouns**
I	me			we			
you				you			
he/she				they			theirs
it							

2. Fill in the blanks with a pronoun:

   A. Our dog, Dogendran, is extremely sensitive about.................... tail.
   B. I asked.............. a question, but she didn't respond.
   C. You're struggling to solve the Rubik's Cube? Rani can. Ask....................
   D. Ravi and Radhika don't have a domestic help. They.................... cook, every day.
   E. She knew who the culprit was. But she didn't tell the police because they never asked.....................
   F. For heaven's sake, don't smoke so much. You are killing.....................
   G. The storekeeper gave you a faulty mobile? But wasn't it..................... responsibility to check the goods before accepting them?
   H. That is not your umbrella, sir. It is..................... (The umbrella belongs to me.)
   I. When the wicketkeeper got hurt, the captain..................... came in to replace her.
   J. In our school, students..................... clean classrooms.

KEY TO ACTIVITIES

Activity 1: A. It (subject pronoun); B. it (object pronoun); C. She (subject pronoun); D. herself (reflexive pronoun).

Activity 2: A. Is this bag yours? B. This umbrella is hers. C. Is that your pen or mine? D. It was my fault, not yours.

52

More Spoken Language and Pronouns

Learning Objectives: This is a continuation of Chapter 51. Here, we will learn more uses of pronouns in spoken English.

52.1 IT'S ME, RADHIKA

In the last chapter, we discussed object pronouns: *me, us, him, her,* and *them* (For example, *My grandma gave me a CD.*) In informal speech, they are also used in the following situations:

- ✓ Who is the captain? —<u>Me</u>. Or: It's <u>me</u>. (You don't say *I*. ✗ Neither do you say: *It's I.* ✗)
- ✓ *Who is there?* —It's <u>me</u>, Radhika.
- ✓ Who painted this picture? —It's <u>her</u>.

When the subject contains two words, like *Ravi + I*, there are two possibilities:

- Formal language: *Ravi and I are going out for dinner.*
- Informal English: *Ravi and me are going out for dinner.*

ACTIVITY 1

Fill in the blanks with: **him, me × 4,** and **them.**

A. 'Who's at the door?' —'It's ...., Rani.'
B. 'Who started the fight?' —'Not us. It was ....'
C. 'Who broke this flower vase?' —'I don't know, but it wasn't ....'
D. Radhika told her friend, 'Ravi and .... are getting married next Sunday.'
E. 'Would all of you like to have an ice cream?' —'Not ....,' said Rani, 'I have a sore throat.'
F. 'Where is Kumaran?' —'Can you see a sleeping man? It's ....'

52.2 A VERSATILE PRONOUN: *IT*

We know that the pronoun *it* refers to a specific animal or a non-living thing:

✓ We went to the church compound, it's a lovely place. We saw Kumaran's dog there. It looks ferocious.

There are several other uses of *it*. We use it in the following situations:

1. To refer to a statement made earlier:
   ✓ 'Has our boss resigned?'—'Yes, it is true.'
   ✓ 'Listen to me carefully; it's important.'

2. To stand as a subject, where the real subject follows:
   ✓ It isn't easy to defeat Italy in football. (Not: To defeat Italy isn't easy.)
   ✓ It takes all sorts to make the world. (= There are all sorts of people in the world.)

3. To talk about weather, time, and distance:
   ✓ It's been/It has been raining since morning.
   ✓ It's/It is 9 o'clock now.
   ✓ How much time does it take to reach the station?
   ✓ How far is it from here to the railway station?

4. *It* is also used to make emphatic statements:
   ✓ It seems the new government will not last five years.
   ✓ It was obvious that he had to hide something.

Focus on the structures above and think when you can use similar expressions. Practise saying them in your head.

ACTIVITY 2

These sentences seem unnatural. Rewrite them beginning with *it*. Follow the model given:

→ Two hands are needed to clap.   ⇨ It takes two hands to clap.
A. Money it was that created all the trouble among the friends. ⇨ ....
B. To ride a motorbike in Delhi is dangerous.   ⇨ ....
C. Let's go, watching this film any longer would be a waste of time.
                                                    ⇨ Let's go, it ....
D. That you can't join us for the picnic is a pity. ⇨ ....
E. To get a job is not easy these days.   ⇨ ....

52.3 THERE IS...

Ravi's friend Gagan has come to visit him from another place:

Gagan: Where are we going for lunch?
Ravi: There is a new restaurant in Park Street. It's good.

Gagan: Good, we can go <u>there</u>. But before that, I need a haircut.

Ravi: <u>There</u> is a hairdresser[1] down the road. It's less than a kilometre from here.

Note that the word ***there*** has been used in two ways in this conversation.

1. To mention something for the first time:
   - ✓ <u>There</u> is a new restaurant…. (Not: A ~~new restaurant is in Park Street~~. ✗)
   - ✓ <u>There</u> are three men at the door.
   - ✓ <u>There</u> was a lot of stress in my previous job.
2. ***There*** also means to/at a place:
   - ✓ We can go <u>there</u>.

ACTIVITY 3

Fill in the blanks with **there is, there are, there was × 2, there were, is it, it was × 3,** and **it wasn't:**

A. ……………… a big crowd at the temple now.
B. 'Did you find it difficult at the station?'—'……………… no problem, but……………… a little crowded.'
C. 'How was your trip?'—'Good, but……………… rather hectic.'
D. 'How was the food at the new restaurant?'—'Not very good, but……………… bad either.'
E. ……………… a good movie;……………… a happy ending.
F. How far……………… from the railway station to your house?
G. ……………… many film stars at the party last night.
H. I've just read your report. I think……………… a few inaccuracies.

52.4 SOMETHING THAT IS GENERALLY DONE

When we talk about something that is generally done or that should generally be done, we often use one of the following words: ***one, you, we, people.***

- ✓ <u>One</u> should try to remain calm in a crisis.
- ✓ <u>One</u> should be aware of <u>one</u>'s limitations.

These are formal expressions. Another point you should note is that in standard British English, you don't say: *One should be aware about his weakness.* ✗

I have often used *you* in this book while talking generally.

- ✓ <u>You</u> don't say: *One should be aware about his weakness.*
- ✓ <u>You</u> shouldn't put an apostrophe after a non-living thing.
- ✓ <u>We</u> should keep our promises.
- ✓ <u>People</u> should keep their city clean.

---

[1] **hairdresser's:** (noun) a place where you get your hair cut, washed, coloured, shaped, and so on.

PRACTICE

1. Fill in the blanks with *it* or *there* and the appropriate form of the verb given within brackets:

   A. ……………………………… non-stop since Monday. (rain)
   B. It took a long time to reach the station because …………………………… a massive traffic jam. (be)
   C. 'How is your new job?'—'…………………… good, but rather stressful.' (be)
   D. ………………………………… a new train from Mumbai to Patna;……'s a superfast train. (be, be)
   E. 'Did you like the film?'—'Yes, ………………………………. fantastic.' (be)
   F. We climbed to the top of the hillock yesterday. ……………………………… rather tiring. (be)

2. Rewrite the following sentences and begin them with *There:*

   A. The fridge is empty → ……………… nothing……………
   B. The book is full of exercises → ……… many exercises…………
   C. The film has some lovely songs. → ………………………………………
   D. This computer has many new features. → ………………………………
   E. This curry is too salty. → ……… too much salt …………
   F. This book has some excellent stories. → ………………………………………

KEY TO ACTIVITIES

Activity 1: A. 'It's me, Rani.' B. Not us, it was them. C. I don't know, but it wasn't me. D. Ravi and me…. E. 'Not me', said Rani…. F. 'Can you see a sleeping man? It's him.'

Activity 2: A. It was money that created all the trouble…. B. It is dangerous to ride a motor bike in Delhi. C. Let's go. It would be waste of time to watch this film any longer. D. It is a pity that you can't join us for the picnic. E. It is not/isn't easy to get a job these days.

Activity 3: A. There is…. B. —'There was no problem, but it was a little crowded.' C. —'Good, but it was rather hectic.' D. —'Not very good, but it wasn't bad either.' E. It was a good movie; there was a happy ending. F. How far is it from the railway station…? G. There were many film stars…. H. I think there are a few inaccuracies.

Test 8:
Adjectives, Adverbs, and Pronouns

1. Form meaningful phrases by combining one word from the first table and another from the second. Follow the given model:

activity	mortally		afraid	journey
candlelight	sole		chair	occupant
church	train		class	rubbish
garden	utter		dinner	spire
lush	quartz		green	watch

1. activity class 2. .... 3. .... 4. .... 5. ....
6. .... 7. .... 8. .... 9. .... 10. ....

2. Given below are snippets from advertisements of three beach resorts in India. Complete them with the words given within brackets:

A. *Green Seas Resort* is spread over of 50 acres of (1) <u>lush</u> green lawns. The resort boasts of a (2) .... beach and offers a (3) .... view of the Balukhanda Reserve Forest. It has 50 cosy rooms and 10 (4) .... cottages. Spending a moonlit night here is an (5)............... experience. **(private, lush, luxurious, panoramic,[1] unforgettable)**

B. (1)............... located in Goa, *Bambolim Beach Resort* makes an ideal base for those wishing to travel around Goa. (2) .... and quiet, and yet just 7 km from Panaji and close to the (3)............... places of sightseeing, the resort makes a (4) .... home to come back to. **(centrally, nice, main, isolated)**

C. Located in one of world's last outposts of (1) .... rainforest islands, the resort overlooks the (2) .... blue waters of the Bay of Bengal. Built (3) .... entirely with the native 'Padouk' wood, the beautiful red timber that is found (4) .... on the Andaman & Nicobar Islands. ... Early morning swims, long (5) .... afternoons, gorgeous sunsets followed by intimate (6)............... dinners. All this and more at *Emerald Resorts*. **(almost, candlelight, lazy, only, pristine,[2] spectacular)**

---

[1] **panoramic:** (adjective) (a view) Covering a wide sweep of land or water.
[2] **pristine:** (adjective) in its original condition.

3. Write the following phrases in the correct order:

→ Labrador/black /small + puppy
⇨ a small black Labrador puppy
A. Royal Bengal/full grown/fierce + tiger ⇨ ....
B. beautiful/silk/embroidered + sari ⇨ ....
C. candlelight/intimate + dinner ⇨ ....
D. stylish/fuel-efficient/Indian + car ⇨ ....

4. Comment on the situations given below, using either a comparative form + *than* or *the* + a superlative form:

→ There are two small rooms in Tania's house; her brother has four large rooms in his house. Tania's house is smaller than her brother's. ....
A. My father is 60 years old; his sister is 58.
....
B. Rajdhani Express reaches New Delhi in 17 hours. Poorva Express takes 23 hours for the same journey.
....
C. The Metro takes you from one end of the city to the other in one hour. No other transport system is as fast.
....
D. Raju is six feet two inches. His best friend Mustak is six one.
....
E. Raju is six feet two inches. No other boy in our class is as tall as he is.
....

5. Write sentences from the hints using the **as… as** or **as not… as** form:

→ Pune/big/Mumbai
⇨ Pune is not as big as Mumbai.
A. A take-away food stall/expensive/a restaurant.
⇨ ....
B. Rajasthan/populous/Uttar Pradesh
⇨ ....
C. Conventional TVs/good/LCD TVs
⇨ ....
D. Mechanical watches/dependable/quartz watches
⇨ ....

6. Rewrite the sentences following the models given:

→ Your speech was brilliant.
⇨ You spoke brilliantly.
A. (Raju is intelligent). He's also hard-working.
⇨ ....
B. Raghu is rather slow in his work.
⇨ Raghu ....

C. She gave me a suspicious look.
⇨
....

D. She ate in a hurry.
⇨
....

E.   Aamir Khan's acting is always good.
⇨
....

F. Akbar .... ruler.
⇨ Akbar ruled wisely.

7. Write sentences based on the information given within brackets:

→ (I made repeated requests to him.)
⇨ I requested him repeatedly.

A. (I look forward to your visit with happiness.)
⇨
....

B. (The bank manager behaved in a rude manner.)
⇨
....

C. (You'll be able to do this sum without difficulty.)
⇨
....

D. (Rani is happy. She is humming a tune.)
⇨
....

8. Select the correct word to complete the following sentences:

A. Please wait for Ravi and	I/me
B. That is Ravi's house, and the one behind is	my/mine
C. It was my fault, not	your/yours
D. He has a broken arm, but he shaves	him/himself
E. The boss has asked you and .... to meet him at 5.00.	I/me
F. It is not for .... to decide, the case is already in court.	they/them

9. Complete the sentences with the appropriate form of the verb given within brackets and any one of **myself, yourselves, himself, herself,** and **themselves:**
A. Ladies and Gentlemen! Will you please ....? (introduce)
B. I .... while hammering a nail. (hurt)
C. He .... to ...., he is talking over the phone. (not talk)
D. The captain, Anil Kumble .... to bowl the first over yesterday. (come out)
E. 'This cake is yummy! Where did you buy it?' —'I didn't buy it, I .... it .... (bake)'
F. Radhika and Ravi don't have a domestic help, they .... the housework .... (do)

10. Rewrite the sentences beginning with the given word(s):

A. This house belongs to me.
⇨ 1. This is ....

B. This is my house.
⇨ 2. This house is ....

C. Rambabu's wife's name is Sita Devi.
⇨ 3. Sita Devi is ....

D. One of my friends is a film actress.
    ⇨ 4. A ....

E. Is this your suitcase?
    ⇨ 5. Is this suitcase ....

F. Tania is one of her friends.
    ⇨ 6. Tania is a friend ....

PART 9

FROM SIMPLE TO COMPLEX LANGUAGE

53

Clauses Can Be Relative

Learning Objectives: This chapter covers vocabulary around describing people and places and some useful collocations. It also covers relative clauses—a most useful structure that is used frequently.

53.1 A NEW EXPERIENCE

Can you recall an experience of moving to a new city, joining a new college, or taking up a new job? It's always exciting, isn't it? Here are five paragraphs of a passage in which I have described the initial days in my first job. But they are not in order. Read the paragraphs quickly and jot down their correct order within the circles. The first one has been identified.

◯

A. Besides observing people from different backgrounds, there was so much to learn from friends. Gopes was an epitome of elegance. Raji would talk straight; she had a healthy disrespect for authority. Just as sincere was Venks, who made no attempt to mask his feelings. Nija was cheerfulness personified, and Thomas was wonderful company. From Sriram, I could have learned how to work hard, but I didn't. But from Damu, I did try to learn something: *not to complain about personal difficulties.* He never did. If—God forbid—you found him in a lifeboat on the sea after a shipwreck, he would still smile and say, 'I am fine.' Good friends are our best teachers.

◯

B. A few weeks later, we were invited to Raji's home for tea. Their sparsely furnished house with its sparkling red floor and white walls was in sharp contrast with the elaborately decorated middle-class homes elsewhere. As I walked in, I felt I was entering an R.K. Narayan book.

◯

C. My new colleagues were young people who could discuss anything under the sun. They tried not to talk shop outside office. Joe was the most well-read among us. He also had a quirky sense of humour. Gopes and Damu were Malayalis who were products of two different army schools; their English didn't have any Malayali accent. On the other hand, there was Mythili from Delhi. Her Malayalam sounded more like English. And in either language, she spoke eloquently.

◯

D. On my first day in office, I met Raji, who has remained a friend ever since. Soon I met the rest of the people who had joined the company along with me. We were a cosmopolitan group from different parts of India. We became friends quickly.

①

E. The place where my first company was located was Thiruvananthapuram. The city, which had small houses with big gardens and thousands of coconut trees, was picturesque.

I believe you have identified the order. Check with the answer at the bottom right corner of this page. The passage with the paragraphs in the correct order is given here. However, before you read it, check the task given in Activity 1 below.

1. The place where my first company was located was Thiruvananthapuram. The city, which had small houses with big gardens and thousands of coconut trees, was picturesque .

2. On my first day in office, I met Raji, who has remained a friend ever since. Soon I met the rest of the people who had joined the company along with me. We were a cosmopolitan group from different parts of India. We became friends quickly.

3. My new colleagues were young people who could discuss anything under the sun and tried not to talk shop outside office. Joe was the most well-read among us. He also had a quirky sense of humour. Gopes and Damu were Malayalis who were products of two different army schools; their English didn't have any Malayali accent . On the other hand, there was Mythili from Delhi. Her Malayalam sounded more like English. And in either language, she spoke eloquently .

4. A few weeks later, we were invited to Raji's home for tea. Their sparsely furnished house with its sparkling red floor and white walls was in sharp contrast with the elaborately decorated middle-class homes elsewhere. As I walked in, I felt I was entering an R.K. Narayan book.

5. Besides observing people from different backgrounds, there was so much to learn from friends. Gopes was, and still is, an epitome[1] of elegance . Raji would talk straight; she had a healthy disrespect for authority. Just as sincere was Venks, who made no attempt to mask his views to please people. From Sriram, I could have learned how to work hard, but I didn't. But from Damu, I did try to learn something: *not to complain about personal difficulties*. He never did. If—God forbid—you found him floating on the sea on a lifeboat after a shipwreck, he would still smile and say, 'I am fine.' Good friends are our best teachers.

ACTIVITY 1

Read the passage and match the definitions with the highlighted words from the passage:

1. the way in which people of a particular country/area pronounce a language	
2. having people from different parts of the world	
3. in great detail	
4. the quality of being graceful in appearance and manners	

Answers: E, D, C, B, A

---

[1] **epitome** is pronounced E.**PI**.TO.MI with stress on the highlighted part of the word.

5.	(to speak) in a fluent and convincing manner	
6.	the highest example of a particular quality	
7.	(to) hide something, such as your feelings	(to)
8.	beautiful in an old-fashioned way (this adjective is used for places)	
9.	unusual, and rather strange but entertaining	
10.	with a few things/people in a relatively large space	
11.	to discuss office or workplace, particularly when others are around (informal)	(to)
12.	if you can discuss anything under the _____, you can talk on any subject	

ACTIVITY 2

Combine the verbs in Column 1 with the words in Column 2 to form meaningful phrases:

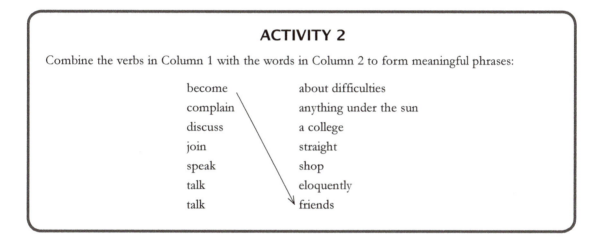

become   about difficulties

complain   anything under the sun

discuss   a college

join   straight

speak   shop

talk   eloquently

talk   friends

53.2 A *CLAUSE?* WHAT IS IT?

Before moving ahead, let's recall the definition of *clause* from Section 4.3 (pages 18-19):

> A *clause* is a group of words that is part of a sentence, but is like a sentence in itself.

For example, the sentence *Joe, who had a quirky sense of humour, was my best friend* has two clauses: (1) *Joe was my best friend* and (2) *Joe had a quirky sense of humour.*

Discussing Issues

We **talk about** issues, but **discuss** them. Some people say, '*We'll discuss ~~about~~ the matter.*' ✗;

This is not Standard English. Don't add *about* after *discuss*. Say: '*We'll discuss the matter.*'

53.3 A FEW EXAMPLES OF *RELATIVE CLAUSES*

Fill in the blanks with the options given in the textbox on the next page:

1. The city.. was Thiruvananthapuram.
2. On my first day in office I made friends with Raji,...
3. Soon I met the rest of the people ....
4. Thomas, ...,
    wrote very well.
5. Nija, ..., was the most cheer-
    ful fellow.
6. The person .... was Sriram.

> A. who has remained a friend ever since
> B. who sang all the time
> C. who had worked as a journalist earlier
> D. who had joined the company along with me
> E. where my first company was located
> F. who was most dedicated to work

Check the answers here: 1E; 2A; 3D; 4C; 5B; 6F

53.4 RELATIVE CLAUSES: IDENTIFYING AND NON-IDENTIFYING

All the clauses in the textbox are known as ***relative clauses.*** They give us information about the nouns that come before them. For example, in Sentence 1 the clause <u>where my first company was located</u> identifies a city. In Sentence 2, the clause <u>who has remained a friend ever since</u> gives more information about Raji. Here's the definition of *relative clause:*

> ***Relative clauses*** are clauses that begin with words such as *who, which, that, whose, where,* and *when,* and either (A) identify or classify or (B) give more information about the noun that comes before.

Let's check three sentences to understand what we mean by (A) ***to identify*** or ***classify*** and (B) ***to give more information about:***

1. Soon I met the people **who had joined the company with me.**
2. People **who are naturally cheerful** make others happy.
3. Nija, **who sang all the time**, was a cheerful fellow.

In the first sentence, the words in bold identify the people I'm talking about. Without this clause, this sentence *Soon I met the people* won't convey a complete idea. (Which people?) In the second sentence, the relative clause (again, the words in bold) refers to a class or group of people (who are of a particular kind) instead of identifying specific individuals. Here too, without this clause, *People make others happy* doesn't make sense.

However, *Nija was a cheerful fellow* is a complete sentence. The clause *who sang all the time* doesn't identify Nija. It just gives more information about him.

Therefore, there are two kinds of relative clauses:

- *Identifying relative clauses* are clauses that identify or classify a noun.
- *Non-identifying relative clauses* are clauses that do not identify or classify a noun. They simply give more information about the noun we are talking about.

[NOTE: Some books refer to them as ***defining*** and ***non-defining*** relative clauses.]

An easy way to check what kind of relative clause it is

If you find the above explanation a little confusing, don't worry. I am sharing with you a trick to identify the two types of relative clauses.

If you have to classify a relative clause, please ask yourself: *Does the sentence stand on its own if we remove the relative clause?*

- If the answer is *No*, it is an **identifying relative clause**. For example, consider the sentence: *The person **who answered your phone last night** is my sister.*
  If we remove the relative clause, *'who answered… last night'*, we get: *The person is my sister.* This doesn't make sense. Does it? We need a relative clause here to identify the person and complete the idea. Therefore, ***who answered your phone last night*** is an identifying relative clause.
- If the answer to the question is *Yes*, it's a **non-identifying relative clause**. Let's take the sentence: *The person who answered your phone last night is my sister, **who has come to visit us.***

This sentence makes perfect sense even if we remove the clause in bold. It only gives additional information about my sister. Therefore, ***who has come to visit us*** is a non-identifying relative clause.

ACTIVITY 3

In these sentences, the **nouns** described by the relative clauses are in bold. *I* stands for identifying and *NI* for non-identifying clauses. Underline the relative clauses and check (✔) the correct options:

	I	*NI*
1. **Thiruvananthapuram**, <u>which had a lot of greenery</u>, was a picturesque city.	*I*	*NI* ✔
2. The **city** <u>where my first company was located</u> is Thiruvananthapuram.	*I*	*NI*
3. On the first day, I met **Raji**, who has remained my friend ever since.	*I*	*NI*
4. The **person** who delivered the speech yesterday is my colleague Damu.	*I*	*NI*
5. Soon I met the rest of the **people** who had joined along with me.	*I*	*NI*
6. **Nija,** who couldn't fit into normal beds, was six feet five inches.	*I*	*NI*

ACTIVITY 4

First, complete the words by filling in the blanks. For sentences 4 to 8 below, underline the relative clauses. Write *I* if the relative clause is an identifying clause and *NI* if it is non-identifying:

1.	The place <u>where I began my career</u> was the p.............. city of Thiruvananthapuram.
2.	The city, <u>which didn't have many outsiders</u>, was not exactly c.................... .
3.	Gopes, <u>whose manners were exceedingly refined</u>, was an e.............. of e...................
4.	Joe, who was really well-read, could discuss anything under the ....
5.	Nija, who used to sing all the time, was a........................... fellow.
6.	The song he used to sing most often was 'Hawa me udta jaye, mera laal dupatta malmalkaa'.
7.	Joe said, 'People who practise yoga regularly r....................... healthy in their old age.'
8.	Those who listen to good speakers carefully can speak e....................

53.5 COMMAS IN THE LIVES OF *RELATIVE CLAUSES*

As we have seen, relative clauses come after the nouns they refer to. In writing, identifying relative clauses are not separated from the noun by a comma. In speech, there is usually no pause after the noun. This is because the idea behind the noun would be incomplete without the relative clause. However, before a non-identifying relative clause, there is always a comma. Compare these:

1. **Identifying:** She married a man <u>who worked for a bank</u>.
2. **Non-identifying:** She married a man from Mumbai, <u>who worked for a bank</u>.

Also, if a non-identifying clause comes in the middle of a sentence, there is also a comma after it:

a. **Identifying:** The friend <u>who always talked straight</u> didn't mind displeasing her bosses.
b. **Non-identifying:** Raji, <u>who always talked straight</u>, was an excellent debater.
c. **Identifying:** People <u>who read a lot</u> can talk on a variety of topics.
d. **Non-identifying:** Joe, <u>who used to read a lot</u>, could discuss anything under the sun.

A NOTE TO BORDERS: *Relative clauses* can be confusing. They can flummox learners, including native speakers of the language. So, if you are still a bit iffy about the concepts, no problem. The next chapter offers you more practice and I believe when you have completed it, you will be able to use the form confidently.

▌PRACTICE

1. Complete the story by filling in the blanks with the options given below:

> **who was either stupid or extremely impertinent²**   **who had a quirky sense of humour**
>
> **when we were working in different places**   **when it was still pitch dark**
>
> **where I had checked in**   **which was highly inadequate to take care of such an emergency**

Our friend Joe, [A]_____ was fond of playing pranks. Many years later, [B]_____ all of us friends visited Kochi to attend a meeting. I reached Kochi a day ahead. The hotel [C]_____ was popular with the employees of our company. Early next morning, [D]_____ there were loud knocks on my door. I woke up when a hotel boy announced, 'Chaya Sir.'

Irritated and still half asleep, I replied in Malayalam, 'I don't want tea!'

There was silence for some time. Then there was louder knocks and the voice said, 'Coffee, sir!'

I yelled, stretching my Malayalam, [E]_____ 'I want neither tea nor coffee!'

After another silence, the hotel boy, [F]_____ replied, 'Sir, naaranga vellam.'

Lemon juice at 5:00 in the morning? Seething with anger, I got up and opened the door, almost ready to hit the stupid fellow.

And lo and behold! My friend Joe was standing there, smiling mischievously.

2. Solve this crossword puzzle with words you have come across in this chapter:

A1→	with lots of details (adjective, 9)	D1↓	Naaseeruddin Shah or Angelina Jolie is an _____ of fine acting (7)
A2→	talking _____ is discussing office matters in presence of others (4)	D2↓	the quality of being graceful and stylish (8)
A3→	a place, city, and the like where there are people from different corners of the world (12)	D3↓	(about a place) beautiful in an old-fashioned way (11)
A4→	to get in touch with someone for the first time (4)	D4↓	to become a member or employee of (4)
A5→	another word for SITUATED (7)	D5↓	a _____ populated area is an area with a few people (8)
A6→	another word for UNUSUAL (6)	D6↓	the opposite of young (3)
A7→	when you speak, this often tells listeners which country you are from (6)		

---

² **impertinent:** (adjective) a person who doesn't show respect, RUDE.

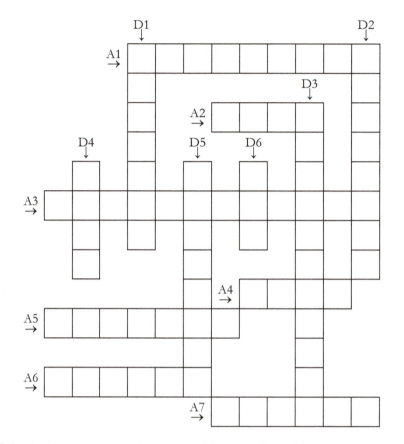

3. Five of the following six sentences are incorrect. Add comma(s) or delete comma(s) to correct them. And put a ✓ next to the correct sentences:

   A. Venks who talked very little was a quiet and sincere fellow.
   B. The people, who worked with us, were friendly and helpful.
   C. The neighbour who I liked most was Mr Kunjakrishna Pillai, an ex-serviceman.[3]
   D. Thiruvananthapuram, where life moved at a slow pace was a good place to live in.
   E. We often went to the famed Kovalam beach which is 16 km away from the city.
   F. My father, who visited Thiruvananthapuram often was exceedingly fond of the place.

4. Combine the two sentences to form a complex sentence with a relative clause:

→	1. In Diwali holidays, we went to Sikkim. 2. Sikkim is the smallest state in India.	In Diwali holidays, we went to Sikkim, which is the smallest state in India.
A.	1. First we went to Gangtok. 2. Gangtok is the capital of Sikkim.	

---

[3] **serviceman:** (noun) a member of the armed forces.

B.	1. Gangtok is remarkably pollution-free.	
	2. No buses or SUVs[4] ply in Gangtok.	
C.	1. Gangtok has a number of monasteries.	
	2. It is an important place for Buddhists.	
D.	1. We stayed in a hotel.	
	2. The hotel was on the slope of a hill.	
E.	1. We went on a day trip to Tsango Lake.	
	2. The lake was completely frozen.	
F.	1. We also went to Zero Point.	
	2. It is at an altitude of 15,000 ft.	
G.	1. We met a lot of people in Sikkim.	
	2. They were courteous and helpful.	

5. Select the correct options:

A. The Kovalam sea beach, **which/where** is 16 km from Thiruvananthapuram, attracts tourists from all over the world.

B. Thiruvananthapuram, **which/that** had few industries, was remarkably pollution free.

C. A city **which/that** has lots of greenery is good to live in.

D. When I visited the place many years ago, it was a sleepy town **that/which/where** had a handful of restaurants.

E. The people, **which/that/who** were warm and hospitable, didn't generally speak English.

F. There was a beautiful palace with a garden at the heart of the city, **which/that** we often visited at weekends.

KEY TO ACTIVITIES

Activity 1: 1. accent; 2. cosmopolitan; 3. elaborately; 4. elegance; 5. eloquently; 6. epitome; 7. (to) mask; 8. picturesque; 9. quirky; 10. sparsely; 11. (to) talk shop; 12. sun

Activity 2: become friends; complain about difficulties; discuss anything under the sun; join a college; speak eloquently; talk straight; talk shop

Activity 3: 2. I; 3, who has remained ... ever since. NI; 4, who delivered .... yesterday. I; 5, who had joined along with me I; 6. who couldn't fit ... beds, NI

Activity 4: 1. picturesque/I; 2. cosmopolitan/NI; 3. epitome, elegance/NI; 4. Joe, who was really well-read, could discuss anything under the sky./NI; 5. Nija, who sang all the time, was a cheerful fellow./NI; 6. The song he used to sing most often was .../I; 7. ...'People who practise yoga regularly remain healthy in their old age'./I; 8. Those who listen to good speakers carefully can speak eloquently./I

---

[4] **SUV:** short form for sport-utility vehicle, which is a large vehicle that is used on rough surfaces. SUVs consume more fuel and hence cause more pollution.

An Adhesive[1] Called Relative Pronoun

Learning Objectives: Continuing from the last chapter, here, we will focus a little more on relative pronouns, discuss how to use them, and when not to use them.

54.1 A QUICK REVIEW

In Chapter 53, to discussed how to use *relative clauses*. Let's recall the two purposes they serve:

1. To identify the person or thing you are talking about. For example:

   i. **The hotel** that we stayed in was on the slope of a hill.
   ii. **People** who practise yoga are likely to be healthy.

2. To give additional information about the person or thing you are talking about. For example, you combine the sentences *We visited Gangtok* and *Gangtok is the capital of Sikkim* into:

   iii. We visited **Gangtok**, which is the capital of Sikkim.

This form is widely used in writing, particularly formal and academic writing. In a language exam such as the IELTS,[2] you wouldn't possibly score high marks in writing if you couldn't handle relative clauses accurately. The structure is also used extensively in essays, dissertations, and theses.[3]

Read the sentences marked (i) to (iii) again and underline the words that join the two clauses in these sentences.

And the answers are: (i) that, (ii) who, and (iii) which.

---

[1] **adhesive:** (uncountable noun) a material that binds or joins two surfaces, GLUE.

[2] *IELTS* is the short form for *International English Language Testing System*. You take this exam if you wish to go to English speaking countries such as the UK, Australia, the USA for job or higher studies.

[3] **theses** is the plural or *thesis,* a long essay that students submit after original research on a topic.

Relative Pronouns

> The words *who, which, where, when, whom, whose,* and *that* act like adhesives that join two clauses together in some complex sentences. They are called ***relative pronouns.***

As the term *relative* suggests, these pronouns put two things in relation, and like all pronouns, they help us avoid repetition of a noun (*the hotel, people, Gangtok*). In this chapter, we are going to look into relative pronouns that we use in different situations and also when we can leave them out.

DIAGNOSTIC ACTIVITY

Let's check how much you already know.

A. Fill in the blanks and add commas where necessary:

    (i)   The lake ⬚ I learned to swim is in South Kolkata.
    (ii)   Later, I went swimming twice a week along with Gautam ⬚ is my best friend.
    (iii) We used to cycle down to the lake early in the morning ⬚ it was still dark.

B. Check (✔) the sentence if it is correct. Correct it if it isn't:

    (i)   The bicycle I had was new.
    (ii)   The cycle, that I had got as a gift on my 13th birthday, was a Hero Ranger.
    (iii) The uncle who, I had got the cycle from, was a keen sportsman.
    (iv) Our swimming coach whose name was Raju Reddy had swum across the English Channel.

Check the answers with the key below. (If you have got all of them right, you don't have to work through this chapter. You can of course do the activities and the practice exercises at the end of the chapter.) If you haven't got them right, it's fine. You'll find answers to all your questions in the following pages.

54.2 USE OF *RELATIVE PRONOUNS* FOR PEOPLE AND THINGS

A. **For people:** We use *who* and *whose* to refer to people. We also use *whom,* but not often.

Identifying Relative Clause	Non-identifying Relative Clause
All the people **who** joined the company along with me had been brilliant students.	My batchmates, **who** had been brilliant students, could discuss anything under the sun.

The colleague **whose** <u>house looked over the sea</u> was Irfan.	Irfan, **whose** <u>house looked over the sea</u>, cycled to office every day.
The friend **whose** <u>bike I borrowed</u> was Nija.	Nija, **whose** <u>bike I borrowed</u>, was most helpful.

In informal communication, we use sentences with **who.** Sentences with **whose** are considered formal. And the following sounds *even more formal*:

✓ **The friend** from whom **I borrowed the bike was Nija.**

In modern spoken (and informal) English, we use **who** instead of **whom** and put the preposition (*from, to,* and the like) at the end of the clause. These sentences sound more natural:

✓ The friend **who** I borrowed the bike **from** was Nija.
✓ The colleague **who** she enjoyed talking **to** was to become her husband.
✓ The officer **who** we first reported **to** was Mr K.C. Oomen.

B. **For things:** We use *which* for objects.

- IDENTIFYING: The bike **which** I borrowed **from** Nija was a Royal Enfield Bullet.
- IDENTIFYING: It was a speech the purpose of **which** I couldn't understand.
- NON-IDENTIFYING: The bike, **which** was quite old, was in excellent condition.

We use *whose* mainly for people. We use it for objects too, but rarely:

- The bike, **whose** condition was excellent, was quite old.
- It was a speech **whose** purpose I couldn't understand.
- It's the house **whose** door is painted red.[4]

Who, Which, and *That*
In **identifying relative clauses**, we often use *that* instead of *who* or *which:*

- The friend **who** lived near the sea was Irfan. = The friend **that** lived near....
- The house **which** Irfan lived in had red doors. = The house **that** Irfan lived in....

However, in a **non-identifying relative clause**, *we do not replace who or which with that:*

- We also visited the Tsango Lake, ~~that~~ was completely frozen. ✗
- We also visited the Tsango Lake, **which** was completely frozen. ✓
- Irfan, ~~that~~ **who** lived near the sea, cycled to office.
- My colleagues, ~~that~~ **who** had been brilliant students, could discuss anything under the sun.

---

[4] OALD, 9th ed., p. 1783.

ACTIVITY 1

Complete the sentences with five of the following. (You can use an option more than once.)

who	who or that	identifying	non-identifying
which, that, or **whose**		**whom** and **whose**	

A. In identifying relative clauses, we commonly use........................ to refer to people.
B. In all relative clauses, we also use........................ to refer to people, but not very often.
C. In modern spoken and informal English, we use.................... instead of *whom* and put the preposition at the end.
D. We use.. for objects.
E. In a/an............................ *relative clause,* we do not use *that* instead of *who.*

ACTIVITY 2

Fill in the blanks with *who, which, that,* and *whose:*

The man [A]................. drove us around Sikkim was Karma Bhutia. Karma, [B]................. family lives in Lachung in North Sikkim, has two children. Lachung, [C]................. is at an elevation of 2,900 m, is a beautiful hamlet[5] at the confluence of two rivers. But Karma, [D]................. takes tourists to all corners of Sikkim, is rarely at home. He loves driving and also loves his vehicle, [E]................. is a Tata Sumo Gold. The vehicle, [F]................. he bought 10 years ago, looks almost new. Karma, [G]................. is extremely hardworking, is polite and helpful. It was a pleasure meeting him.

ACTIVITY 3

Cross out the errors in the following sentences. If a sentence is correct, put a ✓ next to it:

➤ Karma Bhutia, ~~that~~ who drove us through Sikkim, was a cautious driver.
➤ The vehicle that Karma drove was an SUV. ✓
    A. Karma, who drove exceedingly well, was a fine gentleman.
    B. I was surprised to hear that the SUV what looked brand new was actually 10 years old.
    C. Karma lives in Lachung, that is 125 km from Gangtok.
    D. Karma's daughter, who is seven, studies at a boarding school in Gangtok.
    E. Karma, that is keen to educate his daughter well, spends a lot of money on her schooling.

---

[5] **hamlet:** (noun) a small settlement, even smaller than a village.

54.3 *RELATIVE PRONOUNS* FOR PLACES, TIMES, AND REASONS

A. *For places, we use* **where:**

- *The city* **where** *our company had its head office was Thiruvananthapuram.* ✓
- *The place* **where** *we met regularly was the Indian Coffee House.* ✓
- *The place* **that** *we met regularly was the Indian Coffee House.* ✗

B. *To refer to time, we use* **when:**

- *I clearly remember the day* **when** *I met Joe. It was raining heavily.*
- *There used to be a fire drill at our office every six months,* **when** *we would leave everything behind and take the stairs to leave the building.*

C. *To talk about reasons, we use* **why** *or* **that:**

- *The reason* **why** *I went to the Indian Coffee House was to meet Damu.*
- *The reason* **that** *I went to the Indian Coffee House was to meet Damu.*
- *The reason* **why**/**that** *we loved the Coffee House was we could spend hours there, without anyone asking us to get lost.*

ACTIVITY 4

Fill in each blank with a word:

In Thiruvananthapuram, we lived near Edapazhanji, [A]................. there was a wholesale fish market. There used to be a huge hullabaloo in the morning [B]................. hundreds of fishmongers and their customers would converge at the place. Our house, [C]................. was a lovely bungalow with a garden, would often stink of fish. But the reason [D]................. we never thought of leaving the place was our landlords, who were a lovable elderly couple. We all looked forward to Sunday mornings, [E]................. our landlady Saraswati Amma would send us a sumptuous[6] breakfast.

---

[5] **sumptuous:** (adjective) LUXURIOUS (pronounced **SUHMP**.CHOO.UHS).

54.4 CAN WE LEAVE OUT THE *RELATIVE PRONOUN?*

Yes, we can. But my first piece of advice to you would be: *Do not drop relative pronouns in formal written English.* However, the situation is different in informal/spoken English.

> In informal and spoken English, for *identifying relative clauses,* we can leave out the relative pronoun if it is the object of a verb.

Check the table below:

The relative pronoun is an object of the verb, you can drop it in spoken/informal English	The relative pronoun is the subject of the verb—you have to keep it, always
✓ The bike **that/which** Nija had was an Enfield. Or ✓ The bike Nija had was an Enfield.	✓ The bike **which** never let Nija down was an Enfield. ✗ The ~~bike never~~ let Nija down was an Enfield.
✓ The dosa **which/that** Sriram's mom made was delicious. ✓ The dosa Sriram's mom made was delicious.	✓ The café **that** sold excellent dosas at a bargain[7] was naturally popular.
✓ Three of us shared a flat **that** we had rented from an ex-serviceman. ✓ Three of us shared a flat we had rented from an ex-serviceman.	✓ The landlord who often offered us tea and snacks was Kunjakrishna Pillai, an ex-serviceman.
↑ The (identifying) relative pronouns here (*that, which*) are objects of the verbs that follow (*had bought, shared, rented*). In informal English, you can either keep them or drop them.	↑ In these sentences, the (identifying) relative pronouns (*which, that,* and *who*) are all subjects of a clause. We cannot leave them out.

- All the illustrations above have identifying relative clauses. For non-identifying relative clauses, the relative pronoun is never left out.

ACTIVITY 5

Underline the relative pronouns in the following sentences. While speaking, can we drop the relative pronoun in these sentences? Write either *Yes* or *No.*

---

[6] **bargain:** a thing offered for sale much more cheaply than what is expected.

A. The restaurant that we visited often was the Indian Coffee House. ....

B. The Coffee House served excellent omelettes, which we loved. ....

C. We gathered at the Coffee House at weekends, when everyone was free. ....

D. But Sriram, whose office was far away, couldn't join us. ....

E. Sriram now lives in Manama, which is the capital of Bahrain. ....

F. The Coffee House, which was centrally located, was popular with young people. ....

G. Nija used to ride a bike which he had bought years ago. ....

H. Nija had a bike which never let him down. ....

ACTIVITY 6

Combine the two sentences in Column 1. Leave out the relative pronoun if it can be:

➤	We had a boss by name K.C. Oomen. We all admired him.	We had a boss by name K.C. Oomen, who we all admired.
A.	I reported to an officer on the first day. He was K.C. Oomen.	The officer
B.	Oomen was highly placed in our company. He was an epitome of humility.	Oomen, who was highly placed in our company,
C.	Oomen had a phenomenal memory. He knew thousands of employees by name.	
D.	Oomen spoke excellent English. And he looked sad if anyone made a mistake in English.	
E.	Some colleagues called him Mr Webster behind his back. He taught us how to write clearly.	Mr Oomen,

54.5 LET'S CHECK

Please return to the task given at the beginning of this chapter, namely, the Diagnostic Activity. Erase your answers and do the task again.

Are you more confident now?

PRACTICE

1. Write a word or a phrase to match the clues. If necessary, go through the chapter again.

i. Writing in the context of studies, research, and the like	_ _ _ _ _ _ _ _ _ _ _ _ _ _
ii. Something that is offered for sale at a rate much below the usual price	b _ _ _ _ _ _
iii. A short form for bicycle or motorbike	_ _ _ _
iv. A school with an attached hostel where pupils live	_ _ _ _ _ _ _ _ _ _ _ _ _ _
v. Another word for compressed	c _ _ _ _ _ t
vi. A place where two rivers join	c _ n _ _ _ _ _ _ _
vii. The height of a particular place, ALTITUDE	e _ _ _ _ _ _ _ _
viii. An exercise (often done in offices, schools, and so on) to practise what should be done in case of a fire, earthquake, or other emergencies	_ _ _ _ _ _ _ _
ix. You have to do (to someone) this to begin a new job	_ _ _ _ _ _
x. A man who is a member of the armed forces	s _ _ _ _ _ _ _ _ _
xi. A _____ meal is an elaborate and luxurious meal	s _ _ _ _ _ _ _
xii. A long essay that students have to submit to get a PhD	_ _ _ _ _ _

2   Complete each sentence with a relative pronoun and a word from the above list. If the sentence is complete even without the relative pronoun, put a dash in the blank space:

A. Lubna, ... will take the IELTS exam next month, is practising ....
B. Lubna's boyfriend Joe, ... has almost completed writing his ...., should become a PhD soon.
C. Mom organized a .... dinner .... Rohan came at the top of his class.
D. The jacket .... she purchased for Roshan was available at a ....
E. Rohan studies at a ...., ... is located near Gangtok.
F. The place .... Roshan studies is at an .... of 4,000 ft.
G. The school compound, ... is at the .... of two rivers, is picturesque.
H. Last week, there was a .... at Roshan's school, ... everyone had to vacate the school building and gather at the playground.
I. Rohan has an excellent football coach at his school. The coach, ... name is Joseph Mathews, is an ex-.........................
J. At weekends, Roshan .... to Joseph Mathews at 5 AM, ... it is still pitch dark.

3. Solve the crossword puzzle with the clues given below:

A1	A relative pronoun we don't normally use in informal and spoken English	D1	You can use this instead of *who* or *which* in identifying relative clauses

A2	A relative pronoun used for things	D2	The man _____ bike was stolen ....
A3	A relative pronoun used for places	D3	A relative pronoun used for time
		D4	The man _____ I lent some money to ....

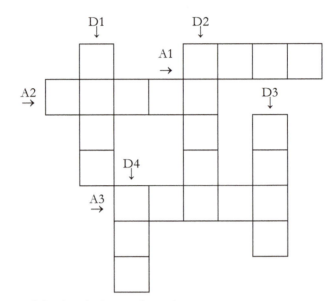

4. Convert the sentences following the instructions given:

   ➤ The friend from whom I borrowed the book was Irfan. [Use *who* instead of *whom*]
   <u>The friend who I borrowed the book from was Irfan.</u>...

   A. Irfan, whose book I borrowed, was one of my best friends. [Use *who* instead of *whose*]
   ....

   B. The colleague to whom I gave the book never returned it. [Use *who* instead of *whom*]
   ....

   C. The colleague who I met first was Raji. [Rephrase this sentence without a relative pronoun]
   ....

   D. A friend from whom I've learned a lot is Damu. [Replace *whom* with *who*]
   ....

5. Complete the sentences by adding the option that matches:

1.	which begins at Yumthang and ends at Lachen
2.	that begins in April
3.	which was once a trading post between Sikkim and Tibet
4.	when he was not smiling
5.	when there are no tourists
6.	who takes tourists to different corners of Sikkim

   A. Karma is from Lachung, ...
   B. Lachung is the base camp for the Rhododendron Valley Trek ....
   C. The Yumthang Valley, ..., attracts a lot of tourists.

    D. Karma, ..., is a busy man.

    E. However, in the winter, ..., Karma gets a break.

    F. Karma is a cheerful fellow. I cannot recall a moment ....

6. Think of four people you know well and four things you are fond of. Write at least one sentence on each of them using relative clauses:

   i. ....
....

  ii. ....
....

 iii. ....
....

 iv. ....
....

KEY TO ACTIVITIES

Diagnostic Activity:

A.

    (i) The lake where I learned to swim is in South Kolkata.

    (ii) Later, I went swimming twice a week along with Gautam, who is my best friend.

    (iii) We used to cycle down ... early in the morning, when it was still dark.

B.

    (i) The bicycle I had was new. ✓

    (ii) The cycle, ~~that~~ which I had got as a gift on my 13th birthday, was a Hero Ranger.

    (iii) The uncle who I had got the cycle from was a keen sportsman.

    (iv) Our swimming coach, whose name was Raju Reddy, had swum across the English Channel.

Activity 1: 1. A. *who* or *that;* B. *whom* and *whose;* C. *who;* D. *which, that,* or *whose;* E. *non-identifying*

Activity 2: A. who/that; B. whose; C. which; D. who; E. which; F. which; G. who

Activity 3: A. ✓ B. I was surprised to hear that the SUV ~~what~~ which looked.... C. Karma lives in Lachung, ~~that~~ is 125 kilometres from.... D. ✓; E. Karma, ~~that~~ who is keen to educate his daughter well, spends a lot of....

Activity 4: A. where; B. when; C. which; D. why/that; E. when

Activity 5: A. that; B. which; C. when; D. whose; E. which; F. which; G. which; H. which
Yes: A and G; No: the rest

Activity 6: A. The officer I reported to on the first day was K.C. Oomen. B. Oomen, who was highly placed in our company, was an epitome of humility. C. Oomen, who had a phenomenal memory, knew thousands of employees by name. D. Oomen, who spoke excellent English, looked sad when someone spoke incorrect English. E. Mr Oomen, who some colleagues called Mr Webster behind his back, taught us to write clearly.

55

Conditions and Results

Learning Objectives: In this chapter, we are going to check complex sentences that contain two clauses—a condition and its expected result.

55.1 WHAT IS A CONDITIONAL STATEMENT?

Ravi and his wife Radhika are talking about their little son Rohan. They are discussing some future possibilities, and the likely outcome thereof. As you read the conversation, focus on the underlined sentences. Are they similar in any way?

Radhika:	If we try hard, we can get Rohan enrolled in a good school this year.
Ravi:	How can *we* try hard? <u>If he does well in the interview, he'll be selected.</u>
Radhika:	That is utter rubbish! Mrs Dubey has been sending her son for special coaching. <u>If Rohan joins a coaching class, he'll sail through interviews.</u> He may even join St Anthony's.
Ravi:	<u>If Rohan doesn't join a school this year, he will join next year.</u>
Radhika:	What kind of a father are you? <u>If you do nothing, he will never join a good school.</u> And…
Ravi:	But Radhika, <u>even if we do nothing, he will only be three next June</u>!

The sentences in italics have two parts: a condition and an expected outcome. If we break them down, they'll look like:

The condition (following If)	The expected outcome/result
If he *does* well in the interview,	he'*ll get through*.
If Rohan *joins* a coaching class,	he *will sail through* interviews.
If Rohan *doesn't join* a school this year,	he *will join* next year.
↑	↑
(In the *simple present*)	(In the *simple future*)

These are called *conditional statements.* Note that the condition, that is, the verb in the *if* clause (*does, try, doesn't join,* and so on) is in the *simple present,* and the expected outcome is in the *simple future.* We do not say: If Rohan ~~will join~~ a coaching class, he *will sail through* interviews.

In these examples, the condition comes first and the likely result next. But often, sentences are framed in the reverse order:

- ✓ If I need any help, I'll tell you. = I'll tell you if I need any help.
- ✓ If I get better, I'll go to the party. = I'll go to the party if I get better.
- ✓ If we don't start now, we'll miss the train. = We'll miss the train if we don't start now.

Please note that in the sentences on the right, there are no commas to separate the clauses.

ACTIVITY 1

Combine the two sentences given below, following the model answer:

→ I might need help. In that case, I'll tell you.
⇨ <u>If I need (any) help, I'll tell you.</u> ....

1. We might require another machine. In that case, we will place an order with you.
⇨ ....
2. Yasmin may wish to join St Xavier's College. In that case, she will have to take a written test.
⇨ ....
3. She might pass the written test. Then she will do an interview.
⇨ ....
4. She may be selected. In that case, she will have to pay the fees within two days.
⇨ ....

55.2 UNLESS

If the condition conveys a negative idea, we can use *unless* instead of *if ... not:*

- ✓ We'll miss the train **if** we **don't** start now. = We'll miss the train **unless** we start now.
- ✓ We will take legal action **unless** you repay your debt within a week.
- ✓ Dr Daruwalla won't get better **unless** he stops drinking.

Admit and *Enrol*

The verb ***admit*** means several things. One of them is 'to allow someone to become a member of an organization, school, and so on'. You can say:

➤ The school admits children from the age of six.

But you do not say: 'I'll admit my son to a school.'
The verb ***enrol*** means 'to arrange for yourself or for someone else to join a school, institute, club, and so on'.

➤ I've just enrolled on a spoken English course at the British Council.

55.3 A LITTLE MORE VARIETY

In our examples so far, the condition is in the simple present tense. But it can also be in the *present perfect*. In fact, this is the only situation when the present perfect is used to talk about a future event:

- ✓ We'll leave when **we have** finished our lunch.
- ✓ No one can get onto the train until the police have **searched** it thoroughly.
- ✓ Raghu: 'Doctor, when can I get back to office?'
  Doctor: 'You can join office only after you **have recovered** completely.'

Another variation is to express the condition in the present continuous:

- ✓ If the doctor **is taking** rest, I'll telephone later.

And also, the likely result/future action may be expressed with the verbs *should*, *may*, *might*, and *can*.

- ✓ If you are going to meet your new girlfriend, you **should put on** a better shirt.
- ✓ If the company doesn't pay bonus, the workers **may go on** strike.
- ✓ If it stops raining, we **might go out** for a walk.

ACTIVITY 2

Read the situation described in the first column and complete the sentences in the second:

→ You have requested your boss for permission to leave office early. He says you can, but the condition is that you finish your work.	The boss says, 'You can leave when you have finished your work.'
1. You have borrowed a book from your friend. You promise to return it after reading it.	You tell your friend, 'I will.......................... when...................................,'
2. Your mother is cooking dinner. She will finish cooking and then call you.	Mother says, 'I'll.......................... ....,'
3. You are a businessman. You tell your son he can join you after graduation.	You say, 'You can join me when...... ....,'
4. Someone phones your grandpa when he is having lunch. You tell the caller that grandpa will call him back after lunch.	You say, 'Grandpa........................... when.......................... his lunch.'

55.4 TYPE 1 AND TYPE ZERO CONDITIONALS

The structures discussed so far in this unit are known as *Type 1 conditional statements*.

If the result or action *automatically* follows the condition, we may use the simple present in both conditions and results. This is also called a *Type Zero conditional statement*.

✓ If it **rains** in summer, the weather **becomes** sultry in Kolkata.
✓ If you **heat** water to 100°C, it boils.

ACTIVITY 3

When Kuttan joined a driving school, this is what his driving instructor told him on the first day. Fill in the blanks with the following verbs to complete the instruction: **get, go, move, stop,** and **turn.**

Learning how to drive is as easy as learning ABC. You just have to learn how to use the accelerator, the brake, and the clutch. If you press the accelerator, the car (1) .... faster. If you press on the brake pedal, the car (2) .... When you press the clutch, the wheels (3) .... detached from the engine. And of course, you have to control the steering. When you turn the steering clockwise, the car (4) .... right. When you turn the steering anticlockwise, the vehicle (5) .... towards the left.

PRACTICE

1. Fill in the blanks to complete the rules:

   A. In Type 1 conditional statements, the verb in the *if* clause is in the .... tense, and the expected outcome is often in the ....

   B. If the result automatically follows the condition, we use the .... in both conditions and results. This is also called a Type Zero conditional sentence.

2. Correct the following sentences:

   A. If we will start now, we will get the 9 o'clock train.
   B. If we miss the train, there can be another train after one hour.
   C. You can leave office when you will finish your work.
   D. If you heat water to 100°C, it is boiling.
   E. If you have lost your ATM card, you will immediately informing your bank.
   F. If you will need a ticket, I can get one for you.

3. Match the sentences in the two columns given below and join them with **if** or **unless:**

→ You break anything.	We will cover 100 km in two days.	
A. We go on polluting the atmosphere.	You learn how to use the computer.	
B. You drive so slowly!	You will have to pay for it.	→
C. You hear Nusrat Fateh Ali Khan once.	The human race will be destroyed.	
D. You won't get a job.	You'll never forget his voice.	

→ If you break anything, you will have to pay for it.

A. ....:
B. ....:
C. ....:
D. ....:

4. Match the two parts of the sentences given below and fill in the blanks with **can, should,** or **may:**

A. If you have finished your work,   you _____ do anything. ( )
B. If you don't have money now,   you _____ report to the police. ( )
C. If you try really hard,   you _____ pay later. ( )
D. If you're getting nasty phone calls,   you _____ leave office. ( )

A. ....:
B. ....:
C. ....:
D. ....:

5. Add *if* and one of the clauses from the list below to complete the sentences. Follow the model given:

~~the computer shows the latest sales figures.~~   the UPS[1] takes over
an alarm goes off   he has to get a passport
the weather becomes sultry   the car moves

(→) <u>If</u> you click on this icon, <u>the computer shows the latest sales figures.</u>

(a) .... you press the accelerator, ...
(b) .... someone touches this safe after 5 PM, ...
(c) .... it rains in Kolkata in summer, ...
(d) .... he wants to go abroad, ...
(e) .... the electricity fails, ...

KEY TO ACTIVITIES

Activity 1: 1. If we require another machine, we will place an order with you. 2. If Yasmin wishes to join St Xavier's College, she will have to take a written test. 3. If she passes the written test, she will have to do an interview. 4. If she is selected, she will have to pay the fees within two days.

Activity 2: 1. I'll return the book when I have read it. 2. Mother says, 'I will call you when I have finished cooking.' 3. You say, 'You can join me when you have graduated.' 4. You say, 'Grandpa will call you back when he has finished his lunch.'

Activity 3: (1) moves; (2) stops; (3) get; (4) turns; (5) goes

---

[1] **UPS:** short form for uninterruptible power supply, a device that supplies electrical power to a machine when there is no electricity.

Tom Sawyer Is Dying

Learning Objectives: In this chapter, we are discussing the grammatical form 'Second Conditional' —that is, the sentence which tells you about an unlikely condition.

56.1 TOM SAWYER ON A MONDAY MORNING

You use the verb *hate* either to express *strong dislike for something,* or to say that *you find something very unpleasant.* Remember this and complete the heading for the passage below. (It is an adaptation from a *Tom Sawyer* story by the celebrated American author Mark Twain.)

Tom Sawyer feels sad on Monday morning because he ....

It is Monday morning. Tom hates Mondays. School begins on Monday and after that, there is a whole week of school. Tom hates going to school! He lies in bed, thinking… *if he was ill, he wouldn't have to go to school.* That is a pity! His head feels all right. His stomach feels all right. He has a loose tooth and that hurts him sometimes. But *if he told his aunt about it, she would pull it out at once.* No, he cannot stay at home for his tooth. What can he do? Then he remembers something. A week before, he cut his toe. Perhaps it was infected. *If it was infected, it would be serious.* That would keep him at home![1]

ACTIVITY 1

In Chapter 55, we saw that a conditional statement has two clauses: one carrying a condition and the other describing its result. The above passage too has three conditional statements, which are in italics. Can you underline the verbs in these statements?

Is there any difference between these three conditional statements and the conditional statements you came across in Chapter 55?

---

[1] I would fill in the blank with: *hates going to school.* What have you written?

56.2 TYPE 1 AND TYPE 2 CONDITIONALS

In Activity 1, the verbs are:

- ✓ If he <u>was</u> ill, he <u>wouldn't have to</u> go to school.
- ✓ If he <u>told</u> his aunt about it, she <u>would pull</u> it out at once.
- ✓ If it (the cut on his toe) <u>was</u> infected, it <u>would</u> be serious.

In these sentences, the conditions are future possibilities, but they are *unlikely* to happen: *Tom is not likely to fall ill, he does not want to tell his aunt about the loose tooth,* and *his toe is not likely to be infected.* As you can see, the (unlikely) possibilities are in **the simple past,** and the (unreal) results are expressed with **would.** (They may also be expressed with **should** or **could.**) We call these sentences Type 2 conditionals.

Compare these with the conditional statements discussed in Chapter 55 (Type 1 conditionals).

- ✓ If Rohan <u>doesn't join</u> a school this year, he <u>will join</u> next year.

The table below contrasts and compares Type 1 and **Type 2 conditionals:**

Type 1 and Type 2 Conditionals

Type 1 Conditionals	**Type 2 Conditionals**
The condition is a **real future possibility.** ↓	The condition is a **future possibility, but it is not likely to happen.** ↓
✓ *(It's morning and it is raining heavily.) If the roads go under water, there will be no school.* ✓ *If you <u>practise</u> regularly, <u>you will be</u> selected for the college team.*	✓ *If there was an earthquake, there would be no school.* ✓ *If you <u>played</u> in the Indian cricket team, you <u>could marry</u> a film star.*
↓	↓
1. The condition is in **present tenses:** the simple present, the present continuous, and the present perfect. 2. The expected result is in **the simple future** or with *can, may, might, should,* and so on.	1. The condition is in **the simple past** or the past continuous. 2. The likely outcome is expressed with **would, should,** or **could** + **the base form of the verb.**

Note: In Type 2 conditionals, you can use **were** instead of **was** in the **if** clause:

- ✓ If he was ill ... = If he were ill ...
- ✓ If I was you ... = If I were you ...

ACTIVITY 2

Are these possibilities real or imaginary for Rani, a two-year-old Indian girl from a middle-class family? Strike off the incorrect options and note the forms of the verbs:

→ When Rani becomes five years old…   ⇨ real/~~unlikely~~
1. If Rani wants to be an engineer…   ⇨ real/unlikely
2. If Rani married a film star…   ⇨ real/unlikely
3. When Rani goes abroad…   ⇨ real/unlikely
4. If Rani went to the moon…   ⇨ real/unlikely
5. If Rani won the Nobel Prize…   ⇨ real/unlikely

ACTIVITY 3

Complete the sentences for Rani, a two-year-old Indian girl from a middle-class family. Use the verbs given within brackets:

1. When Rani becomes five, she …………………… going to school. (start)
2. When Rani ………… to school, she …………………… lots of friends. (go, have)
3. If Rani wants to be an engineer, she …………………… study science in school. (have to)
4. If Rani ………… good in maths, she might study science. (be)
5. If Rani ………… a Bollywood star, she would live in Mumbai. (marry)
6. If Rani ………… the prime minister of India, she …………………… her brother a minister. (become, make)

ACTIVITY 4

Given below are parts of Type 2 conditional sentences. Complete them with your own ideas. Then compare your sentences with the key below:

1. What …………………………………… if you had $20 million in your bank?
2. If I had $20 million in my bank, I ………………………………………
3. …………………………………………, I would travel to space.
4. If Aamir Khan offered me the lead role in his next film, …………………………

56.3 SAME CONTEXT–DIFFERENT MESSAGES

You can use the first and second conditional statements to convey different ideas in the context of the same set of facts. Check the following sentences:

✓ If I take up this job, I will have to travel 25 days every month. (= *I may join the company, I am considering the option.*)
✓ If I took up this job, I would have to travel 25 days every month. (= *I don't think it is a great idea; it is unlikely that I would take up the job.*)

ACTIVITY 5

Frame two sentences each for each set, following the instructions given:

	You don't want it:	*You are positive about it:*
→	If I <u>bought</u> this sofa, my drawing room <u>would look</u> cluttered.	If I <u>buy</u> this sofa, my drawing room <u>will look</u> good.
1.	If you............ that shirt, you............ look funny. (wear, look)	If you............ that shirt, you............ look smart. (wear, look)
2.	If I............ a bank loan, I............ have to........... interest. (take, pay)	If I............ a bank loan, I............ have to........... interest. (take, pay)
3.	If I........... this trip, I........................ spend a lot. (go on, have to)	If I........... this trip, I........................ spend a lot. (take, have to)

PRACTICE

1. Complete the following sentences using the verbs given within brackets:

   A. If I .... ill, I wouldn't have to go to office today. (be)
   B. If I .... rich, I wouldn't live in this one-room flat. (be)
   C. If my boss ...., he could help me. (want)
   D. If I .... (get) the first prize in a lottery, I .... (spend) a night at a hotel made of ice in Northern Europe.
   E. I didn't sleep well last night. If it was a Sunday, I .... till afternoon. (sleep)
   F. I feel sad. If I .... a ticket, I .... to the concert. (have, go)
   G. If it .... raining, we .... out for a walk. (stop, can go)
   H. If wishes .... horses, we .... to success easily. (be, gallop)

2. Write a conditional statement to express the situations given in the first column. Follow the model given:

→ We can't go on long drives because we don't have a car.	If we had a car, we could go out for long drives.
A. Ria won't marry Raghu because she doesn't love him.	If Ria loved Raghu, she
B. I want to swim every day, but there is no swimming pool nearby.	If there
C. Raghu is crazy about films. He wants to see a film every day, but he does not have the time.	If Raghu had
D. I want to call my friend now, but I can't because I can't find my phone.	

KEY TO ACTIVITIES

Activity 2: 1. real; 2. unlikely; 3. real; 4. unlikely; 5. unlikely

Activity 3: 1. will start; 2. goes, will have; 3. will have to; 4. is; 5. married; 6. became, would make

Activity 4: Suggested answers: 1. What would you do if you had $20 million in your bank? 2. If I had $20 million in my bank, I would go around the world every year. 3. If I had $20 million in my bank, I would travel to space. 4. If Aamir Khan offered me the lead role in his next film, I would say, 'Sorry, I have no time.'

Activity 5: 1. If you wore that shirt, you would look funny./If you wear that shirt, you would look smart. 2. If I took a bank loan, I would have to pay interest./If I take a bank loan, I will have to pay interest. 3. If I go on this tour, I will have to spend quite a lot./If I went on this trip, I would have to spend quite a lot./ If I went on this trip, I would have to spend quite a lot.

If Lara Dutta Had Married Brian Lara

Learning Objectives: Continuing from the previous two chapters, we are going to discuss *Type 3 conditional statements* here. You will need these forms often.

57.1 TYPE 3 CONDITIONAL

Imagine that the Cricket World Cup final is going to be held in your city next Sunday. There is tremendous demand for tickets. If you request someone to get a ticket for you, you might get one of these responses:

1. If you want a ticket, I will get one for you.	⇨ This is a serious offer. The condition and the result are both possible.	(Type 1 conditional)
2. If I knew the chairman of the Cricket Council, I could get a ticket for you.	⇨ The speaker is talking about an unlikely possibility. The result is not expected to be true.	(Type 2 conditional)
3. Oh! If you had told me yesterday, I would have got a ticket for you.	⇨ The time for the condition to be fulfilled is over. The result is impossible. (*People often say such things, don't they?*)	(Type 3 conditional)

We discussed the first two types of conditional statements in Chapters 55 and 56. We are going to discuss Type 3 conditionals here.

We use this form when it is too late to fulfil a condition and when the outcome is of no practical value. For example, when actor Lara Dutta married tennis star Mahesh Bhupathi, someone sent me this text message: *If Lara Dutta had married Brian Lara, she would have become Lara Lara.*

Here is one more example. Mirza Ghalib wrote:

Thank God, you said 'No' to me.
If you has said 'yes', I would have died of happiness.

We often use this form to describe things that went wrong. This means sometimes we use this structure to criticize people or to point out mistakes: *If you had driven more carefully, you could have avoided the accident.*

In Type 3 conditional sentences:

- the condition (i.e., the 'if clause') is in the **past perfect** and
- the outcome is in the form **would have/could have/might have + past participle form of the verb.**

ACTIVITY 1

In the following sentences, complete the *if* clause using the verbs given within brackets. (These statements talk about something that didn't happen.)

1. If I .... the alarm, I would have woken up in time. (hear)
2. If I .... in time, I wouldn't have missed the train. (wake up)
3. If I .... the train, I wouldn't have been late for my own wedding. (not miss)
4. If you .... me just a little earlier, I wouldn't have eaten all the potato chips. (ask)
5. If Raju's father .... in an accident, he would have completed his studies. (not die)
6. If I .... that memory chip for virus, my computer wouldn't have crashed. (scan)

ACTIVITY 2

In the following sentences, the *if* clause talks about something that did not happen. Complete the sentences using the verbs given within brackets:

1. If you had come to the party five minutes earlier, you .... Lara Dutta. (meet)
2. If my wife had been here, she .... happy to meet you. (be)
3. If the driver had been more careful, he .... the accident. (can avoid)
4. If Mohan had saved when he was young, he .... more comfortable in his old age. (be)
5. If you had planned your holiday better, you .... these problems now. (not face)
6. If I'd got better marks in secondary exams, I .... a better college. (enrol in)

57.2 COMPARISON BETWEEN TYPE 2 AND TYPE 3 CONDITIONALS

Type 2 and Type 3 conditional statements have been compared and contrasted in the table below:

Type 2 Conditionals	Type 3 Conditionals
The statement is about **the future**.	The statement is about **the past**.
The condition is a **future possibility, but it is *not likely* to happen.** ↓	The condition refers to the **past, something that *did not* happen.** ↓
✓ *If Raghu worked harder, he might pass the exam.* (= The exam is in the future; Raghu can still work hard and pass, but I don't expect him to.)	✓ *If Raghu had worked harder, he might have passed the exam.* (= The exam is over; Raghu has failed.)
✓ *If she missed the flight, she wouldn't be able to present her paper at the conference*	✓ *If Andrej Aplinc hadn't missed her flight, she would have died in the crash.*
↓ 1. The condition is in **the simple past** (or past continuous). 2. The likely outcome is expressed with **would/ should/could/might + the base form of the verb.**	↓ 1. The condition is in **the past perfect.** 2. The likely outcome is expressed with **would/ should/could /might + have + the past participle form of the verb.**

ACTIVITY 3

Frame two sentences for each set of clues, one in the second conditional form and the other in the third conditional:

Clue	An Event in the Future	An Event in the Past
→ I + get a ticket + go to + the concert	*If I got a ticket, I would go to the concert.*	*If I'd got a ticket, I would have gone to the concert.*
1. I + get + a pay hike + I give you a treat		
2. If + rain stop + we + go out for a walk		
3. I lose my pen drive + cannot make the presentation at the conference		

PRACTICE

1. Complete the conversation using the verbs given within brackets:

Irfan:	You couldn't pay the exam fees? If you .... me earlier, I .... something. (tell, can do)
Raju:	If I .... my scholarship in time, there .... no problem. (get, be)
Irfan:	But why didn't you get your scholarship?
Raju:	Well, the head clerk at the university office .... there was no peon to get my file! (say)
Irfan:	This is disgraceful! If that monkey .... his work, you .... a year. (do, not lose)
Raju:	I think if I .... him a bribe, he .... possibly .... his work. (pay, do)

2. Write a conditional statement for the situation described in the column on the left:

A.	I wanted to go to the A.R. Rahman concert. But I didn't get a ticket.	If I had got a ticket, ...
B.	I didn't receive your message. That's why I was not at home.	If I had ....
C.	We reach the cinema late. We didn't get tickets for the film.	If .... a little earlier ....
D.	We didn't top up the tank before starting. We got stuck on the highway.	....
E.	Rani made one careless mistake. Consequently, she didn't score 100 in maths.	....
F.	Rani didn't score 100 out of 100 in maths. She couldn't participate in the Maths Olympiad.	....

KEY TO ACTIVITIES

Activity 1: 1. If I <u>had heard</u> the alarm, I would have woken up in time. 2. If I <u>had woken up</u> in time, I wouldn't have missed the train. 3. If I <u>hadn't missed</u> the train, I wouldn't have been late for my own wedding. 4. If you <u>had asked</u> me just a little earlier, I wouldn't have eaten all the potato chips. 5. If Raju's father <u>hadn't died</u> in an accident, Raju would have completed his studies. 6. If I <u>had scanned</u> that memory chip for virus, my computer wouldn't have crashed.

Activity 2: 1. If you had come to the party five minutes earlier, you <u>would have met</u> Lara Dutta. 2. If my wife had been here, <u>she would have been</u> happy to meet you. 3. If the driver had been more careful, he <u>could have avoided</u> the accident. 4. If Mohan had saved when he was young, he <u>would have been</u> more comfortable in his old age. 5. If you had planned your holiday better, you wouldn't have faced these problems now. 6. If I'd got better marks in secondary exams, I <u>would have enrolled</u> in a better college.

Activity 3: 1. If I got a pay hike, I would give you a treat; If I had got a pay hike, I would have given you a treat. 2. If the rain stopped, we would go out for a walk./If the rain had stopped, we would have gone out for a walk. 3. If I lost my pen drive, I wouldn't be able to make the presentation at the conference./If I had lost my pen drive, I couldn't have made presentation ….

Reporting Another Person's Words

Learning Objectives: In this chapter, we are going to discuss the grammatical forms relating to reporting someone else's speech.

58.1 INTRODUCTION

This passage has been adapted from the C. Rajagopalachari's *Mahabharata*. As you read, focus on how spoken words are expressed when they are written down:

Duryodhana sent a message to Yudhishthira, 'I challenge you to a game of dice. If you are not a coward, accept my challenge.'

Yudhishthira sent back a brief reply, 'I accept the challenge!'

The game was held in an open court and Shakuni, an uncle of Duryodhana, played on his behalf. Yudhishthira was a learned man and a wise king, but in a game of dice, he was a rookie[1] compared to Shakuni who was a master gambler and cheat.

At first, they played with silver, gold, chariots, and horses as stakes. The wise king lost everything. Then Yudhishthira placed as bet his towns, villages, and forests, and went on losing. Then he offered his brothers as bets and lost them too. Shakuni mocked him, 'Yudhishthira, you are a pauper now, I don't think you can offer anything else?'

Yudhishthira said, 'No, I can. Myself. If you won, I would become your slave.'

Once again, Shakuni, the evil genius, triumphed. And he shouted gleefully, 'Ah! All the Pandava brothers are now my slaves!'

A shocked silence fell on the court. However, Shakuni had not finished yet. Turning towards Yudhishthira, he said, 'You are still left with one gorgeous Jewel. Draupadi. Gamble her. If I lose, you get back everything you've just lost.'

---

[1] **rookie:** (adjective) a beginner.

In this story from the Mahabharata, the spoken words have been written down as they were spoken, within inverted commas ("). This is called **the direct speech.**

But you can represent what someone said differently. For example:

1. **Direct speech:**   Yudhishthira replied, 'I accept the challenge.'
2. **Reported speech:** Yudhishthira replied that he accepted the challenge.

58.2 THE REPORTING VERB IS USUALLY IN THE PAST

When we talk about what someone said, the **reporting verb** is usually in the past tense: *Yudhishthira replied*, *Shakuni asked*, and so on. Table 58.1 shows how direct speech is changed into reported speech when the reporting verbs are in past tenses:

TABLE 58.1   Rules for Changing Direct Speech to Reported Speech

The Transformation	Direct Speech	Reported Speech
The simple present becomes the simple past	Shakuni mocked, 'Yudhishthira, you are a pauper.'	Shakuni mocked that Yudhishthira was a pauper.
The present continuous becomes the past continuous	Dhritarashtra asked Vidura, 'What is happening?'	Dhritarashtra asked Vidura what was happening.
The present perfect becomes the past perfect	Vidura told Dhritarashtra, 'Yudhishthira has lost his kingdom.'	Vidura told Dhritarashtra that Yudhishthira had lost his kingdom.
Simple past becomes past perfect	Bhima said, 'Duryodhana tried to kill us many a time.'	Bhima said Duryodhana had tried to kill the Pandavas many a time.
Shall becomes *should; will* becomes *would*	Krishna said, 'Duryodhana and his brothers will be destroyed.'	Krishna said, 'Duryodhana and his brothers would be destroyed.'
The personal pronouns change:	Bhima said, 'I will kill Duryodhana.'	Bhima said he would kill Duryodhana.
I ⇨ he/she; my ⇨ his/her	Shakuni shouted, 'All the five Pandavas are my slaves!'	Shakuni shouted that all the five Pandavas were his slaves!
You can always put *that* between the two clauses in the reported speech.	Bhima said, 'I will kill Duryodhana.'	Bhima said that he would kill Duryodhana.
You can either use or omit *that* after the verbs, *say, tell* or *think*.	Bhima said that he would kill Duryodhana.	Bhima said he would kill Duryodhana.
You have to use *that* if the reporting verb is *respond, reply, announce,* and the like.	Yudhishthira replied, 'I accept the challenge.'	Yudhishthira replied that he accepted the challenge.

Words expressing nearness in time or space are changed into words expressing distance:

this ⇨ that   here ⇨ there   this city ⇨ that city   now ⇨ then

ago ⇨ earlier   today ⇨ that day   last week ⇨ the previous week

tomorrow ⇨ next day

ACTIVITY 1

Yesterday, Tania suddenly met her old friend Catherine in the street. I have jotted down a part of the conversation that took place between the two. Complete the following table by converting *direct speech* into *reported speech* and vice versa:

	Direct Speech	Reported Speech
Tania:	→ Cathy, You here! What a surprise!	Tania said it was a surprise to meet Catherine.
Catherine:	1. Wowee, Tania!	A surprised Catherine said they were meeting after 10 years.
Tania:	2.	Tania said it was true. She enquired how Catherine was.
Catherine:	3. I am fine. I'm married. We have two kids. And you?	....
Tania:	4. I am fine too. But my marriage didn't work out. Raghu and I had a mutual divorce last year.	....
Catherine:	5.	Catherine said she was sorry.
Tania:	6. Well, for me, it's time to move on. I'm new here. I came to Hyderabad only last week.	....
Catherine:	7. What brings you here?	....
Tania:	8. I've taken up a job at the Central University.	....

58.3 THE REPORTED SPEECH IS USED MOSTLY IN ...

If you have done Activity 1, you will see that some of the reported sentences do not sound natural. You will perhaps never say: *Tania said it was a surprise to meet Catherine.* Actually, you do not use the reported speech for informal language often.

The form is widely used in official reports, where people believe they should write *impersonally*. Do Activity 2 to appreciate the point.

ACTIVITY 2

A watchman of a housing society, Hoshiar Singh has caught the infamous thief Charandas Chor under extraordinary circumstances. Inspector Bhola Singh is finding out the details from Hoshiar. Read the conversation below and complete Inspector Bhola's report based on it:

Bhola	→ Congratulations, Hoshiar. You have captured a thief who was evading arrest for a long time. I will recommend a bravery award for you.
Hoshiar	→ Thank you, Inspector Sahab.
Bhola	(A) Tell me did you catch the man?
Hoshiar	(B) Sir, Kewal Ram Varmaji and his family have gone on long vacation. He has given me the keys to his house. At night, I go there. Yesterday too, I went into the bungalow at 10 PM.
Bhola	(C) And what did you find there?
Hoshiar	(D) Nothing unusual, sir. But when I go in, I hear someone snoring. I think a ghost is sleeping in the master bedroom.
Bhola	(E) What do you do then?
Hoshiar	(F) Sir, I run away. I go to my house. I convince my two brothers to join me and all of us go back to Varma Sahab's house. This time, we go into the bedroom and find our neighbour Charandas fast asleep. We jump on him and tie him up with curtains.
Bhola	(G) In that case, I will be forced to think again about the bravery award.

Inspector Bhola Singh's report:

First, I congratulated Hoshiar and told him he had captured a criminal who had been evading arrest for a long time. I also told him I would recommend a bravery award for him. He thanked me. (A) I asked him how .... (B) He said Mr Kewal Ram Varma and his family .... He .... Hoshiar the keys to his house. At night, he .... there. Yesterday too, ... into the bungalow at 10 PM. (C) I asked him what .... (D) He responded by saying he .... unusual. But when ...., he .... He thought .... in the master bedroom. (E) I asked him .... (F) He said .... and .... house. There, he .... his two brothers to join him and all of them .... Mr Varma's house. This time .... and saw their neighbour Charandas fast asleep. They .... and .... with curtains. (G) I .... him in that case, I .... be forced to think again about the bravery award.

58.4 WHAT IF THE REPORTED STATEMENT IS STILL VALID?

Even if the reporting verb is in the past, the tenses of what is being reported may not change if the statement is still valid or applicable. We can often choose whether to keep the original tenses or to change them.

Direct Speech	Reported Speech
The Icelandic[2] tourist said, 'India <u>is</u> a crowded place.'	The Icelandic tourist said India <u>was</u>/<u>is</u> a crowded place. (You can use <u>is</u> here because India continues to be a crowded place.)
The Icelandic tourist said, 'My first impression <u>is</u> that India is a crowded place.'	The Icelandic tourist said his first impression <u>was</u> that India <u>is</u>/<u>was</u> a crowded place
Catherine said, 'I have Tania's email ID.'	Catherine said she has/had Tania's email ID.*

* If you are talking about a recent past, you would say: *Catherine said she has* …. But if you are talking about a distant past, say: *Catherine said she had* ….

58.5 UNIVERSAL TRUTHS

Some statements are always true, at least in our world. They are known as *universal truths*. Universal truths are always in the present, never in past forms:

- ✓ Direct: Yudhishthira said, 'When calamities are imminent, judgement is first destroyed.'
- ✓ Reported: Yudhishthira <u>said</u> when calamities are imminent, judgement <u>is</u> first destroyed.

The following statements are correct. Note the tenses:

- ✓ Tania <u>asked</u> her son to follow the Pole Star as the Pole Star always <u>shows</u> the true north.
- ✓ Before Columbus, people <u>didn't believe</u> the earth <u>is</u> round. They <u>thought</u> it <u>was</u> flat.

58.6 WHEN THE REPORTING VERB IS IN THE PRESENT TENSE

If the reporting verb is in the present, you don't change the tenses of the reported verbs.

- ✓ Direct speech: The prime minister says, 'This is a national crisis. Over 20,000 people have been killed and lakhs have lost their homes.'

Tell or Say?

We use the verb *say* when the person addressed is not mentioned: *Mother **said** she would cook biriyani for dinner.*

But we use *tell* when the person being spoken to is mentioned: *Mother **told me** she would cook biriyani for dinner.*

---

[2] **icelandic tourist:** a tourist from Iceland, a thinly populated country in Northwestern Europe. In 2016, only 3.33 people lived in every square kilometre of Iceland.

✓ Reported speech: The prime minister says this is a national crisis. Over 20,000 people have been killed and lakhs have lost their homes.

PRACTICE

1. Underline the mistakes in the following sentences:

   A. Kabir Khan told his coach he is trying hard to come out of his bad patch.
   B. You assured me that you are doing your best.
   C. She was driving in the wrong direction, but she thought she is right.
   D. When he was a small child, Rajeev once told me he wants to become a pilot.

2. Rewrite these sentences in reported speech:

   A. Rajeev replied, 'I did MSc in physics from Delhi University.'
   ....

   B. Detective Bhola Singh said, 'Last night, I followed Bullet Singh from the airport to his hideout.'
   ....

   C. Dr Ram said, 'I was born before the independence of India.'
   ....

   D. I met my friend Ranjana at the Mumbai airport. She said, 'We are going to Rajasthan.'
   ....

   E. My mother said, 'If you leave the house, there will be no fighting.' (From Mark Tully's *No Full Stops in India*)
   ....

3. Correct the following sentences if they are incorrect. A few of them are correct. Put a ✓ next to them:

   A. Rajeev is a lecturer now. When we met last, he said he is looking for a job.
   B. The men in the teashop told us that we are going in the wrong direction.
   C. He told his wife that he will come back after an hour, but he never returned.
   D. The teacher said she will give us a test the next day.
   E. Christopher Columbus believed that the earth is round.
   F. When I was a small child, my father told me honesty is the best policy.

4. Transform the sentences to reported speech. (The sentences are from Jerome K. Jerome's *Three Men in a Boat*. I have modified them slightly.)

Direct	Reported
Harris said, 'I can prepare excellent scrambled eggs.'	Harris said he could prepare excellent scrambled eggs.
George said, 'I refuse to try your scrambled eggs.'	
Harris: 'You are suspicious by nature.'	
George: 'No, I am merely being cautious.'	

Direct	Reported
Harris: 'A cautious man does not smoke and drink as much as you do.'	
George: 'I remember, the last time I tried a cup of tea made by you, I had a terrible headache.'	
Harris: 'That is utter rubbish. In fact, people who have tasted my scrambled eggs once can't eat anything else for a long time.'	Harris said that George was talking utter rubbish and added that, in fact, those who had tasted his scrambled eggs once couldn't eat anything else for a long time.
George: 'Ha! Here is more of your crap!'	
Harris: 'It is the reality. In fact, they pine away for more of my scrambled eggs and become heartbroken. Some of them even die when they don't get any.'	
George: 'Are you referring to the black lump sticking on your frying pan?'	
Harris: 'You are disgusting. You purposely diverted my attention to get the eggs burnt.'	

KEY TO ACTIVITIES

Activity 1: 1. We are meeting after 10 years. 2 It's true! How are you, Cathy? 3. Catherine said she was fine; she was married and they had two kids. 4. Tania said she too was fine, but her marriage hadn't worked out. She and Raghu had had a mutual divorce the previous year. 5. I am sorry. 6. Tania said, for her, it was time to move on. She added that she was new at the place and she had come to Hyderabad only a week before. 7. Catherine asked Tania what had brought her there. 8. Tania said she had taken up a job at the Central University.

Activity 2: First, I congratulated Hoshiar and told him he had captured a criminal who had been evading arrest for a long time. I also told him I would recommend a bravery award for him. He thanked me. (A) I asked him how he had caught the man. (B) He said Mr Kewal Ram Varma and his family had gone on long vacation. He had given Hoshiar the keys to his house. At night, he went there. Yesterday too, he had gone into the bungalow at 10 PM. (C) I asked him what he had found there. (D) He responded by saying he had seen nothing unusual. But when he went in, he heard someone snoring. He thought a ghost was sleeping in the master bedroom. (E) I asked him what he did next. (F) He said he ran away and went to his house. There, he convinced his two brothers to join him and all of them went back to Mr Varma's house. This time they went into the bedroom and saw their neighbour Charandas fast asleep. They jumped upon him and tied him up with curtains. (G) I told him in that case I would be forced to think again about the bravery award.

Was Majnu Loved by Laila?

59.1 ACTIVE GRANDPA, PASSIVE PEANUTS

Consider the following sentences:

- ✓ Grandpa ate all the peanuts, and
- ✓ All the peanuts were eaten by grandpa

Both the sentences convey the same information but in different ways. The first sentence is in the ***active voice;*** the subject is a person (*grandpa*) who performs an action (*eating*). There is also a direct *object* of the action—*all the peanuts.*

The second sentence carries the same message in a slightly different way. It is in the ***passive voice.*** In this form, the subject of the sentence (*All the peanuts*) does not perform any action. Rather, the subject *is affected* by the action of the verb.

- If the person or thing that performs the action of the verb is the subject of a sentence, the sentence is said to be in the ***active voice.***
- If the subject of a sentence is affected by the action of the verb, the sentence is in the ***passive voice.***

Here are a few more examples:

Active Voice	Passive Voice
Valmiki wrote the Ramayana.	The Ramayana was written by Valmiki.
Laila loved Majnu.	Majnu was loved by Laila.
A faulty brake caused the accident.	The accident was caused by a faulty brake.
Do you love me?	Am I loved by you?

These sentences are in the simple past/simple present. Here are the passive forms for other tenses:

Tense	Active	Passive
Simple present	I clean this room.	This room is cleaned by me.
Present continuous	I am cleaning the room.	The room is being cleaned by me.
Present perfect	I have cleaned the room.	The room has been cleaned by me.
Simple past	I cleaned the room.	The room was cleaned by me.
Past continuous	I was cleaning the room when you telephoned.	This room was being cleaned by me when you telephoned.
Past perfect	By the time the guests came, I had cleaned the room.	By the time the guests came, the room had been cleaned by me.
Simple future	I will clean this room tomorrow.	This room will be cleaned by me tomorrow.

• The general form of a passive sentence is:

Subject	am/is/are was/were is being/are being has been/have been was being/were being had been will be will have been	told invited eaten destroyed and so on …

Note: In a passive sentence, if you wish to mention who performed the action, you use **by**.

ACTIVITY 1

Convert the sentences in active voice to passive and vice versa:

Active	Passive
A. The new store will employ 50 people.	Fifty people will be employed by ....
B. Nandini	This store will be managed by Nandini.
C. A minister will inaugurate the store.	....
D. Nandini is sending out invites for the inauguration.	....
E. She has invited me for the function.	....

59.2 IT DOESN'T MATTER WHO DID IT

When do we use the passive? You will certainly not express every sentence in the passive form. For example, you will perhaps never say: *Am I loved by you?* However, the passive form is often used in the following situations:

- When you look at the action from the point of view of the object of a sentence, you often use this form. For example, if you are reporting an accident, you may write: *The accident was caused by a faulty brake.* If you are writing an essay on the history of films, you will perhaps write: *The moving pictures or the movie was invented by a French engineer, Louis Lumiére.*
- If you are not sure who actually did something, you often use the passive form:
  - ✓ Last night, the statue at the Central Park was vandalized[1] by some people.
  - ✓ A diamond necklace was stolen from a jewellery showroom.
- If the question 'Who did it?' is not important, you may use the passive form:
  - ✓ I wasn't invited to the party.
  - ✓ At last, the problem has been solved!

Except in situations like these, you don't normally use the passive form, particularly while speaking. The active voice is simpler and more direct.

59.3 VERBS OFTEN USED IN THE PASSIVE VOICE

Some verbs are used more often in the passive. Here are a few examples:

arrest	burn	close	damage	destroy	drown
hurt	kill	open	sink	steal	vandalize[1]

ACTIVITY 2

Note the hints and write sentences in the passive voice. Follow the model given:

A. Our car/damage/in an accident/last week.

....

→ It/repair (now)
   It is being repaired.
B. It/paint/too (now)

....

C. Our house/burgle/last month

....

D. My stereo/steal

....

E. The burglar/arrest/by the police/this morning

....

F. The computer network in our office/upgrade/recently

....

G. There was an accident/but no one/hurt

....

H. By the time we reached/the shop/close

....

---

[1] **vandalize:** (verb, usually passive) to damage something, particularly public property.

PRACTICE

1. Complete the table below:

Tense	Active	Passive
Simple present	Raghu repairs mobile phones.	1.
Present continuous	Raghu is repairing my mobile phone.	2.
Present perfect	3.	My phone has been repaired by Raghu.
Simple past	Raghu repaired my phone last week.	4.
Past continuous	When I went to his workshop, Raghu was repairing my phone.	5. When I went to his workshop, my phone....
Past perfect	Raghu had repaired my phone when I went to his workshop.	6.
Simple future	Raghu will repair my phone.	7.
Future Perfect	8.	8. My phone will have been repaired by Raghu by tomorrow evening.

2. Complete the following passage with passive forms of **allow, conduct, control, elect × 2,** and **head.**

In India, the Central and state governments (1) .... by the people every five years. Elections (2) .... by the Election Commissioner, who is an independent authority. Everyone over 18 (3) .... to vote. There are three wings of the government: the executive, the legislative, and the judiciary. While the executive wing (4) .... by the legislative, the judiciary is independent. The executive wing of the government (5) .... by the prime minister. At the head of the three wings of the government, the armed forces, and the constitutional authorities like the Election Commissioner is the President of India. The president (6) .... by the members of the Parliament and the legislative assemblies of the states every five years.

3. This is a report published in a local newspaper about an incident that happened in a small town. Rewrite the report by converting the sentences in active voice into passive and vice versa. Does the rewritten report read better? (I have numbered the sentences for the sake of convenience.)

(1) Last year, a statue of Mahatma Gandhi was installed by our municipality at the Town Hall. (2) Some unknown people vandalized the statue last night. (3) Some leaflets were left behind by the vandals. (4) The leaflets are being examined by the police. (5) The team of detectives that is investigating the crime is being led by Inspector Bhola Singh. (6) They have arrested no one so far.

Last year, ...

....

....

....

....

....

KEY TO ACTIVITIES

Activity 1: A. Fifty people will be employed by the new store. B. Nandini will manage this store. C. The store will be inaugurated by a minister. D. Invites for the inauguration are being sent out by Nandini. E. I have been invited (by her).

Activity 2: A. Our car was damaged in an accident last week. (Or: Our car got damaged….). B. It is being painted too. C. Our house was burgled last month. D. My stereo was stolen. E. The burglar has been arrested this morning. F. Our office computer network has been upgraded recently. G. There was an accident, but no one was/has been hurt. H. By the time we reached, the shop had been closed.

Test 9:
Complex Sentences? They Are Simple!

1. Complete the rules below with these phrases:

do not use	in the simple future tense
does not perform any action	in the simple past

A. When you are talking about real possibilities, the verb in the *if clause* of a conditional statement is in the simple present, and the expected outcome is...

B. In *Type 2 conditional statements*, the (imaginary) possibilities are often ...., and the unlikely results are expressed with *would, should,* or *could*.

C. In reported speech, we report what someone said, but .... their exact words.

D. In *the passive voice*, the subject of the sentence ...., rather it is affected by the action of the verb.

2. Are these conditions real or unlikely? Write Ⓤ if it is an imaginary possibility, and write Ⓡ if it is real:

A. If I get a scholarship ...
B. If we don't pay the bill today ...
C. Unless we start now ...
D. If I were a billionaire ...
E. If I were young again ...
F. When you turn the ignition key of a car ...

3. Match the possibilities above with one of the following and write complete sentences:

- The engine starts.
- We'll miss the train.
- I'd go to the moon.
- I'd study genetics instead of physics.
- I'll go abroad to do a master's in creative writing.
- Our telephone will be disconnected.

A. ....

B. ....

C. ....

D. ....

E. ....

F. ....

4. Complete the sentences below using the verbs given in brackets:

   A. If my wife agrees, we'........................... Leh next summer. (visit)
   B. Darling, I'm stuck in a terrible traffic jam. If I had wings, I .... home. (fly).
   C. If I do well in master's, I'........................ to enroll to for PhD. (try)
   D. If I .... you, I wouldn't resign for such a minor reason. (be)
   E. When water is heated to 100°C, it .... (boil)
   F. If it was a Sunday, I .... through the day. (sleep)

5. Given below are the first parts of some conditional statements. Imagine the possible results/ consequences and complete them:

   A. When you are ready, ...
   B. If you want to watch the match, I ....
   C. If you had told me earlier, I ....
   D. If I hadn't missed the bus, I ....
   E. If Ragini loved Rohit, she ....
   F. When you have finished the first part of the test, you ....

6. Write sentences with **if** and **would have/could have/might have** to describe these situations:

   → Mr Daruwala suffered a heart attack last night. The doctor came much later. Mr Daruwala didn't survive.
   If the doctor had come earlier, Mr Daruwala might have survived.

   → Mohan Bagan got a penalty just before the final whistle. Vincent missed it. The match was drawn.
   If Vincent hadn't missed the penalty, Mohan Bagan would have won.

   A. Kuttan saw a lovely jacket in a store, but he couldn't buy it as he didn't have enough cash on him.
   If Kuttan had
   ....

   ....

   B. Radhika went to a party. The famous actress Madhuri Dixit too attended it. But she had left before Radhika arrived.
   If Radhika
   ....

   ....

   C. Raghu had to make a presentation. But he lost his memory stick and couldn't do it.
   ....

   ....

   D In a recent match, the umpires gave many wrong decisions against India. India lost a match they could have won.
   ....

   ....

7. Rewrite the sentences beginning with the given words:

   A. Louis Lumiére invented the movie.

⇨ The movie ....

....

B. Shyam Benegal has directed this film.
⇨ This film ....

....

C. A nanny looks after our children.
⇨ Our children ....

....

D. Mohan runs this teashop.
⇨ This teashop ....

....

E. Grandpa is eating all the peanuts.
⇨ All the peanuts ....

....

F. I won't miss this opportunity.
⇨ This opportunity ....

....

8. Rewrite the sentences in the reported speech:

A. Louis Lumiére, the French engineer who invented the movie, said, 'My invention might be of some scientific interest, but it has no commercial value.'
B. Albert Einstein said, 'I do not have any special talent. I am merely a little inquisitive.'
C. Spanish author Maria Zambrano said, 'I have never lived outside my homeland. My language is my homeland.'
D. Argentinian poet Antonio Machado said, 'In my solitude, I have clearly seen things that aren't real.'
E. Spanish painter Salvador Dali said, 'When I die, I will not die entirely.'
F. Argentinian author Jorge Luis Borges said, 'I don't know if education can save us, but I don't know of anything better.'
G. Rabindranath Tagore said, 'Trees are the earth's endless effort to speak to the listening heaven.'

A. ....

B. ....

C. ....

D. ....

E. ....

F. ....

G. ....

9. Kuttan has been selected to do master's at a French University. He and his friend Gagan are talking about it. Fill each blank using one word. (In some cases, I have given the relevant verb within brackets.)

Gagan: Congrats! When......... you......... (leave) for France?

Kuttan: I am not sure if I'm leaving. I'… go if I……… a visa.

Gagan: I am sure you will……… you……………… the visa? (apply for)

Kuttan: Yes. I sent the application online to the French Embassy in New Delhi. I……………………… (call) for an interview next week. If I satisfy their requirements, the visa…………………… (issue)

Gagan: And how much time should it take after that?

Kuttan: If the visa……… issued, the university……………… (confirm) my selection. The fall semester……… (begin) on 10 September. I'……………………… (enrol) by 15th of August and leave early next month.

10. When Jules Verne wrote *Around the World in Eighty Days* in 1873, he was challenging man's notions of speed of transportation. If you convert the sentences into direct speech, you get a conversation from the beginning of the novel. The discussion took place among a few friends at a London club.

Ralph, a banker, said a robber had stolen 55,000 pounds from his bank. He added that the police were after the robber.

A friend, Stuart, said that the police wouldn't be able to catch him. The bank would lose all the money.

Phileas Fogg said that the man could go round the world in 80 days.

Sullivan, another friend, agreed and added that it was possible to go around the world in just 80 days.

Stuart said, it might be possible, but Sullivan and Fogg were overlooking many points. He added that if the weather was bad, the ship would arrive late. Trains could be late too. Both trains and ships could catch fire. Many things could happen. Finally, he said that he didn't believe that the man could travel around the world in 80 days.

Fogg said he believed that the man could.

Stuart said that he needed more than 80 days.

Fogg repeated that he could do it in 80 days.

Ralph, a banker, said, 'A robber has stolen 55,000 pounds from my bank. The police are after him.'

PART
10

LET'S TALK BUSINESS

Business Vocabulary: An Introduction

Learning Objectives: In this chapter, we are going to focus on Business English, that is, the language typically used in commerce and industry.

60.1 BUSINESS PHRASES

There are countless professionals who are experts in their respective fields but are not quite successful in career because they don't communicate effectively. Indeed, language proficiency is a prerequisite for success in many fields, so that you can use words to your advantage. With a vocabulary that has the exact words you need, you find it easy to excel in your chosen professional field. In this chapter, we are going to discuss some common business words and phrases.

Table 60.1 lists some words and phrases commonly used in business and industry. You will need them for doing Activity 1.

TABLE 60.1 Common Business Phrases and Their Meaning

hands-on experience	experience that you acquire by working directly on something, as opposed to knowledge acquired by reading
job profile	a description of your responsibilities in office or factory; JOB DESCRIPTION
market leaders	a company that has the largest share of business among all the competitors
site engineer	an engineer who supervises the work at a project site
thrust area	the major activity for any company
time frame	the length of time that is available for doing something

ACTIVITY 1

Read the transcript[1] of an interview that Mangal Ram, a civil engineer, did for a job. Complete the transcript by filling in the blanks with words and phrases given above:

Interviewer: You are a civil engineer working in a bank. What is your (1) j...... p...............?

Mangal Ram: I look after maintenance of the bank's buildings and assist the chief engineer in designing and construction of new offices.

Interviewer: But our company's (2)........... .... is construction of roads and bridges. How will you fit in here?

Mangal Ram: Before joining the bank, I worked for Larsen and Tiwari, (3) the m.............. .... in civil construction, for three years.

Interviewer: Good, but do you have (4).............. .... in construction of roads?

Mangal Ram: Yes, Madam. I worked as a (5)................ .... in several road projects. I supervised construction of highways and concrete bridges. Fortunately, I was able to complete every assignment within the given (6) t.............. ....

Interviewer: Thanks, Mr Ram, we will get in touch with you after we have made a decision.

60.2 JARGON

Every profession has its own special words or expressions called *jargon,*[2] which are often difficult for others to understand. Doctors, lawyers, and engineers frequently use expressions that are understood by a fellow professional, but not others. For example, if you are a computer specialist, you will be familiar with terms such as *bits, bytes, memory chip, RAM, ROM, GUI,* or *GIGO,* although these won't make any sense to most others.

Many professionals have a tendency to use jargon while talking to outsiders and confusing them in the process. This is such a big problem that the word *jargon* itself is often used in a disapproving sense. Please do not use jargon while talking to people who don't know them.

You can live happily even if you don't know engineering or musical jargon, but in the modern world, it is necessary to learn some special words relating to business. You have come across some business vocabulary in Mangal Ram's interview. Now read the following passage taken from the website of a bank and try to guess the meanings of the highlighted words if you do not know them already.

We are in the **services sector** and customers are at the centre of all our activities. Our **company**, which was set up by an internationally renowned **entrepreneur**, strives to achieve 100% customer satisfaction. While banking remains our core strength, we have recently **diversified** in the field of insurance. Thanks to our recent **acquisition** of a health care insurance company *Goodlife Insurance,* we now offer a wide **portfolio** of banking and insurance **products** to our customers. We have a strong **balance sheet** and our **bottom line** has grown steadily over the years. Click on this link to read our latest **annual report.** ∞

---

[1] **transcript:** (noun) a written copy of spoken words.

[2] **jargon** is an uncountable noun.

If you do not know any of the words in the passage above, check them here:

Common business words:

services (usually plural) = the work that a company does for customers without producing goods; the services sector includes banking, insurance, health care, hotels, and so on.

product = a thing that is grown or manufactured, especially for sale; you can also use it for services that are sold. For example: *The main products of a bank are deposits and loans.*

company = an enterprise that sells products or services to its customers and is typically owned by many people, who are known as shareholders

firm = a business enterprise with a few owners, who are known as partners

entrepreneur = a person who invests in business, especially when this involves taking financial risks

CEO = the chief executive officer, a person who is responsible for running a company or firm

annual report = a report made by the CEO of a company or firm to its shareholders every year. It covers important information about how the company performed during a year. The *balance sheet* is a part of this report.

balance sheet = a statement of a company or firm's assets and liabilities, usually at the end of the financial year. (In India, the financial year ends on 31 March.)

assets = (usually plural) all the things of value that a company, firm, or individual owns, which can be sold to repay debts

liabilities = (usually plural), the amount of money that a company/firm/individual owes

profit and loss account = a statement of how much a company or firm has earned and how much it has spent during a financial year. The difference between the two is profit or loss.

bottom line = another name for profit or loss. The last line of a firm's profit and loss account gives the profit (or loss). Hence the name.

top line = the total sale of a company or firm during a period; the first line of a firm's profit and loss account gives this figure.

merger = the process of two companies combining into one

acquisition = the process of a company buying another company

shop floor = the area in a firm's establishment where workers make the goods

greenfield project = an area which has no building, but where construction has been planned. It is a project planned at a new location.

(to) diversify (especially of a company) = to develop a wider range of products or services in order to be more successful

portfolio = the range of products or services sold by a company or firm: a portfolio of clothes

market = a particular area, country, or section of population that buys a particular product; the *domestic market for coffee* means the domestic population that buys coffee.

ACTIVITY 2

Match the business phrases with their meanings:

1. annual report	A. the range of products or services sold by a firm
2. balance sheet	B. a report made by a company's CEO to its shareholders every year
3. bottom line	C. the total sales of a firm or company during a period
4. company	D. the profit or loss of a company during a period
5. market	E. a thing that is grown or manufactured, especially for sale
6. portfolio	F. a statement of a company's assets and liabilities
7. product	G. an area, country, or section of population that buys a particular product
8. top line	H. a business owned by many people called shareholders

60.3 SELLING, MARKETING, AND ADVERTISING

Here are some useful words relating to selling:

consumer	the person who buys and uses a product or service
sales	the number or value of items sold by a company
marketing	the activity of presenting and selling a company's products in an attractive manner
brand	a type of product made by a particular company: *Adidas and Reebok are two leading brands of sports shoes.*
brand loyalty	the tendency of buyers to buy a particular type of product
promotion	activities done for increasing the sale of a product or a service: *The company is doing a promotion of a new brand of precooked noodles.*
cold-calling	telephoning or meeting unknown people in order to sell something to them
telemarketing	trying to sell a product or service by telephoning prospective customers
ad or **advert**	short forms of advertisement (pronounced ad-**vur**-tis-m*uh*nt)
USP	abbreviation for unique selling proposition, that is, the reasons why a particular product or service is better than all others in the market

PRACTICE

1. What do you understand by the following? Write down in your own words:

   A. balance sheet ....
   B. bottom line ....
   C. entrepreneur ....
   D. services ....
   E. shop floor ....
   F. telemarketing ....

2. The following passage has been taken from an annual report of M/s Cutts & Thorats Limited, manufacturers of industrial cutting tools. Complete the report by filling in the blanks with appropriate forms of the verbs/phrasal verbs given within brackets. Also use the following:

| bottom line   financial year   green field   markets   market leaders   portfolio   thrust area |

The economy of our country (1) .... (look up). The gross domestic product (GDP) of the country has grown at the rate of 7% to 9% in the last three years. In the (2) .... ended on 31 March this year, the sales of your company went up by 10% compared to the previous year. Consequently, the company's (3) .... has increased to ₹15 crore, showing a growth of 20% over the previous year.

We are the (4) m .... in the field of manufacture of cutting tools in India. While our (5) .... remains manufacturing chain saws, we (6) .... (diversify) into production of hi-tension hacksaws. These special tools have extra-strong handles and high tension frames with easy tighten knobs. They are lightweight too. The new product line will enable us to offer a complete (7) .... of industrial cutting tools to domestic and international (8) ....

For this purpose, we (9) .... (set up) a (10) .... plant at a remote location in Odisha. As you all know, we applied to the Odisha government for land two years ago. I am happy to inform you that the state government (11) .... recently .... (allot) 50 acres for the plant. The land (12) .... (hand over) to us soon. We plan to start construction of the plant by October.

3. Imagine you are applying for the position of a production engineer at Thompson Press, Delhi, which is one of the most modern printing presses in India.

- You are a first class BTech in printing technology from Jadavpur University, Kolkata. Since graduation, you have been working as a printing technologist in Saraswati Press, Kolkata, for the last two years. You operate and maintain offset printing machines. You have thorough knowledge of printing machinery.
- Your reason for seeking a change: to work with more sophisticated machinery and for better career prospects.

Write a note to your prospective employers about your background and explain why you are suitable for the position. Use the following expressions: **company, job profile, hands-on experience, shop-floor engineer, market leaders,** and **portfolio.**

....
....
....
....
....
....

KEY TO ACTIVITIES

Activity 1: (1) job profile; (2) thrust area; (3) market leaders; (4) hands-on experience; (5) site engineer; (6) time frame

Activity 2: 2-F; 3-D; 4-H; 5-G; 6-A; 7-E; 8-C

Business Communication Is Changing

61.1 A FATHER AND HIS DAUGHTER

Sometime in 1980, Prakash Menon, an executive in an insurance company, went to Calcutta (presently Kolkata), from his headquarters to investigate some unusual insurance claims. After reaching Calcutta, he fell ill and sent this telex message to his boss.

DEAR SIR,

WITH DUE RESPECT, I BEG TO STATE THAT I HAVE FALLEN ILL AFTER REACHING CALCUTTA. TO BE SPECIFIC, I HAVE BEEN SUFFERING FROM ACUTE SHOULDER PAIN AND MUSCLE SPASM, AND I AM HARDLY ABLE TO MOVE MY ARMS OR LIFT ANY WEIGHT. AS A MATTER OF FACT, I HAVE BEEN UNDER MEDICATION SINCE LAST FRIDAY, THAT IS, DURING THE LAST FOUR DAYS.

IN VIEW OF THE ABOVE, ALTHOUGH I HAVE COMPLETED MY ASSIGNED TASK IN CALCUTTA, I AM UNABLE TO RETURN TO BOMBAY TOMORROW AS SCHEDULED, AND I HAVE BEEN FORCED TO RESCHEDULE MY AIR TICKET. I WILL BE TRAVELLING BY THE MORNING FLIGHT ON THURSDAY AS THE ONLY FLIGHT FROM CALCUTTA TO BOMBAY ON WEDNESDAY IS FULLY BOOKED.

I REQUEST YOU TO KINDLY CONFIRM MY ACTION AND ALLOW ME TO WORK AT OUR CALCUTTA OFFICE FOR THE NEXT TWO DAYS. THE INCONVENIENCE CAUSED IS DEEPLY REGRETTED.

THANKING YOU, YOURS FAITHFULLY,

PRAKASH MENON, SENIOR ADMINISTRATIVE OFFICER

Prakash's daughter Rita Menon works for an IT company now. While she was on an official trip to Kolkata recently, she had a similar experience and had to reschedule her programme. Read the SMS and email from Rita to her boss, and note the difference between Rita's language and her father's:

Hi Samir, Unable to travel today because of shoulder pain. Sending you an email. Rita

The text message is followed by this email:

Hi Samir,

Since Friday I have been under medication for shoulder pain and muscle spasms. So, sorry, I won't be able to travel tomorrow. Hope things will improve over next few days. I'll try my best to travel on Thursday. Meanwhile, I will work from our Kolkata office. I hope this is okay with you?

I'll keep you informed.

Regards, Rita

ACTIVITY 1

Read the messages again and note down two main differences between the two:

1. ....

2. ....

61.2 HOW BUSINESS COMMUNICATION HAS CHANGED

Prakash used 150 words to convey the message but his daughter managed with just 59. Prakash wrote in a peculiar language that was born in the offices of East India Company and nurtured by government offices and commercial establishments ever since. For some reason, this style of writing was (and still is, to a lesser extent) considered ideal for business communication. Prakash's language has these problems:

- There are many introductory and connecting phrases: *with due respect, I beg to state, as a matter of fact,* and so on. The main idea gets buried under them.
- An idea has been repeated in the same sentence: *hardly able to move my arms or lift any weight.* If you can't move your arms, does the question arise?
- The message contains several roundabout expressions like *I have been forced to….* Instead of *the inconvenience caused is deeply regretted,* you can write: *I regret the inconvenience.*

A language reflects the community that speaks it. And differences between the styles of communication of the two generations have much to do with the changing lifestyle. In today's world, a professional like Rita does not have time for unnecessary words. In the future, people might criticize her language as too matter-of-fact.[1] But as of now, it is the accepted style.

61.3 NEW CHANNELS OF COMMUNICATION

Telex and telegrams were two of the fastest modes of communication until the end of the last century. They have become obsolete. Long-distance phone calls were unreliable and expensive; they aren't anymore. Today, people use the following channels of communication. (Newer technologies will possibly have hit the market by the time you read this!)

---

[1] **matter-of-fact:** (adjective) said or done without showing any emotion, UNEMOTIONAL.

- Land phone, which is reliable and cheap, but used mainly by offices nowadays.
- Facsimile (fax), which survived the onslaught of new technology, but is fast becoming obsolete as you can easily send scanned documents.
- Mobile phone, reliable and cheap, with the added advantage of connectivity on the move plus a host of other advantages.
- Text (SMS) messaging facility has brought about a revolution not only in communications, but also in human relationships. It has already influenced the behaviour patterns of people and has been changing languages.
- The Internet, email, and a wide range of messaging services.
- Smartphones, namely, iPhones and Android phones, also work like laptops and offer Internet connectivity while you travel. These gadgets offer you predictive texts, and so, in the messages through these gadgets, you don't use texting language.
- Instant messengers or IMs, such as Skype, WhatsApp, KakaoTalk, and the like, which offer you the choice of seeing the person you are talking to.

61.4 A MEETING IS IN PROGRESS

This meeting took place at Sona & Company, a New Delhi-based publishing house, to discuss the publication of a coffee-table book.[2] The participants were Sona, the managing partner and publisher; Putul, the editor-in-chief; Nikhil, the marketing manager; and Gagan, the chief of production. Sona, at 23, was the youngest of the group and Gagan, 32, was the oldest. Note the highlighted words and try to guess their meanings from the context.

Sona: Hi! We are going to discuss Nikhil's proposal to bring out a coffee-table book on the Sundarbans. You have a copy of Nikhil's proposal. He's **flagged** the key points. Still, Nikhil, could you **give us a sense** of the market potential for such a book? Let's not go into details at this stage, just give us the **big picture.**

Nikhil: Well, the mangrove forests of Sundarbans face a huge challenge because of global warming and rising sea-level...

Gagan: Sorry to interrupt, Nikhil. What is mangrove? I've heard only of man-eaters of Sundarbans!

Nikhil: Mangrove is a tropical tree that grows on muddy riverbanks. Its roots are above ground. Every one of them in the Sundarbans might be submerged in the next few decades. Ironically, this has generated new interest in the Sundarbans ecosystem. Next June, the UNESCO[3] will organize a seminar at New Delhi on how to save the Sundarbans. If our book is brought out just before that, it will certainly do well in market.

Gagan: That's fine, but can we **close** the matter by June?

Sona: I think we can, if we **push the envelope.** But let's **park the issue** of scheduling for now. The **bottom line** is whether such a book would do well in the market. Putul, what's your **take** on that?

---

[2] **coffee-table book:** an expensive book printed on art paper with a lot of pictures or photographs; these books are designed for people to look through rather than to read carefully.

[3] **UNESCO:** abbreviated form of United Nations Educational, Scientific and Cultural Organization.

Putul: The subject is indeed interesting, but the **flip side** is that so much **info** is available in the **public domain** nowadays that you don't have to buy books to get general information. And another point is: How good are the existing books on the subject?

Nikhil: I **Googled** for similar publications. And I also checked in several libraries. Most of the available books are for tourists. And the few coffee-table books on the subject that I could find are all **dated**. I agree: A lot of info is available on the Net. But we are targeting readers who don't surf the Net regularly.

Sona: If our print run is 2000 and we go for a 160-page hardbound crown-size book, how much will it cost? Gagan, can you **provide your input** on this?

Gagan: Well, let me do some **back of the envelope** calculations.... My **ballpark figure** is that the production cost will be 12 lakh, that is, ₹600 per copy.

Sona: That should be fine. Putul, can you suggest an **SME,** who can be entrusted with the academic side of the project?

Putul: Well, Nikhil **texted** me about this. So I am ready with a name. I think we can approach Dr Deepak Chatterjee of the Institute of Forest Management in Bhopal. He has done pioneering work on the Sundarbans biosphere.

Sona: You are the best person to judge. Have you thought of **a backup**?

Putul: If Dr Chatterjee is not available, we can approach Dr Rashmi Hattangadi of Bombay University.

61.5 NEW ACTIVITIES CREATE NEW VERBS

The language for business communication has been changing significantly. Here are some verbs and phrasal verbs Rita and Sona use regularly. You won't find most of them in dictionaries published before 2000.

- ✓ **close** something = complete a piece of work you are doing: *We must **close** the matter by tomorrow.*
- ✓ **connect** = (especially North American English) to contact with someone: *If you need something, please connect with me.*
- ✓ **escalate** an issue = to report a matter to the higher authority: *If the cheque isn't credited to my account by tomorrow, I am going to escalate the issue.*
- ✓ **flag** = to put a special mark next to some information: *Please flag the points we have to discuss.*
- ✓ **give** someone **a sense of** something = describe and explain something: *Can you give us a sense of what happened at the board meeting?*
- ✓ **Google** for something = to search for something on the Internet
- ✓ **keep** someone **in the loop =** keep someone informed about developments: *Rita told her assistant, 'I know you can handle this on your own, but please keep me in the loop.'*
- ✓ **park** something = keep aside something for the time being
- ✓ **provide inputs** on something = give your opinion on something
- ✓ **push the envelope** = to go beyond the limits of normal activity: *Our network engineer pushes the envelope to see that our server[4] never fails.*
- ✓ **think out of the box** = to think differently, in a new and imaginative way: *It isn't enough if we follow the usual strategies to increase market share. We have to think out of the box.*

---

[4] **server:** the main computer in a network of computers.

✓ **think laterally** = (especially in British English) to solve a problem by looking at it from a new and essentially different point of view; similar to *thinking out of the box*. Ravi solves problems. The best thing about him is that he can think laterally.

✓ **think on your feet** = to be able to think and react quickly and effectively without preparation: *The customer asked me some unexpected questions. I had to think on my feet to answer him.*

✓ **telecommute** or **log in from home** = to work from home through telephone and Internet: *When Radhika was ill, Ravi telecommuted for almost two weeks.*

✓ **text** someone = to send an SMS message to someone: *I'll be in a meeting at 2 PM, please text me when you arrive.* (**text message** or just **text** = SMS message)

61.6 NEW NOUNS, NOUN PHRASES, AND ADJECTIVES

✓ Given below are some nouns, noun phrases, and adjectives in the context of business:

✓ **attrition rate** = the rate at which a company loses employees to its competitors

✓ **back of the envelope calculations** = a rough and quick calculation

✓ **backup** = a person who takes up your responsibilities if you cannot complete a piece of work

✓ **ballpark figures** = approximate figures

✓ **bottom line** = the essential point (in a discussion): *The bottom line is that we have to complete the project by month-end.*

✓ **the big picture** = the overall situation: *We are individually working on small aspects of the project, but we should keep the big picture in mind.*

✓ **conference call** or **con-call** = a multi-user telephone call where a number of people discuss an issue over long distances. A **video conference** is a conference call in which the participants also see the others on a screen.

✓ **cutting-edge technology** = the latest technology: *Our company uses cutting-edge technologies to produce fuel-efficient trucks.*

✓ **dated** = old-fashioned: *The book on the Sundarbans published in 1989 looks dated.*

✓ **end to end** = the entire process: *Our company provides end-to-end solutions for networking computer systems.*

✓ **flip side** = the negative aspect of a situation; DOWNSIDE

✓ **info** = short form for information

✓ **mail trail** = the series of emails on a particular subject

✓ **on the fly** = if you do something on the fly, you do it quickly while doing something else and without thinking much about it: *Yes, of course, I can pass on the message. I can do it on the fly.*

✓ an **out-of-office response** (or **OOF response**) = An automatic response given by your computer when an email is received, or by your telephone answering machine if someone calls when you are out of office.

✓ **positive energy** = the enthusiasm to perform better. *Corporate social activity or CSA generates a lot of positive energy among employees.*

✓ **negative energy** = opposite of positive energy: *If the boss favours some of the employees, it creates negative energy in office.*

✓ **proactive** = if someone looks ahead and identifies future problems and acts accordingly, he or she is being proactive: People's tastes are changing. We must be proactive and change the designs of our products.

✓ **public domain** = available for everyone to use or to discuss: *Some wonderful resources such as the Wikipedia and the Linux operating system are available in the public domain.*

✓ **reality check** = (informal) an occasion when you are reminded of how things are in the real world, rather than how you would like them to be: *That company thinks they can set up chemical plants anywhere. Well, they are in for a reality check! People are against polluting industries.*

✓ **start-up** = a company that is just beginning to operate

✓ **stretch target** = a target you have over and above the actual target: *Our target is to reach an export figure of $10 million but the stretch target is 11 million.* This means although your target is 10 million, you will try to achieve 11.

✓ **Subject-matter expert** or **SME** = an expert in a particular field who is consulted for specific jobs

✓ **take** something **offline** = In a meeting, when someone says *Let's take this issue offline,* he or she means that *the issue should not be discussed at that time, but later.*

✓ **team player** = someone who is not just out for themselves but works well with others

✓ **upside** = the positive aspect of a generally bad situation: *We have missed the train, but look at the upside: We can see a film.* The opposite is **downside** or **flip side**.

✓ a **win-win** situation = a situation that is good for people on both sides: *After long negotiations, we managed to reach a win-win situation.*

✓ **work–life balance** = the balance between the number of hours you spend working and the hours you spend with your family or friends: *Several senior functionaries of our company have suffered stress-related problems. We ought to have better work–life balance.*

ACTIVITY 2

Complete this telephonic conversation with words/phrases from the above list:

Sona: Hi! Gagan, I just received your (1) t......... m............... You aren't well? What's the problem?

Gagan: Nothing much, Sona. I twisted my ankle last night and the doctor says I have to be in bed for three weeks. (2) So I l......... i...... f......... h............ this morning.

Sona: I am sorry to hear this, Gagan. Hope you'll get better soon. And you can certainly work from home. Can you (3) g.......... me a s.......... of the urgent things you are handling at the moment?

Gagan: Yes, of course. See, the coffee-table book on the Sundarbans is to be published next month, but the works manager of Johnson Press is less than helpful. We'll have to (4)...................... the issue. I was thinking of meeting his boss personally.

Sona: Oh! Don't worry about that. I know the president of Johnson Press personally. (5) I'll c...................... with him.

Gagan: Thanks. Also, a sales rep of Andhra Paper Mills was supposed to meet me at 3.00 today. We have to (6) c................. the deal with them by today, as the paper is to reach the printing press by next Monday. Please check the file in my drawer. (7) I've f...................... the important papers.

Sona: Thanks. Nikhil is in town. I'll ask him to meet this guy.

Gagan: Thanks, Sona. Please (8) k............ me .... l...............

Sona: Yes, I will. Bye for now. Get well soon.

Gagan: Bye!

61.7 SOME MORE NOUNS AND NOUN PHRASES

Finally, let's see some more new expressions that have replaced old ones as shown in the table below:

Modern Nouns and Noun Phrases

Now People Say	Instead of	For Example
core competencies	what you or your company does well	Please focus on your **core competencies** instead of trying to do too many things.
EOD/COB	end of the day/close of business	Let's close the matter by **EOD/COB**.
global footprint	international presence	a company with a **global footprint**
Plan B	contingency plan	This may not work, I have a **Plan B** ready.
take (noun)	opinion, views, and the like	What's your **take** on this?
trade-off	compromise	There is often a trade-off between volume and quality.

ACTIVITY 3

Combine one word from the first row with one from the second to form six two-word phrases. One of them has been done:

	~~attrition~~	ballpark	conference	public	team	reality
	call	domain	~~rate~~	figure	check	player

1. attrition rate   2. .... 3. ....
4. .... 5. .... 6. ....

ACTIVITY 4

Fill in the blanks with the phrases you have just formed:

1. Sorry, Radhika, I'll be late today. I have a .... in the evening with my boss in Seattle and my client in Shanghai.
2. Three engineers resigned from Shanghai last month. The call is about the high .... of the people working on our Shanghai project.

Business English

Business English is English which is especially related to international trade. It is a specialism within English language learning and teaching.... Most of the English communication that takes place within business circles the world over occurs between non-native speakers. In cases such as these, the object of the exercise is efficient and effective communication. The strict rules of grammar are in such cases sometimes ignored....[5]

---

[5] Source: www.dictionary.reference.com

3. We thought our Shanghai project would run smoothly, but we are in for a ....

4. Our company is not looking for brilliant individuals who can't get along with people. We are looking for ....

5. Paul Allen Foundation has done a lot of research on how the human brain works and has put their research findings in the ....

6. The .... for construction of the building was between 5 and 6 lakh, but it actually cost 8.5 lakh.

PRACTICE

1. Complete the phrases below by adding one of these: **call/domain/figure/from home/input/laterally/line/the envelope**

A. bottom......   B. ballpark.........
C. conference...   D. public.........
E. think.........   F. push............
G. provide......   H. log in.........

2. Complete the sentences following the clues given within brackets. Use the following words/phrases:

attrition rate	ballpark	close	COB	dated	flag
give (someone) a sense (of something)			work–life balance	mail trail	on the fly
keep (someone) in the loop		Plan B	push the envelope		SME
stretch target	take (something) offline		think on one's feet		upside

1. 'This approach may not work. Do you have a.........................?' (an alternative plan)
2. 'I don't have the time to read such a long note. Please........................ the important paragraphs.' (put a mark against)
3. 'The share market has crashed. Can you g............. us a s............. what's happened?' (explain)
4. Sona told the chief editor, 'Please contact the .... immediately. And do .... about the developments.' (an expert on the relevant subject, keep me informed)
5. Jaspal Bhatti was a brilliant actor who constantly.............................. of comic satires. (push the limits)
6. A text message to Rita from her boss: 'We have to .... the report by tomorrow. Please see that it's mailed by.............. tomorrow.' (complete, close of business)
7. Our company respects employees' need to have a healthy life. Our employees enjoy a good .... (balance between personal and official lives)
8. 'This is a serious crisis. We don't have time for detailed planning. We must .... (think quickly, without wasting time)
9. The .... is high for IT companies. Many of them provide gyms and playgrounds in the office to keep employees happy. (the rate at which a company loses employees)

10. 'How much will be our loss? You don't have to do precise calculations, just give me a .... figure.' (approximate)

11. 'Who first made the wrong estimate? Find out from the ....' (the sequence of emails on a subject)

12. The chairman said, 'This meeting is for discussing sales targets, but you are talking about staff shortage. Let's t.............. the matter ....' (Let's discuss the matter separately)

13. The share market has crashed. The only .... is that may be a good time to buy stocks. (positive aspect)

14. 'Can you send an email to the managers informing them about the meeting.'—'Yes, I will. I can do it ....' (along with other things)

15. Our target is to close the issue by Friday. But our .... is Thursday. (We will try to do it by Thursday.)

16. The boss doesn't quite like the design. He says it's rather .... (old-fashioned)

KEY TO ACTIVITIES

Activity 2: (1) text message; (2) logged in from home; (3) give (me) a sense of; (4) escalate; (5) connect; (6) close; (7) flagged; (8) keep (me) in the loop

Activity 3: (in any order) 2. ballpark figure; 3. conference call; 4. public domain; 5. reality check; 6. team player

Activity 4: (1) conference call (or con-call or video conference); (2) attrition rate; (3) reality check; (4) team players; (5) public domain; (6) ballpark

International English

Learning Objectives: In this chapter, we are going to analyse the English spoken and written in the Indian subcontinent, how it differs from Standard International English, and what you should keep in mind while interacting with an international audience.

62.1 AN ODE[1] TO MISS PUSHPA T.S.

Read the first two stanzas from a poem by Nissim Ezekiel (1924–2004), an Indian who spoke Marathi and wrote poetry in English. (In the 20th century, Ezekiel was one of the foremost figures among Indians writing in English.) The following lines are in English, of course, but do they sound like English?

Goodbye Party for Miss Pushpa T.S.

Friends,
Our dear sister
Is departing for foreign
In two three days,
And
We are meeting today
To wish her bon voyage.

You are all knowing, friends,
What sweetness is in Miss Pushpa.
I don't mean only external sweetness
But internal sweetness.
Miss Pushpa is smiling and smiling
Even for no reason but simply because
She is feeling.

---

[1] **ode:** (noun) a poem expressing the writer's emotions, usually in irregular metre.

Indian readers will not only follow this poem but will also identify with the emotions expressed in it, although a native speaker of English will find these lines strange and confusing.

This is how lots of people speak English in the Indian subcontinent. In this poem, Ezekiel pokes a little fun at this language, that is, this particular version of English, which is known as **Indian English.** Another word relevant to the topic is **Indianism** (an uncountable noun) which means a word or idiom characteristic of Indian English and which is not used elsewhere.

Moving back to the poem, the light-hearted parody begins in the heading of the poem itself. You say *cocktail party, office party, all-night party,* or in this case, ***farewell party,*** but *goodbye* doesn't collocate[2] with *party*. The expression *goodbye party* isn't English. Also, initials come at the beginning of a written name, you don't say *Pushpa T.S.* like some people from the southern part of India do. Similarly, in the English that is understood globally, people say ***going abroad*** instead of *departing for foreign*, and ***in a few days*** instead of *in two three days*.

Following expressions in the poem too are problematic. We are going to discuss them later in this chapter:

- ✗ You are all knowing
- ✗ What sweetness is in Miss Pushpa
- ✗ Miss Pushpa is smiling and smiling
- ✗ even for no reason but simply because she is feeling
- ✗ I am not remembering now

62.2 IS INDIAN ENGLISH 'INCORRECT ENGLISH'?

A large section of English language experts believes—and I completely agree with them—this question itself is incorrect and unacceptable. For example, English humourist and writer Stephen Fry says: 'There no right language or wrong language any more than are right or wrong clothes. Context, convention and circumstance are all.'[3]

Indian English is a legitimate version of English in the context of South Asia. For example, take the words *brinjal, tiffin box,* or *native place.* They are widely used and understood in this region, although native speakers of English wouldn't know what they mean. These are all right in this particular geographical context. In general, Indian English is fine as long as you are communicating informally within the South Asian community. However, if you are submitting a research paper to an academic journal, making a presentation at a symposium, or dealing with a client based in, say, South Africa, you should be aware of what works globally and what doesn't.

Let me reiterate that you shouldn't hesitate to use *brinjal, godown,* or *ayah* within the Indian English community. However, as an educated person, you had better not use expressions like *You are all knowing, friends, What sweetness is in Miss Pushpa* or *She is smiling and smiling* You must honour some compelling conventions of the English language, which we have discussed through this book. Let's therefore divide the issues relating to Indian English into two parts: *vocabulary* and *grammar.*

---

[2] If you have missed the word *collocation*, see Section 6.3 (pp. 28–29).
[3] https://www.youtube.com/watch?v=Ovi7uQbtKas

62.3 INDIAN ENGLISH VOCABULARY

Hobson-Jobson is the mysterious short title of a book published in the late 19th century. The book, which is still in print, is a dictionary of Anglo-Indian words and terms from Indian languages which came into use during the British rule of India. Many of the words described in the book have fallen into disuse, but many others have become part of English. Here is a sample:

avatar	jungle
bangle	juggernaut
bazaar	khaki
bungalow	loot
catamaran	nirvana
cheroot	pundit
cheetah	pyjamas
chutney	sari
cot	shampoo
cummerbund	shawl
guru	veranda
gymkhana	yoga
hullabaloo	

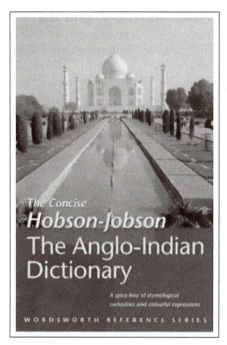

There is no problem with these and other words of Indian origin which have been absorbed by English. You can safely use them! But what is your take on this?

ACTIVITY 1

Read the text below and underline the words that you think won't be understood globally. Compare your answer with the explanation given just below:

My native place is Meenakshipalayam, a small town in South India. My father, a serviceman, had worked for a bank here. He has expired last year. My mother runs a stationery store. She sells pens, pencils, copies, and so on. Besides mom and me, my cousin sister Rehana, a smart, convent-educated girl, lives with us. Rehana loves hanging out with friends and most of the time during the day, she drives her two-wheeler. Recently, Rehana and one of her friends were victims of eve-teasing. It is a shame that some young men do such dreadful things just for timepass. When Rehana's mother, that is, my mom's co-sister, came to know about it, she was mighty upset. But Rehana handled the situation with tremendous courage and put the hoodlums in their place.

> Now, let me talk about our home. We live in a small biscuit-coloured one-storey building opposite to the post office in Murugappa Street. We have bought the house last year for ₹12 lakh. And on the backside of our house there is a godown that stores vegetables such as okra and brinjals. A big building, the godown can be seen while crossing the foot overbridge at the railway station.

Issues (Partly) Explained

Any English-speaking Indian will follow this passage just like the poem quoted at the beginning. However, it will confuse English speakers from around the world mainly because the following are not English words/expressions, although most Indians believe they are!

native place	copy	cousin sister	convent-educated
driving a bike[1]	eve-teasing	timepass	co-sister
biscuit-coloured	opposite to	lakhs[2]	backside[3]
godown	brinjal	foot overbridge	serviceman[4]
expire[5]			

Notes:
1. You don't *drive* a bike, motorbike, or bicycle; you *ride* it.
2. Do not use *lakhs* and *crores* with international clients. Instead of 12 lakh, say 120,000 or 1.2 *million*. Instead of *crore*, say 10 *million*. Indian businessmen regularly create needless confusion by using lakhs and crores while dealing with people from other continents.
3. *Backside* means the two round fleshy parts of the human anatomy on which one sits down. Don't use it to describe what is behind your house, or the person behind you.
4. 'Serviceman' and 'expire' are English words, but they mean something else. A serviceman is a member of the armed forces.
5. 'Expired' means a document, etc. that is 'no longer valid'. Therefore, your driving licence or passport may expire, but you cannot! Good news!

These are some non-standard words/phrases that South Asians often use. English newspapers published here too use most of them (not *backside* or *timepass* perhaps!). Although the line between standard and non-standard English is getting blurred every day, I would advise you *not to use these in formal communications,* particularly to an international audience.

Let's check the standard English equivalents for the common Indian expressions you came across in Activity 1:

native place	⇨ hometown	copy	⇨ exercise book
cousin sister	⇨ cousin	eve-teasing	⇨ sexual harassment
timepass	⇨ pastime	co-sister	⇨ brother-in-law's wife
biscuit-coloured	⇨ beige	on the backside	⇨ behind
godown	⇨ warehouse	foot overbridge	⇨ footbridge/overbridge
brinjal	⇨ aubergine in British English and eggplant in American English		

ACTIVITY 2

Each of the following pairs gives you an Indian English expression and its equivalent that would be understood globally. Put them in the appropriate column in the table below:

1. a month ago, a month back	2. ash coloured, grey
3. bio-data, curriculum vitae/CV	4. cent percent, 100 per cent
5. copy, exercise book	6. discuss, discuss about
7. employee, serviceman	8. eve-teasing, sexual harassment
9. go shopping, go for shopping	10. last night, yesterday night
11. opposite to, opposite	12. Myself Raghu, I am Raghu

Indian English	Understood Globally
1. a month back	a month ago
2.	
3.	
4.	
5.	
6.	
7.	
8.	
9.	
10.	
11.	
11.	

62.4 INDIAN ENGLISH: GRAMMAR ISSUES

Some grammatical structures used widely in the Indian subcontinent are different from their equivalents in the English-speaking regions of the world. And as things stand today, most of them are more or less unacceptable in communication between two educated individuals. The table below gives a list of the problem areas, together with the chapters of this book that cover them:

The Grammatical Form	Example	Relevant Chapter
• Using state verbs *in continuous tenses*	✘ You are ~~all knowing~~…. ✘ simply because she ~~is feeling~~	Chapter 14: *Where Are You Going, My Pretty Maid?* Section 14.6

The Grammatical Form	Example	Relevant Chapter
• Other problems with *continuous tenses*	✗ Miss Pushpa is smiling and smiling ✗ She is coming from a renowned family. ✗ Every day, I am going to office by bus.	Chapter 14: *Where Are You Going, My Pretty Maid?* Section 14.3
• Using time markers of the past with *the present perfect*	✗ My grandpa has passed away last year. ✗ I have met my wife at college, in 2012.	Chapter 18: *The Film Has Already Started…*, Section 18.3
• *The present continuous* instead of *the present perfect continuous*	✗ She is living with us since last year.	Chapter 19: *We've Been Studying English*
• Using *the past perfect* for an event or action in the past	✗ My father had worked for a bank. ✗ I had gone to Delhi last year.	Chapter 23: *The Runaway Bride*, Section 23.2
• Issues with future forms	✗ Grandpa has just fallen off a tree. I am going to take him to hospital. ✗ All arrangements have been made, we'll go to Goa tomorrow.	Chapter 26: *Talking About the Future*
• Improper collocation	✗ Departing for foreign ✗ In two three days ✗ Going to abroad ✗ I gave the exam last week. ✗ I'm going to admit my child to school next month.	Through this book
• Using *the* when not required, and not using *the* when required	✗ Keep the medicines away from the children. ✗ The Delhi University ✗ I studied in University of Wisconsin in USA.	Chapter 35: *A, An, or The?*
• Problems with prepositions	✗ And on the backside of our house there is…. ✗ Our house is opposite to the post office.	Part 4 (Chapters 36 to 38): *Nuts and Bolts of the English Language*
• Direct translation from Indian languages	✗ What sweetness is in Miss Pushpa. ✗ What is your good name?	
• Problems with conditional forms	✗ If you will read this book I would be happy.	Chapters 53 to 55 on the four conditional forms

The Grammatical Form	Example	Relevant Chapter
• Simply unacceptable	✗ ~~Myself~~, Raghubir Singh. ✗ Pleased to meet you, I am ~~coming~~ from Kolkata. ✗ I can't ~~able~~ to do that ✗ Noel, you were not on last week's call—I ~~hope~~ you were not well?	

62.5 THE LAST WORDS… FROM AN EXPERT

Let's keep in mind that while American, Caribbean, British, South African, and Australian English are considered standard English, Indian English is not, yet. But it is almost there!

As India in particular and South Asia in general find their feet in the world, more and more words used in the Indian subcontinent are finding their way into English dictionaries. For example, the *Oxford Advanced Learner's Dictionary* now contains these among other Indian-origin words:

aloo, bhindi, biryani, dal, roti, dosa, samosa, ghagra, churidar, kurta, dhoti, bindi, lathi, tabla, topi…

Let's also note that words from the subcontinent are more widely accepted in literature than in formal usage. Some Indian and Pakistani authors such as Amitav Ghosh, Salman Rushdie, and Mohammed Hanif use innumerable Bangla/Hindi/Urdu words in their novels without bothering to add glossaries.

Finally, let me share with you the views of David Crystal, possibly the most well-known English language expert of our time. He writes:

Many people now realize that labels such as 'sub-standard' and 'broken English' are just as insulting and out of order as any set of racist or sexist names. We have seen a move away from the linguistic subjugation of the prescription era, with people asserting their right to be in control of their language rather than to have it be in control of them.[4]

David Crystal advocates variation in usage of English based on appropriateness of situations and argues that 'zero tolerance' in relation to a language is a profoundly flawed approach. It may just be a matter of time before many expressions I have urged you not to use in formal language are accepted globally.

PRACTICE

1. Strike off the less/least appropriate option:

   1. Have you read the paper **today morning/this morning**?

---

[4] David Crystal, *The Stories of English* (London: Penguin Books, 2005), 534.

2. The **boot/dicky/trunk** of our car is rather small.
3. We watched a movie on television **last night/yesterday night**.
4. We are going to **admit/enrol** our daughter in a school this year.
5. I will **take/give/do/sit** a banking recruitment test this year.
6. He **stood first in/came at the top of** his class.
7. There is a **department/departmental** store near my house.
8. Seven men died after drinking **country liquor/hooch** last night.

2. Change the underlined words with expressions that would be understood globally:

   1. In our last holiday, we went to a <u>town in the hills</u> in Uttarakhand.
   2. My <u>principal</u> language at school was Bangla.
   3. Raghu is always unhappy. He <u>cribs</u> all the time.
   4. I <u>got admitted to</u> a fine arts college after school.
   5. I bought this car a month <u>back</u>.
   6. My <u>cousin sister</u> <u>is having</u> two sons.
   7. I work in a museum; I have my <u>off-day</u> on Monday.
   8. I received a lovely gift <u>today</u> morning.

3. Add or delete a word to correct five of the following sentences. Put a ✓ next to the correct sentence:

   1. We bunked school to see the latest Aamir Khan film.
   2. Our house is opposite to the cinema.
   3. We go for shopping at weekends.
   4. Sorry, I missed your call. We were watching the television.
   5. If you wish to know more about our courses, please request a brochure.
   6. Let's now discuss about our expansion plan.

KEY TO ACTIVITY

Activity 2: The following are Standard English expressions: 1. a month ago; 2. grey; 3. curriculum vitae or CV; 4. 100 per cent; 5. exercise book; 6. discuss; 7. employee; 8. sexual harassment; 9. go shopping; 10. last night; 11. opposite; 12. I am Raghu

THE END GAME, ALTHOUGH THE GAME NEVER ENDS

Appendix A
Irregular Verbs

Key to Practice Tasks and Tests

Irregular Verbs

This appendix lists the common irregular verbs, except the modal verbs (*can, may, should,* and so on. Note that some verbs have more than one past/past participle forms.

Also, the past and past participle forms are different in North American English for some verbs. This list does not contain the North American forms.

For more information on multiple past and past participle forms, usage, pronunciation, and so on, refer to a dictionary.

Base Form	Past	Past Participle
arise	arose	arisen
awake	awoke	awoken
be, am , is, are	was/were	been
bear	bore	borne
beat	beat	beaten
become	became	become
begin	began	begun
behold	beheld	beheld
bend	bent	bent
beseech	besought, beseeched	besought, beseeched
bet	bet	bet
bid	bid, bade	bid, bidden
bind	bound	bound
bite	bit	bitten
bleed	bled	bled
blow	blew	blown
break	broke	broken
breed	bred	bred
bring	brought	brought

Base Form	Past	Past Participle
broadcast	broadcast	broadcast
browbeat	browbeat	browbeaten
build	built	built
burn	burnt, burned	burnt, burned
burst	burst	burst
bust	bust, busted	bust, busted
buy	bought	bought
cast	cast	cast
catch	caught	caught
choose	chose	chosen
cling	clung	clung
come	came	come
cost	cost, costed	cost, costed
creep	crept	crept
cut	cut	cut
deal	dealt	dealt
dig	dug	dug
do	did	done
draw	drew	drawn
dream	dreamt, dreamed	dreamt, dreamed
drink	drank	drunk
drive	drove	driven
eat	ate	eaten
fall	fell	fallen
feed	fed	fed
feel	felt	felt
fight	fought	fought
find	found	found
flee	fled	fled
fling	flung	flung
floodlight	floodlit	floodlit
fly	flew, flied	flown, flied
forbear	forbore	forborne
forbid	forbade	forbidden
forecast	forecast, forecasted	forecast, forecasted
foresee	foresaw	foreseen
foretell	foretold	foretold

Base Form	Past	Past Participle
forget	forgot	forgotten
forgive	forgave	forgiven
forgo	forwent	forgone
forsake	forsook	forsaken
freeze	froze	frozen
get	got	got
give	gave	given
go	went	gone
grind	ground	ground
grow	grew	grown
hamstring	hamstrung	hamstrung
hang	hung, hanged	hung, hanged
have	had	had
hear	heard	heard
heave	heaved, hove	heaved, hove
hide	hid	hidden
hit	hit	hit
hold	held	held
hurt	hurt	hurt
inlay	inlaid	inlaid
input	input, inputted	input, inputted
inset	inset	inset
interweave	interwove	interwoven
keep	kept	kept
kneel	knelt	knelt
knit	knitted, knit	knitted, knit
know	knew	known
lay	laid	laid
lead	led	led
lean	leant, leaned	leant, leaned
leap	leapt, leaped	leapt, leaped
learn	learnt, learned	learnt, learned
leave	left	left
lend	lent	lent
let	let	let
lie*	lay	lain

* (to be or to put in a flat or horizontal position).

Base Form	Past	Past Participle
light	lit, lighted	lit, lighted
lose	lost	lost
make	made	made
mean	meant	meant
meet	met	met
mishear	misheard	misheard
mishit	mishit	mishit
mislay	mislaid	mislaid
misread	misread	misread
misspell	misspelled, misspelt	misspelled, misspelt
mistake	mistook	mistaken
misunderstand	misunderstood	misunderstood
mow	mowed	mown, mowed
offset	offset	offset
outbid	outbid	outbid
outdo	outdid	outdone
outgrow	outgrew	outgrown
outrun	outran	outrun
outsell	outsold	outsold
outshine	outshone	outshone
overcome	overcame	overcome
overdo	overdid	overdone
overdraw	overdrew	overdrawn
overeat	overrate	overeaten
overfly	overflew	overflown
overhang	overhung	overhung
overhear	overheard	overheard
overlay	overlaid	overlaid
overpay	overpaid	overpaid
override	overrode	overridden
overrun	overran	overrun
oversee	oversaw	overseen
overshoot	overshot	overshot
oversleep	overslept	overslept
overspend	overspent	overspent
overtake	overtook	overtaken
overthrow	overthrew	overthrown

Base Form	Past	Past Participle
overwrite	overwrote	overwritten
partake	partook	partaken
pay	paid	paid
plead	pleaded	pleaded
proofread	proofread	proofread
prove	proved	proved, proven
put	put	put
quit	quit, quitted	quit, quitted
read	read	read
rebuild	rebuilt	rebuilt
recast	recast	recast
redo	redid	redone
remake	remade	remade
rend	rent	rent
repay	repaid	repaid
rerun	reran	rerun
resell	resold	resold
reset	reset	reset
retake	retook	retaken
retell	retold	retold
rewind	rewound	rewound
rewrite	rewrote	rewritten
rid	rid	rid
ride	rode	ridden
ring	rang	rung
rise	rose	risen
run	ran	run
saw	sawed	sawn
say	said	said
see	saw	seen
seek	sought	sought
sell	sold	sold
send	sent	sent
set	set	set
sew	sewed	sewn, sewed
shake	shook	shaken
shear	sheared	shorn, sheared

Base Form	Past	Past Participle
shed	shed	shed
shine	shone, shined	shone, shined
shit	shit, shitted, shat	shit, shitted, shat
shoot	shot	shot
show	showed	shown, showed
shrink	shrank, shrunk	shrunk
shut	shut	shut
sing	sang	sung
sink	sank	sunk
sit	sat	sat
slay	slew	slain
sleep	slept	slept
slide	slid	slid
sling	slung	slung
slink	slunk	slunk
slit	slit	slit
smell	smelt, smelled	smelt, smelled
sow	sowed	sown, sowed
speak	spoke	spoken
speed	sped, speeded	sped, speeded
spell	spelt, spelled	spelt, spelled
spend	spent	spent
spill	spilt, spilled	spilt, spelled
spin	spun	spun
spit	spat	spat
split	split	split
spoil	spoilt, spoiled	spoilt, spoiled
spread	spread	spread
spring	sprang	sprung
stand	stood	stood
stave	staved, stove	staved, stove
steal	stole	stolen
stick	stuck	stuck
sting	stung	stung
stink	stank, stunk	stunk
strew	strewed	strewed, strewn

Base Form	Past	Past Participle
stride	strode	—
strike	struck	struck
string	strung	strung
strive	strove, strived	striven, strived
sublet	sublet	sublet
swear	swore	sworn
sweep	swept	swept
swell	swelled	swollen, swelled
swim	swam	swum
swing	swung	swung
take	took	taken
teach	taught	taught
tear	tore	torn
telecast	telecast	telecast
tell	told	told
think	thought	thought
throw	threw	thrown
thrust	thrust	thrust
tread	trod	trodden, trod
typecast	typecast	typecast
unbend	unbent	unbent
underbid	underbid	underbid
undercut	undercut	undercut
undergo	underwent	undergone
underlie	underlay	underlain
underpay	underpaid	underpaid
undersell	undersold	undersold
understand	understood	understood
undertake	undertook	undertaken
underwrite	underwrote	underwritten
undo	undid	undone
unfreeze	unfroze	unfrozen
unwind	unwound	unwound
uphold	upheld	upheld
upset	upset	upset
wake	woke	woken

Base Form	Past	Past Participle
waylay	waylaid	waylaid
wear	wore	worn
weave	wove, weaved	woven, weaved
wed	wedded, wed	wedded, wed
weep	wept	wept
wet	wet, wetted	wet, wetted
win	won	won
wind	wound	wound
withdraw	withdrew	withdrawn
withhold	withheld	withheld
withstand	withstood	withstood
wring	wrung	wrung
write	wrote	written

Key to Practice Tasks and Tests

CHAPTER 2: COMMUNICATION AND LANGUAGE

1 – D; 2 – E; 3 – A; 4 – B; 5 – C

CHAPTER 4: LANGUAGE AND STYLE

1. a. *Somebody's bark is worse than their bite is* used in informal speech to describe someone who is not as bad as they appear: *My boss is actually not a terrible fellow. His bark is worse than his bite.*
   b. You use *between the devil and a deep blue sea* to describe a situation where you are faced with two equally unpleasant choices. If they stay back, they face torture at home. If they migrate, they face hostility in a new country. The poor people are between the devil and the deep blue sea.
   c. *You are out of your depth* when you are unable to understand something because it is too complicated or when you are in a situation you cannot control: *During the first year at university, I was totally out of my depth.*
   d. To *make hay while the sun shines* means to make good use of opportunities while they exist. Property prices are at an all-time low. By a flat now. Make hay while the sun shines.
   e. You use *to make heavy weather of something* when someone makes a task look more difficult than it actually is: *You are making a heavy weather of it. You can solve this problem easily if you use algebra.*
   f. *Running with the hare and hunting with the hound* means to (dishonestly) support both sides in a dispute.
   g. To *sleep like a log* is to sleep very well. After the trek, I slept like a dog.
   h. Stepping into someone else's shoes is taking over a responsible position or task from someone else: *After his father's death, Ramu stepped into his shoes and started running their family business.*
2. a. *A bird in hand is worth two in the bush.* ⇨ Better be satisfied with what you have. Don't try to get much more and lose everything in the process.
   b. *Cut your coat according to your cloth.* ⇨ Live within your means.
   c. *Empty vessels make the most noise.* ⇨ Ignorant people talk too much.
   d. *Fools rush in where angels fear to tread.* ⇨ Unwise people act in haste, without thinking what might happen.
   e. *An idle brain is the Devil's workshop.* ⇨ An idle person does useless things.
   f. *It is never too late to learn.*

g. *A stitch in time saves nine.* ⇨ Deal with problems early, before they become unmanageably big.

h. *There is no use crying over spilt milk.* ⇨ it is pointless to brood over unhappy experiences.

i. *Too many cooks spoil the broth.* ⇨ if too many people try to do the same thing at the same time, things often go wrong.

j. *Where there is a will, there is a way.* ⇨ if you are determined, you can do anything.

CHAPTER 5: DIFFERENT CLASSES OF WORD

1.

a	Mother	gave	me	a	book	yesterday
	noun	verb	pronoun	determiner	noun	adverb

b	The	book	is	The Old Man and the Sea
	determiner	noun	verb	noun phrase

c	It	is	a	novella	by	Ernest Hemingway
	pronoun	verb	determiner	noun	preposition	noun

d	It	is	about	Santiago	an	old	fisherman
	pronoun	verb	preposition	noun	determiner	adjective	noun

e	I	am reading	the	book	now
	pronoun	verb	determiner	noun	adverb

2.

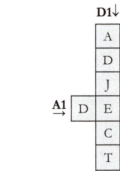

3. Linking words

CHAPTER 6: SENTENCE PATTERNS

1. whisk; 2. toast; 3. strong; 4. sunny; 5. hometown; 6. historic; 7. champions; 8. last; 9. took; 10. fully; 11. while; 12. head
2. a. syntax; b. subject; c. direct object; d. indirect object; e. complement; f. adverbial; g. state
3. The correct options are: a. is; b. are; c. are; d. is; e. is; f. were; g. are; h. wait
4. a. are; b. are; c. has; d. is; e. is
5. A. Ravi repaired <u>his motorbike</u> (last Sunday).
    B. Inspector Bhola put <u>a handcuff</u> on (Bullet Singh)
    C. Mother gave (Kuttan) <u>a music system</u> (on his birthday).

Test 1: Reviewing the Basics

1. B – ✘; C – ✘; F – ✘; I – ✘; the remaining sentences give you good advice.
2. 1 – language; 2 – Language; 3 – speaking; 4. body language; 5. voice
3.

Nouns or noun phrases	years; boyfriend; Aneesh; railway station; Pune; display board; sadness; wedding ring
Pronouns	She; him
Verbs or verb phrases	saw; was looking at; didn't notice;
Adjectives	crowded; shining
Adverbs	carefully
Prepositions	at; in; at; on
Linking words	and
Determiners	many; the; a;

4. Action verbs: A, B, D; State verbs: C and E
5. A. are; B. am; C. is; D. is; E. have; F. are; G. is; H. are
6. A. Radhika bought a <u>camera</u> [at the duty-free shop].
    B. She gave <u>it</u> to (Ravi) [on his birthday].
    C. Ravi held the <u>camera</u> [with evident delight].

CHAPTER 7: EVERYDAY ACTIVITIES AND UNIVERSAL TRUTHS

1. i. I live in a boarding school.
    ii. All of us wake up before 5.15 AM.
    iii. We go to the prayer room by 5.30 AM.
    iv. We hate the prayers, particularly in winter.
    v. After the prayers, we have breakfast.
    vi. Our school ends at 4 PM in the afternoon.

    vii. We play football after school.

    viii. The boys have supper at 9 PM.

    ix. We go to bed by 10.

    x. At that time, the warden switches off the lights.

2. I wake up early, at 5.00 in the morning. At that time, the sky is still dark. Soon, darkness fades away and the sun rises in the east. A pleasant breeze blows in from the north. Birds wake up too and start chirping. Mohan runs a teashop near my house. He lights his stove and makes tea. Rickshaw-pullers drink hot, steaming tea and rush to the station to pick up the passengers who arrive by the first train. Soon, the milkman arrives, riding his old bicycle, with two noisy milk cans hanging on either side. After some time, little girls gather at the junction and wait for their school bus. Their plaits and ponytails swing as they talk excitedly. From my balcony, I see all this. Oh! Here comes the yellow school bus. And I must stop writing, my cup of tea is ready.

3. These are suggested answers. Your answers may be different from these.

    i. The newspaper vendor delivers newspapers every morning.

    ii. The doctor treats patients.

    iii. The architect designs buildings and other structures.

    iv. The English teacher teaches us English.

    v. The vet treats animals.

    vi. The pilot flies aircraft.

4. i. wait; ii. stitch, saves; iii. blames, tools; iv. count, hatched.

CHAPTER 8: I AM FINE, HOW ARE YOU?

1. a. I am a plumber. b. You are a good cook. c. Raju is a carpenter. d. Sachin is an engineer. e. Wasim is a bank manager. f. They are farmers.

2. a. I am not a plumber. b. You are not a great storyteller. c. The players aren't/are not tired. d. The light isn't/is not dim. e. That is not my view on the topic. f. That's not/is not an important point.

3. Although I play cricket regularly, I am not a great cricketer. I'm not an excellent all-rounder. I have to try hard. I think Virat Kohli is a great batsman. He doesn't have many weaknesses in his batting. Therefore, he is my idol. I am not sure that I will be a great success in cricket. But fortunately, my coach thinks so. He even picks me for the school team!

4. a. They are all singers. b. They are actors. c. They are all sportspersons/athletes. d. They are politicians.

Special Test: Vocabulary around Occupations

A.

[1]B	A	[2]R	B	E	R		[3]U	[4]S	H	E	R			[5]C
[6]D		E					T							O
I		[7]P	I	L	O	T	E				[8]R			D
[9]S	T	A	R				W				[10]E	Y	E	
C		O		[11]S	[12]P	E	A	K			A			
[13]J	U	D	G	E		R		R			L		[14]A	
O		R				I		[15]D	O	C	T	O	R	
C		A		[16]P		E					O		C	
K	[17]U	P	H	O	L	S	T	E	R	E	R		H	
E		H		T									I	
Y		[18]D	E	N	T	I	S	T		[19]A	[20]G	E	N	T
	[21]M	R		E							U		E	
[22]D	O	N			R		[23]M	E	[24]C	H	A	N	I	C
	L								A	R				H
[25]L	E	G	I	S	L	A	T	O	R		[26]D	O	G	

B.
1. Rani is a dietician (or nutritionist).
2. Anjali is an air hostess.
3. Sehnaz is a beautician.
4. Bipasha is a model.
5. Mani is a teller.
6. Deepak is a bartender (or barman).
7. Sanjeev is a chef.
8. Raghubir is a ticket examiner.
9. Ram is a lawyer.
10. Sucharita is a copy writer.

C.
1. He is a mechanic. He repairs/operates machines.
2. She is a pilot. She flies aircraft.
3. He is a farmer. He cultivates or tills land.
4. She is an architect. She designs buildings.

D. Suggested answers:
1. Angelica is a nurse. She works at a hospital. She takes care of patients, gives them medicines and injections. She also monitors their health and assists doctors in operation theatres.
2. Gayatri is a fashion designer. She designs beautiful, unusual, and special clothes for men and women. She also designs accessories like hats and belts. She designs clothes that are functional as well as good to look at. She uses a wide range of materials and colours to create such clothes.
3. Shatarupa is an architect. She designs buildings and other structures. She also supervises construction of the buildings she has designed and makes sure they are built properly.
4. Sudeep is a freelance photographer. He works on his own and shoots photographs at weddings and other important functions. He also visits jungles and shoots wildlife pictures and sells them to newspapers and magazines. Occasionally, he organizes exhibitions of his photographs.
5. Barkha is a TV anchor. She hosts talk shows on her channel and often interviews famous people. Barkha is a confident and well-informed woman who can talk to prime ministers and presidents of countries on equal terms.
6. Jagdeesh is a doctor. He works at a hospital. He is an extremely busy person who starts working in the morning and finishes only late in the night. He treats patients suffering from various illnesses and monitors their progress.

CHAPTER 10: TALKING ABOUT OTHERS

1.

¹F	²I	R	³M		⁴R			⁵R	⁶A	⁷W			⁸H
	N		⁹E	N	E	R	G	E	T	I	C		A
	T			S			D		S				Z
¹⁰G	E	N	E	R	O	U	¹¹S		¹²T	E	S	T	Y
	L			U		L							
	L			R		E			¹³M			¹⁴D
	I		¹⁵A	C	C	E	S	S	I	B	L	E
	G			E		P			S			L
¹⁶G	E	N	T	F		Y			E			I
	N			U			¹⁷B	O	R	I	N	G
¹⁸A	T		¹⁹D	U	L	²⁰L			L			H
C					²¹A	N	G	R	Y			T
E				²²Z								E
	²²L	I	V	E	L	Y		²³L	I	V	I	D

2. 1. quick-tempered → calm; 2. brilliant → dim-witted; 3. self-assured → nervous; 4. delighted → sad; 5. down-to-earth → impractical; 6. friendly → stuck-up; 7. generous → mean; 8. alert → absent-minded

3. 1. very sad; 2. very happy; 3. very tired; 4. steadfast; 5. sad; 6. happy; 7. very angry; 8. overweight; 9. sympathetic; 10. active

4. A. People who are <u>laid-back</u> and <u>happy-go-lucky</u> live longer. B. People who are not <u>open-minded</u> often slow down progress. C. When we choose friends, we avoid <u>stuck-up</u> and <u>two-faced</u> people. D. No one likes <u>bad-tempered</u> people.

CHAPTER 11: ASKING QUESTIONS

1. a. <u>What</u> is your name?
   b. <u>Where</u> do you live?
   c. <u>How many</u> children do you have?
   d. At what school do you work?
   e. How many children study in your school?
   f. What are the backgrounds of the students of your school?
   g. How do you spend your day?
   h. When/How do you go to school?
   i. What are your hobbies?
   j. What kind of books do you like?

2. (a) What do <u>you do in the</u> afternoon?
   (b) <u>Do</u> you <u>have</u> a computer at home? Or: <u>Have</u> you <u>got</u> a computer at home?
   (c) <u>What</u> games <u>do</u> <u>you</u> <u>play</u>?
   (d) For how many hours <u>do you play</u>?
   (e) In that case, when <u>do you</u> study?
   (f) How <u>old</u> <u>are</u> <u>you</u>?

3. i. What is your name?
   ii. What languages do you speak?
   iii. Where do you work?
   iv. For which bank do you work?
   v. Where is your office?
   vi. Have you got a car? Or Do you have a car?
   vii. What car is it?
   viii. How do you go to office?
   ix. Are you married?
   x. What does your wife do?
   xi. How many children do you have?
   xii. What does she do?
   xiii. What are your hobbies?
   xiv. What kind of books do you read?
   xv. Who is your favourite author?

CHAPTER 12: COUNTING THINGS

1. a. singular, plural; b. singular; c. plural; d. plural
2. a. blade; b. grain; c. piece; d. strand; e. iota; f. pair
3. i. is; ii. are; iii. are; iv. are; v. is
4. When we reached Darjeeling, all the hotels of the town **was were** full. We had to walk ....
carrying our ~~luggages~~ luggage. .... we could not get the necessary ~~informations~~ information. .... The police **was were** looking for .... I broke my ~~spectacle~~ spectacles and
... they served ~~two fishes~~ two pieces of fish (or two fish) to everyone. .... 'I told you ~~many~~
~~a times~~ many a time not to ....' I said, 'One of my ~~friend~~ friends works for the All India
Radio here, ...'

CHAPTER 13: A SCHOOL OF FISH OR GROUP NOUNS

1. 1 group; 2 collective; 3 bunch; 4 Flight; 5 Cluster; 7 flight; 8 flock; 9 shoal; 10 school; 11 fleet/flotilla;
12 murder; 13 parliament; 14 specific
2. i. is, colony, arm, swam; ii. Flock, comes; iii. herd, enters; iv. pack, lives; v. collection, is; vi. is, cluster;
vii. team, wins; viii. convoy, passes; ix. pile, stands; x. block

CHAPTER 14: WHERE ARE YOU GOING, MY PRETTY MAID?

1. 1. Saudamini is a pilot. She's flying an aircraft.
   2. Raju is a tailor. He's stitching a frock.
   3. Balu is a farmer. He's cultivating land.
   4. Ismail is a carpenter. He's making a table.
   5. Aju is an upholsterer. He's repairing a sofa.
   6. Brinda is an architect. She's drawing a building plan.
   7. Nandini is a teacher. She's teaching maths.
2. a. I am not sleeping, I am listening to music.
   b. My brother isn't playing the match today.
   c. The Indian Republic consists of 28 states and ....
   d. The power supply is erratic here; we depend on ....
   e. My uncle owns two houses.
   f. I don't remember his phone number.
3. a. Are you reading the Gita?
   b. What are you reading?
   c. Is Virat playing today?
   d. Are you reading the newspaper?
   e. Where are you going?
   f. Do you believe in god?
4. Ravi: Why are you repeating the same point?
   Radhika: Because you are not paying attention.
   Ravi: Oh no! I am listening to you.
   Radhika: Are you? I think you are thinking of someone else.

Test 2: Present Tenses

1. I **wake up** early, at five in the morning. At that time, the sky **is** still dark. As I **watch**, darkness fades away and the sun **rises** in the east. A pleasant breeze **blows in** from the north. Birds wake up too and **start** chirping. Mohan runs a teashop **near** my house. He lights his stove and **makes** tea. Rickshaw-pullers **drink** hot, steaming tea and **rush** to the station to pick up the passengers who arrive by the first train. Soon, the milkman arrives, riding his old bicycle, with two noisy milk cans hanging on either side. After some time, little girls **gather** at the junction and **wait** for their school bus. Their plaits and pony-tails **swing** as they **talk** excitedly. From my balcony, I **see** all this. Oh! Here **comes** the yellow school bus. And I must **stop** writing, my cup of tea is ready.

2. i.   I live in a boarding school.
    ii. All of us wake up before 5.15.
    iii. We go to the prayer hall by 5.30.
    iv. We hate the prayer, particularly in winter.

3. i. are; ii. is; iii. is; iv. is

4. i.   What is your name?
    ii. Where do you work? Or, What do you do?
    iii. At which/what school do you work?
    iv. Are you a teacher?
    v.   What subjects do you teach?

5. The correct options are: i. believe; ii. love; iii. don't understand; iv. aren't doing; v. teaches; vi. close

6. 1. freelance journalist; 2. dietician (or nutritionist); 3. bus conductor; 4. teller

7. Durga: It was a (a) <u>stroke</u> of fortune that I met you after 40 years, Lisa. You still look young, although you have a few (b) <u>strands</u> of grey hair. And you haven't put on any weight.
    Lisa: Last month, I had a (c) <u>bout</u> of jaundice. Since then, I've lost some weight.
    Durga: Shall I make (d) <u>some</u> tea for you?
    Lisa: Yes, please. But please don't put (e) <u>any</u> milk in my tea.
    Durga: And sugar?
    Lisa: Just a (e) <u>spoonful</u>.

8. i.   The <u>board</u> of <u>directors</u> decides about bonus every year.
    ii. A <u>herd</u> of <u>elephants</u> are playing among themselves.
    iii. A <u>litter</u> of <u>puppies</u> are suckling at their mother's breast.
    iv. WalMart <u>has</u> a <u>chain</u> of retail stores all over the world.

CHAPTER 17: THREE FORMS OF VERBS

1.

T	A	C	E	P	G	H	J
B	D	K	I	L	L	E	D
F	R	O	Z	E	L	L	N
F	H	J	S	A	I	D	K
J	F	H	G	D	E	C	N
F	L	O	W	E	D	D	E
R	E	S	T	D	Q	W	L
R	W	O	R	E	T	Y	T

2.

Base Form	Past	Past Participle
beg	begged	begged
breed	bred	bred
come	came	come
cry	cried	cried
fly	flew	flown
flow	flowed	flowed
forbid	forbade	forbidden
freeze	froze	frozen
hold	held	held
kill	killed	killed
know	knew	knew

CHAPTER 18: THE FILM HAS ALREADY STARTED

1.　George:　　Howdy, Ravi! Have you seen the latest film of Aamir Khan?
　　Ravi:　　　No, I haven't.
　　George:　　Why? You are such a big fan of Aamir?
　　Ravi:　　　I've been down with a bout of influenza.
　　George:　　Oh! Since when?
　　Ravi:　　　Since last week. I haven't gone to office for the last two days.
　　George:　　Get well soon, buddy.
　　Ravi:　　　Thanks. Have you seen the film?
　　George:　　Yes, I have. It's a brilliant film.

2.　a.　My friend has done PhD.
　　b.　He has also made a film on the slums of Mumbai.
　　c.　The slums in Mumbai have become worse now.
　　d.　'You have made an interesting documentary film.'

3.　a.　I ~~have~~ read *Crime and Punishment* last year. Or: I have read *Crime and Punishment*.
　　b.　My car ~~has broken~~ broke down yesterday.
　　c.　I ~~have~~ fractured my leg last month.
　　d.　I ~~have seen~~ saw Sachin Tendulkar at Dhaka airport in 2010.

4.　2.　You haven't done the right thing.
　　3.　Have you done the right thing?
　　5.　You haven't forgotten your promise.
　　6.　Have you forgotten your promise?
　　7.　They have lived in this city for many years.
　　9.　How long have they lived in this city?
　　10.　Prices have gone up sharply in recent years.
　　11.　Prices haven't gone up sharply in recent years.

CHAPTER 19: WE'VE BEEN STUDYING ENGLISH

1. The correct sentences are:
    (A) I have sent six e-mails today.
    (B) He has been playing cricket since morning.
    (A) I have changed buses twice to reach here.
    (A) The movie has started.
2. a. I have ~~been liking~~ **liked** her performance.
    b. I have ~~been knowing~~ **known** this secret all along.
    c. We have ~~been having~~ **had** this car since 2011.
    d. Ravi and Radhika have ~~been knowing~~ **known** each other since college.
3. Mother: <u>Have</u> you <u>done</u> your homework?
    Boogie: Yes, Amma, <u>I've been studying</u> since morning. I am tired.
    Mother: Which subjects <u>have</u> you <u>studied</u> today?
    Boogie: Maths and English.
    Mother: What <u>have</u> you done in maths?
    Boogie: <u>I've solved</u> 20 arithmetic problems.
    Mother: And what <u>have</u> you <u>learned</u> in English?
    Boogie: Framing sentences in the present perfect tense.
    Mother: What is the present perfect tense?
    Boogie: We use this tense to describe recent events. You and I <u>have</u> <u>been</u> <u>talking</u> in the present perfect tense.
    Mother: Good. Now, please get your geography book.
    Boogie: No! <u>I've</u> <u>done</u> enough for today.

CHAPTER 20: TO THE PAST, ON A TIME MACHINE

1. A. We went to the prayer room by 5.30.
    B. We hated the prayers, particularly in winter.
    C. Our school ended at 4.00 in the afternoon.
    D. We played football after school
2. A. I didn't/did not study at a boarding school.
    B. At school, we didn't/did not participate in many extra-curricular activities.
    C. We didn't/did not have an electronics club in our school.
    D. I didn't/did not become interested in electronic gadgets early in my life.
3. When I was in high school, I never **study**. I **play** from morning to evening. And I didn't **listened** to my parents. Once I bunked off school and **go** to see a film. A friend of my father **see** me in the cinema. But I didn't **knew** that he **see** me. And when I came home ….
4. B. When/In which year did the Second World War end?
    C. When did India achieve freedom from the British rule?
    D. Who was the first President of Bangladesh?
    E. When did Sri Lanka win the Cricket World Cup for the first time?
5. A. never; B. never; C. neither; D. neither, nor; E. neither, nor

CHAPTER 21: I WAS IN HYDERABAD

1. My father was a doctor and my mother, a dietician. My older brother was a freelance reporter. He worked for some TV channels. My sister was a beautician. We lived near the railway station. It was a crowded place. There were five cinemas near our house. They showed Hindi films, but one of them showed/used to show English films on Sundays. On Sundays, we went out/used to go out to see films. After the films, we used to eat/ate ice creams.

2. a. I didn't enjoy my days in college.
   b. You were not the best singer ….
   c. Raju was not the badminton champion.
   d. His uncle was not a professor ….

3. a. How was I as a child?
   b. And how was my sister?
   c. Were we very naughty?
   d. Were we quiet?

4. I am writing from Kasargod, a small town in North Kerala. We **came** to Kerala a few days ago. We **took** a plane from Chennai to Thiruvananthapuram. The air-craft **took off** at 7.00 in the morning and **reached** Thiruvananthapuram in one hour. The flight **was** fantastic. We **flew** low over a green carpet of coconut trees. Before landing, the plane **took** a turn over the famed Kovalam beach. The view from above **was** breathtaking.
   We **spent** two days at Kovalam, which **is** 16 km away from Thiruvananthapuram. After spending three days at Kovalam, we **went** to Thekkady. Thekkady **is** a lovely wildlife reserve beside the Periyar Lake. We **saw** a herd of elephants frolicking in the lake. This morning, we **have arrived** at Kasargod …

5. 2. Jamsedhi Jamsedji Tata established Tata Steel in 1907 at an undeveloped area in Bihar. It was a defining moment in Indian history. At that time, in the colonial state of India, it was unthinkable that an Indian could set up a modern, large-scale industry. Jamshedji had a rare ability for modern thinking. For example, Tata Steel introduced an 8-hour working day as early as in 1912. At that time, in England, the legal requirement was only a 12-hour working day. Tata Steel was also the first company in India to introduce leave-with-pay. The company also started a provident fund for its employees as early as in 1920.

   3. In 1888, Laxmanrao Kashinath Kirloskar set up his first venture at Belgaum, Karnataka. It was a cycle repair shop. Laxmanrao wanted to manufacture useful things for people. His first industrial product was an iron plough. Over time, his companies manufactured lots of essential machinery such as water pumps, electric transformers, and so on. At present, Kirloskar group of companies is a major player in the machinery manufacturing sector in India.

CHAPTER 22: I WAS SLEEPING WHEN MY BOSS WALKED IN

1. 1-C, 2-B, 3-A
2. A. Raghu was sleeping when his boss walked in.
   B. I was reading the newspaper when the phone rang.
   C. The cat ate my food while I was standing at guarding the entrance.
   D. A fire broke out at the astrologer's house when he was making Raghu's horoscope.

3. a. …. Waves after waves <u>were splashing</u> on our boat. b. …. A pleasant breeze <u>was blowing</u> in from the north. c. … it <u>was snowing</u> in Manali…. c. …. Stars <u>were twinkling</u>.

4. i. The head clerk was telling a visitor to come back after a week. ii. Four employees were playing cards in the lunchroom. iii. An employee was reading a newspaper. iv. Two employees were discussing the unexpected election results. v. A lady typist was typing a memorandum. vi. A record-keeper was filing papers in the records room. vii. Two employees were planning their next vacation. viii. Two lady employees were knitting sweaters.

CHAPTER 23: THE RUNAWAY BRIDE

1. i. the past perfect, D; ii. the simple past, A; iii. the present perfect, B; iv. the simple past, C

2. A. didn't move; B. passed; C. switched off, went; D. had failed; E. bought, had saved; F. had got; G. told, hadn't/had not; H. lost, had been; I. defeated, lost; J. had gone

3. Three monkeys, who ¹<u>lived</u> on the ground floor of a two-storey building, ²<u>had come</u> to the city in search of jobs. On the first floor of the building ³<u>lived</u> a young couple, who ⁴<u>had</u> just <u>got</u> married. The wife ⁴<u>was</u> exceedingly beautiful.

    On a Sunday morning, the monkeys ⁵<u>woke up</u> and ⁶<u>heard</u> the couple fighting. It ⁷<u>was</u> a noisy argument. The leader monkey ⁸<u>sent</u> the youngest one to check what ⁹<u>had gone/was wrong</u> upstairs.

    As the little monkey ¹¹<u>didn't/did not return</u> after a long time, the senior ¹²<u>sent</u> the second monkey to enquire. He too ¹³<u>did not come back</u>.

    After some time, the leader himself ¹⁴<u>went</u> up. He ¹⁵<u>found</u> the two younger monkeys … saying: 'We have a chance …. Yes, of course, we have a chance!'

    Inside the flat, the wife ¹⁶<u>was shouting</u> at her husband: 'If I had known you were so useless, I would have married a monkey. Indeed, I should have married a monkey.'

CHAPTER 24: HE HAD BEEN SAVING ALL HIS LIFE

1. a.   … I had been searching for it for months.
    b.   … he had been fighting a legal battle to get his flat back.
    c.   … Rainwater had been seeping in for some time.
    d.   The workers had been repairing the boiler when the accident occurred.
    e.   I felt sleepy because I hadn't been able to sleep the previous night.
    f.   Amla had been batting brilliantly when he was injured.

2. A. He'd ~~been loving~~ loved her for years, but didn't have the courage …. B. … I ~~had been liking~~ had liked their work. C. Sorry, I had doubted your intentions when …. D. I ~~had been seeing~~ had seen the point even before ….

3. 1. D. When Ravi met Radhika at a restaurant, it had been raining for hours.
    2. B. Radhika had been angry because she had been waiting for an hour.
    3. C. Ravi's eyes were red because he'd been working … for 10 hours.
    4. A. Radhika was delighted to see the gold chain Ravi had been hiding under his jacket.

Test 3: The Blast That Wasn't *(A Test on Describing the Past)*

1. →

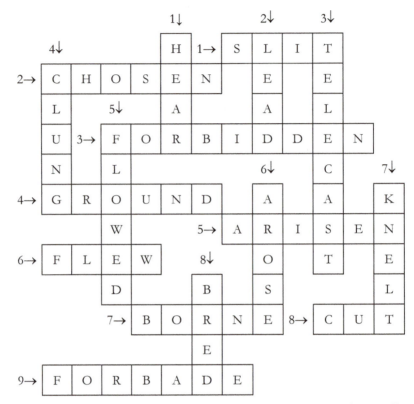

2. Yesterday, I had some work in Kharagpur, a small town about 130 km away from Kolkata. I ~~start~~ from my house at 6.00 in the morning. While I ~~drive~~ along Alipur Road, I saw an old friend, Tausif. He was wait for a bus. Tausif ~~didn't saw~~ me, but fortunately, I saw him. It ~~is~~ a happy coincidence; Tausif too ~~went~~ to Kharagpur. So he ~~get~~ on to my car and we start chatting. We had breakfast at a roadside eatery. Tausif ~~didn't allowed~~ me to pay for the breakfast. While we ~~crossed~~ the bridge over the Rupnarayan River, a car just ahead of us collided with a vehicle coming from the other side. Fortunately, no one is hurt. But there was a massive traffic jam after the accident. We ~~reaching~~ Kharagpur only in the evening.

3. i. (2) has burst; ii. (1) lived; iii. (1) was; iv. (2) The luggage was; v. (1) were searching; vi. (2) used to go; vii. (2) has left; viii. (3) were crossing; ix. (2) had been; x. (3) 'd been playing

4. A. Good morning, sir. I am a graduate engineer.
   B. I did my BTech from IIT Kanpur.
   C. Electronics.
   D. I was born in Lucknow. When I was five, my family moved to New Delhi. I did my schooling at a Kendriya Vidyalaya.

5. i. Where were you born?
   ii. At which school did you study?
   iii. When/In which year did you pass higher secondary exams?
   iv. What subjects did you study at high school?

v. What was your overall percentage of marks in higher secondary?

vi. From where did you do BTech?

6. It **happened** in 2006. …. While I **was going** to the station, our bus **had** an accident. I just **managed** to reach the Chhatrapati Shivaji station in time. It **had been raining** when I reached the station. And then, I suddenly **realized** that **I had left** the ticket behind …. I **telephoned** home. But no one **picked up** the phone. Actually, my mother and father **were watching** TV and so **did not hear** the phone.

… my father … **heard** the phone. He … **could not reach** ….

In the normal course, the train should have left by then, but a strange thing **had happened** in the meantime. Shortly before the train was to leave, someone **had noticed** an abandoned bag ….

A few months earlier, there **had been** a series of bomb blasts …. Over 200 innocent people **had lost** their lives that day. The memory of that tragedy **was** still fresh in people's minds. Naturally, the passengers **panicked** and **got off** the train. Policemen immediately **came in** with sniffer dogs. They cordoned off the platform and **searched** the bag carefully. Fortunately, they **found** only two coconuts. That **delayed** the train and I could travel that day.

CHAPTER 26: TALKING ABOUT THE FUTURE

1. a. the **be going to** form; b. the **will be doing** form; c. the **simple present**; d. the **simple future**

2. a. … Tania will become a doctor. b. The sun will turn into a giant red star …. c. I think the East Bengal Club will win …. d. The film begins/will begin at 6.30. e. We are going to visit/are visiting Agra next Sunday. f. … I'll get a pen and paper. g. … There'll be/'s going to be trouble …. h. The Venezuelan prime minister is visiting/is to visit India …. i. … Mandira will lead the Indian women's cricket team someday. j. … It is going to rain. k. … It's going to be a sunny day. l. … I'll open the window.

3. a) I am buying a flat next year. b) Our club is organizing a picnic on 1 Jan. c) Abhishek is acting in the next film of Karan Johar. d) Coca-Cola is launching a new soft drink.

4. You: Good evening, I <u>am travelling</u> to Ahmedabad by …. Is the train on time?
    Railway official: Yes, it <u>is</u>.
    You: On which platform <u>will</u> the train <u>arrive</u>?
    Railway official: Platform no. 1.
    You: I <u>have</u> an unconfirmed ticket. <u>Can</u> you please <u>check</u> the present status …?
    Railway official: Yes, of course. Please <u>tell</u> me your PNR number.
    You: It's 450-3522494.
    Railway official: Your reservation <u>is</u> confirmed, sir. Coach S-10, berth 72.
    You: Thank you. Where exactly <u>will be</u> coach S-10?
    Railway official: We <u>haven't received</u> the position of the coaches yet. I'll be able to tell you ….
    You: At what time <u>shall</u> I <u>check</u> with you again?
    Railway official: Please <u>come</u> back around 7.30.

CHAPTER 27: I'LL BE TRAVELLING NEXT SATURDAY

1. Ravi: George, would you like to join us for dinner tomorrow?
    George: Sorry, Ravi. Tausif and I<u>'ll be watching</u> a football match ….

Ravi: What match?
George: Don't you know? Lionel Messi <u>will be playing</u> in Kolkata.
Ravi: Messi?
George: Yes, Messi. Argentina <u>will be taking on</u> Venezuela in a friendly ….

2   (i)   It's sad that you can't come to the party. We'**ll be missing** you.
    (ii)   I guess I'**ll be eating** biriyani every day.
    (iii) And I'**ll be buying** as many Charlie Chaplin films as I find.
    (iv)   We are **spending/going to spend** a week in Delhi. We'**ll** also **be going** to Agra.
    (v)   'I **will stop** at Paris for a day on my way to New York.'—'<u>**Will**</u> you **be visiting** the Louvre?'
    (vi)   Grandpa will be admitted to hospital tomorrow. He **will be undergoing** an MRI scan.

CHAPTER 28: THE FUTURE IS PERFECT

1. By the year 2100, the mean sea level will have risen by 50 to 100 cm.
2. By the year 2100, the snow caps of the Himalayas will have melted completely.
3. By 2100, perennial rivers like the Ganga will have become dry.
4. By 2100, rising sea waters will have submerged many islands like the Maldives.
5. By 2100, many low-lying coastal regions will have gone under water.
6. By 2100, doctors will have invented medicines to cure cancer and AIDS.
7. But millions of people will have died in floods, storms, and forest fires.
8. By 2100, the energy problem of the world will have been solved.
9. By 2100, scientists will have been able to produce electricity from water.
10. By 2100, human beings will have set up colonies on the moon.

Test 4: Can We Review the Future?

1.   I.   Planned actions: A, H, J
    II.   Instant decisions: C, G
    III.   Predicting future based on some evidence: E
    IV.   A future activity that is part of a timetable: D, I
    V.   A neutral statement about the future: F
    VI.   A future possibility: B

2. a.   I think Rita ~~goes~~ **will go** to college tomorrow.
    b.   Her college reopens tomorrow after the … vacation. ✓
    c.   Rita and I have booked tickets for …. We ~~will see~~ **are going to see** it next Saturday.
    d.   Oh! … Sorry ~~I am going to~~ **will** sign it in a moment.
    e.   Thanks for your letter. I'**ll** ~~m going to~~ **pass** it on to my manager.
    f.   The sky is dark, it's going to rain. ✓
    g.   I will have reached Jaipur by 4 PM tomorrow. Or: I will reach Jaipur at 4 PM ….
    h.   I ~~certainly~~ might change my job next year.

3. (a) are arriving; (b) reaches; (c) are coming; (d) will be; (e) are organizing; (f) will attend; (g) will have/ are going to have

4. [Suggested answer:] I am going to retire next year. Before that, I am going to build a new house in my village. Sometime after retirement, I will visit Egypt to see the pyramids. I might also visit China. Hopefully, I will read the complete works of Rabindranath Tagore after I retire. I will also learn how to play the sitar. I might put my only son at a residential college. I will settle down in my quiet village with lots of books and a good music system. There will be no TV in my home.

CHAPTER 30: RANI LOVES DANCING

1. I love/I enjoy/I don't like/I hate/I don't care much for …
    A. playing football
    B. cooking
    C. waiting for a bus
    D. travelling by local trains
    E. gardening
    F. shopping
    G. watching TV

2.

Father:	Last night, I couldn't finish <u>checking</u> the exam papers. Could you please stop <u>making</u> so much noise?
Kuttan:	I wasn't making noise, dad. I was singing. You know that I love <u>singing</u>.
Father:	You were singing? How could you play so many instruments?
Kuttan:	The new music system that amma gave me has karaoke. It is a system for <u>playing</u> the music as you sing along yourself. Now, whenever I feel like <u>singing</u>, I turn on the music too.
Father:	That is most unfortunate, son. Your mother should stop <u>spoiling</u> you. And how can we avoid <u>hearing</u> the noise?
Kuttan:	OK, if you wish to deny yourself the pleasure of <u>listening to</u> the finest of modern music, it's your problem! I won't sing when you are at home.
Father:	No, not at all, son. I only suggest <u>keeping</u> the volume a bit low. And one more thing, would you mind <u>closing</u> the door when you sing?
Kuttan:	Not at all, dad. Thanks!

CHAPTER 31: IN JAPANESE, IKIRU MEANS TO LIVE

1. a. T; b. F; c. T; d. T
2. a. Radhika … needs ~~leaving~~ **to leave** early.
    b. It's easy ~~learning~~ **to learn** English.
    c. Rajiv has gone to the post office **to** collect a parcel.
    d. I don't mind waiting for a little while. ✔
    e. I was disappointed not ~~seeing~~ **to see** my name ….
    f. My boss let me ~~to~~ leave early.
    g. She was too exhausted ~~for talking~~ **to talk**.
    h. I'm always happy to help. ✔
3. (a) to extract; (b) to eat; (c) to see; (d) to eat; (e) to eat; (f) to play; (g) to be; (h) to bring; (i) to look; (j) to entertain

CHAPTER 32: VERBS + PREPOSITIONS: WERE YOU WAITING FOR THIS BOOK?

1. i. Please answer — my question.
    ii. We must approach — the problem with an open mind.
    iii. We demand — justice.
    iv. We do not enter — a temple wearing shoes.
    v. I requested — a day's leave.
    vi. There was a fire, but we managed to control — it in minutes.
    vii. Do you still believe <u>in</u> communism?
    viii. Let us discuss — the problem of water shortage.
    ix. Please state the main points alone. Don't go <u>into</u> details at this stage.
    x. He doesn't know when to stop. He just went <u>on</u> and on.
2. i. –; ii. for; iii. off; iv. into; v. –, to; vi. for; vii. at; viii. for, to; ix. with; x. –; xi. for; xii. –
3. A. He is going abroad next week.
    B. He arrived at Dadar last night.
    C. He has come from his home town, Durg.
    D. His train was delayed by an hour.
    E. Tomorrow, he is flying to Barcelona by Air India.

CHAPTER 33: PHRASAL VERBS: DON'T DROP OFF AS YOU READ THIS

1. 1. blow up = to explode; 2. call at (some place) = to visit a place; 3. call on = to visit a person; 4. look up = to improve; 5. take after (someone) = to look/behave like someone; 6. take over = to get control of (something)
2. A. go into; B. go on; C. found out; D. blew up; E. hold on; F. come across
3. A. called; B. blow; C. up; D. looking; E. after; F. out; G. off; H. came
4. A. I <u>called up</u> the bank.
    B. I'll <u>put you through</u> to Dr Ram in a moment.
    C. The minister <u>called at</u> the hospital ….
    D. Do you really need a bigger house? Please <u>think it over</u>.
    E. I'm sorry, we had to <u>call off</u> the function ….
    F. … Give me some time, I will <u>go into</u> it carefully.

CHAPTER 34: MORE PHRASAL VERBS

1. A. … Sashi always **gets** her ideas **across** clearly. B. … a man **was giving out** a map …. C. … I'**ll give** it **back** after an hour. D. … I just wanted to **get away**. E. OK, I **give up**. How do you solve this puzzle? F. Raghu, the store-keeper, **checks off** long lists of goods every day. G. She pulled the car to the side and **turned off** the engine. H. … and checked into a hotel by midday.
2. A. Can you please **turn up** the radio?
    B. … Have you **checked into** a hotel?

C. At what time do we **check out**?

D. … I **gave up** after three months.

E. Can you **turn** the table lamp **around**?

F. All the seats have been filled; the college is **turning away** new applicants.

G. I **switch off** when I return from office.

H. She usually **gets across** her ideas easily.

Test 5: Joe Was Shocked to Find His Wallet Empty

1. A. – T; B. – F; C. – T; D. – T

2. A. The teacher said, 'Children, stop ~~to make~~ **making** noise!'

   B. Radhika asked Rohan **to** put on a sweater.

   C. My boss allowed me ~~leaving~~ **to leave** early.

   D. ~~To acting~~ **Acting** on stage is not easy.

   E. It was nice meeting you. ✓

   F. It was nice to meet you. ✓

3. I love **trekking**. On a Sunday, I decided **to climb** to the top of the hill near our village. I asked my friend Gautam, 'Would you like **to join** me for a short trek?'

   Gautam said, 'Generally, I hate **walking** unless there is a strong reason, but for a change, I don't mind **accompanying** you today.'

   On the way, we saw thousands of butterflies **dancing** around flowers. We also heard birds **chirping**, but we didn't see many birds. It was a very hot day, and after three hours, we found it difficult **to walk**. Gautam sat down under a tree and said, 'You seem to be strong enough **to reach** the top, but I am too tired **to walk** even one more step. It was a mistake **to accept** your crazy idea.'

   I pretended **to be** hurt, but actually, I was much relieved to hear what my friend said. We had our lunch and decided **to lie down** under a tree. When we woke up, the sun was about **to set** on the horizon.

4. and 5.

   1. It happened sometime in the 1980s, long before credit or debit cards. My friend Joe was in Mumbai **to attend** a meeting.

   2. After the meeting, he went to an expensive restaurant **to have** dinner.

   3. When he took out his wallet **to pay** the bill, he was shocked **to find** it empty.

   4. He didn't know what **to do**.

   5. For the first time after growing up, he decided **to pray** to God.

   6. And he appealed to God **to bail** him **out** of the awkward situation.

   7. And God appeared in the shape of an old friend, Madhusudan Rao, who happened **to walk into** the restaurant at that precise moment.

6. A. Volker and Linda arrived **in** New Delhi this morning, shortly after midnight.

   B. Tomorrow, they are leaving ~~at~~ **for** Kolkata from New Delhi.

   C. Volker phoned ~~to~~ me **to** say they had arrived.

   D. I needn't worry about Volker and Linda. They can look ~~about~~ **after** themselves.

7. A. The match was called **off** because of bad weather.

   B. The meeting has been put **off** to next Monday.

   C. Do you still believe **in** communism?

   D. Which university did you study **at**?

8. A. We cannot **give up** at this stage.

   B. The police **are looking into/have looked into/will look into** the complaint.

C. 'I've misplaced my keys. I'**m looking for** them.'

D. I **called at** Raghu's office yesterday ….

E. Listen carefully, they **are calling out** the names.

F. The room is stuffy. Please **put on** the fan.

G. He speaks English fluently, but **puts on** a strange accent.

H. I left early because I was **put off** by her rudeness.

I. I **explained** the problem **to** the headmaster ….

J. I **prefer** coffee **to** tea.

K. I don't know, I'll **check with** the station manager.

L. I've reached Chennai and have just **checked into** Hotel Savera.

9. Once George and I were **travelling to** New Delhi **by** train for a job interview. We had decided **to prepare** for the interview during the journey. After we settled down in the train, I suggested, 'Let's **play** a game of chess. Then we'll open the books.'

But unfortunately, we didn't stop **playing** until late night. The next morning, I realized I had forgotten **to bring** my toothbrush and paste. My friend had brought his toothbrush, but he too didn't have toothpaste. So George decided **to get off** at Patna **to buy** toothpaste. As I anxiously waited for him **to return**, the train began **to move**.

After some time, the train stopped at Danapur. And I was pleasantly surprised **to see** George **walk** in with a broad smile on his face and a toothpaste tube in his shirt pocket. Said he, 'When the train left, I decided **to take** a taxi. …'

CHAPTER 35: A, AN, OR THE?

1. (A) the; (B) the; (C) a; (D) a; (E) the; (F) the; (G) the; (H) the; (I) the; (J) the; (K) a; (L) –; (M) the

2. (i) the, –, –; (ii) the, The, the, the; (iii) a, the; (iv) the, a, the, –

3. (i) The sun rises in the east. (ii) The doctor says it is a hopeless case. (iii) The musician was as ancient as his tanpura. (iv) Have you seen a tiger in the open? (v) A flimsy wooden bridge joined the two sides of the river. (vi) ✓; (vii) Dr Reddy is the headmaster of our school. (viii) The project failed because of shortage of funds.

4. ~~The~~ Computers have changed our lives. ~~The~~ Information is so easily available these days. For example, take the case of ~~the~~ Irfan, one day, he was searching the Internet to gather information on the Commonwealth Games. He stumbled upon a site about ~~the~~ scholarships available to students from the Commonwealth countries. And would you believe it? Next summer, Irfan is going to ~~the~~ Auckland University of Technology to do masters in ~~the~~ Artificial Intelligence.

CHAPTER 36: NUTS AND BOLTS OF THE ENGLISH LANGUAGE

1. (i) over; (ii) below; (iii) over; (iv) above; (v) under; (vi) beside/with; (vii) off; (viii) between; (ix) around; (x) towards; (xi) beside; (xii) around or round

2. (i) We stopped **at** Dubai for three hours **on** our way to London.
   (ii) Our boat was **on** the river Godavari.
   (iii) London is **on** the river Thames.
   (iv) Darjeeling is 7000 ft **above** the sea level.

(v)   He put the letter **in** an envelope and affixed a stamp **on** it.

(vi)   He dived **into/in** the water.

(vii) When we were going **to** Delhi, we bought some wooden toys **at** the Varanasi station.

(viii) There were not many people **at** the rally.

(ix)   I didn't see you **at** the party.

(x)   She hid his letter **in** the cupboard **under** some clothes.

(xi)   Our train went **through** a tunnel on the way to Aruku Valley.

(xii) Mr Ismail sits **at** the last desk.

CHAPTER 37: TALKING ABOUT TIME

1. A. since; B. for
2. A. I have been waiting ~~since~~ **for** two hours.
    B. He gets up early ~~at~~ **in** the morning.
    C. I have to attend a meeting in **on** Monday.
    D. We admit children between 4 ~~to~~ **and** 5 years.
    E. I passed higher secondary exams long ~~before~~ **ago**.
    F. Finally, I received the passport for which I had applied six months ~~since~~ **before/earlier**.
3. A. I am tired. I've been waiting <u>for</u> more than an hour!
    B. I am tired. I've been waiting <u>since</u> morning!
    C. Durga Puja will be held <u>in</u> September this year.
    D. George and Rini married last year. They had met five years <u>before/earlier</u>.
    E. A band played music <u>during</u> the half-time of the match.
    F. A troop of dancers entertained the spectators <u>while</u> the players were having lunch.
4. A. We stopped **at** Dubai **for** three hours **on** our way **to** London.
    B. I am going **on** a short trip **to** Goa **at** the weekend.
    C. My grandfather goes **for** a walk **in** the morning.
    D. We will issue admission forms **from** 4th July **to** 9th July. (**between** 4th July **and** 9th July)
    E. The Nilgiris, Kurinji flowers bloom once **in** 12 years.
    F. I'll be attending a short course **in** baking **during** the summer vacation.
5. Next month, I am going abroad **for** three years. **Before** that, I have to do a lot of work. I applied for visa two weeks **ago**, but I haven't received it yet. I must telephone my travel agent again **on** Monday. I had to submit a report in my present office last week, but I couldn't. I fell **behind** schedule because of various reasons. But today I will leave the office sharp **at** 5 PM because I have to go to my friend Ravi's house **in** the evening.

CHAPTER 38: MORE ON PREPOSITIONS

1. a) My friend works **with/~~by~~** sincerity.
    b) I came to know **~~of~~/from** a friend that a new shopping mall would come up in our city.
    c) For a long time, I had dreamed **of/~~for~~** setting up my own store.
    d) We wanted to check with the builders of the shopping mall **for/~~of~~** whatever it was worth.
2. a) You should be sorry **~~by~~ about** what you have done.
    b) Cloth is sold **~~for~~ by** the metre in India.

c) How much does milk cost?—Rs. 20 ~~by~~ **per** litre.
d) I am writing with a pen given by my dad. ✓
e) Ravi was senior ~~than~~ **to** me in office.
f) I don't think Sony laptops are inferior ~~than~~ **to** Toshiba laptops.

3. a) with; b) of; c) at; d) at; e) for; f) than; g) to; h) with

TEST 6: NEW ZEALAND BURGLAR WITH A CONSCIENCE

1. B. We use/~~do not use~~ *the* before names of oceans, seas, rivers, mountains, and the like.
   C. We use/~~do not use~~ *the* before names of books that are known to everyone.
   D. We use/~~do not use~~ *the* before names of musical instruments.
   E. We ~~use~~/do not use *the* before the name of an institution that begins with the name of a person or place.
   F. If the name of an institution doesn't begin with the name of a person or place, we use/~~do not use~~ *the* before its name.
   G. We ~~use~~/do not use *the* before uncountable nouns used in a general sense.
   H. We ~~use~~/do not use *the* before plural countable nouns used in a general sense.

2. A. a; B. an; C. a; D. the; E. an; F. a

3. A. the; B. The, the; C. the, the; D. The; E. the; F. the; G. – ; H. The

4. A. into/in; B. in; C. on; D. on; E. on; F. on; G. across; H. over; I. through; J. out of; K. on; L. at

5. Nisha: … Aamir Khan's next film will be released <u>on</u> Friday, the 20th of March.

   Rani: That's day after tomorrow. I am a great fan <u>of</u> Aamir. I'd love <u>to</u> see the movie. Besides, I haven't seen any film <u>since</u> the holidays ended.

   Nisha: I have two tickets <u>for</u> the premiere. Why don't you come <u>with</u> me?

   Rani: Wow! The first show of *Taare Zameen Par?* Thanks a heap, Nisha!

   Nisha: You're welcome Rani. The premiere will be <u>at</u> the Regal Cinema.

   Rani: <u>At</u> what time?

   Nisha: The film starts <u>at</u> 6.00 in the evening.

   Rani: And where do we meet?

   Nisha: Let's meet in front <u>of</u> the theatre at 5.45.

   Rani: That should be fine. But Nisha, I'll pay <u>for</u> the tickets.

   Nisha: No, you won't. I didn't give you anything <u>on</u> your birthday. …

   Rani: … do you know anything <u>about</u> the film?

   Nisha: … I think it's <u>about</u> the relationship <u>between</u> a child and his teacher.

   Rani: I heard that Aamir has made the film <u>in</u> less than a year.

   Nisha: In fact, he wanted to complete it <u>in</u> six months. The project was delayed <u>by</u> a few months.

6. New Zealand Burglar <u>with</u> a Conscience

   Associated Press, Queenstown, New Zealand, 31 August: <u>A</u> burglar visited Graeme Glass's home twice <u>in</u> one day, first to steal some goods and later to return them along <u>with</u> a heartfelt apology note.

   The thief struck while Glass was <u>at</u> work on Tuesday.

   <u>The</u> burglar smashed <u>a</u> window to gain entry and made off <u>with</u> a laptop computer, <u>a</u> camera, and Glass's wallet <u>with</u> an American Express credit card. The thief returned the goods later <u>in</u> <u>the</u> day, along with <u>a</u> new basketball and two pairs <u>of</u> gloves bought <u>with</u> the stolen credit card.

Glass and his wife Shirley discovered <u>the</u> loot piled <u>on</u> their kitchen table <u>with</u> a neat, handwritten full-page note <u>from</u> the burglar saying he was sorry <u>for</u> 'violating the safety and security <u>of</u> your home.' The robber also promised <u>to</u> leave cash <u>in</u> Glass's mailbox <u>to</u> pay <u>for</u> the smashed window when he had enough money.

'I have never written truer words when I say that I wish that I had never done this <u>to</u> you and your family,' <u>the</u> note read. '<u>From</u> the bottom <u>of</u> my heart I am sorry.'

CHAPTER 39: I CAN SPEAK ENGLISH FLUENTLY

1. a. Take a taxi, you **will** ~~can~~ **be able to** reach ....
    b. ... I think she can take care of herself there. ✓
    c. ... Ravi ~~could~~ **was able to walk** to his office.
    d. ... I managed to pass the exam. ✓
    e. It was a difficult book, but I ~~could~~ **was able to** finish it.
    f. As our train was crossing ... we could see the Taj Mahal. ✓
2. (1) could climb; (2) could speak; (3) could teach; (4) couldn't cook; (5) can recite; (6) managed to/was able to swim; (7) can break; (8) could break; (9) was able to/managed to defeat; (10) will be able to participate; (11) hasn't been able to pass; (12) were able to/managed to reach
3. 1. ... we could see it from Eastern India.
    2. ... we could understand it clearly.
    3. ... you will be able to reach Kottayam by sunset.
    4. ... I'll be able to return it to you next week.

CHAPTER 40: SUGGESTIONS AND PERMISSIONS

1. B and D - ✗; A, C, E, and F - ✓
2. 1. <u>Could</u> I <u>open</u> the window please? Or: <u>Can</u> I ...
    2. ... We <u>can take</u> a taxi. Or: We <u>could take</u> ...
    3. <u>Could</u> I <u>borrow</u> this book for a day?
    4. ... <u>May</u> I <u>work</u> from home ...?
    5. You <u>can park</u> your car here.
    6. Employees <u>can put</u> their infant children in the crèche ....
    7. Visitors <u>are not allowed to sit</u> on the lawn.
    8. Passengers <u>are allowed to carry</u> only one hand baggage ....
    9. ... You <u>are not allowed to smoke</u> here.
    10. ... Visitors <u>must not use</u> their mobile phones here.
3. A. Smoking <u>is not allowed</u> here.
    B. You <u>can</u> smoke here. Or: You <u>are allowed to smoke</u> here.
    C. Parking <u>is not allowed</u> on this side of the road.
    D. <u>You are not allowed to take a U-turn here.</u>

CHAPTER 41: TALKING ABOUT POSSIBLE FUTURE EVENTS

1. 1. ... We<u>'ll start</u> within an hour.
    2. ... I <u>am going to walk</u> to office.

3. ... He <u>won't change</u> his job.
4. ... We <u>may/might not reach</u> the station in time.
5. ... I <u>might study</u> computer science.
6. ... We <u>might visit</u> Goa.
7. ... I am not sure, he <u>might</u>.
8. Aamir Khan <u>might win</u> an Oscar this year.
9. If God offered me a boon, I <u>would ask</u> for a pair of wings.
10. My boss ... said he <u>might go on leave</u> for a week.

CHAPTER 42: POSSIBILITIES NOW ...

1. A. ... 'It must have <u>been</u> a great experience?'
   B. ... He might <u>be</u> unwell.
   C. ... He must have <u>been</u> ill.
   D. ... she must <u>be</u> tired.
   E. ... He must <u>be</u> delighted!
   F. ... He must <u>be</u> disappointed.
2. The sentences that talk about the present: B, D, E, F
   The sentences that talk about the past: A, C
3. A. You must be joking.
   B. He must have been tired.
   C. He must have been upset.
   D. You must have been sleeping.
   E. Radhika couldn't have got it yesterday.
   F. He must have worked hard during the year.

CHAPTER 43: WE SHOULD, WE MUST, WE'VE GOT TO ...

1. A. diligent; B. reckless; C. graceless; D. rude; E. behind time; F. sporadically
2. B. You shouldn't have been so reckless. C. I shouldn't have been rude. D. You shouldn't have been ungracious. E. Do you have to be behind time every month?
3. (a) must; (b) have to; (c) must; (d) should / must; (e) have to; (f) have to / must; (g) must / has to; (h) mustn't; (i) shouldn't; (j) shouldn't
4. A. You should have explained your difficulties to your boss. B. Raghu shouldn't have complained against his colleagues. C. You should have booked the tickets earlier. D. She should have consulted a doctor much earlier. E. You shouldn't have forgotten to pay your telephone bill in time.

CHAPTER 44: THE VERSATILE *WOULD*

1. Suggested answers:
   A. I <u>wouldn't like</u> to live in a house without windows.
   B. I <u>would be delighted</u> to watch a play by Naseeruddin Shah.

   C. I <u>wouldn't enjoy</u> a visit to New Delhi in summer.

   D. It <u>wouldn't be</u> a good idea to get into a fight with a professional boxer.

   E. … I'<u>d love</u> to have a shower.

2. A. I <u>would love to sing</u>, but I have a sore throat.

   B. I <u>would love to visit</u> Kashmir, but I don't have any leave.

   C. I <u>would love to buy</u> a car, but there is no parking space ….

   D. It <u>would love to use</u> a computer, but there is no electricity ….

   E. I <u>would love to watch</u> the match, but it's completely sold out.

3. A. I <u>would have loved</u> to sing, but I had a sore throat.

   B. I would have loved to visit Kashmir, but I don't have leave.

   C. I would have loved to buy a car, but don't have money.

   D. I would have loved to use a computer, but there is no electricity in our village.

   E. I would have loved to watch a match, but I don't have a ticket.

4. B. Would you like to have a cup of tea?

   C. Would (Or: Could) you please come back after five minutes?

   D. Would (Or: Could) you please show your ID card?

   E. Would (Or: Could) you please send the goods to my home?

CHAPTER 45: WISH YOU GOOD LUCK

1. A. I **wish** you every success in life.

   B. I **hope** you'll find a good job soon.

   C. **Hope** it won't rain during our picnic.

   D. I **wish** you success in your new job.

   E. I **hope** you'll come at the top of your class.

   F. I **hope** income tax rates will be reduced.

   G. My boss **wished** me good luck for promotion.

   H. I **wish** my boss was more sensitive.

2. (a) Wish you a long and happy married life.

   (b) Best wishes for your exam./Wish you all the best.

   (c) Safe journey./Wish you a pleasant journey.

3. A. I wish my friend Joe was here.   Present

   B. I wish I was not so forgetful.   Present

   C. I wish I hadn't been so rude with her.   Past

   D. I wish she kept her words more often. Present

   E. I wish I hadn't forgotten my wife's birthday.   Past

4. A. I wish I wasn't unwell./I wish I could be there in your wedding.

   B. I wish you hadn't forgotten to book the tickets in time.

   C. I wish my accountant had filed the tax return on time.

   D. I wish I was less forgetful./I wish I was not so forgetful.

   E. I wish I had renewed my passport./I wish I had a valid passport

Test 7: Modal Verbs

1. A. **Could/~~Will~~** I have a glass of water please?

   B. **Could/~~Shall~~/~~Should~~** you hold my bag for a moment?

　　　C. **Will**/**May**/~~Would~~ I come in?
　　　D. **Shall**/**May**/~~Will~~ I join the meeting half an hour later?
　　　E. **Could**/~~Shall~~/~~Will~~ I borrow your bicycle for a day?
　　　F. **Could**/~~Shall~~/~~Will~~ you please pass the salt?
　　　G. ~~Could~~/~~Shall~~/**Would** you have a cup of coffee?
　　　H. We are going to see a film. ~~Could~~/~~Shall~~/**Would** you like to join us?

2. A. could; B. can; C. was able to; D. was able to; E. could; F. were able to
3. A. You should/ought to use a firm chair with arms.
　　B. You shouldn't/should not sit at the computer for hours at a stretch.
　　C. You should/ought to get up and walk around for a few minutes every hour
　　D. You should also do some stretching exercises. Or: Also, you should/ought to do ….
　　E. You should fix an anti-glare screen on your monitor.
　　F. You should splash cold water on your eyes after a few hours.
4. A. must be; B. can't be or cannot be; C. must been; D. might have
5. A. … You must be joking.
　　B. … He must have been exhausted.
　　C. … He must have been upset by something.
　　D. Radhika might not have (or would not have) got it.
6. I haven't yet decided what I'**d** do after secondary exams. I **might** visit my uncle in Mumbai. There is only one problem. My uncle **will** go to Europe on some work during that time. But I **might** still go, my aunt and cousin Arun **will** be in Mumbai. My friend Gautam said he **might** join me for the trip, but he is not sure. I hope he **will** be able to go. We **might** visit Matheran too, but I am not certain about it.
7. A. might; B. should; C. should; D. must; E. needn't; F. must; G. Wish; H. hope
8. A. TV channels shouldn't show so much violence.
　　B. The government should make primary education compulsory.
　　C. You needn't reserve a seat in advance for this bus.
　　D. To work in a call centre, you must speak English or a foreign language fluently.
9. Sentences B, E, F, and H are correct. The rest are incorrect.
　　A. Pauls said they ~~may~~ **might** join us for dinner yesterday, but they didn't.
　　C. You are suffering from cough. You ~~don't have to~~ **must not** smoke.
　　D. You ~~need~~ **must** not carry inflammable materials such as gas stoves on a train.
　　G. No, you ~~couldn't~~ **cannot** leave before 5 o'clock.
10. A. Wish you all the best for your exam./Wish you all the best./All the best.
　　B. Wish you a speedy recovery./Get well soon, Grandma.
　　C. Congrats/Congratulations! Wish you a long and happy married life.

CHAPTER 46: 'HOW GREEN WAS MY VALLEY'

1. A. broad daylight; B. circumstantial evidence; C. close friend; D. crowning glory; E. slender lead; F. definite information; G. mutual benefit; H. white lie
2. (1) middle-aged; (2) broad; (3) definite; (4) circumstantial; (5) notorious; (6) ghastly; (7) slim; (8) former; (9) close; (10) unwritten
3. A. Look at the ~~asleep~~ sleeping man. B. The doctor says the ~~unwell~~ woman who is unwell will recover soon. Or: The doctor says the ~~unwell~~ sick woman will recover soon. C. The teacher took the ~~afraid~~ scared girl to her home.

4. a. awake; b: barren tree; c: unfashionable or old-fashioned; d: loose, baggy; e: easy; f: modern or fashion-able; g: total; h: sad

5. A. baggy/loose clothes; B. a barren tree; C. a modern office; D. an old-fashioned car

CHAPTER 47: A BIG BROWN FURRY DOG

1. (1) lush; (2) green; (3) tall; (4) leafy; (5) meandering; (6) cascading; (7) blue; (8) rough; (9) tiny; (10) undulating

2. →

Reporter:	Batting for 50 overs in the hot sun must have been *exhausting?*
Cricketer:	I wasn't excited, just a little tired.
Reporter:	But right now, you don't look tired. Rather, you look relaxed.
Cricketer:	Yeah! A hot water bath at the end of the day is always relaxing.
Reporter:	You couldn't hit the winning shot. How disappointed were you?
Cricketer:	Not much, but indeed, it is disappointing to get out when you are only two runs short of victory.
Reporter:	You are in the finals. The next match should be exciting. What are the chances of the Bangladesh team?
Cricketer:	Well, we are excited about the finals. Our chances? I would say it's fifty-fifty.

CHAPTER 48: COMPARING CATS WITH DOGS

1. A. She has scored ~~low~~ **lower** marks this time than in the last exam. B. John is not less ~~richer~~ **rich** than Abraham. C. The minister claimed it was the ~~most~~ **grandest** rally of all times. D. Virat Kohli is ~~elder~~ **older** than Kuldeep Yadav. E. ~~Less~~ **Fewer** students passed secondary exams this year … F. The ~~last~~ **latest** position of the test match?

2. A. **the most beautiful** monument; B. one of **the most active** volcanoes; C. **the biggest** planet; D. **the most populous** city; E. **the coldest** place F. **The hottest** place on earth ….

3. A. the best; B. stranger; C. the best; D. mightier than the sword; E. better than cure; F. greener

4. 1. I would like to go to a quieter place. 2. … I wish I had a more dependable car. 3. … I wish the roads were less congested. 4. But his younger brother Mukesh is richer/wealthier. 5. Have you seen the latest Aamir Khan film? 6. Flats are costlier in Mumbai than in Kolkata.

5. A. Papayas are not as tasty as mangoes. B. Abhishek is as tall as Ritwik. C. Govind is not as tall as Abhishek. D. Rakhi is as beautiful as Rekha.

CHAPTER 49: UNFORTUNATELY, BULLET SINGH SLIPPED AWAY

1. A. T; B. T; C. T; D. F; E. T; F. F

2. **Once,** an Oraon woman gave birth to an **exceedingly** beautiful girl. As the little girl grew up, she became **even** more beautiful. People wondered if such a lovely girl had **ever** come to the world before. But one day, some soldiers came and announced that the girl was **actually** the daughter of the

snake-king Nagraj, who lived under water. Nagaraj had ordered them to take the girl back. (You can also say, Nagaraj had ordered them to take back the girl.) The Oraon villagers cried **helplessly**. **Then** they went to the Nagaraj and begged him not to take **away** the girl (or not to take the girl **away**). **Initially**, the king did not agree. But **later**, he felt sorry for the villagers. **Finally**, he decided that the girl would live in our world for six months **every year**. For the rest of the year, she would live under water.

It has been like that **ever** since. When the beautiful girl comes up to our world, trees grow new leaves and bloom with flowers. Birds chirp. The fields are filled with golden harvest. But when she goes **away**, trees become totally barren, birds stop chirping, and a great sadness descends on earth.

3. (1) badly; (2) very; (3) highly; (4) carefully; (5) Unfortunately

4. A. Tania suddenly saw ~~suddenly~~ her old friend Catherine on a bus. B. Tania came ~~last month~~ from Nagaland last month. C. She met ~~by chance~~ Catherine by chance. D. She met Catherine after 10 long years ~~Catherine~~.

5. (A) Raghu brushes his teeth **almost** every day. (B) Brett bowls **real** fast. (C) Gandhiji could write **equally** well with either hand. (D) The fridge is **quite** empty. (E) You are **probably** right. (F) Raju is intelligent, he is hard-working **too**. (G) Sriram **never** eats fish. (H) Sonia doesn't **often** eat fish.

CHAPTER 50: HOW HOT IS YOUR TEA?

1. i. already; ii. yet, already; iii. still; iv. yet; v. yet; vi. still; vii. any more; viii. still, yet; ix. hardly; x. yet

2. i. Hritik loves dancing <u>very much</u>. ii. Your blood pressure is <u>marginally</u> high. iii. I've finished the work <u>already</u>. iv. Haven't you done your homework <u>yet</u>? v. The booking counter hasn't opened <u>yet</u>. vi. I am <u>still</u> struggling with my homework. vii. … He is <u>still</u> there. viii. … They <u>no longer</u> manufacture it. ix. I don't play computer games <u>any more</u>. x. … I could see the road <u>clearly</u>.

3. Yasmin quite enjoys driving. But the night was very dark. She could hardly see the road. And the road was awfully bad. She was driving very slowly. She had already driven for two hours. But she had hardly covered 46 km. She was rather tense. Her husband was sleeping peacefully by her side. She was exceedingly annoyed with him.

CHAPTER 51: SPEAKING: SHE, HER, HERSELF, HERS

1. →

Singular				Plural			
Subject	Object	Reflexive Pronouns	Possessive Pronouns	Subject	Object	Reflexive Pronouns	Possessive Pronouns
I	me	myself	mine	we	us	ourselves	ours
you	you	yourself	yours	you	you	yourselves	yours
he/she	him/her	himself/herself	his	they	them	themselves	theirs
it	It	itself	–				

2. A. its/his; B. her; C. her; D. themselves; E. her; F. yourself; G. your; H. mine; I. herself; J. themselves

CHAPTER 52: MORE SPOKEN LANGUAGE AND PRONOUNS

1. A. **It has been raining** …. B. … **there had been** a massive traffic jam. C. **It's good**, but …. D. **There is** a new train from Mumbai to Patna; **it's** a super-fast train. E. Yes, **it is/was** fantastic. F. … **It was** rather tiring
2. A. There's/There is nothing in the fridge. B. There are many exercises in this book. C. There are some lovely songs in the film. D. There are lots of new features in this computer. E. There's too much salt in this curry. F. There are some excellent stories in this book.

Test 8: Adjectives, Adverbs, and Pronouns

1. 1. activity class; 2. candlelight dinner; 3. church spire; 4. garden chair; 5. lush green; 6. mortally afraid; 7. sole occupant; 8. train journey; 9. utter rubbish; 10. quartz watch
2. A. (2) private; (3) panoramic; (4) luxurious; (5) unforgettable
   B. (1) Centrally; (2) Isolated; (3) main; (4) nice
   C. (1) pristine; (2) spectacular; (3) almost; (4) only; (5) lazy; (6) candlelight
3. A. a fierce full grown Royal Bengal tiger; B. a beautiful embroidered silk sari; C. an intimate candlelight dinner; D. a stylish fuel-efficient Indian car
4. A. My father is older than his sister.
   B. Rajdhani Express is faster than Poorva Express.
   C. The Metro is the fastest transport system.
   D. Raju is taller than his best friend Mustak.
   E. Raju is the tallest boy in our class.
5. A. A take-away food stall is not as expensive as a restaurant.
   B. Rajasthan is not as populous as Uttar Pradesh.
   C. Conventional TVs are not as good as LCD TVs.
   D. Mechanical watches are not as dependable as quartz watches.
6. A. … He also works hard.
   B. Raghu works slowly.
   C. She looked at me suspiciously.
   D. She ate hurriedly.
   E. Aamir Khan always acts well.
   F. Akbar was a wise ruler.
7. A. I happily look forward to your visit.
   B. The bank manager behaved rudely.
   C. You'll be able to do this sum easily.
   D. Rani is happily humming a tune.
8. A. me; B. mine; C. yours; D. himself; E. me; F. them
9. A. Ladies and Gentlemen! Will you please <u>introduce yourselves</u>?
   B. I hurt <u>myself</u> when I was hammering a nail.
   C. He is <u>not talking</u> to <u>himself</u>, he is talking over the phone.
   D. The captain, Anil Kumble <u>himself</u> <u>came</u> to bowl the first over ….
   E. … 'I didn't buy it, I <u>baked</u> it <u>myself</u>.'
   F. Radhika and Ravi … <u>do</u> the household work <u>themselves</u>.

10. A. This is **my house**.
    B. This house is **mine**.
    C. Sita Devi is **Rambabu's wife**.
    D. A **friend of mine is a film actress**.
    E. Is this suitcase **yours**?
    F. Tania is a friend **of hers**.

CHAPTER 53: CLAUSES CAN BE RELATIVE

1. A. who had a quirky sense of humour, B. when we were working in different places, C. where I had checked in, D. when it was still pitch dark, E. which was highly inadequate to take care of such an emergency, F. who was either stupid or extremely impertinent

2.

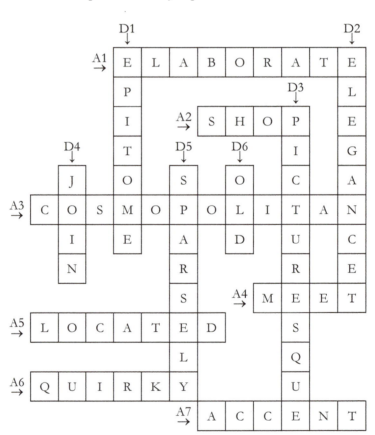

3. A. Venks, who talked very little, was a quiet and sincere person.
   B. The people who worked with us were friendly and helpful.
   C. The neighbour who I liked most was Mr Kunjakrishna Pillai, an ex-serviceman. ✓
   D. Thiruvananthapuram, where life moved at a slow pace, was a good place to live in.
   E. We often went to the famed Kovalam beach, which is 16 km away from the city.
   F. My father, who visited Thiruvananthapuram often, was exceedingly fond of the place.

4. A. First, we went to Gangtok, which is the capital of Sikkim.
   B. Gangtok, where no buses or SUVs ply, is remarkably pollution-free.
   C. Gangtok, which has a number of monasteries, is an important place for Buddhists.
   D. We stayed in a hotel which was on the slope of a hill.
   E. We went on a day trip to Tsango Lake, which was completely frozen.
   F. We also went to Zero Point, which is at an altitude of 15,000 ft.
   G. We met a lot of people in Sikkim, who were courteous and helpful.
5. A. The Kovalam sea beach, **which/~~where~~** is 16 km from ….
   B. Thiruvananthapuram, **which/that** had few industries, was ….
   C. A city **which/that** has lots of greenery is good to live in.
   D. When I visited the place …, it was a sleepy town **that/which/~~where~~** had ….
   E. The people, **~~which~~/that/who** were warm and hospitable, didn't ….
   F. There was a beautiful palace with a garden at the heart of the city, **which/~~that~~** we often visited at weekends.

CHAPTER 54: AN ADHESIVE CALLED *RELATIVE PRONOUN*

1. i. academic writing; ii. bargain; iii. bike; iv. boarding school; v. compact; vi. confluence; vii. elevation; viii. fire drill; ix. report; x. serviceman; xi. sumptuous; xii. thesis
2. A. Lubna, <u>who</u> will take the IELTS Exam next month, is practising <u>academic writing</u>.
   B. Lubna's boyfriend Joe, <u>who</u> has almost completed writing his <u>thesis</u>, should become ….
   C. Mom organized a <u>sumptuous</u> dinner <u>for</u> Rohan's friends <u>because/as</u> he came at the top of his class.
   D. The jacket <u>which/that</u> she purchased for Roshan was available at a <u>bargain</u>.
   E. Rohan studies at a <u>boarding school</u>, <u>which</u> is located near Gangtok.
   F. The place <u>–</u> Roshan studies is at an <u>elevation</u> of 4,000 ft.
   G. The school compound, <u>which</u> is at the <u>confluence</u> of two rivers, is picturesque.
   H. Last week, there was a <u>fire drill</u> at Roshan's school, <u>when</u> everyone had to vacate ….
   I. Rohan has an excellent football coach at his school. The coach, <u>whose</u> name is Joseph Mathews, is an ex-<u>serviceman</u>.
   J. At weekends, Roshan <u>reports to</u> Joseph Mathews at 5 AM, <u>when</u> it is still pitch dark.
3.

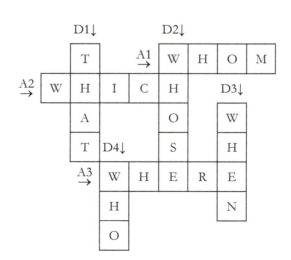

4.   A. Irfan, who I borrowed the book from, was one of my best friends.
      B. The colleague who I gave the book to never returned it.
      C. The colleague I met first was Raji.
      D. A friend who I have learned a lot from is Damu.
5.   A. – 3; B. – 2, C. – 1; D – 6; E – 5; F. – 4

CHAPTER 55: CONDITIONS AND RESULTS

1.   A. In Type 1 conditional statements, the verb in the if clause is in the <u>present tense</u>, and the expected outcome is often in the <u>simple future</u>.
      B. If the result automatically follows the condition, we use the <u>simple present</u> tense in both conditions and results. This is also called Type Zero conditional sentence.
2.   A. If we ~~will~~ start now, we will get the 9 o'clock train.
      B. If we miss the train, there ~~can~~ **will** be another train after an hour.
      C. You can leave office when you ~~will~~ finish your work.
      D. If you heat water to 100° centigrade, it ~~is boiling~~ **boils**.
      E. If you have lost your ATM card, you ~~will immediately informing~~ **must/should immediately inform** your bank.
      F. If you ~~will~~ need a ticket, I can get one for you.
3.   A. If we go on polluting the atmosphere, the human race will be destroyed.
      B. If you drive so slowly, you will cover 100 km in two days.
      C. If you hear Nusrat Fateh Ali Khan once, you won't forget his voice ever.
      D. Unless you learn to use the computer, you won't get a job.
4.   A. If you have finished your work, you <u>may</u> leave office.
      B. If you don't have money now, you <u>may</u> pay later.
      C. If you try really hard, you <u>can</u> do anything.
      D. If you are getting nasty phone calls, you <u>should</u> report to the police
5.   (a) <u>If</u> you press the accelerator, <u>the car moves faster</u>.
      (b) <u>If</u> someone touches this safe after 5 PM, <u>an alarm goes off</u>.
      (c) <u>If</u> it rains in Kolkata in summer, <u>the weather becomes sultry</u>.
      (d) <u>If</u> he wants to go abroad, <u>he has to get a passport first</u>.
      (e) <u>If</u> the electricity fails, <u>the UPS takes over</u>.

CHAPTER 56: TOM SAWYER IS DYING

1.   A. If I <u>was</u> ill, I wouldn't have to go to office today.
      B. If I <u>was</u> rich, I wouldn't live in this one-room flat.
      C. If my boss <u>wanted</u>, he could help me.
      D. If I <u>got</u> the first prize in a lottery, I <u>would spend</u> a night at a hotel ….
      E. I didn't sleep well last night. If it was a Sunday, I <u>would sleep</u> till afternoon.
      F. I feel sad. If I <u>had</u> a ticket, I <u>would go</u> to the concert.
      G. If it <u>stopped</u> raining, we <u>could go</u> out for a walk.
      H. If wishes <u>were</u> horses, we <u>would gallop</u> to success easily.

2. A. If Ria loved Raghu, she would marry him.
    B. If there were a swimming pool nearby, I would swim every day.
    C. If Raghu had time, he would see a film every day.
    D. If I could find my phone, I would call my friend.

CHAPTER 57: IF LARA DUTTA HAD MARRIED BRIAN LARA

1. Irfan: You couldn't pay the exam fees? If you <u>had told me</u> earlier, I <u>could have done</u> something.
    Raju: If I <u>had got</u> my scholarship in time, there <u>would have been</u> no problem.
    Irfan: But why didn't you get your scholarship?
    Raju: Well, the head clerk at the … office <u>said</u> there was no peon to get my file!
    Irfan: … If that monkey <u>had done</u> his work, you <u>wouldn't have lost</u> a year.
    Raju: I think if I <u>had paid</u> him a bribe, he <u>would possibly have done</u> the work.
2. A. If I had got a ticket, I would have gone to the A.R. Rahman concert. Or: I would have gone to the A.R. Rahman concert if I had got a ticket.
    B. If I had received your message, I would have stayed at home.
    C. If we had reached the cinema a little earlier, we would have got tickets for the film.
    D. We got stuck on the highway because we hadn't topped up the tank before starting.
    E. If Rani hadn't made one careless mistake, she would have scored 100 in maths.
    F. If Rani had scored 100 in maths, she would have participated in the Maths Olympiad.

CHAPTER 58: REPORTING ANOTHER PERSON'S WORDS

1. A. Kabir Khan told his coach he <u>is</u> **was** trying hard to come out of his bad patch.
    B. You assured me that you <u>are</u> **were** doing your best.
    C. She was driving in the wrong direction, but she thought she <u>is</u> **was** right.
    D. When he was a small child, Rajeev once told me he <u>wants</u> **wanted** to become a pilot.
2. A. Rajeev replied he <u>had done</u> MSc in physics from Delhi University.
    B. Detective Bhola Singh said he had followed Bullet Singh from the airport to his hideout the previous night.
    C. Dr Ram said that he had been born before the independence of India.
    D. My friend Ranjana, who I met at the Mumbai airport, said that they were going to Rajasthan.
    E. My mother said if I left the house, there would be no fighting.
3. A. Rajeev is a lecturer now. When we met last, he said he <u>is</u> **was** looking for a job.
    B. The men in the teashop told us that we <u>are</u> **were** going in the wrong direction.
    C. He told his wife that he <u>will</u> **would** come back after an hour, but he never returned.
    D. The teacher said she <u>will</u> **would** give us a test the next day.
    E. Christopher Columbus believed that the earth is round. ✓
    F. When I was a small child, my father told me honesty is the best policy. ✓
4. George said he refused to try Harris's scrambled eggs.
    Harris said George was suspicious by nature.
    George said it was not true, he was merely being cautious.
    Harris said a cautious man did not smoke and drink as much as George did.

George said that he remembered, the last time he had tried a cup of tea made by Harris, he had had a terrible headache.

George laughed and said it was more of Harris's crap.

Harris said it was the reality and in fact, they pined away for more of his scrambled eggs and became heart-broken. Some of them even died when they didn't get them.

George asked if Harris was referring to the black lump sticking to his frying pan.

Harris said George was disgusting. He had purposely diverted Harris's attention to get the eggs burnt.

CHAPTER 59: WAS MAJNU LOVED BY LAILA?

1. 1. Mobile phones are repaired by Raghu.
   2. My mobile phone is being repaired by Raghu.
   3. Raghu has repaired my phone.
   4. My phone was repaired by Raghu last week.
   5. When I went to his workshop, my phone was being repaired by Raghu.
   6. My phone had been repaired by Raghu when I went to his workshop.
   7. My phone will be repaired by Raghu.
   8. Raghu will have repaired my phone by tomorrow evening.
2. (1) are elected; (2) are conducted; (3) is allowed; (4) is controlled; (5) is headed; (6) is elected
3. (1) Last year, our municipality installed a statue of Mahatma Gandhi at the Town Hall.
   (2) The statue was vandalized by some unknown people last night.
   (3) The vandals left behind some leaflets.
   (4) The police are examining the leaflets.
   (5) Inspector Bhola Singh is leading the team of detectives that is investigating the crime.
   (6) No one has been arrested so far.

The rewritten report reads better. The passive form has been used more naturally here.

Test 9: Complex Sentences? They Are Simple!

1. A. When you are talking about real possibilities, the verb in the *if clause* of a conditional   statement is in the simple present, and the expected outcome is usually in the simple future tense.
   B. In *Type 2 conditional statements*, the (imaginary) possibilities are often in the simple past, and the unlikely results are expressed with *would, should,* or *could*.
   C. In reported speech, we report what someone said, but do not use their exact words.
   D. In the *passive voice*, the subject of the sentence does not perform any action, rather it is affected by the action of the verb.
2. A. If I get a scholarship …   R
   B. If we don't pay the bill today …   R
   C. Unless we start now …   R
   D. If I were a billionaire …   U
   E. If I were young again …   U
   F. When you turn the ignition key … R
3. A. If I get a scholarship, I'll go abroad to do a master's in creative writing.
   B. If we don't pay the bill today, our telephone will be disconnected.

    C. Unless we start now, we'll miss the train.

    D. If I were a billionaire, I would go to the moon.

    E. If I were young again, I would study genetics instead of physics.

    F. When you turn the ignition key of a car, the engine starts.

4. A. If my wife agrees, we<u>'ll visit</u> Leh next summer.

    B. Darling, I'm stuck in a terrible traffic jam. If I had wings, I<u>'d fly</u> home.

    C. If I do well in the master's, I would enrol for a PhD.

    D. If I <u>were</u> you, I wouldn't resign for such a trivial reason.

    E. When water is heated to 100 °C, it <u>boils</u>.

    F. If it was a Sunday, I <u>would sleep</u> through the day.

5. Suggested answers:

    A. When you are ready, <u>we will start</u>.

    B. If you want to watch the match, <u>I'll get a ticket for you</u>.

    C. If you had told me earlier, <u>I could have helped you</u>.

    D. If I hadn't missed the bus, I would have reached in time.

    E. If Ragini loved Rohit, <u>she would marry him</u>.

    F. When you have finished the first part of the test, <u>you can open the second booklet</u>.

6. Suggested answers:

    A. If Kuttan had cash, <u>he could have/would have bought the jacket</u>.

    B. If Radhika had reached the party a little earlier, <u>she would have met Madhuri Dixit</u>.

    C. If Raghu hadn't lost his memory stick, <u>he would have made the presentation</u>.

    D. If the umpires hadn't given so many wrong decisions against India, <u>they would have won the match</u>.

7. A. The movie was invented by Louis Lumiére.

    B. This film has been directed by Shyam Benegal.

    C. Our children are looked after by a nanny.

    D. This teashop is run by Mohan.

    E. All the peanuts are being eaten by grandpa.

    F. This opportunity won't be missed by me.

8. A. Louis Lumiére, the French engineer who invented the movie, said his invention might be of some scientific interest, but it had no commercial value.

    B. Albert Einstein said he did not have any special talent, he was merely a little inquisitive.

    C. Spanish author Maria Zambrano said she had never lived outside her homeland. Her language was her homeland.

    D. Argentinian poet Antonio Machado said that in his solitude, he had clearly seen things that hadn't been real.

    E. Spanish painter Salvador Dali said when he died, he would not die entirely.

    F. Argentinian author Jorge Luis Borges said he didn't know if education could save us, but he didn't know of anything better.

    G. Rabindranath Tagore said trees are the earth's endless effort to speak to the listening heaven.

9. Gagan: Congrats! When <u>are</u> you <u>leaving</u> for France?

   Kuttan: I am not sure if <u>I'm leaving</u>. I<u>'ll go</u> if I <u>get</u> a visa.

   Gagan: I am sure you will. <u>Have</u> you already <u>applied</u> for the visa?

   Kuttan: Yes. I sent the application online to the French Embassy in New Delhi. I <u>will be called</u> for an interview next week. If I satisfy their requirements, the visa <u>will be issued</u>.

   Gagan: And how much time should it take after that?

   Kuttan: If the visa <u>is</u> issued, the university <u>will confirm</u> my selection. The fall semester <u>begins</u> on 10 September. <u>I'll enrol</u> by 15th of August and leave early next month.

Gagan: I am sure you will.
10. Ralph, a banker, said, 'A robber has stolen 55,000 pounds from my bank. The police are after him.'
   A friend, Stuart responded, 'The police won't be able to catch him. The bank would lose all the money.'
   Phileas Fogg said, 'The man can go round the world in 80 days.'
   Sullivan, another friend, agreed, 'Yes. It is possible to go around the world in only 80 days.'
   Stuart said, 'It might be possible, but you and Fogg are overlooking many points. If the weather is bad, the ship will arrive late. Trains can be late too. Both trains and ships can catch fire. Many things can happen. I don't believe that a man can travel around the world in 80 days.'
   Fogg said, 'I believe he can.'
   Stuart said, 'No, he needs more than 80 days.'
   Fogg said again, 'He can do it in 80 days.'

CHAPTER 60: BUSINESS VOCABULARY: AN INTRODUCTION

1. A. balance sheet = a statement of a company or firm's assets and liabilities, usually at the end of the financial year
    B. bottom line = profit or loss of a firm or company during a period (of one year, six months, and so on)
    C. entrepreneur = a person who invests in business, especially when this involves taking financial risks
    D. services = (usually plural) the work that a company does for customers, without producing goods; the services sector includes banking, insurance, healthcare, and so on
    E. shop floor = the area in a firm's establishment where workers manufacture goods
    F. telemarketing = trying to sell a product or service by telephoning prospective customers
2. (1) is looking up; (2) financial year; (3) bottom line; (4) market leaders; (5) thrust area; (6) are diversifying; (7) portfolio; (8) markets; (9) are setting up; (10) greenfield; (11) has … allotted; (12) will be handed over

CHAPTER 61: BUSINESS COMMUNICATION IS CHANGING

1. A. bottom line; B. ballpark figure; C. conference call; D. public domain; E. think laterally; F. push the envelope G. provide inputs; H. log in from home
2. 1. Plan B; 2. flag; 3. give … sense; 4. SME, keep me in the loop; 5. pushed the envelope; 6. close, COB; 7. work–life balance; 8. think on our feet; 9. attrition rate; 10. ballpark; 11. mail trail; 12. take … offline; 13. upside; 14. on the fly; 15. stretch target; 16. dated

CHAPTER 62: INTERNATIONAL ENGLISH

1. 1. Have you read the paper ~~today morning~~/**this morning**?
    2. The **boot**/~~dicky~~/**trunk** of our car is rather small.
    3. We watched a movie on television **last night**/~~yesterday night~~.
    4. We are going to ~~admit~~/**enrol** our daughter in a school this year.

5. I will **take**/~~give~~/**do**/**sit** a banking recruitment test this year.
6. He ~~stood first in~~/**came at the top of** his class.
7. There is a **department**/~~departmental~~ store near my house.
8. Seven men died after drinking ~~country liquor~~/**hooch** last night.

2. 1. hill station; 2. main; 3. complains; 4. enrolled in; 5. ago; 6. cousin has; 7. day-off; 8. this morning

3. 1. We bunked **off** school ....
   2. Our house is opposite ~~to~~ the cinema.
   3. We go ~~for~~ shopping at weekends.
   4. Sorry, I missed your call. We were watching ~~the~~ television.
   5. If you wish to know more about our courses, please request a brochure. ✓
   6. Let's now discuss ~~about~~ our expansion plan.

INDEX